A Practical Guide to Localization

The LANGUAGE INTERNATIONAL WORLD DIRECTORY is a series of international listings on subjects pertaining to language related practice such as language policy and planning, training, translation, modern tools for teaching, lexicography, terminology, etc.

The LANGUAGE INTERNATIONAL WORLD DIRECTORY is published under the auspices of *Language International: The magazine for language professionals.*

THE LANGUAGE INTERNATIONAL WORLD DIRECTORY

1. *Language International World Directory of Sociolinguistic and Language Planning Organizations* compiled by Francesc Domínguez and Núria López, 1995.

2. *Language International World Directory of Translation and Interpreting Schools* compiled by Brian Harris, 1997.

3. *A Practical Guide to Software Localization* by Bert Esselink, 1998.

4. *A Practical Guide to Localization* by Bert Esselink, 2000.

Volume 4

Bert Esselink

A Practical Guide to Localization

A Practical Guide to Localization

Bert Esselink

Development Editor: Arjen-Sjoerd de Vries

Copy Editor: Shiera O'Brien

JOHN BENJAMINS PUBLISHING COMPANY
AMSTERDAM/PHILADELPHIA

The paper used in this publication meets the minimum requirements of American National Standard for Information Sciences – Permanence of Paper for Printed Library Materials, ANSI Z39.48-1984.

Library of Congress Cataloging-in-Publication Data

Esselink, Bert

A Practical Guide to Localization / [Bert Esselink]. -- [Rev.ed.]

Rev. ed. of: A practical guide to software localization

p.   cm. -- (Language International World Directory, ISSN 1383-7591 ; vol. 4)

Includes bibliographical references and index.

1. Software localization   2. Software documentation. I. Esselink, Bert. A practical guide to software localization   I. Title   II. Series

QA76.76.D63E87   2000

005.1 -- dc 21   00-058639

ISBN 90 272 1956 7 (Eur.)/1-58811-006-0 (US) (Pb;alk. paper)   CIP

ISBN 90 272 1955 9 (Eur.)/1-58811-005-2 (US) (Hb;alk. paper)

John Benjamins Publishing Co. • P.O. Box 75577 • 1070 AN Amsterdam • The Netherlands

John Benjamins North America • P.O. Box 27519 • Philadelphia, PA 19118-0519 • USA

Preface

The preface of the first edition of this book started with "Writing about software localization is like fighting against time." In the two years that have passed since the first edition was published, the localization industry has changed quite dramatically. The web has taken over the world and new, web-based localization providers are challenging the larger, established localization vendors by offering advanced translation workflow automation solutions. Translation technology has evolved quickly, with an even greater number of translation tools available than ever before. Global or local web sites have become a necessity rather than a luxury, and more than half of all web pages are now in languages other than English.

Many of these changes are reflected in the second edition of A Practical Guide to Software Localization. For this second edition, I have elected to omit the word "Software" from the title, because the book covers a wide variety of topics useful to people localizing and translating material in other areas, such as web sites or "traditional" documentation.

In this new and totally revised edition, a lot of information has been added on translating and engineering HTML and XML documents, multilingual web sites, and HTML-based online help systems. Other important changes include the addition of new chapters on internationalization, software quality assurance, and desktop publishing.

Because information on localization becomes outdated very quickly, some sections from the book have been moved to the web. At www.locguide.com you will find many links to useful online resources related to localization and translation. The web site also contains updates to the book, exercises, and some sample files.

A big thank you to my colleagues at International Software Products, ALPNET, and Lionbridge Technologies for everything they have taught me over the past years. Special thanks to Amancio Quant for designing the new layout, Alex Eamis and Carmen Andrés Lange for reviewing some of the chapters, and Arjen-Sjoerd de Vries, Bob Clark, and Sue Ellen Wright for volunteering to review the book in its entirety. Shiera, thanks for doing such a great job copy-editing the book.

Last but never least, thank you Caroline for your continuing support and patience.

Bert Esselink, Haarlem 2000

Table of Contents

Chapter 1:
Introduction

This introduction contains information on the basic principles of localization, including definitions for commonly used terms, an overview of the localization industry, and a description of a typical localization project, which serves as an outline for the rest of this book.

This chapter includes the following sections:

1. Introduction
2. Definitions of Terms
3. Localization Industry
4. Localization Projects
5. Further Reading

1   Introduction

Over the past decades, localization has progressed from being an added effort by some software publishers to a multi-billion dollar professional industry. Localization, web site globalization, language engineering, and software internationalization have become important issues for companies that want to market and sell their products in international markets. In many cases, localization has proven to be the key factor for international product acceptance and success.

As explained later in the Definitions section, many different definitions exist for the term "localization". Generally speaking, localization is the translation and adaptation of a software or web product, which includes the software application itself and all related product documentation. The term "localization" is derived from the word "locale", which traditionally means a small area or vicinity. Today, locale is mostly used in a technical context, where it represents a specific combination of language, region, and character encoding. For example, the French spoken in Canada is a different locale to the French spoken in France.

Before the Internet and World Wide Web transformed software development and localization, a typical localization project would encompass full translation and engineering of a software application, its online help files, a set of printed manuals, and reference and registration cards included in the product box. Many current localization projects still fit this description. However, because of new web-based publishing and distribution technologies, localization can now also include the translation and adaptation of web-based applications and database-driven web sites.

Traditionally, translation is only one of the activities in a project where material is transferred from one language to another. Other activities in traditional translation projects include terminology research, editing, proofreading, and page layout. In localization, many more activities have been added to this list. Examples of activities in localization which are not necessarily part of traditional translation include multilingual project management, software and online help engineering and testing, conversion of translated documentation to other formats, translation memory alignment and management, multilingual product support, and translation strategy consulting.

Most large, multi-language localization agencies focus on these additional activities, while outsourcing core translation activities to freelance translators. Only final language quality assurance is performed in-house by these vendors.

Another key difference between localization and translation is the fact that traditional translation is typically an activity performed after the source document has been finalized. Localization projects, on the other hand, often run in parallel with the development of the source product to enable simultaneous shipment of all language versions. For example, the translation of software strings may often start while the software product is still in beta phase.

The key reasons why software publishers localize their products are local market and legal requirements. In most countries, computer users prefer to work with software in their native language. In order to increase sales opportunities in target countries, software publishers have to localize their products, while local law often requires all imported hardware or devices to be accompanied by a user manual in the local language.

2   Definitions of Terms

Many different definitions and descriptions for *localization* are used in the software and translation industry. Below you will find a commonly used definition, as well as descriptions of some related terms, including: Internationalization, Localization, Globalization, Translation, and Language Engineering.

Explanations of many other commonly used terms can be found in Appendix A, Glossary of Terms.

2.1   Internationalization

The Localisation Industry Standards Association (LISA) defines internationalization as follows:

"Internationalization is the process of generalizing a product so that it can handle multiple languages and cultural conventions without the need for re-design. Internationalization takes place at the level of program design and document development."

In general, a product is internationalized during the product development cycle, as a precursor to the localization of a product.

An important aspect of internationalization is the separation of text from the software source code. Translatable text, i.e. text which is visible to the user, should be moved to separate strings-only resource files. This will prevent translators from changing – or breaking – the program code, because the resource files only contain translatable components and no coding.

Central to internationalization is the ability to display the character sets and support local standards of a particular language and country. For example, before a software product can be translated into Japanese, it must support double-byte characters. If the application has been programmed to support only Western European languages, it must be *double-byte enabled* first, for example by using Unicode character support. Likewise, different foreign keyboard layouts, input methods, and hardware standards must be supported.

Internationalization is not limited to software. Online help, documentation, and web sites, in particular, also need to be internationalized. For technical writers this process is often called "writing for translation" or "writing for a global audience". In the case of web sites, internationalization, translation, and adapting the content to specific target markets is usually referred to as "web site globalization."

Internationalization is often abbreviated to "i18n", where "18" indicates the number of letters between the "i" and the "n". For more information on internationalization, refer to Chapter 2, Internationalization.

2.2 Localization

The Localisation Industry Standards Association (LISA) defines localization as follows:

"Localization involves taking a product and making it linguistically and culturally appropriate to the target locale (country/region and language) where it will be used and sold."

Note that some publishers consider localization as an integral part of the development process of a product. In some cases, special country-specific releases of software products are called *localizations*. In this book, we will refer to all localization-related activities taking place during development of the original product as *internationalization*.

Localization projects usually include the following activities:

- Project management
- Translation and engineering of software
- Translation, engineering, and testing of online help or web content
- Translation and desktop publishing (DTP) of documentation
- Translation and assembling of multimedia or computer-based training components
- Functionality testing of localized software or web applications

Approximately 80% of software products are localized from English into other languages because the majority of software and web applications are being developed in the United States. In addition, software manufacturers in other countries often develop their products in English, or have them localized into English first and use this version as a basis for further localization.

A well-localized product enables users to interact with a software application in their native language. They should be able to read all interface components such as error messages or screen tips in their native language, and enter information with all accented characters using the local keyboard layout. "L10n" is often used as an abbreviation for localization.

2.3 Globalization

The Localisation Industry Standards Association (LISA) defines globalization as follows:

"Globalization addresses the business issues associated with taking a product global. In the globalization of high-tech products this involves integrating localization throughout a company, after proper internationalization and product design, as well as marketing, sales, and support in the world market."

Globalization is a term used in many different ways. For example, there is the top, geopolitical level that deals with globalization of business as an economic evolution. Secondly, there is the globalization of an enterprise that establishes an international presence with local branch or distribution offices. Thirdly, there is the process of creating local or localized versions of web sites, which we will refer to as "web site globalization". Web site globalization refers to enabling a web site to deal with non-English speaking visitors, i.e. internationalizing the site's back-end software, designing a multi-lingual architecture, and localizing the site's static or dynamic content.

In the context of this book, globalization covers both internationalization and localization. Publishers will "go global" when they start developing, translating, marketing, and distributing their products to foreign language markets. The concept of globalization ("g11n") is typically used in a sales and marketing context, i.e. it is the process by which a company breaks free of the home markets to pursue business opportunities wherever its customers may be located.

2.4 Translation

Translation is the process of converting written text or spoken words to another language. It requires that the full meaning of the source material be accurately rendered into the target language, with special attention paid to cultural nuance and style.

The difference between translation and localization can be defined as follows:

"Translation is only one of the activities in localization; in addition to translation, a localization project includes many other tasks such as project management, software engineering, testing, and desktop publishing."

In localization there is stronger emphasis placed on translation tools and technology compared to the traditional translation industry.

2.5 Language Engineering

The following definition for Language Engineering was extracted from The Euromap Report published on behalf of the EUROMAP Consortium in 1998:

"Language engineering is the application of knowledge of written and spoken language to the development of information, transaction and communication systems, so that they can recognise, understand, interpret, and generate human language. Language technologies include, for example, automatic or computer assisted translation, speech recognition and synthesis, speaker verification, semantic searches and information retrieval, text mining and fact extraction."

Language engineering and computer aided translation (CAT) are discussed briefly in this book. Most language engineering applications are not yet utilized on a large scale in the localization industry, even though this is changing rapidly. Many language engineering techniques such as sentence parsing, terminology extraction, or text mining are now integrated in CAT tools used in localization.

A company that is very active in the language engineering field is Lernout & Hauspie (www.lhsl.com). Another good resource for more information on language engineering is the Human Language Technologies web site at www.linglink.lu.

3 Localization Industry

The localization industry is relatively young. Until the early 1980s, U.S. based software publishers did not appreciate the need for internationalized and localized products. This has changed dramatically since the early 1990s. The growth of the Internet, in particular, has made it much easier for software publishers to market and distribute their products in other countries.

Business reasons aside, many companies are translating and localizing their products for legal reasons. In many countries, such as some Baltic countries, importing or even using products which are not in the country's native language is not permitted.

3.1 History

In the early 1980s, most software publishers either started in-house translation departments, or outsourced translation work to freelance translators or in-country product distributors.

The increasing size and complexity of localization projects soon forced companies to an outsourcing model. Most software publishers simply did not have the time, knowledge or resources to manage multilingual translation or localization projects.

In the mid 1980s, the first multi-language vendors (MLVs) were formed. New companies such as INK (now Lionbridge) or IDOC (now Bowne) specialized in the management and translation of technical documentation and software. Existing companies with other core competencies, such as Berlitz, started translation divisions that could handle multilingual translation and localization projects.

At the same time, many software publishers were still experiencing bottlenecks in their multilingual product release cycles. For example, in their engineering and testing departments, they were suddenly faced with the task of testing multiple language versions instead of just one English version. As a result, an extended outsourcing model took off in the beginning of the 1990s. In addition to translation services, MLVs then began offering engineering, testing, desktop publishing, printing, and support services.

This development kickstarted the transition from translation into localization. In 1990, the Localisation Industry Standards Association (LISA) was founded, in an attempt to bring together the IT industry and localization service providers.

In the second half of the 1990s, the localization industry began to consolidate. Since the mid 1990s, the 30 largest translation and localization service providers have been reduced to a dozen multi-language providers with a global presence. Examples of these MLVs are Lionbridge Technologies, ALPNET, and Berlitz GlobalNET.

3.1.1   SERVICE PROVIDERS

Today, most software publishers outsource translation and localization activities to localization service providers. In the 1980s, large in-house localization divisions were commonplace in software firms. These divisions were either closed or reduced to just a coordination or quality assurance department.

A localization manager or vendor manager is now often the key person at the publisher site, serving as the link between the development department and the localization service provider.

3.1.2   OUTSOURCING

Most large software or web publishers today are interested in working with multi-language vendors (MLV) which can take charge of a range of target languages and language-related activities. MLVs are specialized firms, very often with expertise in both language services and technology. The main benefit to this approach is that project management and technical activities are typically centralized in one location by the vendor. Benefits for publishers are that they can focus on their core competencies and have one point of contact for all languages as opposed to a different one per language.

Despite consolidation activity, many single-language vendors (SLVs) are still active in the localization industry. Most SLVs specialize in only one target language and may have limited technical capacity. Many of them work with MLVs, or may have signed strategic partnerships with MLVs that guarantee business volumes in exchange for an exclusive business relationship.

Another approach often preferred or combined with the use of MLVs is risk spreading, where publishers divide – sets of – languages or products between different localization service providers to spread the risk if projects go wrong and to avoid bottlenecks when many languages are involved. Because localization service providers want to be able to offer as many languages as possible, many of them have subsidiaries or partners (often SLVs) in countries where no wholly-owned offices exist.

3.1.3 CONSOLIDATION

In the second half of the 1990s, major mergers and acquisitions took place in the localization industry, which created about a dozen service providers with offices spread out across the world. Not only have many global localization companies acquired smaller ones; many partnerships were also formed to create worldwide service networks such as Lernout & Hauspie, ALPNET, Lionbridge, and Berlitz GlobalNET.

Examples of consolidations that took place in the late 1990s are the acquisitions of LMI by Berlitz, ITP by SDL, and INT'L.com by Lionbridge.

3.1.4 IRELAND

Even though it seems localization vendors are now moving activities to many locations across the globe, Ireland established itself as the leader in the localization industry during the 1990s. Over the past 10 to 20 years, the Industrial Development Authority (IDA) had the mandate as a semi-governmental body to move Ireland forward industrially by attracting foreign investment. Back in the 1980s, a high concentration of manufacturing type companies started in Ireland, including some hi-tech companies. The Irish government at the time was providing what they called turnkey factories, where a large multinational was offered a certain amount of government subsidy per employee, plus facilities and grants, and a corporate tax rate of 10%, as an incentive to invest in Ireland.

After some failed investments and the increased competition from manufacturing in cheap labour markets, the Irish government changed strategy to focus on Research and Development and the hi-tech, blue-chip companies, i.e. with a more long-term strategy in mind. Most large software and web companies now have a presence in Ireland, with the bulk of their localization being managed from there, including Microsoft, Oracle, Lotus Development, Visio International, Sun Microsystems, Siebel, and FileNET.

The key benefits they offered these companies included:

- Government grants – A certain amount of money per employee, 10% corporate tax rate, exemption from VAT (Value-Added Tax). All products, including software, exported to Europe are exempt from VAT in Ireland.

- Competitive labour costs – With social costs at approximately 12-15% per employee, it is cheaper to employ in Ireland than in many of the European Union countries. Compared to the United States, development costs are still lower in Ireland.

- A young, well-educated, and motivated work force – Approximately 50% of the population was under 25 at the beginning of the 1990s.

The Irish government has invested a great deal of subsidy in education. There now is a strong push to offer additional computer courses to cope with the growing demand for IT and localization staff. This, combined with the fact that Ireland is an English speaking nation on the edge of Europe that serves as a gateway to Europe and the Euro zone, made many U.S. based companies decide to base their European headquarters or distribution centers in Dublin.

3.2   Market Developments

Historically, the largest markets for localized products have been France, Germany, and Japan. Medium-sized markets include Brazil, Italy, Spain, Sweden, Norway, and the Netherlands. Software publishers typically localize their products into FIGS (French, Italian, German, Spanish) and Japanese first. Swedish, Norwegian, Danish, Dutch, or Brazilian Portuguese often follow as second tier languages.

Because the localization industry is growing, on average by 30% annually, the need for localization specialists is more obvious than ever. Translators need a greater knowledge of computer technology, and engineers better language skills. Many translation schools and universities recognize this market potential and are now offering localization courses.

Inevitably, the localization industry will mature over the coming years. Competition in the localization industry is very strong, and service providers will have to distinguish themselves by offering value-added services such as internationalization consulting, functional software testing, multilingual product support, and structured document authoring and management. At the same time, many software publishers are moving towards "total outsourcing" models, where all globalization and localization-related activities are outsourced to large, multi-language localization vendors.

3.3   Organizations

In 1990, the Localisation Industry Standards Association (LISA) was founded in Switzerland. LISA defines its mission as "promoting the localization and internationalization industry and providing a mechanism and services to enable companies to exchange and share information on the development of processes, tools, technologies and business models connected with localization, internationalization and related topics".

LISA organizes forums and regular workshops, where members can share information on the latest developments in the industry and attend training workshops. For more information, visit the LISA web site at www.lisa.org.

In Ireland, two organizations were founded in the nineties to establish contacts between software publishers, localization service providers, and universities in and around the Dublin area. The Localisation Research Centre (LRC) was established at the University of Limerick in April 1998 as the result of a merger between the Centre for Language Engineering and the Localisation Resources Centre. The Software Localisation Interest Group (SLIG) is a special interest group for all parties involved in localization, and focuses specifically on the business interests of the localisation industry in Ireland and was founded in February 1984. For more information on LRC and SLIG visit their web sites at lrc.csis.ul.ie and www.slig.ie respectively.

3.4   Technology

The late 1990s have also brought important changes in international software and web development. In many current software applications, users are able to produce multilingual content without any special international software support or add-ons.

Software engineers also seem to be more aware of internationalization issues and are learning how to integrate international support in their products.

One important technology development that has affected the localization industry to a large extent is the Unicode standard. Unicode offers a solution for character set issues, i.e. it offers support for all scripts that are being used around the world today. The Unicode standard uses two bytes (16 bits) for all characters instead of just one byte for standard European characters and has been implemented throughout the Microsoft Windows platforms, Apple Mac OS, and other computing platforms. For more information on Unicode, visit the Unicode Consortium web site at www.unicode.org.

Another important change in international software development has been the introduction of a "single world-wide binary", i.e. development of one version of a program that supports all languages. This single binary is often combined with "resource-only .dll files", where all user interface text elements, such as dialog box options, menus and error messages, are centralized. All program code is separated from the resources, which means that applications can be run in another language by replacing the resource-only .dll with a localized version. A good example of this technology can be found in Microsoft Windows 2000, and Microsoft Office 2000, where users can run the applications using the user interface in their preferred language and preferred regional settings without impacting the functionality.

3.5 Training

Until quite recently, finding language graduates with computer or localization skills was virtually impossible. All translation and localization service providers had to develop internal training for new employees on localization-specific computer usage and translation tools.

Linguists working for a localization vendor are normally expected to have the following skills or qualifications:

- Native speakers of their target language
- Advanced knowledge of computer applications
- Experience using computer aided translation tools, e.g. translation memory
- Subject matter knowledge, e.g. expertise in the financial or medical field
- Professional approach to schedules, budgets, and quality of deliverables
- Basic knowledge of terminology management

Many translation schools and universities are now reviewing their curricula to meet industry requirements. In many cases, general computer training or localization classes have been introduced. Some universities, such as the University of Limerick in Ireland, offer postgraduate courses in localization, covering subjects such as language engineering, localization process, computer programming, technical communication, and quality control in localization. The Monterey Institute of International Studies in California (www.miis.edu) and Kent State University in Ohio (appling.kent.edu) are training language and translation students in localization and project management.

Groups of industry and education specialists, such as LEIT and LETRAC, have researched available courseware and industry needs on internationalization, globalization, and localization.

LEIT is short for LISA Education Initiative Taskforce, a commission that was founded in March 1998. The commission consists of representatives from universities in the U.S. and Europe and has been commissioned to evaluate the status of localization-related education. In 1998, LEIT released the Industry Needs Survey report with facts and figures from a preliminary survey. The LEIT web site at www.lisa.org/leit contains this report and a growing list of existing educational material and courseware.

LETRAC is short for Language Engineering for Translators Curricula, a project funded by the European Commission, DG XIII, within the Telematics Application Programme of the Fourth Framework. LETRAC was an initiative that concluded in early 1999. The aim of the project was to "investigate the requirements and changing working environments of prospective employers of translators in both the private and public sectors to determine qualification requirements from an industry point of view." For more information on the LETRAC project and an overview of the findings, visit the LETRAC web Site at www.iai.uni-sb.de/LETRAC.

4   Localization Projects

This section provides an overview of a typical software localization project, i.e. components, people involved, and the localization process. The text contains references to other sections in the book that cover certain steps in the process in more detail.

4.1   Project Components

Traditionally, localization projects involve the following components:

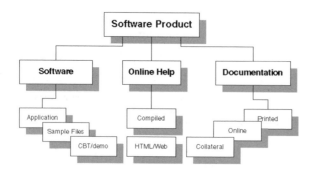

Today, localization projects increasingly include additional support material, such as web-based technical support data. In some cases, software products are partially localized for certain target markets. For example, a software publisher may decide to translate the software and not documentation, or only parts of the complete documentation set, based on sales and marketing requirements and return-on-investment expectations. A common choice for non-desktop applications is to translate the installation guide and getting started guide, and to include administrator or reference manuals in English.

Below you will find more detailed descriptions for each of the project components shown in the chart.

4.1.1 SOFTWARE FILES

A software product is usually distributed on CD-ROM or through the Internet. Setup disks contain compressed installation files that are unpacked and copied to the hard drive by a setup program, or installer.

Most software applications install the following file types on a computer's hard drive:

- Program files
- Online help or online documentation files
- Readme files

On PCs with Microsoft Windows installed, program files typically have file extensions such as .exe, .dll, and .ocx. Online help files have extensions such as .chm (HTML Help) or .hlp (WinHelp), and online documentation files often are in Adobe Acrobat PDF format. Readme files usually have .txt, .wri or .doc extensions. On Apple Mac OS computers, files have no file extensions but internal file type definitions and custom icons.

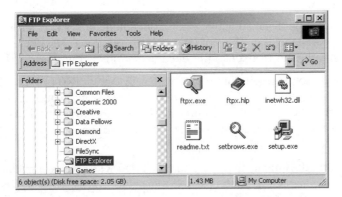

Software publishers often include sample files, tutorials, demos, and trial versions of other products with their application. Some, or even all of these files may also require localization.

For more information on translating software, refer to Chapter 3, Software Translation.

4.1.2 ONLINE HELP

Online help consists of documents that can be viewed on-screen and contain hypertext links that enable the user to jump from one topic to another. These documents can normally be accessed from within the application. Most online help systems are context-sensitive, which means that from within a particular section of the application it is possible to directly access help information on that section, for example a dialog box or a particular option.

Increasingly, online help is distributed in HTML format. In the case of Microsoft's HTML Help standard, a set of HTML files is compiled into one central online help file that can be searched, printed, and annotated.

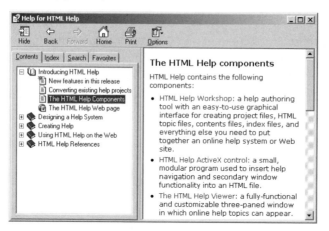

For more information on translating online help files, refer to Chapter 6, Online Help Translation.

4.1.3 DOCUMENTATION

In most cases, software publishers include online documentation with their products instead of printed documentation. This not only reduces printing costs, but also makes it easier to distribute updates or fixes to the documentation via the Internet.

Many shrink-wrapped software products come with only one or two printed manuals, typically an installation guide and a getting started guide. The installation guide tells the user how to install the application; getting started guides provide a short introduction to the application. Detailed procedural information can be found in the online help or online documentation.

Other types of printed documents that are often included with software packages are quick reference cards, marketing materials, and registration cards. These types of documents are often referred to as *collateral material*. Other examples of collaterals are CD labels and the product packaging.

Online manuals are usually provided in an electronic exchange format, such as Adobe's Portable Document Format (PDF). Online manuals can be opened and viewed using a helper application, which can also be used to print sections or pages. Adobe Acrobat Reader is the freeware viewer for PDF files.

The main difference between online help and online documentation is in their use. Online help is frequently accessed from within the application, can be searched, and enables users to jump between topics to find related information. Although many of these features may also be present in online documentation, it is less focused on on-screen use. Much more important is that users can view the online documentation and print the pages they need.

For more information on translating (online) documentation, refer to Chapter 8, Documentation Translation.

4.1.4 WEB SITES

Global enterprises often provide information on their web site in a number of languages, enabling visitors to choose the required language from the opening page. They usually not only require the company and product or service information translated, but also their entire product catalog, e-commerce, and support pages.

Today's web sites are often based on a database repository that publishes text and other information dynamically to HTML or ASP pages. With the introduction of XML, the use of databases to create web site content will become even more widespread. For web site localization this means that where traditionally large sets of HMTL pages and images needed to be localized, now database tables with structured content will be translated. As a result, web site localization is more comparable to software localization than online help localization, i.e. extensive linguistic and functional testing will be required.

Another complex issue when localizing web sites is the speed at which content is updated; ideally all updates on multilingual web sites are published simultaneously in all target languages. For this reason, many web integrators and localization vendors are designing translation workflow solutions that transfer changed or updated content to vendors or individual translators and post the translations back to the web site.

Even though this book does not contain a chapter dedicated to web localization, most of the information provided is relevant to localizing web sites and web-based software applications, especially the HTML and XML sections in the online help chapters.

4.2 People Involved

Traditionally, any or all of the following parties are involved in a localization project:

- The publisher, utilizing centralized in-house project management, engineering, and translation support staff
- The publisher's subsidiary or distributor in the target language country
- A localization service provider

Today, with companies globalizing and the web cutting out many of the middlemen, increasingly publishers are dealing directly with localization vendors to integrate localization in the overall development process. Many localization vendors are even setting up infrastructures that enable developers or publishers to interact directly with individual translators or single-language vendors in order to achieve simultaneous release of all language versions.

Software and web publishers normally outsource localization work to specialized localization and translation service providers to avoid setting up large in-house localization groups that only have work for limited periods of time, e.g. the months before the release of a new product. In addition to translation and localization, in many cases, software publishers also outsource other activities to service providers, such as functional testing, document authoring and management, internationalization, or multilingual product support.

The following diagram displays a high-level overview of the people who are directly involved in localization projects, both on the localization vendor and publisher side.

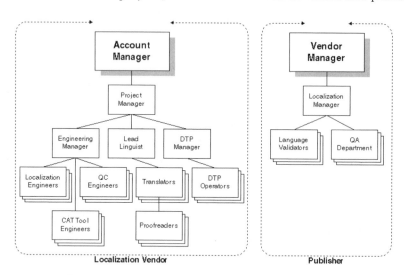

4.2.1 SOFTWARE PUBLISHERS

Large software publishers that localize their products in a number of languages usually employ one or more full-time vendor managers and localization managers, and may also have a dedicated quality assurance department. These people are responsible for managing, supporting, and monitoring the overall localization process as the work is produced by the localization vendors.

Vendor Manager

A vendor manager is responsible for all business relationships with localization service providers and works with vendors on much of the non-project-specific issues. The tasks of a vendor manager may include:

- Creating requests for quotation (RFQ) or requests for proposal (RFP) that are sent out to localization service providers prior to new projects.
- Developing long-term partnerships with strategic localization vendors.
- Visiting, assessing, and selecting vendors, based on specific internal quality and time to market goals and requirements.
- Negotiating prices and conditions with selected vendors.
- Supervising vendor contract administration.

- Monitoring the quality delivered by the selected vendors.
- Creating and monitoring localization budgets.

Small software publishers often combine the function of vendor manager and localization manager in one role. In many cases, this role is more advisory than decision making, but this does not apply to all organizations.

Localization Manager

A localization manager typically coordinates the projects that are ongoing. The tasks of a localization manager include:

- Organizing kick-off meetings for new projects.
- Defining processes and contact points for localization vendors.
- Distributing project materials and guidelines to vendors.
- Overseeing overall project progress, budget, and contracts.
- Coordinating post-localization release activities, such as CD creation, printing, or electronic distribution.
- Assisting the vendor manager in selecting the right localization vendor.
- Managing or coordinating project teams on the vendor side.

Localization managers are sometimes called program managers or project managers. They are ultimately responsible for the timely localization of a product.

Quality Assurance Department

The quality assurance department of the software publisher performs a final quality check on all localized components received from the localization service provider to look for problems or bugs in the language or functionality. The QA group also usually performs quality checks on samples during the project.

Depending on the degree of outsourcing that the software publisher has decided upon, localized versions of the product are tested by the internal QA department. However, software publishers increasingly also outsource full functional testing to the localization provider, to prevent bottlenecks just before all localized versions are to be released. In many cases, localization providers are required to hand-off gold-master versions of the localized product, which have been fully tested and are ready for release.

In-country Language Reviewers

Most large publishers ask in-country reviewers working in their local offices, or product distributors to review samples of the files that have been localized by the localization service providers. This review or validation is not the same as editing or proofreading; reviewers must focus on technical consistency, completeness, and adherence to agreed terminology and language standards.

Often, these reviewers are in direct contact with the lead translators of the localization service provider to discuss linguistic issues.

4.2.2 LOCALIZATION SERVICE PROVIDERS

At localization service providers, the people involved in a typical project are:

Account Manager

The account manager, sometimes called program manager, is the direct contact for publishers on all non-project related issues, such as contract negotiations, finances, general, and quality issues. In the case of serious project-related issues, account managers may get involved as well. Account managers are often also responsible for generating new leads and developing new business.

Project Manager

Project managers schedule projects, assign resources, communicate with clients about project-related issues, and monitor the project progress and budget.

For more information on project management, refer to Chapter 14 of this book.

Localization Specialist/Senior Translator/Translator

Localization specialists or senior translators review the work that in-house translators or freelance translators do. They also set style standards and manage terminology.

Often linguists who translate software applications are called "localizers" because they also get involved in other project activities such as software user interface resizing.

Proofreader/QA Specialist

A dedicated proofreader or reviewer proofreads translated software, online help, and documentation files. A proofreader does not necessarily focus on the *translation* quality, but especially on the final *linguistic* quality of the product. Proofreading is a final language check for spelling errors, grammar mistakes, and consistency.

For more information on proofreading, refer to the Reviewing Documentation section in Chapter 8 of this book.

Localization Engineer/Testing or QC Engineer

Localization engineers are responsible for all technical aspects of localization projects, including project preparation, software and online help engineering, compiling and testing. Often, dedicated testing or quality control engineers take responsibility for the final, functionality testing of a translated product.

Another task that is often performed by localization engineers is the creation of screen captures which are embedded in the localized online help or documentation files.

For more information on localization engineering and testing, refer to Chapters 4, 5, 7, and 10 of this book.

CAT Tools Specialist

A Computer Aided Translation Tools Specialist is usually part of the engineering team, and specializes in the correct and efficient use of CAT tools such as translation memory and software localization tools.

Tasks performed by CAT Tools Specialists include extracting, importing, and processing of text using tools, selecting the right tools for specific file formats, and creating customized filters or parsers using scripting languages.

For more information on computer aided translation tools and other translation technology, refer to Chapter 11.

DTP Operator

DTP operators take responsibility for the layout of the printed or online material and usually prepare localized files for pre-press production, or conversion of printed documentation to online format.

For more information on desktop publishing, refer to Chapt er9.

4.3   Localization Process

No two localization projects are the same. Each project has its surprises, in a positive or negative sense. Sometimes, projects that were announced as huge, technically complex operations are over before you know it. On the other hand, it is equally possible that small projects can turn into never-ending nightmares.

Each task in the localization process, including linguistic, technical, and project management steps, should be defined accurately before project initiation so the scope of the project is fully clear. Preparation is key in every project!

The workflow of a typical localization project can be summarized in the following steps:

1. Pre-Sales Phase
2. Kick-Off Meeting
3. Analysis of Source Material
4. Scheduling and Budgeting
5. Terminology Setup
6. Preparation of Source Material
7. Translation of Software
8. Translation of Online Help and Documentation
9. Engineering and Testing of Software
10. Screen Captures
11. Help Engineering and DTP of Documentation
12. Processing Updates
13. Product QA and Delivery
14. Project Closure

Please note that the order of these steps can differ substantially depending on the project. Besides, two or more tasks can run simultaneously.

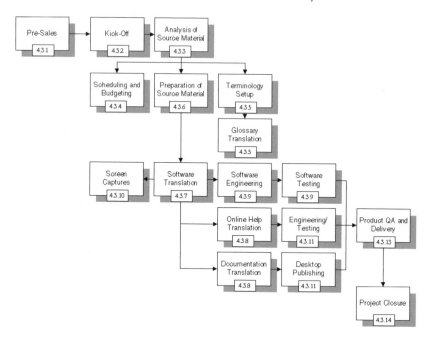

The following sections provide a more detailed overview of these steps and other issues that need to be taken into consideration during localization projects.

4.3.1 PRE-SALES PHASE

Before a project is awarded to a localization vendor, the vendor manager of the software publisher usually sends out requests for quotation (RFQ) or requests for proposal (RFP) to multiple vendors in order to get the most competitive bid.

RFQs are usually accompanied by a CD containing source material in order to enable localization vendors to create a realistic quotation and project proposal. The vendor evaluates the source material and then provides a quotation with a breakdown of all project activities and volumes. For more information on evaluating source material, refer to Chapter 13, Project Evaluations.

For more information on RFQs and creating quotations, refer to Chapter 14, Project Management.

4.3.2 KICK-OFF MEETING

Once the project has been awarded to a vendor, software publishers often organize kick-off meetings for translators, localization engineers and project managers for product training, to provide an overview of the project, to explain the localization procedures and methods, and – last but not least – to meet.

4.3.3 ANALYSIS OF SOURCE MATERIAL

When files for a localization project are received from a publisher, they first need to be analyzed by production specialists, i.e. engineers for the software and online help components, and DTP operators for documentation. Source files are mostly sent directly from a publisher's development department in a localization kit that includes the following:

- Running version of the English product
- Build environment for the software including source files
- Build environment for the online help including source files
- Documentation folder containing all book files, chapter files and graphics
- If appropriate, previously translated versions of the product or existing glossaries or translation memories

Larger localization vendors have a project evaluation team in place that analyzes all aspects of a new localization project, identifies problem areas, selects tools and approach, and provides the project managers with all information necessary to create a project schedule, budget, and resourcing plan.

Examples of information required by project managers are the project scope, the volumes, the recommended localization approach, and additional investments that may be necessary.

For more information, refer to Chapter 13, Project Evaluations.

4.3.4 SCHEDULING AND BUDGETING

Scheduling is a critical task in localization. Many issues endanger the time schedule set at the beginning of a project, the most likely one being late delivery of the source material by the publisher. Because many software publishers are aiming for simultaneous release – also called *simship* – of all language versions of their product, most localization vendors experience heavy workloads towards the end of a project.

For more information on scheduling localization projects, refer to the Scheduling section on page 443.

4.3.5 TERMINOLOGY SETUP

Most localization projects start with the creation of a multilingual product-specific glossary, which should ideally be approved by the publisher before any localization work is done.

This basic terminology list, also called project glossary, would typically contain terms that are commonly used in the product user interface or support documentation. A project glossary would also clearly indicate which essential terms, such as product names, should *not* be localized. For more information on glossaries, refer to the Project Glossaries section on page 403.

Please note that in professional terminology management, source terms are not just *translated*, but multilingual equivalents are established by research. In fact, translated terms are only valid when the translations are found in several reference documents in the target language; obviously the web is a great resource for terminology research.

To obtain accurate multilingual equivalents from the very beginning of the project, provide terminology researchers with sufficient reference material, such as the running application or online help file. Translating key terms or finding equivalent terms in the target language without any contextual information on the product may result in major terminology changes later in the project.

In most cases, the project glossary is sent to the publisher for review and approval. After validation of the glossary, translation of the project's source material can start. During the project, the terminology database should be maintained and updated.

For more information on Terminology Management, refer to Chapter 12, Terminology.

4.3.6 PREPARATION OF SOURCE MATERIAL

When the engineers and DTP operators have analyzed the source material, spotted potential problems and test-compiled all source material, a translation kit is created for the translators. Especially for multilingual projects, project preparation is a vital step because problems caused by insufficient preparation are multiplied by the number of target languages of the project.

Preparing a translation kit includes investigating leveraging possibilities for the software, i.e. checking whether existing translations can be automatically re-used. If previous translations of the software resource files exist, the localization engineer should try to re-use these translations as much as possible to avoid unnecessary work for the translators. This not only improves consistency, it also decreases the number of words to translate, i.e. speeds up the software translation process and reduces the cost for the publisher. For more information on the preparation of software files for translation, refer to Chapter 4, Software Engineering.

The same issues apply to online help and documentation files. If translation memories exist, they need to be included with the localization kit, along with files that have been pre-processed for use in a translation memory tool. If no translation memories exist, but an earlier version of the online help or documentation files has been translated, the possibility of *alignment* needs to be considered. Chapter 11, Translation Technology, provides more information on aligning translated text to create translation memory databases.

For more information on the preparation of online help and documentation files for translation, refer to Chapter 7, Online Help Engineering and Testing, and Chapter 9, Desktop Publishing.

The technical and linguistic information should be combined into one coherent set of instructions that is given to the translator along with all source material.

4.3.7 TRANSLATION OF SOFTWARE

Ideally, software is translated first in localization projects. Translators edit resources in text-only files, in a resource editor, a translation memory tool, or in a software localization tool. For more information on translating software files, refer to Chapter 3, Software Translation.

The recommended order in which to translate software application resources is: dialog boxes, menus and strings. Usually, the string section contains most of the translatable text, i.e. error messages, status messages, and help text.

Once dialog box resources and menus have been translated, it is possible to create a preliminary user interface glossary – or even a preliminary software build – of these translations, which can be used as a reference point for translators of online help and documentation. Likely, most of the software references in help and documentation contain dialog box items and menu names, so it is not recommended to start translation of help and documentation before these items have been localized. For more information on creating software glossaries, refer to the Creating User Interface Glossaries section on page 409.

Once all resource files have been translated, the software application is compiled and dialog boxes resized. For more information on compiling and resizing localized software applications, refer to Chapter 4, Software Engineering.

Next, a linguistic test is performed to validate the translations in context in the running application. Once linguistic testing of the localized software is completed, the terminology of the application should be final and frozen. This means that a localized software version can be sent to the client for an acceptance test. In addition, vendors can now start creating screen captures for inclusion in the online help and documentation. For more information on creating screen captures, refer to the Creating Screen Captures section on page 349.

4.3.8 TRANSLATION OF ONLINE HELP AND DOCUMENTATION

As soon as a software glossary or a preliminary build of the localized software is available, translation of online help and documentation can start.

For more information on translating online help and documentation, refer to Chapter 6, Online Help Translation, and Chapter 8, Documentation Translation.

4.3.9 ENGINEERING AND TESTING OF SOFTWARE

Engineering localized software primarily involves resizing the user interface, assigning unique hot keys, and compiling the localized resource files into a running application. For more information on engineering localized software applications, refer to Chapter 4, Software Engineering.

Many different types of testing are possible in a localization project. The first testing type, linguistic testing, is often seen as part of the translation process and should be done by a translator or linguist, if possible with the help of a localization engineer or test scripts.

If included in the statement of work for the project, functionality testing is performed by localization engineers or dedicated testing and QC teams. Often the publisher provides test scripts, which guide engineers through the testing process. If no guidelines or scripts are provided, ask the software publisher how much time should be scheduled for functionality or compatibility testing of the localized versions of the software. Typically, a subset of the test scripts used for the English version is created to test the functionality of the localized versions.

Refer to Chapter 5, Software Quality Assurance, for more information on testing localized software applications.

4.3.10 SCREEN CAPTURES

Screen captures are pictures of user interface elements of the running software that are used in online help or documentation to show a task situation or context, the objects being described, or the result of performing a procedural step. For example, a screen capture can show a dialog box with certain options selected.

Screen captures need to be created for each target language. Without screen captures of the localized software, no online help file or manual can be finalized. Therefore, it is recommended to start creating screen captures as soon as the linguistic testing of the software is completed and the user interface terminology has been frozen.

For more information on creating screen captures, refer to the Creating Screen Captures section on page 349.

4.3.11 HELP ENGINEERING AND DTP OF DOCUMENTATION

As soon as all graphics and screen captures have been localized and reviewed, desktop publishing of documentation and testing of online help projects can start. Although it is possible to perform DTP and online help testing when the graphics have not been localized yet, using the original graphics, this will require an additional check after the graphics have been translated. For example, image sizes may change in localized versions because of resizing of dialog boxes. As a result, page flows may change so DTP work needs to be re-done.

For more information on engineering and testing online help files, refer to Chapter 7, Online Help Engineering and Testing. For more information on desktop publishing, refer to Chapter 9, Desktop Publishing.

4.3.12 PROCESSING UPDATES

Translation often starts when the English product is still being developed. This means that first one or more beta versions or release candidates of the product are translated before the final version is released to localization.

If vendors are not using a translation memory system for translation, they need to manually process updates using file compares, copying and pasting, etc. Translation memory systems enable the user to process new files and automatically re-use the translations that were already completed. Refer to Chapter 11, Translation Technology, for more information on the use of translation memory tools.

When desktop publishing for printed documentation or testing of online help has already started, it is more difficult to process updates. After translation in a translation memory tool, files are converted back to their native formats, and after that point additional edits or corrections are no longer stored in translation memory. In case of these last-minute updates, either process the updates using the translation memory tool and lose all desktop publishing or testing work, or insert the changes in the files that are being worked on. In the latter case, the translation memory will not be up-to-date anymore, unless it is updated separately.

Most of the time, there will be too much time pressure to re-do desktop publishing and testing work, and the latter procedure will be chosen.

To prevent unnecessary software engineering, testing, or desktop publishing work, project managers should always agree with their clients if – and when – updates can be expected.

4.3.13 PRODUCT QA AND DELIVERY

Before delivery, a quality assurance check should be performed on all translated material. At this stage, the software publisher may also ask to see the files for sign-off.

This pre-delivery QA check includes:

- Proofreading all translations. For more information on proofreading, refer to the Reviewing Documentation section on page 315.
- Delivery test of the software. For more information on this type of testing, refer to the Delivery Testing section on page 154.
- Finalizing bug or problem reports. For more information on bug reports, refer to the Bug Tracking section on page 160.
- Reviewing the instructions given in the initial hand-off or statement of work from the publisher to ensure that all steps were covered.

When the QA checks have been completed, the translated material can be delivered to the publisher. After all translated files have been delivered and approved by the publisher, all project materials are archived.

4.3.14 PROJECT CLOSURE

Many publishers organize a post-mortem – or project audit or wrap-up meeting – with the localization vendor after a project has been completed. Issues discussed in these meetings include:

- Process-oriented evaluation of the completed project
- Evaluation of technical and linguistic quality of deliverables
- Identification of areas for improvement
- Suggestions for process modifications for future projects

Please note that these meetings work both ways; both parties need to provide input on each other's performance.

During the post-mortem meeting, one of the attendees should take notes and distribute a summary of all topics discussed to both parties. This document could function as a starting point for new projects.

5   Further Reading

Not many books have been written covering software localization or the localization industry. The following references cover different aspects of the localization industry. For example, Robert Sprung's book deals with business case studies of localization vendors and publishers, and Hickey's book is a collection of daily job and task descriptions of various people working for a localization vendor, from project managers to translators and engineers.

Hickey, Tim. ed. 1999. *The Guide to Product Translation and Localization.* Computer Society, ISBN 0-769-50022-6.

Hoft, Nancy. 1995. *International Technical Communication.* John Wiley & Sons, ISBN 0-471-03743-5.

Sprung, Robert. ed. 2000. *Translating Into Success: Case Studies in Translation, Localization, and Internationalization.* John Benjamins, ISBN 1-556-19631-8.

Chapter 2:
Internationalization

This chapter is aimed at software publishers or web developers who want to learn more about the internationalization of their products. The chapter provides an overview on internationalization and further relevant information for managers, software programmers, web developers, and technical writers.

This chapter includes the following sections:

1. Introduction
2. Language
3. Software
4. Web Sites and HTML
5. Documentation
6. Creating Localization Kits
7. Further Reading

1   Introduction

The localization of a product does not begin with the delivery of source material to the localization vendor. Publishers can influence the success of their localization and globalization effort to a large extent by preparing their products for foreign markets during the development phase, in other words, by internationalizing them properly.

As mentioned in the introduction, the Localisation Industry Standards Association (LISA) defines internationalization as follows:

"Internationalization is the process of generalizing a product so that it can handle multiple languages and cultural conventions without the need for re-design. Internationalization takes place at the level of program design and document development."

There are two key reasons for internationalizing software and (online) information:

1. To ensure that a product is functional and accepted in international markets.
2. To ensure that a product is localizable.

In the first case, the product is designed to support features such as international character sets, keyboard layouts, date and time formats, and currencies. The online help and documentation should be concise, clear, and not contain any jargon or slang, and its contents should be free of culture-specific examples or references.

The second reason above will help to reduce localization costs by developing the product in a way that ensures a smooth localization process, both for the software publisher and the localization vendor. One way to do this in the software is to externalize all translatable components of a software application to make them easy to identify and translate. In the online help and documentation, using generic country-independent examples, or creating multi-layered images reduces costs considerably.

Here is an example of problems that may be prevented by internationalizing products during development:

- Incorrect display of accented characters. If the product has no built-in support for character sets that fall outside the range of the standard ASCII set, accented characters may display incorrectly or garbled. Unicode support in a product guarantees support, i.e. correct processing and display, for all of the world's language scripts.

- Text truncations. Translated text is normally about 30% longer (sentences) than the English original, but the increase may be as much as 100 percent (single words). If there are significant length restrictions in the user interface of a software application, translators will have to abbreviate items or choose synonyms, which may affect the quality of the localized product or confuse the end user. If this is the case, the user interface may have to undergo extensive resizing, which will increase production time and costs. This is a particular problem in ideographic languages, such as Japanese or Chinese, where abbreviations are not used and vertical expansion may also be required.

- Fixed date, time, number, or currency formats. Apart from different separators, e.g. 1/6/2001 in the United States and 1.6.2001 in German, the order is also important. For example, 6/10/2001 means 10 June 2001 in the United States and 6 October 2001 in European countries.

- U.S. specific icons or graphics. Icons may have different meanings in different countries. When Apple first used the Trashcan icon, it was interpreted as a mail box to European Mac OS users.

"Enablement" is a term that is commonly used in the context of internationalization. It refers to the process of adjusting software to make it functional in certain countries or geographical regions. For example, a software product can be "double-byte enabled" to process and display text in Asian languages.

Internationalization can be applied to the online help and documentation, as well as software. Here are some examples of internationalization issues in documentation:

- Jargon or U.S. specific language. Many internationalization problems have been found in sample files, such as document templates, which were not designed with international users in mind.
- Manually generated table of contents or index. If the source material does not contain an automatically generated table of contents or index, these elements need to be recreated manually for each target language. Getting the index page numbers right is a very time-consuming process, and leaves a considerable margin for errors. Automating this process will help avoid any problems.
- Text in graphics. Adding large chunks of text in icons or bitmaps will increase localization costs and add to the translation and editing time for graphics. Ideally, the level of text in graphics should be kept to a minimum, and should be highlighted at the internationalization phase and the implications understood.

The following sections describe some of the methods used to internationalize a software product, along with examples, check lists, and tools that may simplify the internationalization effort.

2 Language

To date, the majority of software products have been developed in the United States. As a result, the bulk of software localization work is performed on English source language products for other languages. Influencing the way language is used in the English product can have a great impact on the acceptance and localizability of the product.

Typical examples of product components that often pose difficulties during the translation cycle are sample files and template documents. With these types of documents, it is advisable to use generic examples and models which can be used internationally with little or no modification.

2.1 Overview

Most software publishers employ a group of technical writers and authors who write and develop the online help and documentation text. It is not an easy task for writers whose native language is English to "write globally", i.e. use examples that can be understood world-wide, because this will often limit the type of examples they can use and the style they can adopt.

The most important thing in a written text is that the text must be understood by non-native readers. The terminology and style used should, therefore, be basic and uniform. Furthermore, the text must be written with translation in mind, so the translator can work quickly and accurately, without the need for clarifications, rewrites, or cultural modifications. Typical examples of a writing style that could make the translation work easier are short sentences, simple vocabulary, consistency in terminology, and careful use of punctuation.

Moreover, a structural consistency in the source files greatly improves leveraging of information within the same files and also across file sets, especially where CAT tools are used in the translation process.

2.2   Check List

Ensure technical writers keep the following issues in mind:

2.2.1   TERMINOLOGY

✓ Create a glossary of terms relating to the product, company or industry, and apply this consistently across all documentation and online help sets.

✓ Use consistent phrases and terminology. The importance of simple, concise language is magnified when writing for translation. For example, decide at the outset if you want to use phrases like "click on", "click", "choose", or "select", when describing software commands.

✓ Maintain consistency between the documentation or online help text and the software user interface.

2.2.2   STYLE

✓ Ensure that the text is clear and unambiguous, for example refrain from using verbs like "may" or "might"; use "can" instead.

✓ Avoid the use of "telegraphic English", i.e. write full sentences.

✓ Use short, concise sentences, preferably in active voice. For example, "Choose the Copy command" is much clearer than "the Copy command should now be chosen."

✓ Do not use culturally-specific text or jargon, e.g. humor, political references, slang, references to TV shows, national monuments, sports equipment, hand gestures, or ethnic stereotypes. Equivalents in other languages can probably be found, but this requires much more effort than straight translation and increases costs.

✓ Avoid references to or images of animals. In some Asian regions, for example, this may be considered offensive. Be careful in using references to religions, sacred objects, or symbols.

✓ Avoid references to seasons, time zones, weather, or holidays, such as Christmas trees or Halloween pumpkins.

✓ Avoid using acronyms and abbreviations, e.g. NBA (National Basketball Association). Abbreviations are often difficult to reproduce in other languages. If acronyms have to be used, spell them out in the first occurrence in the text.

✓ Avoid using long modifier chains or ambiguous phrases, such as "required disk slot". This phrase can be interpreted as "the slot for a required disk" or a "disk slot which is required".

✓ Consider measurement conversion. For example, consider adding "(2.54 cm)" when referring to "1 inch". This will also avoid inconsistencies between the conversions done in different target languages; some translators may leave the "1 inch" unchanged, others may completely replace it with the conversion. Anticipate any confusion.

✓ In marketing material, avoid comparative statements on competitor's products. In many countries outside the U.S. this is unusual or even illegal.

2.2.3 EXPANSION

✓ Leave sufficient space for text expansion in tables, flow charts, and illustrations, i.e. anticipate text expansion, particularly in software user interfaces.

✓ When text is localized into double-byte languages, anticipate vertical expansion.

✓ Use only one space between sentences and after all punctuation marks.

2.2.4 COUNTRY-SPECIFIC ELEMENTS

✓ Write dates out fully, e.g. write "6 November 2000" instead of "6/11/2000" because the month/date order varies in some languages.

✓ Be aware that many countries have different calendars, e.g. in India and Thailand the calendar starts from Buddha's birth.

✓ In telephone numbers and addresses, always include the country code and country name. Specify the hours and time zone when customer support services are available.

✓ When including examples such as a person's name, use generic examples that are known world-wide.

✓ Check if the warranty and technical support text is relevant and valid in the target countries. If not, consider having them translated or reviewed by legal in-country staff or consultants.

Some of the items listed above are standard issues for technical documentation authoring, nevertheless it is advisable to list all items in an internal, international style guide for the authoring team. This style guide could be based on standard works like the *Chicago Manual of Style* or the *Microsoft Manual of Style*.

2.3 Controlled Language

Controlling or structuring the use of language is an important factor in reducing the costs of writing online help and documentation, and the time needed to develop and update it. Controlled language, controlled English, easy English, structured authoring, or simplified English is a writing system or method which helps technical authors avoid ambiguity, and improve the readability of their text. There is no single standard for controlled language; several systems have been developed and applied with varying degrees of success.

A controlled language is a subset of a natural language and is used to write technical documentation, usually for a particular company or industry sector. Its basic components can include a set of approved terms for certain concepts, a list of words and phrases to be avoided, along with their approved synonyms, and a set of grammar rules.

Using controlled language has the following advantages:

- The information presented can only be interpreted in one way, so ambiguity is reduced and readability improved.
- Consistent use of style and terminology is enforced.
- The translatability of the text is improved, especially when computer-assisted translation tools, e.g. machine translation, are used in the localization process.
- The time to market for localized products can be shortened because translation speed will be increased, often up to 25%.

Several companies have developed software applications that assist writers in using controlled language. These can be run in conjunction with the editor used by technical writers. Most of these tools work either in batch mode or interactive mode, presenting grammar and vocabulary suggestions in an external word processor or desktop publishing application. The tools basically place constraints on the vocabulary and syntactic structures that an author can use.

Even though the resulting documents may be easier to read and understand, they are not necessarily easier to write. A few examples of these constraints include a maximum or restricted number of words per sentence, no passive clauses, restrictions on the use of tenses that may be difficult to translate, and a defined terminology domain.

Controlled language has been used for years in the aerospace and automotive industries, and is gradually finding its way in the IT industry, often combined with SGML- or XML-based content creation and document management systems. One of the first companies to develop a controlled English, called Fundamental English, was Caterpillar Tractor Corporation. In the aerospace industry, the AECMA Simplified English standard was released in 1986. Both systems outline style and grammar rules and list both allowed and proscribed vocabulary.

Here are some examples of commercially available tools for controlled language writing:

- ClearCheck by Logica Carnegie Group – more information at www.logica.com or www.cgi.com
- LANT®MASTER by LANT – www.lant.com
- MAXit by SMART Communications – www.smartny.com

Further information on Controlled English can be found at www.eamt.org.

3   Software

Internationalization of software code has always been a complex task. More often than not, software products have been developed without any consideration for localization issues. This makes it very difficult to re-design the code for a localized version.

The best approach to take when developing software is to maintain language independence throughout the entire programming code. No portion of the software should contain code that is specific to any one language. Product development and internationalization should be treated as a single, integrated process. Moreover, the code should rely on language support offered by the operating system or another qualified language application programming interface (API).

Most development environment manuals contain chapters on developing software for international markets. Microsoft, for example, includes chapters on internationalization in their Visual Studio documentation. This can be accessed through the Microsoft MSDN web site at msdn.microsoft.com (search for "internationalization").

3.1   Overview

Software publishers have to deal with several design issues when internationalizing software code for foreign markets. The most important issues are listed below:

1. Character encoding
2. Location of *translatables*, e.g. user interface text
3. User interface design
4. Regional standards

In the following sections, tips and resources are provided that may help you in internationalizing a software product. Remember that re-engineering a product after development is more time-consuming and problematic than addressing internationalization issues from the very beginning!

3.1.1   CHARACTER ENCODING

Apart from having the capability to *display* all foreign characters in the software user interface, users should also be able to *input* international data in a software application, using a localized keyboard or other preferred input method.

The best advice for software publishers who want to enable their products for international markets is: Go Unicode! Unicode is a fixed-width, 16-bit character set, which means it can represent more than 65,000 characters. The Unicode standard is destined to replace the ASCII and other single- and multi-byte character sets currently in existence. Unicode encompasses scripts and general-purpose symbols for writing text in nearly every language.

If a software publisher considers localizing products for Far Eastern or Middle Eastern markets, making the source code and application Unicode compliant is worth the investment. Unicode is already supported by most current operating systems, including

Mac OS and Windows. The main advantages of Unicode support are the ability to represent all text with one unambiguous encoding, and the ease with which multilingual text can be supported.

For more information on Unicode, visit the Unicode Consortium web site at www.unicode.org.

3.1.2　LOCATION OF TRANSLATABLES

For the location of translatables in source code, there are several approaches, the most common of which is centralizing all localizable items in external resource files.

According to Microsoft's development guidelines, the most efficient way to design a software application is to split the application into two conceptual blocks: a code block and a data block. The data block contains all user interface items and no programming code, which means it is the only element that requires localization. All information from the data block can be centralized in a resource file which compiles into a resource-only language .dll. If a multilingual user interface is required, for example a button for switching between languages, name the resource-only .dll files with an easily identifiable language code, e.g. `res_fr.dll` for the French version.

Externalizing all translatables to one resource file has the following advantages:

- Efficiency – for each new language version of the application, only the resource file needs to be adapted.
- Security – localizers or vendors do not need to access the source code.
- Quality – reduces the chance of missing translatable strings, and limits the level of functional testing required.

For translators or localization vendors, dealing with source code that contains translatable text can pose some challenges, particularly where code and translatable text are indistinguishable. A string like "COPY" could be a status bar string, but could also be an internal command that would corrupt the application when changed.

In addition to externalizing all localizable strings to one file, it is advisable to create a build environment that is truly multilingual. Here is an example of a folder structure for a multilingual software build environment:

If separate folders containing language-specific resource files are used, create different project files to compile each language version.

3.1.3 USER INTERFACE

There are many things to consider when developing a software user interface. The most important thing is to allow for text expansion. Add approximately 30% extra space to each control or button in the dialog boxes. Ensure the menu tree fits on all screen resolutions. For example, the German translation for the Edit menu is "Bearbeiten", and "Wiedergabe" for the View menu. In both cases, the text has been expanded by 100%. For this reason, many Windows applications in European languages use a question mark symbol (?) instead of the word "Help" on menu bars.

3.1.4 REGIONAL STANDARDS

Software applications should, of course, support all regional standards of the countries or regions where they are being shipped. Here are some examples of regional standards that should be supported by applications:

- Sorting rules, e.g. in Traditional Chinese sorting is based on the number of strokes in the character. In Swedish the letter Å sorts after Z, not near A.
- Measurement formats, e.g. inches in the U.S. versus centimeters in Europe
- Number formats, e.g. decimal separators
- Time/date formats
- Calendar formats
- Currency formats
- Address formats
- Phone numbers

Most development environments support the *locale* model, i.e. a collection of standard settings, rules and data specific to a language and geographical region.

3.2 Check List

Here is a check list for foreign character support:

- ✓ Ensure the product supports international sorting standards.
- ✓ Ensure the product is multi-byte enabled, for example by using Unicode.
- ✓ Verify that the users can successfully cut/paste text that contains accented (or double-byte) characters to other applications.
- ✓ Verify that the application can open and save files with accented characters.
- ✓ Ensure the product supports international code sets, and supports both input and output (display) of accented characters.

Here is a checklist for location of translatables:

- ✓ Keep track of all resource files and *include files* (bitmaps, icons) to be localized.
- ✓ Avoid using too many separate, small resource files. Ideally all translatable text should be centralized in one or two files.

- ✓ Use variable names that are not "real" words to avoid translation of non-translatable strings.
- ✓ Use comments with code to provide context for translators.
- ✓ Exclude all non-translatable text strings from the resource files, unless they include comment text for translators.

Here is a checklist for the user interface design:

- ✓ Allow for text expansion, make buffers and UI large enough to accommodate translated text. French and German, for example, are usually up to 30% longer than the English originals.
- ✓ Use text-wrapping features instead of manual wrapping using \n control codes.
- ✓ If possible, restrict the use of "dynamic" dialog boxes, i.e. dialog boxes with options where text is retrieved from the strings section and dynamically inserted.
- ✓ Avoid concatenating strings, i.e. combining strings at run-time to form new strings. Composite messages are often very hard to translate.
- ✓ Avoid hardcoding keyboard commands.
- ✓ Make sure shortcut key combinations are accessible from international keyboards, e.g. use Function keys instead of letters in shortcut key combinations, e.g. Ctrl+F3.
- ✓ Delete any obsolete text or strings from the resource files.
- ✓ Avoid hardcoding coordinates of dialog box or control sizes.
- ✓ Avoid using placeholders or variables, such as %s, or include a comment line explaining to the localizer what will be inserted at run-time. Never add grammatical endings (such as the plural "s") to variables.
- ✓ Allow localizers to change the font and font size of options in dialog boxes.
- ✓ Ensure custom, third-party controls in dialog boxes are localizable.
- ✓ Be cautious about using icons or bitmaps showing people, hand gestures, holiday symbols, or body language. Use generic images that do not have to be localized or adjusted for target locales.
- ✓ Avoid using colors or color combinations associated with national flags or political movements.
- ✓ Avoid using fixed variable orders.
- ✓ Limit the use of text or letters in bitmaps and icons.
- ✓ When variables are used within a string, add at least one extra line to text boxes.

Here is a checklist for locale support:

- ✓ Build in support in for DBCS (Double-Byte Character Sets) for Asian languages, i.e. Japanese, Chinese and Korean, to enable users to enter, store, process, retrieve, distribute, display, and print DBCS languages.
- ✓ Build in support for IME (Input Method Editor) handling for Asian languages.

✓ Use language support from the operating system running the software product.

✓ Ensure the product supports different calendars, date formats, and time formats.

✓ Ensure the product supports different number formats, currencies, weights, and measurement systems.

✓ Ensure the product supports international paper sizes, envelope sizes, and address formats.

3.3 Tools

Several tools have been developed to help developers determine how well their products have been internationalized.

Two types of internationalization tools are available: code analyzers and software that modifies the code to support different locales and character sets using international libraries. The following sections provide some examples of these tools.

3.3.1 I18N EXPEDITOR

I18n Expeditor analyzes source code (C/C++ and Java) before compilation to detect and (often automatically) correct internationalization errors, such as hard-coded strings and character literals.

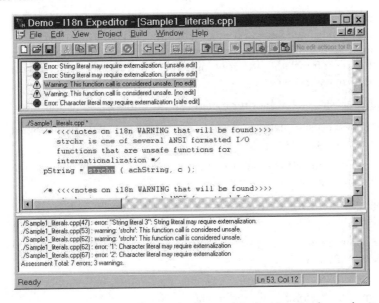

For more information on I18n Expeditor, visit the OneRealm web site at www.onerealm.com.

3.3.2 GLOBAL CHECKER

Uniscape's Global Checker is a software scanning utility that identifies issues with internationalization and provides solutions. It scans Java, C or C++ type source files and searches for language support issues based on the language and platform specified.

Uniscape's Global C provides programmers with a basic set of routines and functions providing platform-independent internationalization services, such as Unicode API's, message catalogs, and a locale definition utility.

For more information on Global Checker and Global C, visit the Uniscape web site at www.uniscape.com.

3.3.3 ALIS BATAM

Alis Batam offers instant, global language support to an existing Windows application. It creates an open, multilingual application, unrestricted by the Windows version it runs on, as input, character sets and display are all handled by the internationalization library and include full Unicode support.

For more information on Batam, visit the Alis web site at www.alis.com.

4   Web Sites and HTML

Like software, web sites and HTML documents should be designed and developed with foreign language support in mind. Internationalization of web sites implies developing the site content to simplify hosting and display of localized information. This applies to graphics, placement of text, and local content.

Because web site internationalization is very much integrated with localization, the process of publishing web sites in foreign languages is usually referred to as web site globalization. A well globalized and internationalized web site allows localization vendors to focus on translating the content, as opposed to processing a wide range of complex file formats and types.

In short, the web site globalization process can be summarized as follows:

1. Choose a web site platform, server, and software palette that supports multilingual site hosting.

2. Evaluate the site architecture to determine what should be changed to facilitate the localization process.

3. Identify which parts of the site can be translated and which parts must be re-written specific for a target country – local content versus global content.

4. Create a multilingual web site structure or content database with language folders and navigation system.

5. Choose a toolset, for example combining a multilingual content management system with tracking tools and translation memory.

6. Develop a site update and maintenance plan.

After these initial internationalization steps, select a localization vendor to translate the web site content, or create local content. If applicable, involve your local or regional offices in the content creation or review process for their locale.

4.1   Overview

It is not unusual to see web sites changing frequently, both from a content and design perspective. Web pages are often generated dynamically using templates, scripts, and databases. Maintaining web sites in several languages can be a tedious process if it is not well thought-out from the beginning.

For more information on multilingual web site development, visit the Localization and Internationalization web page from the World Wide Web Consortium at www.w3c.org/ international. Other good references for web site internationalization and globalization are the Worldpoint web site at www.worldpoint.com, the Idiom web site at www.idiominc.com, Mark Bishop's book *How to Build a Successful International Web Site*, and the www.multilingualwebmaster.com web site.

4.1.1   WEB SITE DESIGN

When planning a web site, anticipate localization even if the initial version will be in one language only.

First of all, determine which pages will be language-specific, e.g. product descriptions, and which ones will be generic, e.g. product graphics or icons, and build a multilingual folder structure for the web site based on specific language folders. At this point it is important to decide whether it is preferable to have one central web site running a content database that contains all language versions of web site, or separate web sites for each target language or region. The latter is an option often favored by larger companies with a significant physical presence in each country.

Maintaining one central, multilingual web site is the most common solution for companies that maintain a relatively small web site or do not publish in a large number of languages. For example, the high-level folder structure of a centralized, multilingual web site may be set up as follows:

```
index.html
\us
\us\images
\fr
\fr\images
\de
\de\images
\shared images
```

The index.html home page contains links to all language folders and contains a language selection menu. The \us, \fr, and \de folders contain the English, French, and German files. Each language folder has its \images folder to store localized images, and there is a \shared images folder containing non-localized art, such as logos or bullet symbols.

It is also very important to consider a multilingual navigation system that enables users to select their language or country first, and then guides them through all pa̲g̲ ̲ ̲ ̲their native language. Ideally, the system should track the visitor's language pre̲ example by leaving a cookie on the local machine. It is advisable to inclu̲d̲ choice button on every page, because users may access the page throu̲ engine instead of the site's home page. List the languages in a selection menu with localized language names.

Many web sites today are database-driven or have a transaction processor, i.e. so-called dynamic web sites. Ensure that the database and platform chosen support content in foreign languages, particularly if there is a plan to localize into multi-byte languages. Check if common internationalization issues such as currency conversions and date or time formats are supported. A good way to verify language support is to run a pseudo-translation of the web site, including accented characters in all strings, or increasing the string length using a search and replace tool.

A properly internationalized web site has the following features:

- Support for non-Roman languages and character encodings, for example through the use of Unicode
- A scalable design which makes the localization process more efficient, for example, by limiting the use of text within graphics
- Clear separation of code and content, for example, by including all interface text in one central content database, or using cascading style sheets for sets of HTML pages
- Web page layout which is determined by language-specific style sheets or templates

A web site ready for localization would be Unicode compliant, stores all content in a database format, and publishes information dynamically using internationalized HTML templates and style sheets that allow for text expansion. Ideally, the site should have a tracking tool which would automatically detect changed or new content and send it directly to the assigned localization vendor and/or reviewers before it is returned and inserted in the content database.

4.1.2 CULTURAL ADAPTATION

You need to clearly classify the pages on the web site under the following headings:

- Pages that require heavy cultural or regional adaptation

- Pages that require straight translation
- Pages that require no translation

Pages that require real "localization", i.e. many adaptations to regional standards and conventions, such as marketing text, may need to be rewritten by local authors in each of the target languages. Involving in-country offices or contacts in this process is recommended. Localizing this type of content goes way beyond translation because it is an integral part of the company's global branding initiative. Pages that contain no country-specific information, such as technical product information, can be sent directly for translation. Examples of pages that require no translation are local advertising campaigns or local office information.

Tip: Web sites that contain a lot of *local* content, as opposed to localized or translated information, tend to increase the comfort level of international visitors. For example, do not just translate your company information into German, but also include additional information about your German operations, your activities in Germany, or local case studies and client references.

If a web site offers online purchasing capabilities which need to be localized, ensure there is a strategy for the following:

- Local payment facilities
- Local product mix
- Local distribution system
- Local laws for taxes, tariffs, etc.

Obviously, true web site globalization in the case of e-commerce sites requires far more effort than just localizing the content.

4.1.3 UPDATE MANAGEMENT

It is important to consider web site localization as part of the development process, because web site content is often more frequently updated than any other medium. It is essential to use a localization vendor with strong project management skills and advanced translation technology. Develop a long-term relationship and update/maintenance plan with this vendor, as repeated and quick turnaround times will be needed from this vendor.

Essential to update management of multilingual web sites is the use of translation memory systems. For advanced, large web sites published in many different languages, the employment of a "multilingual content management system" or version control software is recommended. These systems compare new or updated documents to the pre-existing memory files, and will only extract the new and previously untranslated text. After the new text has been translated, it is automatically reinserted into the HTML pages or database and uploaded to the web site.

Several tools have been developed to monitor web site content and automatically transfer new or changed content to translators. Examples of such tools are LionTrack by Lionbridge Technologies (www.lionbridge.com) and SDL WebFlow by SDL International (www.sdlintl.com). These tools automate the file transfer of frequently updated content and are usually integrated with a translation memory system.

4.1.4 HTML PAGES

In addition to the overall setup and design of the web site, the individual HTML pages also need to be internationalized.

It is advisable to use the latest version of the HTML standard if there is a plan to publish multilingual web pages. Version 4 of the HTML standard supports Unicode and allows use of multiple languages and character sets in HTML pages. It is also possible to enable foreign language searching and sorting functions by using the right language, region, and character set encoding tags in the pages. For more information on inserting language tags, refer to the Engineering HTML section on page 264.

It is best to avoid using too many graphics with text on web pages. If graphics with text need to be used, create image files where the text is stored on a separate text layer to make them easier to localize. Keep the foreign target audiences in mind when designing web pages with images. Many countries do not yet have an advanced high-speed internet infrastructure, so restrict the number of graphics.

Where Active Server Pages (ASP) are used or HTML pages containing heavy scripting, include comments for translators, explaining which elements should be translated and where or how they will be displayed. ASP pages often contain a combination of static content, which is translatable, and dynamic information that is retrieved from a database or external files. The dynamic content should be translated in the source, i.e. the content management system or database, not on the ASP page itself.

The most efficient way to design HTML pages for localization is to create subsets for each language in which all path settings and links have already been adjusted to the target language folders and images, and where all language and character set encoding tags are set correctly. This way the localization vendor will only require this subset of the HTML files, which can be merged directly into the central web site after localization. For example, provide the vendor with the contents of a \de folder with HTML files that already link to the \de\images folder where the localized images will be stored.

Consider creating separate HTML templates or style sheets for each language or set of languages. For example, style sheets for Asian languages could define a different font set to be used on the localized HTML pages.

For more information on HTML internationalization, visit the World Wide Web Consortium web site at www.w3c.org/international.

4.2 Check List

When designing a web site, follow these guidelines:

✓ Decide on either a central, multilingual web site or a distributed, language or region-specific web site.

✓ Create a folder structure or database architecture that clearly separates generic content from language-specific content.

✓ Develop a navigation system that guides foreign users through the web site in their native language.

✓ Create a clear language selection menu on the home page; use the translated name of the language (for example "Deutsch" for German), as opposed to flags. Flags will not work in countries with several languages, e.g Switzerland, where French, German, and Italian are spoken.

✓ Add the language selection option on all pages because users do not necessarily access the site through the home page; they may enter the site through a search engine, for example.

✓ Ensure the back-end web site database or transaction processor supports foreign language character sets, particularly for multi-byte languages.

✓ Allow for local formatting conventions, such as address formats, date/time formats, currencies, telephone and fax numbers, etc.

✓ Develop an efficient site update and change management strategy.

When developing HTML pages, follow these guidelines:

✓ Use generic icons.

✓ Avoid using too many graphics with text, and for all graphics containing text keep the original graphic files with the translatable text on a separate text layer.

✓ Always include the `charset` parameter in the HTML header. This is important even for standard iso-8859-1 (Latin-1). Even though the HTTP protocol says this is the default, many localized browsers do not accept it as the default.

✓ If (text) layers are not used for graphics, keep the blank image backgrounds. With blank images, localizers do not need to recreate the image background.

✓ Use variable names that are not words to avoid overtranslation.

✓ Define and use a consistent and limited set of tags.

✓ Avoid complex formatting, and create a resizable layout structure.

✓ Avoid using fonts as a design feature, because the specified fonts may be overruled by browser settings, or the fonts may not support accented or double-byte characters.

✓ Avoid using em- and en-dashes. They are not always displayed correctly in all browsers.

✓ Avoid broken functionality in the source files. Harmless tagging errors will cause the localization vendor to question whether the error was introduced at the translation phase.

✓ Add `<!-- -->` comments for translators to explain scripts, applet codes, etc.

✓ Avoid using tabs or spaces to format text.

✓ Allow tables to resize dynamically, and allow for sufficient text expansion in table cells.

✓ Create language-specific versions of the HTML pages, including the correct language encoding tags, to be sent out for translation.

4.3 Tools

Several companies offer tools that aid the development, maintenance, and management of international and multilingual web sites. Most of these tools contain capabilities that extract all of the text from HTML pages and insert it into a database. This makes content creation, synchronization, version control, and translation management easier.

4.3.1 WORLDSERVER

The Idiom WorldServer software offers a full global web site management solution, including features that allow the user to collaborate effectively with translators, reviewers, and site managers. WorldServer makes extensive use of XML and open APIs. One of the biggest advantages is that it is highly customizable.

For more information on WorldServer, visit the Idiom Technologies web site at www.idiomtech.com.

4.3.2 GLOBAL CONTENT MANAGER

Global Content Manager is a software agent that integrates Uniscape.com with a company's corporate web site to recognize changes in web content, automatically initiate translation of corresponding multilingual content and update the site when completed.

For more information on Global Content Manager, visit the Uniscape web site at www.uniscape.com.

4.3.3 AMBASSADOR

Ambassador by GlobalSight is a web site maintenance utility that allows users to maintain databases of the translated material. When a change is made in one language, flags are used to mark the equivalent places in the other languages.

GlobalSight Ambassador also enables the user to transform a single-language web site into a centrally managed multilingual web site.

For more information on Ambassador, visit the GlobalSight web site at www.globalsight.com.

4.3.4 PASSPORT

According to WorldPoint's web site, Passport is "the Internet's first comprehensive software solution for creating, managing, and delivering complex multilingual web sites." Passport manages multilingual content development, management, and delivery using a centralized database architecture.

For more information on Passport, visit the WorldPoint site at www.worldpoint.com.

4.3.5 WEBPLEXER

WebPlexer allows users to maintain international versions of a web site, generate the correct linguistic version of a requested page, track the locales, languages, and pages receiving the most impressions or hits, etc. Its main features are language navigation capabilities and options.

WebPlexer stores all text in a database. To translate the files, text is exported to RTF format. Conversion to HTML is done automatically upon re-insertion in the system.

For more information on WebPlexer, visit the Language Automation web site at www.lai.com.

4.3.6 UNISITE

UniSite by Glides is a database-driven platform for creating and managing global web sites, particularly multilingual or multi-regional sites. UniSite is structured with an SQL database to run on Windows NT and Windows 2000 servers. It can also interface with Oracle and Sybase databases.

For more information on UniSite, visit the Glides web site at www.glides.com.

4.3.7 TRANSERVER

TranServer by Wholetree.com is a translation server that allows for the exchange of data between publishers and translators. The server can receive files from SiteTrak, which is a technology designed to maintain updates to companies' multilingual web sites.

For more information on TranServer and SiteTrak, visit the Wholetree.com web site at www.wholetree.com.

5 Documentation

There are many issues to be considered when selecting an authoring and publishing environment for printed or online documentation.

In addition to teaching technical authors how to write with an international audience in mind as described in the beginning of this chapter, there are several other – practical – aspects in documentation creation that can largely influence the efficiency of creating multilingual versions of a document, such as the application and fonts used, the template design, compatibility with CAT tools, and the final output requirements.

5.1 Creation

The page layout or document production application for creating printed or online documentation needs to be chosen carefully.

Formatting work after translation typically represents 30 to 40% of the total localization cost of a printed manual, and picking a suitable page layout application may reduce those costs considerably. For example, ensure the application you use supports automatic generation of table of contents and indexes. Doing this manually will multiply this expense by the number of target languages. Converting documents to a database publishing solution will further reduce DTP costs.

Base decisions on issues such as type of document, supported languages, final output, and compatibility with CAT tools.

5.1.1 DOCUMENT TYPE

The application chosen to create documents will depend to a large extent on the type of document being produced. For example, when creating a quick reference card, product box, or registration card, an application such as QuarkXPress is most suitable because Quark was designed for the creation of short documents containing many graphics, colors, and images.

Disk or CD labels are usually created with graphics applications such as Adobe Illustrator or MacroMedia Freehand.

When creating a large product manual, a document production application such as PageMaker or FrameMaker is most suitable. Both applications enable the user to automatically generate table of contents, indexes, and cross-references. Word processors such as Microsoft Word can best be used for short documents such as customer letters, errata, and other relatively small documents.

When publishing large amounts of documents, in multiple formats, versions, and languages, choosing a document management or content creation system may be the best option. For example, an SGML-based document management system (DMS) enables the user to create documents from information elements selected, based on version, author, language, etc. in multiple output formats, for example PostScript files for printing, and PDF files for online distribution. Examples of such content and document management systems are Documentum (www.documentum.com) and Interleaf (www.interleaf.com). Commonly used SGML editors are FrameMaker/SGML (www.adobe.com) and Epic Editor (www.arbortext.com).

For more information on structured documentation standards, visit the OASIS (Organization for the Advancement of Structured Information Standards) web site at www.oasis-open.org.

5.1.2 SUPPORTED LANGUAGES

Remember that document creation applications do not necessarily support all languages. Before writing product manuals in a particular application, ensure that this (version of the) application supports all languages required. Translators should be able to use the same application and version for their translation work, and not have to rely on some sort of conversion or a localized version of the application.

For example, when translating manuals into Asian languages, ensure the application used to create the manuals supports input, display, and kerning of double-byte characters. If the manuals are to be published in multilingual format, verify that different languages can easily be combined within one document.

Another important aspect is the availability of dictionaries and hyphenation modules for the application chosen.

5.1.3 FINAL OUTPUT

Consider carefully the final output required when choosing a document creation application: if the final output to the printer has to be color-separated PostScript files, ensure the application supports color separations. For example, creating color separations from Microsoft Word is a very difficult process, whereas producing the same color separation in an application such as FrameMaker is only a matter of selecting some print options.

For PostScript files, ensure the PostScript driver and printer description files support the target languages of the documents. If files are to be distributed electronically, for example in PDF format, ensure that the online file format supports all character sets of the target languages.

5.1.4 TEMPLATES

Designing templates for all language versions of the documentation can make the localization process more efficient, particularly when using the same number of pages for all languages or if you're producing a multilingual booklet.

The choice of fonts used in the templates or style sheets is important. Make sure to select fonts that exist in foreign language versions and contain all required accented characters. The basic idea behind designing templates is to minimize the amount of manual layout overrides.

To save time during the page formatting process, create language-specific templates containing the correct page size, fonts, language settings, document properties, etc. for each target language or group of languages. For example, when creating a standard template for all documentation translated into Chinese, with the correct Chinese fonts defined in each style, the DTP operator need only to attach this template, which will save a lot of time and gives documents a consistent look, regardless of the language.

If only one template is used for all languages, select a "universal" page format, and leave sufficient room for text expansion in tables, page margins, space between paragraphs, leading, etc.

A template which is well set-up makes it easier to keep a one-to-one page correspondence, which may be important for the final output.

5.1.5 CAT TOOL COMPATIBILITY

Now that the majority of localization vendors use computer aided translation (CAT) tools, such as translation memory systems, to perform their translations, make sure that the application chosen to create documents is compatible with these CAT tools.

Check with the localization vendor which CAT tool they will use, and verify that the tool supports the file format of the application being used for generating the documentation. Alternatively, research which file formats are best supported by the most commonly used CAT tools, and use these formats to develop the documentation.

5.2   Graphics

Many things can be done to ensure that graphics are easily localized. The best way is to create layered graphics, with the text in editable format on a separate layer. For example, create Adobe Photoshop images with one background layer, and several text layers for each language. The text in the layer can then be translated, the required layers enabled and the image saved in a format supported by the authoring application.

Here is an example of a graphic showing a baby's face and the overlaying text that needs to be localized. For the localization vendor, it will be difficult to recreate the background on which the text is placed. However, if the vendor is provided with a PhotoShop image file where the text is placed on a separate layer, all the translator needs to do is replace the text on the layer with a translation, and save the file in the desired file format, e.g. GIF or TIF.

When using an application such as Illustrator or CorelDraw to create artwork for manuals, ensure that the fonts are not outlined. Outlined text cannot be edited or translated. It is better to supply the localization vendor with the source files containing editable text.

Please note that linked – or referenced – graphics are easier to process in multiple languages than embedded graphics, especially when the output of the translated documents will be generated in several different formats, such as HTML, printed manuals, and PDF. Different output formats typically require different image formats or resolutions. In order to avoid having to embed or paste all graphics several times in the translated documents, try linking them instead.

Captions of graphics should be placed in the running text so they can be translated using a translation memory tool, and to avoid time-consuming image editing.

If the document contains screen captures that are difficult to reproduce or create, include detailed instructions for the localization vendors. Screen capture scripts can shorten the time required to create captures in various languages considerably.

5.3   Check List

Here are some guidelines for creating documentation:

✓ Choose an application that suits the document type, and supports all target languages and output formats.

✓ Design templates to be used for all languages, or language-specific templates.

✓ Use standard fonts, and if localizing into Asian languages, ensure fonts are used that have Asian variants.

✓ Check if it is possible to use combined fonts, i.e. fonts containing both Asian and Roman character sets, in cases where the translated text will contain many English words or sections.

✓ Ensure consistent text flow and linking, and use styles consistently.

✓ When working with character styles, for example Character Tags in FrameMaker, create a character style for all software user interface references. A different color for this style makes it easier, both in the original and translated versions, to perform a software consistency check on the documentation.

✓ Leave sufficient space for text expansion when creating a document where no pages can be added, such as a registration card or product box.

In addition to selecting the most appropriate application, there are many other things that can be done to ensure that CAT tools are used effectively:

✓ Avoid using manual hard returns in running text.

✓ Avoid placing (index) markers in the middle of words or sentences. Place index markers outside of the sentence instead.

✓ Avoid using (manual) hyphenation, if possible.

✓ Import graphics by reference, i.e. link graphics instead of embedding them.

✓ Avoid using conditional text, especially at character level.

✓ Maintain a single text flow.

✓ When using revision marks or change bars when creating documents, make sure all revisions are accepted and no marks are left in the documents before being delivered to the vendor.

✓ Keep documents (or chapters) shorter than 50 pages; this will improve the performance of CAT tools.

Here are some guidelines for the use of graphics:

✓ Create artwork which is generic and internationally acceptable.

✓ Create graphics with text using a separate text layer.

✓ Ensure that screen captures are reproducible, and use the default color scheme and font settings.

✓ Link graphics to the documents, as opposed to embedding them.

✓ Do not outline text in graphics or illustrations.

✓ Create graphic captions in the document text, not in the graphic.

6 Creating Localization Kits

A well-prepared localization kit will save the localization vendors a considerable amount of time evaluating and preparing the project material. This is particularly important when sending the kit out to multiple vendors, where multiple languages have been split between vendors. Any work that can be done before the kit is sent out will prevent duplication of effort, which will eventually be reflected in the total project costs.

Localization Kit is defined in Nadine Kano's book *Developing International Software (Microsoft Press, 1995)* as: "A subset of tools, source files, binary files, test scripts and appropriate instructions that can be used to create a localized edition of a program. Generally given to translators, localization agencies or international distributors."

Distributing localization kits will also allow a publisher to obtain detailed project quotations and proposals before vendors are selected and production starts.

In general, a localization kit contains the following components:

1. Localization guidelines and schedule information

2. Build environments and source files

3. Reference materials

The localization kit should be divided into sections specifically built for the team working on the project, e.g. a section for project managers, one for online help engineers, etc. The kit should use a well-organized folder structure. Provide a road map on the contents of the kit and ensure no irrelevant or extraneous files are inadvertently included, as these are bound to cause confusion.

6.1 Localization Guidelines

Localization kits should include detailed guidelines for all the team members involved in the project, such as project managers, engineers, desktop publishers, and linguists.

The most important information for the project managers is an overview of project scope, milestones and requirements. Engineers expect guidelines on compilers and versions that need to be used for the online help or software, while desktop publishers need to know which application version, fonts, platform, and output settings to use.

6.1.1 PROJECT MANAGEMENT GUIDELINES

Project managers working for localization vendors would need the following information:

- Required tasks, services, and deliverables, e.g. only translation, or full engineering and testing. Refer to the List Of Expected Services and Deliverables section on page 51.

- Project scope overview, e.g. components, number of words to localize, languages, number of pages for DTP, number of updates that can be expected

- General project release schedule, including milestones such as hand-offs, review cycles, and deliveries
- Quality steps, e.g. number of language reviews, online help functionality validation, software testing scope
- References to information on the product or product terminology, e.g. web sites or subject-matter dictionaries
- Contact information and communication methods

When scheduling a project, try to incorporate a realistic time frame for localization into the flow chart for product development. If something slips, adjust the time scheduled for localization accordingly.

6.1.2 SOFTWARE ENGINEERING GUIDELINES

Localization engineers need to know what resource files need to be localized, the hardware or software required to build the software, and how the compilation and testing phase is to be conducted.

Make sure the localization kit includes information on the following:

- Any specific requirements for the computer setup, such as hardware, platform, path settings, third party software, memory, etc.
- The version of the compiler that should be used to compile the localized software
- Instructions about compilation process, e.g. location of project files, language settings to change, batch files that need to be run
- List of files that require localization, and instructions on the text that needs to be localized and text that should stay in English
- For cosmetic testing of dialog boxes, include instructions on the operating system version and resolution settings that should be used
- Software testing approach/requirements. If functional testing is required, include test scripts.

6.1.3 ONLINE HELP OR HTML ENGINEERING GUIDELINES

Online help or HTML engineers need to know how to compile the help files, and how to test them.

For Windows Help, HTML Help or web site localization projects, include the following information:

- Compilation procedure, i.e. the compiler version to be used, or a third-party application such as Robohelp to be installed
- List of files that require localization, and instructions on the text that needs to be localized and text that should stay in English

- Specifications for the images or screen captures, i.e. monitor resolution, color palette, file format, or fonts
- Specification of editor, i.e. version of Microsoft Word, or HTML Editor
- A list of platforms, viewers, browsers and browser versions with which the localized online help or HTML project should be tested
- An overview of the authoring, multimedia and validation tools to be used on the source files
- An explanation of filtering processes used to load the source files in a translation memory tool, if applicable
- Testing approach, for example operating system, browser and browser version to be used for testing
- Specification of the language settings that need to be changed in the localized files, for example META tags in HTML files

6.1.4 DOCUMENTATION GUIDELINES

Include a documentation section in the localization kit containing information on:

- The desktop publishing application to be used, and the platform and version
- List of files that require localization, and instructions as to what text needs to be localized and what text should stay in English
- General document setup guidelines, i.e. should the manual contain all languages, or should a separate manual be created for each language?
- Printer driver version and printer description file to be used, e.g. Adobe PostScript Printer Driver version 5 with the Linotronic 530 description file
- Guidelines for text expansion, i.e. what to do when the translations are longer than the original: add pages, decrease font size, change margins?
- Fonts and font types to be used, for example Type I fonts or TrueType fonts, and fonts to be used for Asian languages
- Specifications for the images or screen captures, i.e. monitor resolution, color palette, file format, or fonts
- Country-specific standards requirements, for example quotation marks and hyphenation
- Language-specific information, such as part number, address or distributor information, trademarks, and URLs
- Detailed final output specifications, e.g. PostScript or PDF settings, crop marks, color separations, etc.
- Where relevant, steps to produce online manuals
- Test specifications for online manuals, e.g. monitors and monitor or printer resolutions to test, links verification

If possible, include the style guide used by the technical writers of the source files specifying all style conventions, typography, and naming conventions.

6.1.5   LIST OF EXPECTED SERVICES AND DELIVERABLES

A localization kit should contain a statement of work, listing all expected services and deliverables.

Required services will typically include:

- Translating, reviewing, and proofreading all project materials according to the guidelines provided
- Consistency check of software references found in the online help or documentation
- Using and updating terminology glossaries with key terms
- Compiling, engineering and testing online help files according to the guidelines provided
- Compiling, engineering, and visual testing all software components according to the guidelines provided
- Processing updates using the software tools described in the localization kit
- Producing PostScript and/or PDF files of the translated documentation files with the layout and output according to the guidelines provided

Where there are updates or changes to the original source language material, some publishers include the updated source files in the list of deliverables. A vendor should agree with the publisher as to who will be responsible for updating the source files in the case of last-minute changes or updates.

The statement of work should be as clear, complete, and concise as possible. It should also include a description of any collateral services required, such as status reporting or sample hand-offs.

A detailed list of deliverables should be provided, for example:

- Complete and up-to-date translation memories for all components
- An up-to-date project glossary
- Compiled and fully functional tested software files, including all localized resource files and the build environment
- Compiled and fully functional tested help files, including all localized source files, and images
- DTPed and checked documentation files in the following formats: 600 dpi laser hardcopy, PostScript (one file per chapter), and PDF for onscreen display
- Signed copies of all quality assurance check lists

A statement of work could also include information on delivery methods and requirements, for example via FTP using particular file naming conventions.

It is advisable to add a version number to the statement of work, because updates may be necessary during the project.

6.1.6 CONTACT INFORMATION

The contact information in the localization kit should include the name and phone number of the project managers, as well as contacts for technical issues or language issues, e.g. in-country reviewers.

This section should also include the name of the person to be contacted for various aspects of the project, e.g. who should receive status reports or be copied on e-mails concerning serious quality problems.

During a kick-off meeting, contacts between vendor and publisher need to be established, and responsibilities assigned.

6.2 Build Environments and Source Files

The information below outlines what should be included in a localization kit to enable a localization vendor to deliver quality products.

6.2.1 SOFTWARE

Where full software engineering and cosmetic testing is expected from the localization vendor, they should be supplied with the following files:

- A full build environment, including all resource files, *include* files, project files, etc.
- Batch files that automatically set any required system parameters, settings, or compiler settings
- Batch files that allow engineers to compile each language, or all languages in batch mode
- Any proprietary compilation or translation tools
- Resource files and/or glossaries of previously localized versions of the software
- Localized versions of any third-party components, e.g. localized standard dialog boxes for installation scripts

If full functional testing is required, include the following information and files:

- A test plan indicating team size, hardware and software resources, and setup required, responsibilities for fixing bugs, schedule, etc.
- A test suite containing test scripts, both for manual testing and automated testing. These test scripts should ideally be a subset of the scripts used on the original product and should contain additional, localization-specific sections, for example double-byte support test cases.
- Automated test scripts in case manual testing is combined with automatic testing tools such as Segue QA Partner (www.segue.com)
- Sample files or tools required to perform the tests included in the test scripts

- Access to or a copy of the bug tracking database created by the engineers at the publisher's site for the vendor testing team. This database will allow the vendor testing team to enter functionality bugs that need to be fixed by the publisher's engineering team.
- The most suitable skills profile required for the person who will run the tests, e.g. a linguist or a software engineer

6.2.2 ONLINE HELP OR HTML

If a localization vendor is expected to provide full online help engineering and testing, they should receive the following information and files:

- All source files, both text and images, categorized in a proper directory structure
- Project files used to compile the online help project
- Any include or header files required for compilation
- Compiled versions of the online help or HTML Help projects
- Copies of non-standard or proprietary tools or compilers
- (If applicable) templates or style sheets required for formatting the help documents
- (If available) layered versions of non-screenshot graphics containing text

6.2.3 DOCUMENTATION

If a localisation vendor is expected to deliver full documentation desktop publishing and production, they should receive the following information and files:

- All source files, text and artwork, categorized in their proper folder structure
- Printer drivers and printer description files, and printer and screen fonts
- PostScript files, hardcopy, and PDF files of the source documents
- (If applicable) templates or style sheets required for formatting the documents
- (If available) layered versions of non-screenshot graphics containing text

6.3 Reference Materials

Here are some examples of reference materials that should be included in a localization kit:

- A (beta) version of the running software, including online help
- Background information on the product
- A copy of previously localized versions of the product
- Other localized products from same manufacturer
- Glossaries of previous versions of the product, or other localized products
- Operating system glossaries

- Translation memories of previous validated translations
- Linguistic style guides from language reviewers
- Quality check lists or tracking sheets from QA department
- Software user interface design guidelines from software publishers
- Internal style guides and terminology list from technical authors

7   Further Reading

Many books have been written about internationalizing software code. The books listed below cover different aspects of product internationalization and globalization. Some discuss user interface design issues or specific platforms, while others discuss double-byte languages or web site design.

Information on the publication dates has also been included. This is important to note when considering the speed at which internationalization technologies have changed over the past decade and are still changing.

Apple Computer. 1992. *Guide to Macintosh Software Localization*. Addison-Wesley, ISBN 0-201-60856-1.

Apple Computer. 1993. *Inside Macintosh: Text*. Addison-Wesley, ISBN 0-201-63298-5.

Bishop, Mark. 1998. *How to Build a Successful International Web Site*. Coriolis Group Books, ISBN 1-576-10158-4.

Carter, Daniel R. 1991. *Writing Localizable Software for the Macintosh*. Addison-Wesley, ISBN 0-201-57013-0.

Daniels, Peter T. and William Bright. 1996. *The World's Writing Systems*. Oxford University Press, ISBN 0-195-07993-0.

Darnell, Rick. 1997. "Chapter 39: Internationalizing HTML Character Set and Language Tags". *HTML Unleashed*. Sams.net Publishing, ISBN 1-575-21299-4.

Digital Guide to Developing International Software. 1991. Digital Press, ISBN 1-555-58063-7.

Fernandes, Tony. 1995. *Global Interface Design*. AP Professional, ISBN 0-122-53790-4.

Galdo, Elisa del and Jakob Nielsen. 1996. *International User Interfaces*. Wiley & Sons, ISBN 4-711-4965-9.

Hall, P.A.V. and R. Hudson. 1997. *Software Without Frontiers: A Multi-Platform, Multi-Cultural, Multi-Nation Approach*. John Wiley & Sons, ISBN 0-471-96974-5.

Hoft, Nancy. 1995. *International Technical Communication*. John Wiley & Sons, ISBN 0-471-03743-5.

Kano, Nadine. 1995. *Developing International Software for Windows 95 and Windows NT*. Microsoft Press, ISBN 1-556-15840-8.

Latham, Lance. 1997. Standard C Date/Time Library: Programming the World's Calendars and Clocks. R&D Books, ISBN 0-879-30496-0.

Lunde, Ken. 1993. *Understanding Japanese Information Processing*. O'Reilly and Associates, ISBN 1-565-92043-0.

Lunde, Ken. 1998. *CJKV Information Processing*. O'Reilly & Associates, ISBN 1-565-92224-7.

Luong, Tuoc V. and James S.H. Lok, David J. Taylor. 1995. *Internationalization: Developing Software for Global Markets*. John Wiley & Sons, ISBN 0-471-07661-9.

Madell, Tom and Clark Parsons, John Abegg. 1994. *Developing and Localizing International Software*. Prentice Hall, ISBN 0-133-00674-3.

Martin O'Donnell, Sandra. 1993. *Programming for the World: A Guide to Internationalization*. Prentice Hall, ISBN 0-137-22190-8.

O'Hagan, Minako. 1996. *The Coming Industry of Teletranslation*. Multilingual Matters, ISBN 1-853-59325-7.

Ott, Christopher. 1999. *Global Solutions for Multilingual Applications: Real World Techniques for Developers and Designers*. John Wiley & Sons, ISBN 0-471-34827-9.

Schmitt, David A. 2000. *International Programming for Microsoft Windows: Guidelines for Software Localization With Examples in Microsoft Visual C*. Microsoft Press, ISBN 1-572-31956-9.

Taylor, Dave. 1992. *Global Software: Developing Applications for the International Market*. Springer Verlag, ISBN 0-387-97706-6.

Tuthill, Bill and David Smallberg. 1997. *Creating Worldwide Software*. (2nd edition). Sun Press - Prentice Hall, ISBN 1-349-4493-3.

Uren, Emmanuel and Robert Howard, Tiziana Perinotti. 1993. *Software Internationalization and Localization: An Introduction*. Van Nostrand Reinhold, ISBN 0-442-01498-8.

Unicode Consortium. 1996. *The Unicode Standard Version 2.0*. Addison-Wesley, ISBN 0-201-48345-9.

Chapter 3:
Software Translation

This chapter contains information for software translators (or localizers). Topics include translation of resource files, editing resources on Windows and Mac OS platforms, as well as several examples of commonly used tools and procedures.

This chapter includes the following sections:

1. Introduction
2. Translation Guidelines
3. Windows
4. Mac OS
5. Further Reading

Chapters related to these topics are Chapter 4, which has information on engineering localized software, and Chapter 5, which has information on testing localized software.

1 Introduction

In general, "software translation" refers to the translation of all graphical user interface (GUI) components of a software application, such as dialog boxes, menus, and error or status messages displayed on screen. In the screen captures below, all translatable components of the user interface have been marked. They include the document title, menu tree, dialog box title, dialog box options and fields, and a status bar message. The image on the right shows the localized Swedish version of the GUI.

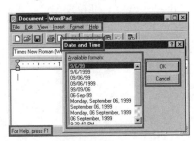 

As this example shows, the date formats have been fully "localized", so that the list only shows available date formats that are used in Sweden.

Most localization projects start with the software translation. Translation of online help and documentation should not begin until the software is fully translated and reviewed, because online help and documentation typically contain many references to the software user interface. For example, if an online help file contains a sentence such as "Choose the Page Setup command from the File menu", the translators will need to know the correct translations for the menu items "Page Setup" and "File" if they are to provide the correct translation and be consistent with the software.

This section discusses all localizable components of a software product and the methodology for localizing the software, i.e. the translation approach. It also describes the contents of a typical Windows software resource file.

1.1 Software Components

In a software application, the following UI components would normally be translated:

- Dialog boxes
- Menus
- Strings

1.1.1 DIALOG BOXES

Dialog boxes are the windows or screens used to change options or settings. Most operating systems support the use of *tabbed* dialog boxes.

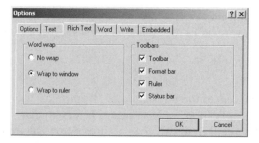

1.1.2 MENUS

Menus are the drop-down lists used to select commands and options, or to access dialog boxes. Menu commands that are displayed with an ellipsis (three dots), open dialog boxes. Choosing a menu command without dots immediately executes a task.

1.1.3 STRINGS

Strings contain the error messages, status messages, questions, and tool tips that are used in the application.

In most software applications, the string section is the most complicated and time consuming task in the translation process. This is mainly because the strings do not contain contextual information. Items used in menus and dialog boxes are usually grouped so the translators can view the context of these items. An example of this kind of problem is where all the options used within one particular dialog box would be displayed together. When working with software strings, translators very often have to guess if, how, and where a particular string may be displayed in the software application.

1.2 Translation Approach

Software applications are usually developed by programmers who create a set of code and resource files. These are then compiled into binary program files. In a Windows application, for example: a set of .rc files is compiled into a .dll file using the Visual C++ compiler.

Resource files contain user interface components, such as menus and dialog boxes. These are the main components to be translated, as mentioned in the previous section.

Software can be translated either in the resource files, which are typically in text format, or directly in the compiled program files, which are normally in binary file format. The method chosen will depend on the software developer. Direct binary translation is becoming the preferred method to prevent accidental changes in the text-only resource files.

Text-only resource files can be translated using a text editor, a resource editor, or a translation memory tool. Binary program files can only be translated using either a resource editor or a software localization tool. More information on resource editors can be found in the Windows and Mac OS sections later in this chapter. Information on localization tools can be found in Chapter 11, Translation Technology.

In text-only resource files, translatable text is usually embedded in coding, such as dialog box definitions and size coordinates. In Windows resource files, translatable text is normally placed between quotation marks (" and "), as can be seen in the example on page 60. It is important that surrounding code is not changed during translation.

If a translation memory tool is used to translate software resource files, ensure the tool has a filtering component that processes only the translatable text, and not the surrounding code. Most translation memory tools have a standard filter for Windows .rc files, or parsers that allow the user to create filters for customized file formats. An example of this would be where single quotes are used as text delimiters rather than double quotes.

Resource files contain all user interface information for an application and are compiled into program files using a resource compiler such as Microsoft Visual C++ or Borland C. Because resource files are in text-only format, they contain no formatting, such as bold or italic text.

Resource files for Windows applications are easily identified by the extension .rc or .dlg. The software build environment may also contain files with other extensions, such as a .str, .txs, .dlg, .msg or .txt. These files should also be translated, according to the instructions provided by the software publisher. Resource files for Mac OS applications typically have the .r extension.

A localization engineer or technical translator should identify the files that require translation. Refer to the Preparing for Translation section on page 102 for more information.

1.3   Resource File Contents

Irrespective of the development platform, most resource files contain the following components: dialog boxes, menus, strings, version information, and comment lines.

1.3.1   DIALOG BOXES

Here is an example of a dialog box section in a Windows resource file:

```
14 DIALOG FIXED IMPURE  0, 0, 356, 196
STYLE DS_MODALFRAME | DS_3DLOOK | DS_CONTEXTHELP | WS_POPUP |
WS_VISIBLE | WS_CAPTION | WS_SYSMENU
CAPTION "Page Setup"
FONT 8, "MS Sans Serif"
BEGIN
        GROUPBOX        "Paper",1073,8,9,224,56,WS_GROUP
        LTEXT           "Si&ze:",1089,16,24,36,8
        COMBOBOX        1137,64,23,160,160,CBS_DROPDOWNLIST | CBS_SORT |
                        WS_VSCROLL | WS_GROUP | WS_TABSTOP
        LTEXT           "&Source:",1090,16,45,36,8
        COMBOBOX        1138,64,42,160,160,CBS_DROPDOWNLIST | CBS_SORT |
                        WS_VSCROLL | WS_GROUP | WS_TABSTOP
        GROUPBOX        "Orientation",1072,8,69,64,56,WS_GROUP
        CONTROL         "P&ortrait",1056,"Button",BS_AUTORADIOBUTTON |
                        WS_GROUP |
                        WS_TABSTOP,16,82,52,12
    ...
        DEFPUSHBUTTON   "OK",1,190,174,50,14,WS_GROUP
        PUSHBUTTON      "Cancel",2,244,174,50,14
        PUSHBUTTON      "&Printer...",1026,298,174,50,14
        GROUPBOX        "Preview",34,240,8,108,158
        CONTROL         "",1080,"Static",SS_WHITERECT,254,46,80,80
        CONTROL         "",1081,"Static",SS_GRAYRECT,334,50,4,80
        CONTROL         "",1082,"Static",SS_GRAYRECT,262,122,80,4
END
```

Here is an example of a compiled dialog box from a running software application:

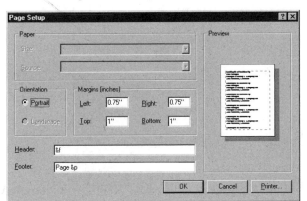

In this example, the word DIALOG in the first line indicates that the section defines a dialog box. All dialog box objects, called controls, have identifiers such as PUSHBUTTON (a button), GROUPBOX (field title) or LTEXT (option).

The ampersand (&) characters in the resource file define the hot keys. Refer to the Hot Keys section on page 70 for more information.

As a rule, all text displayed between double quotes in software resource files requires translation. There are some exceptions to the rule. In the dialog box example on page 60, "MS Sans Serif" is the name of the font used in the dialog box, and this text should not be translated or changed. Another example is "Button", which indicates the control type.

Other examples of words in .rc files that should typically remain in English are:

- Custom1
- Generic1
- Button1
- User1
- Caption
- Static

Note that these words indicate control *types*, not control *labels*.

The numbers at the end of each line contain information on the size and position of the item. In the example on page 60, the numbers in the "Paper" control line indicate that the Paper field starts 8 positions from the left, and 9 positions from the top side of the dialog box. The width of the Paper field is 224 and the height is 56.

Size values very often need to be adjusted to make a translated string fit in a button or dialog box. This resizing work is done in a resource editor or manually in the text-only resource files. Refer to the Dialog Box Resizing section on page 120 for more information.

1.3.2 MENUS

Here is an example of a menu section in a Windows resource file:

```
6 MENU FIXED IMPURE
BEGIN
    POPUP "&File"
BEGIN
            MENUITEM "&New...\tCtrl+N",              57600
            MENUITEM "&Open...\tCtrl+O",             57601
            MENUITEM "&Save\tCtrl+S",                57603
            MENUITEM "Save &As...",                  57604
            MENUITEM SEPARATOR
            MENUITEM "&Print...\tCtrl+P",            57607
            MENUITEM "Print Pre&view",               57608
            MENUITEM "Page Set&up...",               32771
            MENUITEM SEPARATOR
            MENUITEM "Recent File",                  57616, GRAYED
            MENUITEM SEPARATOR
            MENUITEM "Sen&d...",                     57611
            MENUITEM SEPARATOR
            MENUITEM "E&xit",                        57665
    END
    MENUITEM SEPARATOR
    MENUITEM SEPARATOR
END
```

Here is an example of a compiled menu text from a running software application:

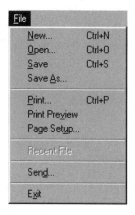

In this example, the word MENU in the first line indicates that the section below it defines a drop-down menu. The MENUITEM lines define the individual commands and separation lines.

The ampersand (&) characters define the hot keys. Refer to the Hot Keys section on page 70 for further information.

Some of the commands are followed by three dots. These dots indicate that there is a dialog box which will open when the user selects the menu item. The \t variable inserts a tab in the menu command during compilation. Several commands are followed by Control key assignments, e.g. Ctrl+P. Refer to the Control Keys (Shortcut Keys) section on page 72 for more information.

1.3.3   STRINGS

Here is an example of a string section from a Windows resource file:

```
STRINGTABLE FIXED IMPURE
BEGIN
    100    "OLE initialization failed. WordPad cannot continue."
    102    "Failed to create object. "
    103    "Can't find record %s."
    104    "%d%% complete. Formatting ... please wait"
    105    "%d%% copied"
    106    "Do you wish to save this file in a different format?"
    107    "Do you want to save changes to %1"
    108    "%1 already exists.\nDo you want to replace it?"
    109    "Changes page layout settings\nPage Setup"
    110    "Sets Options\nOptions"
    111    "Inserts a bullet on this line\nBullets"
    112    "EXT"
    113    "CAP"
    114    "NUM"
    115    "Rich Text"
    116    "Word 6"
    117    "%s to %s"
    118    "&Delete"
END
```

In this example, the word STRINGTABLE indicates that the section contains strings. Strings may contain error messages (item 100-103), status messages (104-105), questions (106-108), tool tips/status bar messages (109-111), keyboard modes (112-114), list items (115-116), variable strings (117), or dynamic menu or dialog box options (118).

String sections are the most complex and most time-consuming translatable components of a software file. Messages are often quite cryptic or require in-depth programming, product or context knowledge. A good example of this is single word messages, such as the word "NONE". In many languages, this word can have several translations or grammatical variations, depending on the context. The same applies to words like "Copy": This could interpreted as a verb or a noun, and translated as "to copy", "a copy", or it could be used as "Copy *filename*"? In many languages, there are often three or more translation options for a single word, depending on the context.

Take the example of the word "None". This string is often used in combination with several other strings, for example with "File" and "Directory". In German, "None" in combination with *File* (*die* Datei) would be "Keine"; "None" in combination with *Directory* (*das* Verzeichnis) would be "Kein."

1.3.4   VERSION INFO

Windows resource files usually contain a Version – or version stamp – section, in which the company name, application name, copyright, version number, and language edition of a program are specified.

Here is an example of a version stamp:

```
/////////////////////////////////////////////////////////////////
//
// Version
//

1 VERSIONINFO
 FILEVERSION 4,0,950,0
 PRODUCTVERSION 4,0,0,0
 FILEFLAGSMASK 0x3fL
#ifdef _DEBUG
 FILEFLAGS 0x1L
#else
 FILEFLAGS 0x0L
#endif
 FILEOS 0x4L
 FILETYPE 0x1L
 FILESUBTYPE 0x0L
BEGIN
   BLOCK "StringFileInfo"
   BEGIN
     BLOCK "040904e4"
     BEGIN
       VALUE "CompanyName", "Microsoft Corporation\0"
       VALUE "FileDescription", "WordPad MFC Application\0"
       VALUE "FileVersion", "4.00.950\0"
       VALUE "InternalName", "wordpad\0"
       VALUE "LegalCopyright", "Copyright © Microsoft Corp. 1995\0"
       VALUE "OriginalFilename", "WORDPAD.EXE\0"
      VALUE "ProductName", "Microsoft Windows (TM) Operating System\0"
       VALUE "ProductVersion", "4.0\0"
     END
   END
   BLOCK "VarFileInfo"
   BEGIN
       VALUE "Translation", 0x409, 1252
   END
END
```

In the above example, only the value text following the `FileDescription`, `LegalCopyright`, and `ProductName` value names should be translated. Never translate the value names!

The version stamp also defines the language ID (`0x409`) and code page (`1252`) of the .rc file. Refer to the Language Settings section on page 116 for more information on setting languages in a resource file.

1.3.5 COMMENT LINES

Most software resource files contain strings that are enclosed or preceded by comment delimiters. These strings contain comment text that has been manually added by the programmer or automatically inserted by the compiler.

Here are examples of comment delimiters for programming languages:

Java, C or C++ files:

```
// commentcommentcommentcomment.
or
/*commentcommentcommentcomment.*/
```

Pascal or Delphi files:

```
{ commentcommentcommentcomment. }
or
{*commentcommentcommentcomment.*}
```

Because these strings have been *commented out*, they are not included in the compilation and will never be displayed to the user in the program. Unless otherwise instructed, these comments should not be translated.

Programmers often include information for software localizers in the comment strings, for example useful context information, length restrictions, etc. If a set of strings should not be translated, for example, it may be marked by a `//Do not translate` comment line.

Note that sample files, batch files, .ini or .inf files, or other non-compiled configuration files may contain comment text that needs to be translated. This should be clarified before the translation starts.

2   Translation Guidelines

This section covers general guidelines for software translators and localizers. Most of the guidelines also apply to the translation of binary files in resource editors or software localization tools.

2.1   General Guidelines

Follow these guidelines when editing resource files or software text:

- Translatable text strings are usually placed in quotation marks (" and "), so the use of quotation marks *within* strings should be avoided, where possible. If they are absolutely necessary, enter double quotation marks. If a string needs to be translated using double quotes, such as `"Press OK to continue"`, a possible German translation would be `"Drücken Sie ""OK"" um weiter zu machen"`.
- Avoid deleting or adding leading or trailing quotation marks. Each string should begin and end with a quotation mark.
- Avoid deleting leading or trailing spaces. Where a string such as `"Copying "` is followed by a file name at run-time, an inadvertent deletion of the trailing space would force an Italian translation to be displayed as: `"CopiaSYS32.DLL"`.
- Avoid using the ampersand character (&) in translations. Use the word "and" instead. The ampersand is often used specifically for hot keys (see Hot Keys section on page 70). Using ampersands in running text will confuse the software

compiler and corrupt hot key functionality. If there is no other option but to use ampersand characters, double them (&&).

- If software resource files contain strings defining date, time or number formats, e.g. mm/dd/yyyy hh:mm AM/PM (displayed as for example 03/25/2000 9:00 PM) and if these need to be changed in the target language, do not change them in the resource file. It is better to consult a localization engineer or the software publisher. Very often these codes should remain untouched, because the software program will retrieve the date and time formats from the operating system.

- Never translate file names or file extensions, unless specifically requested by the software publisher. If the software resource file contains the string "README.TXT" consult a localization engineer or the publisher to see whether the file name should be translated here or in the installer script files.

2.2 Language Guidelines

Here are some general guidelines on language and style in software translations:

- Try to be creative, i.e. avoid literal translations of software options. Always verify the meaning or function of each software option, and use a word in the target language that accurately describes that feature.

- Ensure that the translation of software strings is consistent within and between software products.

- Choose terminology which is consistent with the target operating system, for example use standard Apple Mac OS or Microsoft Windows terminology. Some software publishers make their standard terminology freely available over the web.

- Avoid using the first person (I or we) anywhere in messages, and avoid using second person.

- Always try to use the imperative mood, as this makes the text easier to follow.

- Where exclamation marks are used in the English software, do not automatically include these in the translations, unless absolutely necessary. In many languages, it is less common to use exclamation marks.

- If menus or options are used to open a dialog box, use consistent translations for both the option and dialog box. For example, if the "Save As..." command opens a dialog box which has the same title, in Swedish both items should be translated as "Spara som".

- Adjust capitalization to the standards of the target language. In English, software options are usually written in title case, e.g. Open File. In many other languages grammatical rules will dictate how it should be written. In German, for example, this would be written as "Datei öffnen", where "open" is in lower case.

- Use a consistent style and grammatical form for specific types of user interface components. It is better to use the imperative form for menu commands and dialog box options or buttons. Also try to be consistent when translating status bar messages.

- Adapt the language in the user interface to suit local conventions. For example, if the English user interface says "Congratulations, you have successfully installed this application" the translation may need to be more formal, so delete the word "Congratulations".

2.3   Space Restrictions

Each software translator will have work with space and length restrictions. Most European language text is longer than the English text, often by as much as 30 percent more. Here is an example of a dialog box, where part of an option or button text is truncated. This will only become evident when the localized software is compiled.

The software localization tools, as a rule, will allow the user to resize the items in dialog boxes to make translations fit in the control boxes. These tasks are generally performed by localization engineers, but with improvements in resource editors and localization tools, translators can resize dialog boxes before the files are recompiled. This is becoming more of an issue with increased pressures on localization vendors to turn products around and deliver them faster to the publishers.

In some development environments, fixed form or dialog box layouts are used. An example of this is where one screen layout is used for all languages. Here, the translators need to be very creative and select shorter translations or abbreviate words. A translator may be forced to vary the length of specific terms due to space or length restrictions. A good example is the term Connection Speed, which can have two length variants: Conn. Speed or CoSp. It is important to be consistent with every abbreviation that is used. Consistent abbreviations are often necessary in firmware translations, for example messages displayed on a printer or mobile phone display. It is important to include these standard abbreviations or length variants in the terminology management application to ensure consistency throughout the software user interface translation.

The localized main menu bar (File, Edit, etc.) should fit on the screen, irrespective of the screen resolution. If the menu bar does not fit, change the Help menu name to a question mark. This has almost become a standard in localized versions of many Microsoft Windows compatible products.

Strings in the Windows environment typically have a length restriction of 255 characters, including spaces. Always keep this restriction in mind when translating software strings.

As a general rule, keep menu names, commands, and other software text as short as possible when translating user interface items. Try to adopt a concise and clear translation style for software strings. This will reduce engineering time and keep resizing efforts to a minimum.

2.4   Variables

Programmers use many variable parameters – or placeholders – in strings. Examples of variables can be seen in strings 104, 105, 107, 108, 117-120 in the example shown on page 63.

Variables are characters that are usually preceded by a percentage (%) sign and replaced by another word, value or string at application run-time. For example, string 105 in the example may be displayed as "65% complete" in the application, and string 107 may be displayed as "Do you want to save changes to SAMPLE.DOC?"

If one string contains two variables, do not change the word order in the translated string. For example, a string such as *Choose %s to copy %s* should not be translated as *To copy %s, choose %s*. This may display a garbled screen message such as *To copy Continue, choose SAMPLE.DOC*.

Programmers often include plurals that are constructed at run-time. Here is an example of a string section with plurals:

```
1. "Copying %d file%s."
2. "Copying %d folder%s."
3. "s"
```

At run-time, the program will insert the letter *s* when the variable %d is two or more. This will introduce problems during the translation. For example, if *file* were translated with the German word *Datei*, and *folder* with *Ordner*, a uniform plural extension would not be possible. The plural of *Datei* is *Dateien*, the plural of *Ordner* is *Ordner*. An option would be to delete the %s variable (not the entire string resource!) and use translations that incorporate both singular and plural variables, such as *Datei(en)*.

The following table displays common variables, and the parameters replacing them.

Variable	Parameter
%s	string
%d	decimal integer
%ld	decimal long integer
%x	integer in hexadecimal form
%g	floating point value
%u	Unicode character
%p	page number

2.5 Control Codes

Control codes provide formatting information to be displayed within strings. If required, these formatting codes can be moved to enhance the visual display of the string.

In the example, the string `"%1 already exists.\nDo you want to replace it?"` will be displayed on two separate lines in the message box, because \n is the line break control code.

The \n control code is also used to separate status bar text from tool tips. In string 109 on page 63, for example, the `"Changes page layout settings"` string will be displayed in the status bar of the application window when the command is selected. The `"Page Setup"` string is the "help balloon" string, which will be displayed when the cursor is positioned on the command icon.

Here is a table showing the most common control codes:

\012 or \r	line feed/carriage return
\015 or \n	line break
\011 or \t	tab character

2.6 Non-Translatables

String sections may contain items that should not be translated. It is important to note that if these items are translated, they could corrupt the entire software program.

Here are some examples of non-translatable text or items:

- Words in all caps, such as EDIT
- Words containing underscores, such as size_is
- Word combinations, such as ConnCount

However, it is sometimes difficult to differentiate between strings that look translatable, but may not be, such as Copy. In these instances, these strings should stay in English because they may be internal software commands.

Typical examples of software elements that should not be translated are command line commands (COPY), parameters, and command line switches (-F).

It is a valuable exercise to have a localization engineer or developer spend time preparing and marking translatable strings and inserting translation comments. This will help enormously in reducing the number of bugs and errors introduced during the translation cycle. Whenever in doubt about a certain string or group of strings, consult an engineer or the application developer.

2.7 Concatenated Strings

Programmers often concatenate strings. Concatenation is the process of adding text elements or strings together to form a longer string.

A good example is the Undo command. In this case, the last executed command is usually added to Undo at run-time. Many applications concatenate `"Undo "` and a command name such as "Cut" to generate a more specific "Undo Cut" menu item. If the application is then localized in German, the concatenation will be displayed as "Widerrufen Ausschneiden", which is grammatically incorrect. "Ausschneiden widerrufen" is the correct translation, so the word order is changed.

If it is not possible to reverse the order of this concatenation, try placing a colon after the translation of `"Undo"`, so the localized version would read "Widerrufen: Ausschneiden".

2.8 Hot Keys

On most operating systems, menu commands and dialog box options are usually displayed with one letter marked or underlined. This is referred to as the hot key (sometimes known as the accelerator, mnemonic key, or hit key). This key is used to activate a certain command by pressing it in combination with the Alt key. Hot keys provide an alternative way to access menu commands or dialog box options.

Since the hot keys are underlined, avoid using letters with descenders such as p, j, q, g as hot keys, as the underline will be difficult to see on the screen. Where feasible, use the first letter of the option, for example, in Copy, underline the letter "C".

Please note that in ideographic languages, such as Japanese, Chinese, and Korean, the hot key letter assigned in the source language is added after the translation. The following example shows the Windows Notepad File menu in English and Korean:

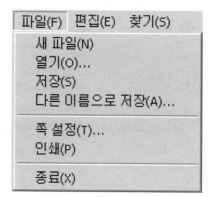

The hot keys between brackets are typically displayed in uppercase.

2.8.1 HOT KEY SYMBOL

In Windows resource files, hot keys are preceded by the ampersand (&) symbol. The menu string `"&Open..."` in a resource file, for example, will appear as O̲pen... in the running application. Files written in Visual Basic use the tilde (~) instead of the ampersand.

Because the ampersand symbol is used as the hot key symbol in Windows resource files, as mentioned previously, this should be doubled when used as a substitute for the word "and". A menu item such as Save & Close, would look like this in a resource file: `"&Save && Close"`. The French translation of this string would be `"&Enregistrer && Fermer"`.

2.8.2 UNIQUENESS

A hot key assignment can only be used once in each menu or dialog box. In the following example, the same hot key (F) is used for two different options, which will corrupt its functionality:

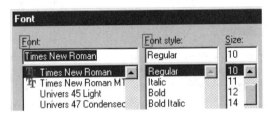

Localization engineers will normally use user interface verification tools to ensure that each menu or dialog box contains no hot keys clashes. Refer to the Checking Hot Keys section on page 122 for more information.

Submenus are considered separate menus, and as such, a hot key used in a main menu may be re-used in a submenu. Here is an example of a re-used hot key:

The Strings section of a resource file often contains menu or dialog box items that are used dynamically in the application at run-time. A good example is where a menu contains an item that toggles, such as the Show/Hide Toolbar command. Here, the standard menu resource contains only Show Toolbar, while the Hide Toolbar string is retrieved from the string section. Always verify in the application where these strings show up, and whether they cause hot key conflicts with other menu or dialog box items.

2.8.3 OPERATING ENVIRONMENT

It is important to be consistent with the hot keys used in the target operating environment. This is particularly relevant for the standard commands, such as Open, Save, Print, Copy, and Paste, where consistent hot keys should always be used.

Here is a good example: In Windows applications the hot keys for the menu options *Open...* and *Save...* are always the letters *O* and *S*. In German, the translations are consistently *Öffnen* and *Speichern*, with the standard hot keys on *f* and *S*.

For Windows 3.x-based software, translations and hot keys for common commands are provided in the *Microsoft GUI Guide* manual. Terminology extracted from Windows 9x/NT/2000 and other Microsoft software can be found on the Microsoft Developer Network CD-ROMs or the Microsoft FTP server at ftp.microsoft.com/developr/msdn/newup/glossary.

2.8.4   ACCENTED CHARACTERS

Avoid using accented characters as hot keys, because standard keyboard layouts will not necessarily support the accented characters proposed as hot keys. For example, if the German translation for the Open command, *Öffnen*, had a hot key on the first letter, users with a non-German keyboard or keyboard setting would be unable to type the hot key letter in combination with the Alt key. Accented characters should only be used as accelerators when there really are no other letter or character options available.

2.9   Control Keys (Shortcut Keys)

In most applications, it is possible to activate commands by pressing the Ctrl key in combination with a function key or letter. For example, in most Windows-based applications, pressing Ctrl+S saves the current file, while pressing Ctrl+P prints the file. On the Mac OS, users press the Command key in combination with standard letters to activate commonly used commands, such as Open, Save, Print, Cut, Copy, Paste, etc.

A Control or Command key can only be used once in an application. When Ctrl+P is assigned to the Print command, it cannot be used for another command.

2.9.1   FUNCTION KEYS

Ctrl keys that are used in combination with function keys (such as Ctrl+F12 for the Preferences command) should never be changed in the localized software.

2.9.2   LETTERS OR SYMBOLS

Combinations of the Ctrl key with a letter, such as Ctrl+C for Copy, or a number or symbol, such as Ctrl+= or Ctrl+9, may be changed by the translator or localization engineer. However, it is better to use the Control key settings in the original version. Check the localized versions of any Windows or Mac OS product to check whether the Control keys have been translated, for example in Wordpad or any Office application.

Changing Control key combinations may be necessary where certain key combinations cannot be used on a local keyboard. Characters such as   @ $ { } [ ] \ ~ | ^ ' <> can cause problems on non-English keyboards. Local keyboard images can be found on Microsoft's GlobalDev web site at www.microsoft.com/globaldev.

On a French keyboard, using Ctrl key combinations with numbers causes problems, because the numbers are always entered using the Shift key. Always discuss the preferred key combinations with the localization engineers, to avoid any problems.

2.9.3 KEY NAMES

In many European languages, key names on the keyboard are localized. For example, the Shift key is called *Umschalt* in German and *Maj* in French.

2.9.4 OPERATING ENVIRONMENT

There are many standard hot key combinations in certain operating environments. For example, Ctrl+B is used to "bold" characters in Microsoft Windows applications. Many target languages also have standard hot key combinations. Refer to the operating system glossaries or a Windows or Mac OS version in the language, to ensure that the standards are being used.

If a Control key needs to be changed, make sure to change it in the menu resource item, as well as in the Accelerator section of the resource file. For example, if the menu item is MENUITEM "&Paste\tCtrl+V", 57637, and the Control key is to be changed to Ctrl+U, locate the Accelerator section of the resource file, which will have one or more items with the same menu ID number 57637 and a "V" key definition. Ensure that the Accelerator section is also changed to reflect changes to the Control keys.

2.10 Examples

When translating string sections of software applications, translators will frequently be faced with many issues and problems that need to be resolved, such as lack of context, fixed sentence orders, unclear variables, etc. This section includes some examples of problematic strings, along with an explanation and possible solutions.

```
STRINGTABLE FIXED IMPURE
BEGIN
    100    "%s to %s."
    101    "Change Fancy First Letter"
    102    "Can't find record "
    103    "ppexcept.ini"
    104    "&Delete"
    105    "Please call 1-800-876-5075 or (716) 871-6513 at any time to
register your product."
    106    "Parse stack underflow while reading object."
    107    "This is not a valid %s."
    108    "%1 already exists.\nDo you want to replace it?"
    109    "ClickToCreate\0"
    110    "dddd, mmmm d, yyyy"
    111    "Click on the Continue button to close this window."
    112    "Mon"
    113    "Software\\Microsoft\\Shared Tools\\Graphics Filters\\Import"
    114    "The file '%s' is stored on a disk called '%s'. Please insert
this disk."
    115    "All"
END
```

100   "%s to %s."
This string contains two variables, which can be replaced with many different words

by the application at run-time. For example, the string can be used as "Monday to Friday", "Copying file.dll to c:\windows\system", or "23 to 54", depending on how the programmer has defined the variables. In most languages, the word "to" will have different translations in each of these possibilities, so it is important to check how the string will be displayed before choosing a translation. Consult the software developer or run the application.

101   "Change Fancy First Letter"
Try to avoid translating the English string literally, as this may cause problems in a language where a more formal style is required, which can provide a more accurate description of what a command does. The Swedish translation for this string, for example, was "Byt anfang", which is shorter and more suited to Swedish.

102   "Can't find record "
This string contains a trailing space, and a character or string of characters may be inserted after the string at run-time, for example a record number, as in "Can't find record 23". In most languages the sentence order will need to change to reflect the grammatical rules of the target language. A good example of this is German, where the verb is placed at the end of the sentence, depending on the sentence structure, verbs, and tenses used. If the word order is not changed, the error message will be displayed incorrectly as "Kann record nicht finde n23". This is clearly a case of poor internationalization. If the string cannot be changed by the developer, you will have to find an alternative solution. For example, try making the translation more generic, e.g. "Can't find the record numbered: ".

103   "ppexcept.ini"
This string contains a file name. File names are sometimes translated in the localized product, but the safest option is to leave all file names in English, especially in this example, where the string contains the name of a settings file. Translating this string could generate a major bug in the localized application.

104   "&Delete"
If commands such as Delete are included in the strings section of a software application, the chances are this command is inserted dynamically in a dialog box or menu, for example in a context-sensitive menu. Before assigning a hot key to a letter in the translation of this command, check where the command will be used. Hot key conflicts are often caused by dynamically inserted items.

105   "Please call 1-800-876-5075 or (716) 871-6513 at any time to register your product."
Support or registration information is often included in software strings. These are often displayed in the splash screen of an application. In the example above, two American phone numbers are provided as contact numbers. These are probably not applicable, and in the case of the 800 number not accessible, for the target country. Check with the software publisher how this information should be adjusted. In most cases, publishers will request a change in the strings, so that they display as "... please contact your local office or distributor...".

106 "Parse stack underflow while reading object."
Many programmers add debugging messages like this one to the string section of a software application. These types of messages are very difficult to translate, and not of any relevance to the end user of the application, so it is better to leave them in English. This also facilitates the debugging of localized versions for the developers of the English product. The vendor and publisher should agree on the preferred approach.

107 "This is not a valid %s."
Depending on the word that is inserted at the location of this variable, the grammatical form of the word "valid" will vary. This will also depend on the gender of the word that is inserted. In such cases, try creating separate strings for all possibilities.

108 "%1 already exists.\nDo you want to replace it?"
This case is similar to string 107. The gender of the word replacing the %1 variable will determine the translation of the word "it" in the second sentence. Again, it is advisable to create separate strings for all possibilities.

109 "ClickToCreate\0"
This string contains an internal command or variable and should not be translated.

110 "dddd, mmmm d, yyyy"
This string defines how a date is displayed and formatted. Avoid changing these formats because the operating system defines such regional settings. In any case, the letters (d for day, m for month, y for year) should not be changed because of their links to internal variables. The vendor and publisher should agree on whether the date format should be adjusted to reflect local settings.

111 "Click on the Continue button to close this window."
This string contains a reference to a button in the application's user interface. Ensure the correct translation for the "Continue" button is used, and check the application at run-time for consistency.

112 "Mon"
In English, most days are abbreviated to one or three letters. In the target language, this may be different, for example "Må" is used in Swedish. The vendor and publisher should agree on the number of letters to be used.

113 "Software\\Microsoft\\Shared Tools\\Graphics Filters\\Import"
Strings containing two backslashes are usually path settings stored in the Windows Registry settings of the application. These are not normally translated, but this should be agreed before the translation cycle begins. In the case of the \Program Files folder, installed with Microsoft Windows, for example, the name of this folder has been localized in some languages, while in other languages it remains in English.

114 "The file '%s' is stored on a disk called '%s'. Please insert this disk."
The word "disk" in English is used for hard drive, CD-ROM, and diskette disks. Most languages have different translations for these variants, so never assume that the English string refers to a "diskette".

115 "All"
These one word strings can have many different translations depending on the context.

The Danish Windows NT glossary, for example, contains the following translations: Alle, Alt, and Vis alle. Always verify the context of these type of strings before choosing a translation or grammatical form.

3   Windows

The majority of localized software products run on the Windows platform and the most commonly used development environment is Microsoft Visual Studio.

3.1   Introduction

A Microsoft Windows software application contains a set of files that can be subdivided into four categories:

- Executables (.exe or .com)
- Additional binary program files such as drivers (.drv) or dynamic link libraries (.dll)
- Online help files (.hlp, .cnt, or .chm)
- Readme files (.txt, .doc, .html, or .wri)

All of these file types may contain translatable strings or text. The executables and program files often contain the menus, dialog boxes, commands, and messages associated with the application.

3.1.1   TRANSLATION APPROACH

Software developers are increasingly including all user interface elements in a separate .dll file, called a satellite .dll or a resource-only .dll, as this is the only file that requires translation. In Microsoft Windows and Office 2000, for example, all user interface elements have been isolated from the binary code to enable users to switch the language and regional settings of the user interface.

As mentioned in the beginning of this chapter, software files can be translated in two ways, either in text-only *resource files* or directly in the binary *program files*:

- *Resource files* (typically files with the extension .rc or .dlg) are text-only files that contain all localizable application components, such as messages, menus, dialog boxes, default settings for languages, and country codes. These files can be translated using a Windows-based text editor or word processor. After translation, they need to be compiled into binary program files. More information on translating resource files can be found in the first section of this chapter.
- *Program files* (files with the file extension .dll or .exe) need to be translated in a resource editor, such as the one included in Microsoft Visual Studio, or a software localization tool, such as Corel Catalyst. The advantage of translating .dll files in a resource editor as opposed to translating text-only resource files, is that it is possible to see immediately how the translation will be displayed in

the actual dialog box or menu. Translators know immediately what impact their translations will have on the user interface layout. In addition, dialog boxes can be resized directly in these files to make translations fit. Most software localization tools also allow direct translation of the program files. Examples of these tools can be found in the Software Localization Tools section on page 383.

It is also possible to open and translate text-only resource code files directly in a resource editor, such as the one included in Microsoft Visual Studio, which has all the advantages of translating directly in binary program files. The only risk is using different resource editors or different versions of the same editor may change the structure of the resource files. So, if .rc files are delivered from the publisher which have been created using Microsoft Visual C++ version 4, never open or edit them in Visual C++ 6 or later versions!

It is now more common for translators to work directly on the program files when translating. These .dll files or .exe files can be edited by the translator without the need for compilation.

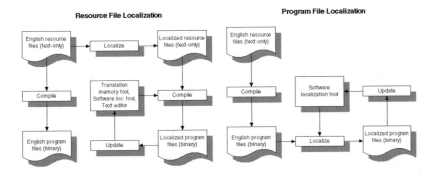

16-bit applications, .dll and .exe files can be edited using the Microsoft App Studio (included in Microsoft Visual C++ 1.x) or Borland Resource Workshop resource editor. 32-bit program files can be translated in Microsoft Developer Studio (Visual C++ 4.x) or Microsoft Visual Studio (Visual C++ 5.x and later versions), Borland Resource Workshop, or in a software localization tool.

Tip: It is impossible to edit and save 32-bit program files using Visual C++ in a Windows 9x environment. The resource editor needs to be run under Window sNT or 2000.

3.1.2 TERMINOLOGY

A software application that runs on a Microsoft Windows platform will probably contain many terms or options which are also available in the Windows operating system or other Microsoft applications. Some examples are standard commands or options such as File, Save, Edit, and Exit or buttons such as Cancel and Apply.

The translation of these terms should be consistent with the operating system which will be used to run the application. To ensure the translations are consistent with the localized Microsoft operating systems and applications, refer to Microsoft's product glossaries, which are available in many languages from the following ftp site: ftp.microsoft.com/developr/MSDN/NewUp/Glossary.

Refer to Chapter 7, Terminology, for more information on standard terminology for specific operating systems.

3.2   Resource Editors

Resource editors are usually integrated in development environments, such as Microsoft Visual Studio. They are used to create and edit a software user interface.

Most resource editors have similar functionality, in that they display a list of resource types and resources, and allow the user to translate and edit all components of the user interface.

3.2.1   MICROSOFT APP STUDIO

Microsoft App Studio is included in Visual C++ version 1.x and 2 and can be used to open and edit resource scripts (.rc), executables (.exe), dynamic link libraries (.dll), resource files (.res), bitmaps (.bmp), icons (.ico), and cursors (.cur).

App Studio only handles 16-bit executable or .dll files, i.e. applications that run on Windows 3.1. When a 32-bit program file is opened in App Studio, the following warning message is displayed:

When a 16-bit executable or dynamic link library is opened, a screen with resource types and resources is displayed:

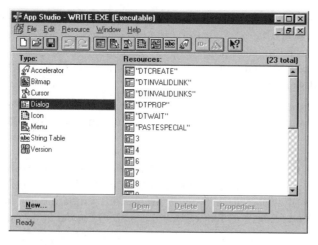

The following sections cover each of the translatable resource types: dialog boxes, menus, string tables, and other file types.

Dialog Boxes

To translate dialog boxes, follow these steps:

1. Click on the Dialog resource type, and double-click on the first item in the Resources list.

2. In the displayed dialog box, double-click on each text item, and translate the text in the Caption field of the property window.

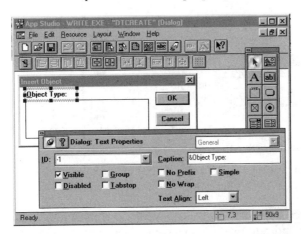

3. When all text has been translated, close the dialog box resource by pressing Ctrl+F4 and open the next item in the Resources list.

Tip: Click on the pushpin button in the property window to keep it open. Clicking on a text item in the dialog box automatically displays the text in the Caption field.

Please note that the ampersand (&) symbol defines the hot keys. Refer to the Hot Keys section on page 70 for more information.

Once a dialog box is translated, run a test it by choosing Test from the Resource menu, or pressing Ctrl+T. This test mode enables the user to type in text, select options, choose commands, and test hot keys.

The coordinates in the lower right corner of the window show the position and dimensions of the item. Refer to the Dialog Box Resizing section on page 120 for more information on resizing dialog box controls.

Menus

To translate menus, follow these steps:

1. Click on the Menu resource type, and double-click on the first item in the Resources list.

2. In the open screen, double-click on each menu and submenu item, and translate the text in the Caption field of the property window.

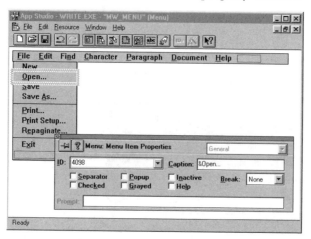

3. Once the text is translated, close the menu resource by pressing Ctrl+F4 and open the next item in the Resources list.

Do not delete the three dots that follow some of the commands. As mentioned previously, these dots indicate that the command opens an additional dialog box.

If a menu item contains a Control key definition that needs to be changed, such as Ctrl+C for the Copy command, follow these steps:

1. Open the Accelerator resources.

2. Locate the menu ID of the menu item that needs to be changed.

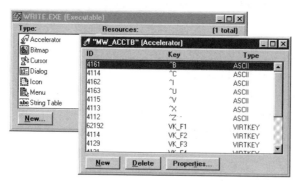

3. Change the Control key letter accordingly.

Refer to the Menus section on page 58 for more information on translating menu resources. Refer to the Checking Hot Keys section on page 122 for more information on checking hot keys in menu resources. Refer to the Control Keys (Shortcut Keys) section on page 72 for more information on assigning Control key letters.

Strings

To translate strings, follow these steps:

1. Click on the String Table resource type, and double-click on the first item in the Resources list.

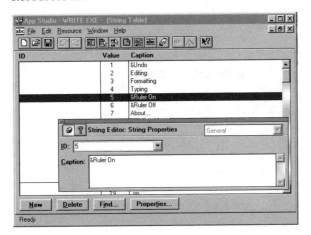

2. In the open screen, double-click on each string item, and translate the text in the Caption field of the property window.

3. Once all the text is translated, close the menu resource by pressing Ctrl+F4 and open the next item in the Resources list.

Refer to the Strings section on page 91 for more information on translating string resources.

Other Resource Types

Resource types such as bitmaps, cursors, and icons may also contain translatable text or letters. To browse through a list of bitmap resources, click on the first item, choose the Properties button, click on the pushpin button, and browse down the list using the arrow keys. This is the quickest way to search for translatable text in images.

If a bitmap contains text, it can be translated in the integrated bitmap editor, or the bitmap can be exported and edited it in a graphics editor, such as Adobe Photoshop or JASC Paint Shop Pro, and re-imported.

An example of bitmaps that may be translated are the buttons for Bold, Italic, and Underline.

In some languages, these buttons are translated. Start the Wordpad application in the localized Windows version to check whether they are translated in the target language.

Refer to the Bitmap Editing section on page 112 for more information.

3.2.2 MICROSOFT VISUAL STUDIO

Microsoft Visual Studio is a shell for Microsoft Visual C++ 4.x and later versions. The 32-bit resource editor is incorporated in this shell.

With Microsoft Visual Studio, it is possible to open program files for translation. Editing and saving 32-bit program files, for example .dlls, is only possible when running Visual Studio on a Windows NT platform.

Opening a program file displays a screen containing a list of all resource types:

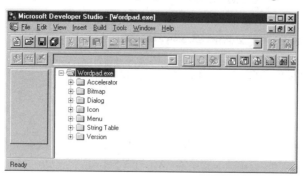

Clicking on the plus sign next to a resource type opens a list of resources. For more information on translating the different resource types in Microsoft Visual Studio, follow the steps in the Microsoft App Studio section on page 78.

Tip: Please note that in Visual C++ 5 and later versions, Resource should be selected in the Open As field of the Open dialog box, otherwise the file opens as a project workspace.

There are a number of differences between translating resources in Visual Studio, and working in App Studio:

- In Microsoft Visual Studio, it is possible to specify the language of each resource. Refer to the Language Settings section on page 116 for more information.

- Visual Studio can verify that no duplicate hot keys exist in a dialog box or menu. Refer to the Checking Hot Keys section on page 122 for more information.

- The menu resource property window contains an additional field, called Prompt. This field may contain the status bar text and tooltip for the selected menu command. This prompt text is stored in the String Table resources. It can be translated in the Menu Item Properties window or in the string section.

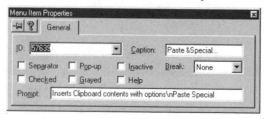

When the entire build environment of a program file is located on the localizer's machine and includes all .rc or .dlg files, .rc files can be opened for editing. RC or .dlg files in Microsoft Visual Studio are translated in the same way as program files. The only difference is that included files such as icons and bitmaps are located in a separate resource folder in the build environment.

3.2.3 BORLAND RESOURCE WORKSHOP

Borland (now Inprise) Resource Workshop is available as part of the Borland C++ and Turbo C compiler packages or as a separate package up to version 4.5. Unlike Microsoft Visual Studio, Resource Workshop enables the user to edit and save 32-bit program files under Windows 9x. When translating .rc files, it is important to use the same compiler and resource editor that was used to create the project file.

To translate resources in Borland Resource Workshop, follow these steps:

1. Choose the Open Project command from the File menu, and select the program file (.exe, .dll) or resource file (.rc, .dlg) to be edited.

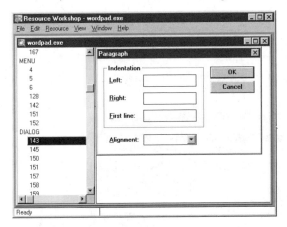

2. In the Resource Workshop window, scroll down the resource types (bitmaps, menus, dialog boxes, etc.) and double-click on a resource to open it.

3. Double-click on the item that needs to be translated, and enter the translation in the Caption field.

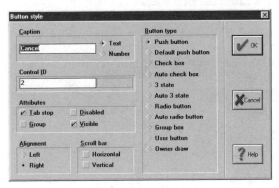

4. Alternatively, translate the controls by changing their properties, and selecting Show Properties from the Options menu. Click on an item, select the Caption property, and enter the translation in the text box.

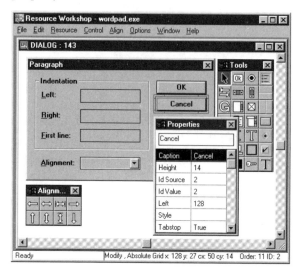

5. For menu resources, translate the menu item in the Item Text field and the status bar text in the Item Help field.

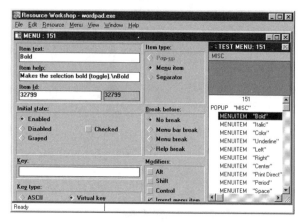

6. To save the translations, choose the Save Project command from the File menu

For more information on Borland C++, visit the Inprise/Borland web site at www.inprise.com.

4   Mac OS

Although the volume of localized Mac OS software is significantly lower than the volume of PC-based or Windows software, the success of Apple's iMac and Gx product lines has meant that many software publishers are now shipping Mac OS versions of their software.

Localizing software for the Mac OS has traditionally been easier and more intuitive than Windows-based software. Many of the tools required are free, and MacOS software development is well-standardized with respect to tools and designs.

4.1   Introduction

Most software for Mac OS computers is translated directly in the program files. This means that instead of editing text-only resource files that need to be recompiled after translation, most translators work directly in the executable of a Ma cOS application.

4.1.1   TERMINOLOGY

Terminology for applications used on the Ma cOS platform may differ from standard Microsoft Windows terminology. Like Microsoft, Apple has published standard operating system glossaries in a number of languages.

When translating Mac OS-only products, it is advisable to use the standard terminology. For cross-platform products, however, where the product is shipping both in a Mac and a Windows version, consider adapting the terminology of the Mac version to suit the Windows version. There are some disadvantages to this, for example, in some languages translations of the standard commands (Open, Save, Print, etc.) differ from the localized Mac OS. The advantages are that translations can be leveraged between platforms, and allow the user to create one set of translated online help files or documentation that can be used for both platforms.

The Apple international glossaries can be found on the Apple Developer Connection CDs and at the Apple FTP server at ftp.apple.com/devworld/Tool_Chest/ Localization_Tools/Apple_Intl_Glossaries.

4.1.2   LOCALIZATION TOOLS

This section covers some of the most commonly used resource editors and tools for translating Mac OS applications.

The resource editor traditionally used for translating Mac OS applications is called ResEdit. ResEdit is a powerful resource editor from Apple Computer. Refer to the Resource Editors section on page 87 for more information.

Other development and localization tools for Mac OS applications include Apple's MPW, Metrowerks CodeWarrior, Resorcerer, Icepick, ViewEdit, AppleGlot, and PowerGlot.

- MPW (Macintosh Programmer's Workshop) is a text-based Ma cOS resource compiler.

- Metrowerks CodeWarrior is a development tool that contains an editor, compiler, linker, and debugger. CodeWarrior is used mostly by developers when creating cross-platform products.

- Resorcerer is comparable to ResEdit, but is often considered faster and easier to use. Refer to the Resource Editors section on page 87 for more information.

- Icepick and ViewEdit are small tools that are only used to translate coded MacApp VIEW resources.

- AppleGlot is a localization utility that was developed by Apple Computer. It contains advanced functions for automatically updating and translating extracted resource files. Refer to the AppleGlot section on page 389 for more information.

- PowerGlot is a commercially available resource translation tool that extracts, sorts, and provides a very comprehensive overview of all translatable text contained in an application. Refer to the PowerGlot section on page 391 for more information.

For more information on Apple's development and localization tools, visit the Apple Developer Connection site at www.apple.com/developer (search for "localization").

4.1.3 RESOURCE TYPES

Every Mac OS application contains a number of resources. All resource type names are four characters long. In every resource, a specific component of the application is coded. Examples of resource types are menus (MENU), dialog boxes (DITL), and strings (STR#).

The following table shows common localizable components and their resource types:

Resource Type	Description
aedt	AppleEvents
ALRT	Alert window definition
cicn	Color icon
CMNU	Command menus (MacApp)
CNTL	Control definitions (buttons)
crsr	Color cursor or mouse pointer
CURS	Cursor or mouse pointer
DITL	Dialog box
DLOG	Dialog box definition
hdlg	Balloon help for dialog boxes
hfdr	Balloon help for Finder icon

hmnu	Balloon help for menus
hwin	Balloon help for windows
ICN#, icl4, icl8	icon (1-bit, 4-bit, 8-bit)
ICON	Icon used in dialogs or menus
MENU	Application menus
PICT	Picture (bitmap)
PPob	PowerPlant resources
STR	Strings
STR#	List of strings
TEXT	Text
Vers	Finder version info
View	Dialog box definition
WIND	Document window definition

4.1.4 PREPARATION

Always make sure to work on copies of the original file. If the Macintosh crashes while the user is editing a program file in ResEdit or Resorcerer, there is a strong possibility that the file will be corrupted. Therefore, it is very important to save copies of the file you are working on regularly, preferably every 15 minutes. To make a copy of a program file, click on the file in the Finder and press Command-D. The file is duplicated and the word *copy* is added to the name. Replacing the word *copy* with a number makes it easy to keep control of the version of the file being edited.

Never open a copy of the file in the same folder as the original file. ResEdit may save changes to the wrong file or to both files. It may be easier for the translator to run the application while working on the translation in ResEdit. This way the translator can view every dialog box at run-time while translating the file.

Before translating a Mac OS application, check whether there is a previously translated version available. The translator can then use the existing translations to automatically update the new version. Refer to the Updating Software section on page 133 for more information.

4.2 Resource Editors

Unlike the Windows platform, resource editors on the Mac OS are usually not part of the development environment. Mac resource editors are separate utilities, except Metrowerks Constructor, which is incorporated in the CodeWarrior development environment.

ResEdit is the most commonly used tool for Mac OS software localization and translation. Although newer versions are available, version 2.1.1 is the most stable one. ResEdit can be downloaded from the Apple FTP server at ftp.apple.com/devworld/ Tool_Chest/Developer_Utilities.

More information on the use of ResEdit and resource types can be found in the ResEdit Reference guide, which can be downloaded from the Apple Developer Connection web site at www.apple.com/developer (search for "ResEdit Reference").

Tip: Detailed information on the use of ResEdit can be found in the *ResEdit Complete* manual by P. Alley and C. Strange.

Resorcerer is a commercially available resource editor that has additional features and functionality. For more information on Resorcerer and a demo version, visit the Mathemaesthetics web site at www.mathemaesthetics.com.

It is advisable to start on the resource files by translating the menus and dialog boxes, followed by the strings and other resources. When a M acOS program file is opened with ResEdit or Resorcerer, a window with resource types is displayed:

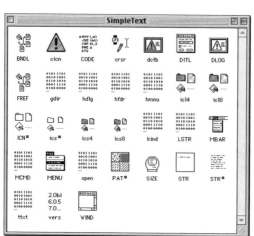 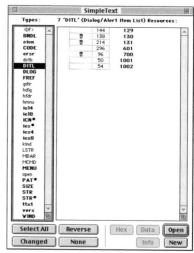

Double-clicking on a resource type opens a window with numbered resources. The next section provides information on specific resource types and ways to translate them. The information refers to both Resorcerer and ResEdit.

4.2.1 MENUS

The MENU and CMENU resource types contain all menus and drop-down list boxes. To edit a menu, open it, select the title or menu item and type the translation in the Title or Text box. Do not delete the three dots or the shortcuts following some commands.

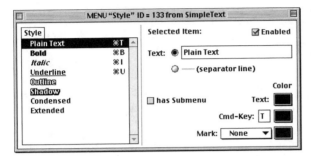

The translator may choose to change the Command key for a menu item by typing another letter in the Cmd-Key field. However, these key combinations should typically remain identical to the source. Refer to the Control Keys (Shortcut Keys) section on page 72 for more information.

4.2.2 DIALOG BOXES

The DITL, DLOG, ALRT, and WIND resource types contain all window and dialog box definitions. The contents of most dialog boxes can be found in the DITL (Dialog ITem List) resources. The DLOG and WIND resources are used to define dialog box or window sizes, and to translate the titles. ALRT resources are a subset of the DITL resources that report errors or alerts. They usually contain only buttons and icons.

To translate DITL resources, follow these steps:

1. Double-click on the DITL icon to open a list of dialog boxes. Each dialog box has an ID number.

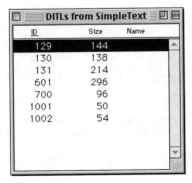

2. Double-click on the first item to open the dialog box. Press the Option key to display the borders and ID numbers of all items in the dialog box. Select the

Show Item Numbers option in the DITL menu if there is a preference to make the borders and numbers display by default.

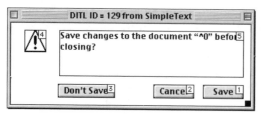

3. To open an item in the dialog box, double-click on the item. Alternatively, choose Select Item Number in the DITL menu and type the number of the required item. Opening items this way is preferable when items overlap one another.

4. The translation can be entered in the display window. In this window, it is also possible to change the size of the item box. Never resize by dragging with the mouse button because this will not provide accurate and consistent sizes. For example, when resizing the Cancel button, the new size should be consistent in all dialog boxes of the applications.

Tip: When resizing items, make sure the Show Item Numbers option in the DITL menu (ResEdit) or Item menu (Resorcerer) is selected to prevent overlapping other (hidden) items!

Before resizing items on Mac OS 8 or later versions, set the system font to Chicago, as the default Charcoal system font is smaller and can introduce truncations when the application is run on a 7.x version of Mac OS. According to Apple's *Mac OS 8 Human Interface Guidelines*, "Chicago provides the best basis for text layout; in fact, it is the metric standard upon which Charcoal is based. It is very important for you to design your dialog boxes and control panels with Chicago text, so they will look good in any System font the user selects."

After translating and resizing all items within a certain DITL, either continue with the next DITL, or translate the title of the DITL just completed. To change the size or title of a dialog box, open the DLOG, ALRT or WIND resource with the ID number that corresponds to the DITL number.

Tip: To open all items in a dialog box, press Command-A to select, and Command-O to open them. To close items one by one, press Command-W.

Double-clicking on a DLOG resource displays a window containing an image of the desktop with the associated dialog box in it. Use the Left, Right, Top and Bottom fields to change the size of the dialog box.

When increasing the dialog box size, it is important to ensure that the box will fit on all possible screen sizes. To determine whether a dialog still fits on all Mac screens, select several screen types from the MiniScreen menu once a DLOG has been opened.

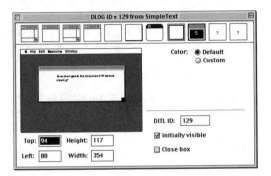

To translate the title of the dialog box, choose the Set DLOG Characteristics command in the DLOG menu and enter the translation in the Window Title box.

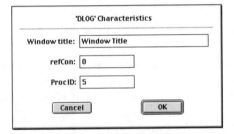

After all DITLs and DLOGs have been translated, open the ALRT resources. ALRTs and WIND resources are translated and resized in the same way as the DLOGs.

4.2.3 STRINGS

Open the STR, STR# and TEXT resource types to check whether they contain translatable text. The STR# resources usually contain error messages, but they may also include menu items or dialog options. Refer to the Strings section on page 63 for more information on translating strings.

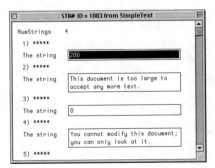

4.2.4 CONTROLS

Controls are button definitions or labels that are often used in several forms or dialog boxes, e.g. the Cancel button. To translate controls, double-click on a Control resource (CNTL) and translate the text in the Title field.

The location of the buttons can often be adjusted by changing the corresponding RECT resources.

4.2.5 IMAGES

The PICT resources contain the images used in the application, such as splash screens. To edit the text in a bitmap, open the resource, press Command-C and paste the image in an image editor like Adobe Photoshop. Color PICTs should be edited in indexed color mode, monochrome PICTs in bitmap mode.

Tip: When choosing the New command in Adobe Photoshop after copying a bitmap from a resource to the clipboard, the new image should have the same dimensions as the resource bitmap on the clipboard. Press Command-V in Photoshop to paste the bitmap in the new image.

After editing, paste the bitmap back in the resource, and close and save the resource. Refer to the Bitmap Editing section on page 129 for more information on editing bitmaps from Mac OS resources.

The ICN# and ICON resource types contain the icons for all program files. Double-click on an icon resource to open an icon editor in which the icon text can be edited. An example of translatable icon text is *PREFS*, which is displayed on preferences file icons. To activate translated icons, restart the Macintosh and rebuild the desktop. The desktop can be rebuilt by holding down the Option-Command key combination when booting the Macintosh.

The CURS resource type contains cursors and mouse pointers that sometimes contain localizable text or letters. Double-click on a cursor resource to open a cursor editor in which the cursor text can be edited.

4.2.6 BALLOON HELP

The hfdr, hdlg, hmnu, and hwin resource types contain balloon help text. Balloon help text is displayed when the Show Balloons command is selected in the Finder's help menu. These strings are hard-coded and need to be translated using a ResEdit template. Resorcerer supports Balloon Help templates by default:

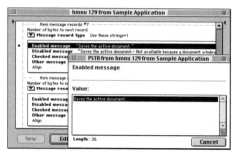

To translate help balloon text, open the balloon help resource, select the Help Message line and click on the Edit button. Then enter the translation in the displayed window.

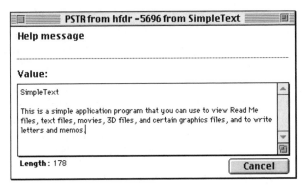

Please note that each balloon help string is limited to 255 characters. The length of the string being translated is displayed in the Length field of the hfdr resource window.

Balloon help hmnu resources often contain links to text in STR# resources. In this case, the hmnu resource will contain references to these STR# resources.

4.2.7 VERSION

Vers resources contain the language version and the copyright information that is shown when Get Info is selected from the Finder's File menu with the application icon selected. Double-click on a vers resource item to open the version info window. Change the Country Code to the target language and translate the text in the Long Version String box.

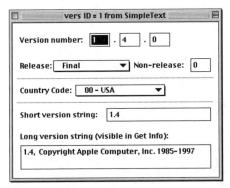

4.2.8 CUSTOM RESOURCES

Both ResEdit and Resorcerer contain template editors that let you edit custom resources in a dialog box format, with fields where the source text can be replaced with the translation.

For example, if an application contains resources created using Metrowerks CodeWarrior, particularly PPob resources, either a template needs to be created or provided, or Constructor should be used. Constructor is the CodeWarrior resource editor used to translate and resize these types of resources. Before creating a template, check whether a template is available from the software publisher.

4.3 Installers

Most Mac OS installers can be translated in "translator applications" that are created using the Installer VISE application. Refer to the Creating Installers section on page 130 for more information on Installer VISE.

A translator application enables the localizer to translate all disk names, file information, file descriptions, package information, and easy install text included in the localized installer. Most of the standard interface components will already be localized in the localized installer files, which are included with Installer VISE.

To translate a translator application, follow these steps:

1. Double-click on the file named "English to *language*" to launch the translator application.

2. Click on the Disk Information window and enter the translation in the right-hand column. The left-hand column contains the folder names of the original application archive.

3. Click on the File Information window to translate the names of the files and folders to be installed. Choose the File List option from the Windows menu.

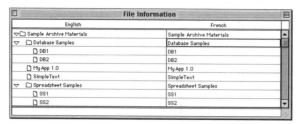

4. Click on the Package Information window, or select Package List from the Windows menu to translate the names and descriptions of the packages. The packages are typically called Easy Install and Custom Install.

5. Next, click on the Easy Install Text window, or select Easy Install Text from the Windows menu to translate the text to be displayed in the installer when the easy install option is selected.

6. To save the translations, choose the Save command from the File menu.

If a previously translated version of the translator application exists, select the Import Translator command from the File menu. The target column in the new file will be filled with any matching information from the old translator application that corresponds to the text in the left-hand column.

5   Further Reading

There is very little information available to translators of software applications. This is mainly because the translation approach and tools largely depend on a number of factors: the software publisher, file format, and the translation vendor selected to work on the project.

Here is a list of useful references for translators localizing software. References to books covering general technical translation issues can be found in the Further Reading section on page 224.

Alley, P. and C. Strange. 1994. *ResEdit Complete*. Addison-Wesley, ISBN 0-201-62686-1.

Apple Computer. 1992. *Guide to Macintosh Software Localization*. Addison-Wesley, ISBN 0-201-60856-1.

Carter, Daniel R. 1991. *Writing Localizable Software for the Macintosh*. Addison-Wesley, ISBN 0-201-57013-0.

Hickey, Tim. ed. 1999. *The Guide to Product Translation and Localization*. Computer Society, ISBN 0-769-50022-6.

Chapter 4:
Software Engineering

This chapter contains information on the engineering of localized software files for Windows and Mac OS. Topics include software compiling, dialog box resizing, hot key validation, and processing updates.

This chapter includes the following sections:

1. Introduction
2. Evaluation and Preparation
3. Compiling and Engineering
4. Windows
5. Mac OS
6. Other Environments
7. Further Reading

Chapters related to these topics are Chapter 3, which contains information on translating software applications, and Chapter 5, which contains information on testing localized software products.

1   Introduction

Software localization engineering is a central component of the whole localization process. Engineers usually have a wide range of tasks and responsibilities, including:

- Project evaluation and setup
- Compilation and resizing
- Processing updates
- Cosmetic testing
- Supporting linguists and project managers
- Editing graphics

Please note that these tasks and responsibilities will vary from one company to another.

Because software localization vendors usually have a wide portfolio of clients, localization engineers need to familiarize themselves with a huge number of development platforms, tools, and file formats. In addition to the platform and tool knowledge they need to have, localization engineers often have responsibility for both the software and the online help components.

This chapter covers the basic tasks performed by a localization engineer on localized software applications, and includes specific information on the Windows and Mac OS platforms. Chapter 7, Online Help Engineering and Testing, contains information on engineering activities related to localized online help systems. Chapter 10, Graphics Localization, contains information on editing graphics and creating screen captures.

As mentioned above, localization engineers require an in-depth knowledge of many different operating systems, utilities, translation tools, development environments, and localization models.

Most localization vendors expect, as a minimum, that their engineers have the following skills:

- Working knowledge of installation and configuration management for the most common operating systems and platforms
- Experience in industry-standard development and programming environments, e.g. Microsoft Visual Studio, Java Development Kit, Metrowerks CodeWarrior
- Experience using setup technologies such as InstallShield and WISE
- Understanding of internationalization and character set issues in software applications, for example the basics of Unicode
- Knowledge of database systems, scripting languages, and graphical user interface development
- Professional and creative attitude approach to problem-solving and bug-fixing
- Awareness of localization models and workflows, and project scheduling issues
- Experience selecting and using computer aided translation (CAT) tools
- Knowledge of Internet technology, communication software and protocols
- Excellent communication skills, both written and oral
- Foreign language skills (preferred)

Software localization engineers need to have a wide range of software applications at their disposal to produce the highest quality localized software. In addition to the standard Office and Internet applications, a localization engineering "toolkit" will most likely include the following:

- Microsoft's MSDN and/or Apple's Developer Connection subscriptions
- Advanced text editor, such as TextPad or Programmer's File Editor
- Image editor, such as Paint Shop Pro or Adobe Photoshop
- Screen capture utility, such as Collage Complete
- Version control software, such as Microsoft Visual SourceSafe
- File management utilities, such as diff tools and file synchronizers

- (Evaluation versions of) all commonly used software localization tools, such as Corel Catalyst, RC-WinTrans, AppLocalize

In this chapter, there are many references to the Microsoft Developer Network CDs and the Apple Developer Connection CDs:

- Microsoft Developer Network (MSDN) is an online subscribed service that provides developers with a set of CDs containing development kits and tools, localized versions of Microsoft operating systems and applications, glossaries, beta versions of new releases, etc. The MSDN has three subscription levels: library, professional, and universal. For more information on MSDN, visit the Microsoft's MSDN web site at msdn.microsoft.com.

- Apple provides a similar subscription to its Apple Developer Connection CD series. This is a series of quarterly CD-ROMs that provide developers with the latest Apple technical information, system software, and development utilities. The Tool Chest CDs, containing localization tools, are part of the CD series. For more information on membership, visit the Apple Developer Connection web site at www.apple.com/developer.

In addition to these resources, reference works such as Nadine Kano's *Developing International Software For Windows 95 and Windows NT* are invaluable to a localization team. This book and the manuals for all development tools included in Microsoft Visual Studio, are available online at Microsoft's MSDN web site at msdn.microsoft.com (search for "Developing International Software").

2 Evaluation and Preparation

It is important, when working with software products, to do a full and thorough evaluation and preparation of the source materials. The consequences of not checking can be quite significant, for example, if files that contain errors are sent out for translation into 14 languages, any errors originating in the source files will need to be fixed 14 times!

The purpose of project evaluation is to try to spot potential problems with source materials before the translation cycle. Apart from evaluating and checking the source files, all material needs to be prepared for translation in the most efficient and cost-effective way.

At this point in the project, localization engineers should focus on the following tasks:

- Checking source material
- Configuring build environments
- Test-compiling
- Preparing files for translation

The end of this section provides a check list that may help determine whether the source material is complete and ready for translation.

2.1   Checking Source Material

In the localization kit, locate the files necessary to build the software and check whether all source material is valid and complete. The source material must be checked in several stages:

1. Is the localization kit complete, i.e. does it contain all files that are needed to localize and build the application?

2. Were instructions or guidelines included?

3. Are all files valid and virus-free?

4. Does the localization kit include file types that are unknown or unreadable?

5. Are duplicate files included, or does the kit contain files with identical names but different dates or properties?

6. Does the localization kit include files that are relevant to project management, such as schedules or word counts? These files should be handed over to the project manager.

7. Does the kit include files that are important for translators/localizers, such as previously localized versions or glossaries? These files should be forwarded to the translators.

It is advisable to copy all contents of a localization kit to the hard drive and browse through the folders and files. It is also important to read the guidelines very carefully, to check whether there are any special hardware or software requirements for building or testing the software.

2.2   Configuring Build Environments

If the engineering team is responsible for compiling, engineering and testing the localized versions of a software application, the setup and configuration of the software build environment should be completed before files are sent out for translation.

Here are some important issues to consider when configuring a build environment:

- Operating system
- Compiler
- Path or variable settings

It is essential to know the version and language of the operating system on which the compiler will run. Most localization engineers use English versions of Windows NT or the latest Mac OS to compile software. Make sure all software compilation and engineering is done on a computer other than the one used to run or test beta software!

An even more important factor is the compiler and compiler version used to build the software. If the English software has been developed using Microsoft Visual C++ 4.2, compiling it with a different version will change file structures and content. If there are no compilation guidelines included in the publisher's kit, check with the publisher to determine which compiler to use.

Most build environments require path or environment variable settings on an operating system. Professional localization kits should contain batch files that automatically set the right variables. If different path settings are required for each language compilation, such as a path setting for localized resource files, then create compilation batch files for each language because the localized versions will probably need to be compiled a number of times.

When all required hardware and software has been installed, and the build environment has been correctly configured, test-compile the English version of the software application.

2.3 Test-Compiling

Here are some advantages to be gained from running a test-compilation on the source material:

- Compilation problems are identified early in the process.
- Missing files are highlighted.
- Configuration issues are flagged at an early stage.
- The validity of the compiled executable can be addressed.

If there are problems compiling the English product, these problems should be resolved before the translation cycle. The localization engineer should ideally perform a *pseudo-translation* during the test-compilation phase. A pseudo-translation is an exercise where each translatable text string in the software is replaced with a longer string or a series of accented characters. This will help to identify any potential problems in compiling and executing the localized files.

Instruction documents, included in the localization kit, usually describe how the application is compiled. If there is any uncertainty on how to proceed or if any problems arise while compiling, consult the publisher. The localization engineers should discuss these issues directly with the publisher's development department to avoid any confusion.

Once the original application compiles with no errors, check whether the file being built, i.e. the .dll or .exe file, has the same byte size as the file installed with the original application. If there is a substantial file size difference, it is worthwhile checking with the publisher whether an increase in file size will cause any problems. Then replace the original installed executable or .dll with the *pseudo-translated* .dll, and check whether the application still runs without errors.

2.4   Preparing for Translation

Once all the source material is complete and compiles without errors, it is important to address the following issues:

- Which files need to be translated?

- Are existing translations available that can be re-used, or leveraged?

- What is the most efficient translation method or approach?

- Do marks or comments need to be inserted in the strings for the translation team?

- How can the software code be protected, for example by using a filter, tagger, or parser for a translation memory tool? If no existing filter, tagger or parser is available, is it possible to create a customized tool?

If the source material is well prepared, the translation kit will make life easier for translators, and avoids unnecessary re-translation of previously translated text.

2.4.1   TRANSLATABLE FILES

If the localization kit does not contain a list of "translatable" files, locate them in the build environment. In Visual C++ or Visual Basic projects, translatable strings are usually included in .rc files. It is advisable to check all files, as programmers often include translatable text in files with extensions such as .str, .txs, .dlg, .msg or .txt. If there is any uncertainty about the translatable files, create a list of these files and verify this with the publisher.

On the Mac OS platform, translatable resources are usually embedded in the executable itself. Here, it is more important to identify which resource types within the executable require translation.

In addition to the resource files, it is important to identify any image files that may need to be localized, such as bitmap images of splash screens, or buttons used in the software.

2.4.2   LEVERAGE

With most software localization projects, it is possible to re-use existing translations from the following sources:

- Project glossaries

- Previously localized versions of the software application

- Localized versions of other applications from the same publisher

- Operating system glossaries

Re-using existing translations not only reduces the word counts, it also increases the speed of translation and improves terminology consistency. For example, if version 4 of a Windows application was being translated, it may be possible to pre-translate 90% of the application if a localized version3 exists.

If no previously localized versions exist, it is possible to leverage translations from operating system glossaries. Most applications contain standard commands or menu items such as File, Edit, Save As, or buttons such as Cancel and Apply. Try pre-translating these items using the operating system glossaries before sending source material out for translation. For more information on operating system glossaries, refer to Chapter 12, Terminology.

The way in which existing translations can be leveraged depends entirely on the file format and the translation method chosen. Most software localization tools include features that enable the user to import previous translations or glossary items. Some localization tools, such as Corel Catalyst, also enable the user to re-use resizing information from previously translated and resized versions.

When using a translation memory tool to translate software resource files, convert software glossaries to translation memory databases before the translators start working on the files. For more information on translation memory, refer to Chapter 11, Translation Technology.

2.4.3 TRANSLATION METHOD

The translation approach depends largely on the tools strategy adopted by the software publisher, i.e. whether they have developed their own tool set or elected to use the standard commercial tools?

Either way, the vendor will need to decide, if the publisher has not already decided, how to send the files out for translation. In general, one of the tools listed below is used for software translation:

- Text editor
- Resource editor
- Software localization tool
- Translation memory tool

The choice of tool should be based on the criteria below:

- Publisher instructs the vendor to use a specific industry standard tool.
- Publisher instructs the vendor to use a proprietary tool. Some software publishers, such as Lotus and Oracle, have developed their own localization tools, which have to be used on all projects.
- Did the publisher instruct you to use a specific tool, or were you provided with a proprietary tool? Some software publishers, such as Lotus and Oracle, have developed their own localization tools, which have to be used for all their projects.
- Are the investments for developing or purchasing a translation tool justifiable? For example, a 3000 word software user interface project may not justify the costs of purchasing a professional tool like Corel Catalyst.

- Which method is safest, i.e. how can we minimize the risk of translators damaging or altering the software code? If the software is translated using a text editor, it is very easy to inadvertently alter the code surrounding translatable strings.

- Is the file format supported by the tool? For example, binary software files such as .dll files are not supported by translation memory tools.

- Is it possible or easy to re-use translations if updates need to be processed during the project?

- Does the tool support all target languages, especially double-byte or bi-directional languages?

In most cases, a software localization tool should be used on binary files (such as .dll files or Mac OS executables) and standard resource file types, and a translation memory tool should be used on custom resource file types or database strings in text format.

In the case of custom software file types a text filter or parser will need to be created using regular expressions in a scripting language such as Perl or Awk. Regular expressions are patterns used for searching text in data. For more information on filters, refer to the Translation Memory tools section in Chapter 11, Translation Technology.

2.4.4 MARKING

Depending on how well the source files have been programmed, localization engineers should browse through all text strings and include marks and comments if necessary. Here are some examples of comments that could be added to strings:

- Do not translate!

- Do not use more than *xx* characters.

- Translation leveraged from operating system glossaries, please review.

- This message is concatenated with message ID *xx*.

- Do not delete hot key symbols.

- Leave trailing space in string.

- Do not change order of variables.

If the developer of the source material has internationalized the application fully, i.e. separated all translatable text from software code, it should be relatively easy to comment or mark the strings. However, if the resource files contain many strings that should remain in English, marking the strings will be quite a time-consuming task, but it is worthwhile doing this on multilingual projects, where the same items will be translated for all languages.

2.5 Check List

If the publisher has not supplied detailed guidelines or instructions, ask the following questions to get a complete overview of the work to be performed and the services and deliverables expected.

2.5.1 SOFTWARE COMPILATION

Here is a list of questions on compilation issues for the software project. If these issues are unclear from the localization kit, they should be discussed with the publisher.

- ✓ Does compilation require any special procedures or steps?
- ✓ Which version and which compiler should be used?
- ✓ What is the name of the program file being compiled?
- ✓ Are specific tools required for compiling the software?
- ✓ Which path settings or environment variables are required for compiling?
- ✓ Can controls, such as buttons, and dialog boxes be resized?
- ✓ Do the files contain country-specific information that needs to be changed, such as default page sizes, currency symbols, etc.?
- ✓ Should *locale* information be changed in the resource files?

2.5.2 SOURCE MATERIAL

Here is a list of questions on the source material for the software project. If these issues are unclear from the localization kit, they should be discussed with the publisher.

- ✓ Which software resource files need to be translated?
- ✓ Which tools should be used to translate the resource files?
- ✓ Which bitmaps or icons need to be translated?
- ✓ Are blank or layered versions and font information for the bitmaps available?
- ✓ Are there space restrictions that translators should consider?
- ✓ Are previously translated versions of the resource files available?
- ✓ Are source files available for each component that contains user interface text?

2.5.3 TESTING

Here is a list of questions on testing issues for the software project. If these issues are unclear from the localization kit, they should be discussed with the publisher.

- ✓ Should the localized software also be tested?
- ✓ What type of testing should be done, i.e. linguistic testing, or functionality, compatibility, and regression testing?
- ✓ On which platforms should the software be tested?
- ✓ Will automated testing tools be used?
- ✓ Are test scripts available?

For more information on testing methods and types, refer to Chapter 5, Software Quality Assurance.

A well-constructed localization kit should address most of these issues. Refer to the Creating Localization Kits section on page 48 for more information on localization kit contents.

3   Compiling and Engineering

When files are returned from translation, localization engineers need to compile the localized versions to create executables or .dll files, unless the translation was entered directly in the binary files. Once the files have been compiled, begin checking the translated files and resizing dialog boxes. Files do not always need to be recompiled, for example, in the case of many Ma cOS software localization projects. In this case, the engineering can begin immediately.

3.1   Compiling

If the source material has been carefully prepared, localization engineers can follow the steps below:

1. Check the translated files for completeness, file format, etc. Check whether all file components and strings have been translated and whether the files have been saved in the correct file format.

2. Copy the translated files into the build environment, replacing the source language or pseudo-translated files.

3. Change the language settings for the project files, and each individual resource file.

4. Compile the translated versions, resize the dialog boxes, fix the hot keys, and test the localized applications.

In many cases, compilation problems are encountered when translated files are compiled. These problems are often caused by errors introduced during translation. Here are some examples below:

* Deleted quotation marks. Each software string should start and end with a quotation mark.

* Added quotation marks, i.e. where the translator has introduced additional quotation marks within the translated strings, the compiler will regard the first quotation mark as the end of the string.

* Strings containing too many characters. Many compilers have a length restriction of 254 characters for software strings. When more characters are used, the compiler will display an error message.

Here is an example where the translator has inadvertently deleted a quotation mark:

```
GROUPBOX        "Papier,1073,8,9,224,56,WS_GROUP
```

To fix this error, simply type a quotation mark at the end of the text string:

```
GROUPBOX     "Papier",1073,8,9,224,56,WS_GROUP
```

Here is an example where quotation marks have been introduced by the translator to highlight the dialog box name:

```
102     "Öffnet das Dialogfeld "Farben". "
```

If the translator wants to use quotation marks, the marks should be duplicated or single quotation marks should be used instead:

```
102     "Öffnet das Dialogfeld ""Farben"". "
```

```
102     "Öffnet das Dialogfeld 'Farben'. "
```

Here are some examples of errors that do not interfere with the compilation, but that may appear in translated resource files:

- Missing leading or trailing spaces
- Duplicate hot keys
- Missing ellipses (...)
- Overtranslation, i.e. strings that should remain in English have been translated.
- Added or deleted hot key symbols, i.e. the translator has inserted a hot key symbol in the string but has not deleted the original, or has deleted the entire hot key symbol.
- Added or deleted variables, control codes, or control keys

Some software localization tools contain features that automatically check for common errors. In the Corel Catalyst tool, Validate Expert allows the user to select error types to be checked in translated software files:

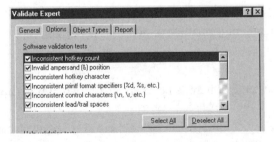

If the translated software fails to compile, and the compiler does not indicate the line number containing the error, the engineer will have to find the string causing the problem through trial-and-error. One way to do this is to compile the product using the English version, and paste small sections of the translated file into the original version until the compiler reports the error. Then, repeat this process for the isolated section until the error is located. Where possible, use a text editor that displays line numbers when working this way.

3.2 Dialog Box Resizing

When software resource files have been translated, the dialog boxes need to be adjusted to make all options fit on the screen. Changing the size and/or positioning of elements in a localized dialog box to accommodate expanded or reduced translations is called dialog box resizing. If the software has been well internationalized, i.e. sufficient space is reserved for text expansion, the resizing effort should be minimal. After resizing a dialog box in a resource editor, check the results in the running application. Depending on the system fonts or screen resolution, the running application may distort the dialog boxes or display them incorrectly.

It is not always possible to resize dialog boxes or on-screen forms. A good example of this is where applications use the same screen layout for all languages. This often is the case with UNIX or database-driven applications. In such cases, translators should be instructed to abbreviate their translations to make them fit in the available space.

Please refer to the Dialog Box Resizing section on page 120 for resizing guidelines for Windows applications, and refer to the Dialog Box Resizing section on page 128 for information on Mac OS applications.

3.2.1 GENERAL GUIDELINES

Here are some general guidelines that apply to the resizing of localized (controls in) dialog boxes:

- Localized dialog boxes should contain exactly the same number of buttons and options as the English version.
- Default buttons have default sizes, e.g. the Cancel button should be the same size in all dialog boxes, where possible. Where possible, buttons should be the same size within a dialog box.
- Avoid adjusting the space between buttons. Try, in particular, to avoid moving two buttons closer to each other.
- Verify that controls do not overlap. This also applies to controls without text.
- Follow the original alignment format for options, i.e. left, right, top, or bottom.
- Follow the original Tab key order for the options displayed in the localized dialog box.
- Avoid abbreviating text, unless there is no alternative. If an abbreviation is required, always consult the translation team!
- Avoid reducing the size of controls, even when there is space available. There may be some text in the controls, which is only inserted at run-time. This will be truncated when the control size is reduced.
- Always try to make the dialog box title or caption fit in the title bar.
- Avoid changing the size of a dialog box. Changing the box size will have an impact on the size of dialog box screen captures. This will also affect the DTP or HTML engineering, for example, in HTML, the image size coordinates need to be adjusted manually when the image size has changed.

- Never change font attributes of items in dialog boxes, unless non-Roman languages are being localized.
- Dialog boxes should fit on a standard VGA screen with 640 x 480 resolution.

Each item in a dialog box has position and size coordinates. In the following example, the position of the Cancel button is 29 units from the left of the dialog box, and 44 units from the top of the dialog box. The button height is 14 units, and the button width is 32 units.

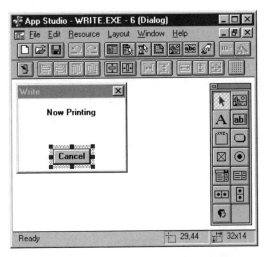

Always refer to these coordinates when resizing controls or dialog boxes, and never drag item borders using the mouse. It is impossible to be exact, when relying on hand-eye coordination! A consistent and esthetically correct user interface leaves users with a much more professional impression than a user interface where dialog box buttons have different sizes or locations.

Here is an example. If the size of the Cancel button has increased by 10 points in one dialog box, apply this coordinate across all occurrences of the Cancel button in the application. This is exactly why engineers should never use auto-resize features that are included with some resource editors or localization tools.

Engineers should familiarize themselves with the graphical user interface design rules for each individual platform. Refer to Microsoft's Windows Interface Guidelines for Software Design, or Apple's Human Interface Guidelines. The Microsoft reference book can be accessed through Microsoft's MSDN web site at msdn.microsoft.com (search for "Windows Interface Guidelines for Software Design"). The Apple manual can be downloaded from the Apple Developer Connection web site at www.apple.com/developer (search for "Human Interface Guidelines").

If no resource editor is available or the engineers are working with custom resource file formats, the engineers need to alter strings and coordinates directly in the text-only resource files and then compile the translated files to view the results.

This process is time-consuming and can generate many errors, because, for each change entered, the software needs to be compiled in order to view the results.

Coordinates are typically displayed as ID, position from left, position from top, width, and height. In the following example, to increase the width of the translated Cancel button with 10 points, the engineer would change 50 to 60.

```
PUSHBUTTON          "Abbrechen",2,244,174,50,14
```

It makes sense to search the resource file for `"244,174,50,14"` and replace this with `"244,174,60,14"` to ensure consistent resizing of the Cancel button throughout the file.

3.3   Checking Hot Keys

The function and assignment of hot keys is described in the Hot Keys section on page 70. Assigning hot keys in localized software is a task ideally suited to the software translator, but it is the responsibility of localization engineers to check localized software for duplicate or missing hot keys.

Some compilers, such as Microsoft's Visual C++ allow the user to automatically identify duplicate hot keys in resources, as explained in the Checking Hot Keys section on page 122. Some software localization tools also have this functionality, but it may vary from one to another.

The engineering team should check for hot key clashes in dynamic menus or dialog boxes, i.e. menus or dialog boxes containing items that are inserted at run-time. An example of this is where menu items in Windows Explorer will vary depending on the item that is selected at run-time, such as a file or a folder. These menus are automatically generated, so hot keys can only be checked during run-time and not in the program resources.

Here is a checklist for software localization engineers to use when checking hot keys:

- No duplicate hot keys are used in menus and dialog boxes, including dynamically generated menus or dialog boxes.
- No items have missing or multiple hot keys.
- All hot keys work on localized keyboards or keyboard layouts. Nadine Kano's book *Developing International Software for Windows 95 and Windows NT* contains an appendix showing all local keyboard layouts. Local keyboard images can also be found on Microsoft's GlobalDev web site at www.microsoft.com/globaldev.
- In ideographic languages, such as Japanese, Chinese, and Korean, the hot key letter assigned in the source language is added between brackets after the translation cycle. An example can be found in the Hot Keys section on page 70.
- Hot key assignments are consistent with operating environment standards.
- Accented characters and letters with descenders such as p, j, q, g are not used as hot keys when other alternatives are available.

Hot keys are not used on all operating platforms. Mac OS applications, for example, do not normally have hot key assignments.

3.4 Processing Updates

Most software localization projects *are* either updates to a previous version of a product, e.g. version 4 is an update of version 3, or *contain* interim beta build updates that need to be processed by localization engineers after the project has started. It is not unusual to start the translation during the development cycle of the source language product. As a result, localization vendors are forced to process several product updates or milestones before a final translation is produced.

The main reason for working this way is that ship dates for localized versions are moving ever closer to the domestic product ship date, and in some instances, there may be a simultaneous shipment ("simship"), where the localized version goes out the same day as the English.

To avoid a lot of rework by the translation team, there are many things that can be done to accelerate the updating process, varying from copying and pasting existing translations to automatically importing existing translations from a translation memory database. The procedure selected will, of course, depend on the extent of the update and the file format/translation approach involved.

If, for example, resource file version 3.1 has been translated, and version 3.2 is sent out for translation with 10 new words and no other changes, it would be better to do a file compare on source 3.1 and source 3.2, then use the translated version 3.1 resource files and copy and paste in the new words once they have been translated. If the update is larger, with a 20% text change to the updated file, the best approach is to use the new 3.2 resource file and try to import (or leverage) as many translations as possible from version 3.1, so that the unchanged 80% of the text can be automatically pre-translated.

There are many ways to leverage existing translations, but this will depend on file formats and tools used. If the software resource files have been translated in a translation memory tool, with no engineering or resizing work done on the files, the updated or new files can be loaded into the translation memory tool, and any matching translations will automatically feed from the translation memory database.

In the case of binary files or resource files where resizing or other engineering information needs to be re-used, it is better to use a software localization tool. Some tools, Corel Catalyst for example, not only automatically re-use translations and hot key assignments, but also utilize resizing information for translated controls and dialog box items from previous file versions. For more information, refer to the Software Localization Tools section on page 383.

If a vendor receives multiple updates from a publisher, it may make sense to accumulate a number of updates and then process them in batch mode, rather than individually. Vendors and publishers should agree on the number of updates expected and the percentage change anticipated in each update. Update management is critical and can be very problematic, particularly when working on a multilingual project. It is vital that the project manager uses a revision or version control mechanism or tool to keep track of updated files. Microsoft Visual SourceSafe is a tool that is commonly used for localization projects. Where possible, the vendor should mirror the version control mechanism used by publisher. Another option is to set up a database replication system between the vendor and publisher, where both teams update the database with any new material in the project on a regular basis, be it source material, glossaries, instructions or completed translations.

3.5   Bitmap Editing

Any bitmaps (with text) located in software resource files will need to be edited using a bitmapped graphics editor. The most common graphics editors are Adobe Photoshop or JASC Paint Shop Pro.

If the translation is done in the compiled .rc files, the `// Bitmap` section in the .rc file will indicate which bitmaps will be included in the compiled program file. If the bitmap section contains a reference like `BITMAP MOVEABLE PURE "bmp403.bmp"`, locate the `bmp403.bmp` file in the build environment and edit it using a graphics editor. The bitmaps are usually stored along with the icon and cursor resource files, in one folder in the build environment.

If the translation is done directly in a program file, such as a .dll file on the Windows platform or a Mac OS executable, open the bitmap resource using the integrated bitmap editor of the resource editor or software localization tool. In most cases, bitmap resources can be exported and re-imported after editing.

Bitmaps may often contain images that are very specific to a particular culture, and may even cause offense in other cultures. For example, a mailbox icon displaying a U.S. mailbox may have little meaning to a user in another country. In cases like these, it is best to consult the publisher on how the bitmap should be localized. Another example is the "Home" button which is displayed in many web browsers. In many languages "home page" is translated as "starting page" or "front page". Using the icon depicting a house on a localized web page may not make sense for users in the target languages.

If a bitmap contains translatable text pasted on a gradient of photographic background, ask the software developer to provide *blanks* of the bitmap, i.e. bitmaps without the text. Using these original graphics will be much easier than recreating or patching up backgrounds. When editing bitmap images used in software applications, ascertain which font was used to create the original bitmap. To see which font was used, place a text block containing the original text on top of the text in the original bitmap. For more information on bitmap or image editing, refer to Chapter 10, Graphics Localization.

3.6   Cosmetic Testing

Once the dialog boxes have been resized, the hot keys have been fixed, and all components have been localized and compiled, the user interface needs to be tested visually in the running application. This type of testing is called *cosmetic testing*.

Cosmetic testing should always be performed on the running application. Looking at the dialog boxes and menus in a resource editor or localization tool will not suffice, as strings or options may only be visible at run-time, and a system font may completely alter the display of dialog box items.

For more information on visual or cosmetic testing, refer to the Cosmetic Test section on page 151.

4   Windows

Software applications for the Windows environment are usually developed in an object-oriented programming environment such as Visual C++ or Visual Basic or a web-based development environment such as Java.

In the case of Visual C++ based projects, software developers can choose to have the text-only resource files (.rc) translated, or the compiled executables (.dll or .exe). In the first case, compilation is almost always necessary. In the other case, the translator will need a tool to support binary file translation, such as a resource editor or software localization tool, for example Microsoft Visual Studio or Corel Catalyst respectively.

These tools all have their own features and specifications, and here we focus on the first scenario, where engineers are compiling text-only resource files that have been translated. More information on the tools mentioned above can be found in the Resource Editors section on page 78 and the Software Localization Tools section on page 383.

In the following sections, we will concentrate on applications developed in Visual C++ with standard Windows resource files. For information on the localization of applications created in other development environments, refer to the Other Environments section on page 137.

4.1   Evaluation and Preparation

To evaluate and prepare a Windows software localization project, follow all the steps in the Evaluation and Preparation section on page 99.

Briefly, the steps are:

- Check the source material.
- Set up the build environment.
- Test-compile the source material.
- Prepare all translatable files for translation.

If the build environment is only set up to compile one language, create a multilingual build environment by creating subfolders for the resource files in each language. In this case, create batch files that will set the right paths and instruct the compiler to use localized files.

Make sure to check whether all the correct variables are set on the system when compiling from a DOS Command Prompt using a batch file. Most compilers require specific path and environment variables. For Microsoft Visual C++ projects, for example, run the MSVCvars32.bat file, which can be found in the \Bin folder. It is important to read the documentation on the compiler being used.

Corel Catalyst is one of the software localization tools that allows the user to perform a pseudo-translation on .rc files. This is always recommended, particularly when working with double-byte languages, or Cyrillic character sets.

4.2 Compiling

Windows applications are normally built from a project file or makefile (.mak) containing all project and compilation settings. Makefiles are opened using Microsoft Visual Studio and link to resource (.rc) files, .h files, and other source files. Refer to the File Types section on page 115 for a listing of file types found in a build environment.

Do not edit, save, or compile resource or project files using other versions of a compiler other than the one used originally to create the files. This may change the file structure considerably and cause serious problems! Information on compiler versions can often be found in the header of the project or makefile. If it is not clear which version of a compiler should be used, do not edit the .rc files directly in the compiler's resource editor. Enter all changes manually in the .rc files, which can then be recompiled to reflect the changes.

A project file instructs the resource compiler to create a binary resource file (.res) from an ASCII resource file (.rc). The .res file is then appended to the executable file (.exe or .dll) of a Windows application. It is now more common for programmers to include translatable resources in a separate .dll, called a satellite .dll or resource-only .dll, which is completely separate from the program code.

To compile the translated product, replace all English .rc files with localized ones (or copy them to separate language folders, depending on how the build environment was set up). Open the makefile using Visual C++, and choose the Build command. Change the language settings in the compiler before building the .dll or .exe file. In Microsoft Visual Studio, open the Project Settings window and select the required language in the Resources tab.

4.2.1   FILE TYPES

The following table lists different file types that are most likely to be included in a localization kit. It also indicates whether the file can be localized or translated:

Extension	File Type	Localizable?
.aps	binary version of the resource script file	no
.bat	batch file used for compiling	no
.bmp	bitmap resource file	yes
.clw	class wizard file	no
.cpp	C++ module used for .dll	no
.cur	cursor resource file	yes
.def	module definition file	no
.dlg	dialog resource script file	yes
.dll	dynamic link library	yes
.fnt	font	no
.h	header file	no
.ico	icon resource file	yes
.inf	setup file	yes
.mak or .mdp	file containing project build instructions	no
.mc	messages	yes
.mnu	menu resource file	yes
.rc	resource script file (text-only)	yes
.rc2	resources that are not edited directly	no
.reg	registry files	yes
.res	resource file (binary)	yes
.vcp	project configuration file	no
.ver	version information header file	no

4.2.2 LANGUAGE SETTINGS

Windows-based software resource files contain several language settings that may need to change before compiling the translated files.

When editing .rc files using a text editor, change the header information and the version stamp manually. The preferred way is to open the .rc file using the resource editor and then set all the language options.

The header of an .rc file may contain the following lines:

```
/////////////////////////////////////////////////////////////////////
/////////
// English (U.S.) resources

#if !defined(AFX_RESOURCE_DLL) || defined(AFX_TARG_ENU)
#ifdef _WIN32
LANGUAGE LANG_ENGLISH, SUBLANG_ENGLISH_US
#pragma code_page(1252)
#endif //_WIN32
```

This info block contains four language settings that need to be changed:

- The `English (U.S.) resources` comment line indicates that the resources that follow will be English. The end of a language block is defined by `#endif // English (U.S.) resources`.

- `AFX_TARG_ENU` indicates the language of the resource .dll to be used. The three letter language codes are only valid in Windows9x and NT. ENU is the language code for U.S. English. For a list of language codes, refer to the Locale Codes and IDs section on page 118.

- The `LANGUAGE` line defines the locale to be used in the compiled file. `LANGUAGE` is one of the keywords introduced with 32-bit .rc files. The two parameters following the keyword set the language and sublanguage, for example language French and sublanguage Canadian French. For a list of locales, refer to the Locale Codes and IDs section on page 118.

- The pragma code page defines the Windows character set to be used. The code page is an array that maps the integer code to the character of the character set. The number 1252 stands for the default Latin-1 ANSI code page. Code page 1252 is used for English and most European languages. Other examples of code pages are 932 (Japan), 949 (Korean), 950 (Taiwan), 1200 (Unicode), 1250 (Eastern European), 1251 (Cyrillic), 1253 (Greek), and 1254 (Turkish), 1255 (Hebrew), and 1256 (Arabic). For more information on character sets, refer to www.microsoft.com/typography.

To set the language of resources when you are using the resource editor integrated in Microsoft Visual Studio, follow these steps:

1. Open the resource file or binary program file (.dll or .exe) to be edited.

2. Select one or more resources where the language is to be set. As a default, all resources are selected.

3. Right-click on the selection and choose the Properties command.

4. In the Properties window, select a language from the Language drop-down menu.

The version stamp in a resource file specifies the company name, application name, copyright, version number, and language edition of an application.

A `Version` section in a resource file contains a language ID in the `StringFileInfo` and `VarFileInfo` blocks. The `StringFileInfo` block contains the user-defined string information, and the variable file information (`VarFileInfo`) block contains a list of languages supported by this version of the resource file.

```
BEGIN
BLOCK "StringFileInfo"
BEGIN
BLOCK "040904e4"
BEGIN
VALUE "CompanyName", "Microsoft Corporation\0"
VALUE "FileDescription", "WordPad MFC Application\0"
VALUE "FileVersion", "4.00.950\0"
VALUE "InternalName", "wordpad\0"
VALUE "LegalCopyright", "Copyright © Microsoft Corp.\0"
VALUE "OriginalFilename", "WORDPAD.EXE\0"
VALUE "ProductName", "Microsoft Windows (TM)\0"
VALUE "ProductVersion", "4.0\0"
END
END
BLOCK "VarFileInfo"
BEGIN
VALUE "Translation", 0x409, 1252
END
END
```

In the example above, change `"040904e4"`, the `"0x409"` language ID, and `1252` character set specification to reflect the settings for the target language. The `"040904e4"` is an ASCII hexadecimal representation of "0x409" and "1252". The first part can be retrieved from the table in the following section, for the second part (for example `04e4` for `1252`, the ANSI code page), use a hexadecimal converter. Refer to the following section for a table of language IDs and codes.

To change the version stamp of the resource file when using Microsoft Visual Studio, follow these steps:

1. Open the .rc file or binary program file (.dll or .exe) that you are editing.

2. Open the Version resource.

3. Double-click on the Block Header line.

4. In the Block Header Properties window, select a language and code page for the file or project.

If you are working with a large set of resource files, it may be quicker to assign the language to the resources in one of the .rc files. Next, copy the language definition heading from one file into the other files using a text editor or word processor.

4.2.3 FONT SETTINGS

In many cases, the font to be used in dialog boxes is defined in the .rc file, at the start of each dialog box section, for example:

```
PICKFONT DIALOG DISCARDABLE   0, 0, 348, 308
STYLE WS_CHILD | WS_VISIBLE | WS_BORDER
FONT 8, "MS Sans Serif"
```

For multi-byte languages, this font attribute needs to be changed because the MS Sans Serif font set does not include any Asian characters. For example, for Chinese you would use New Ming Li, for Japanese MS Gothic or Mincho.

Check the default system font of the localized operating system using the Appearance tab in the Display Properties Control Panel to see which fonts are used for dialog box components such as options and buttons. Next, insert this font name in the localized .rc files and re-compile.

4.3 Locale Codes and IDs

The following table shows the IDs and language codes that are used to identify locales in Windows software resource files. For a complete list of locale IDs, refer to Microsoft's

MSDN web site at msdn.microsoft.com (search for "locale IDs"). A complete listing of locales can be found on the Unicode web site at www.unicode.org.

Language	ID	Code	Locale
English	0x409	ENU	LANG_ENGLISH
English (UK)	0x02	ENG	SUBLANG_ENGLISH_UK
English (US)	0x01	ENU	SUBLANG_ENGLISH_US
French	0x40c	FRA	LANG_FRENCH
French	0x01	FRA	SUBLANG_FRENCH
French (Belgian)	0x02	FRB	SUBLANG_FRENCH_BELGIAN
German	0x407	DEU	LANG_GERMAN
German	0x01	DEU	SUBLANG_GERMAN
German (Austrian)	0x03	DEA	SUBLANG_GERMAN_AUSTRIAN
German (Swiss)	0x02	DES	SUBLANG_GERMAN_SWISS
Italian	0x410	ITA	LANG_ITALIAN
Italian	0x01	ITA	SUBLANG_ITALIAN
Italian (Swiss)	0x02	ITS	SUBLANG_ITALIAN_SWISS
Spanish	0x40a	ESP	LANG_SPANISH
Spanish (Modern Sort)	0x03	ESN	SUBLANG_SPANISH_MODERN
Spanish (Traditional Sort)	0x01	ESP	SUBLANG_SPANISH
System Default	0x02		SUBLANG_SYS_DEFAULT

In programming environments, a *locale* is a combination of primary (language) and sub language (country) codes. Locale information includes currency symbol, date/time/ number formatting information, localized days of the week and months of the year, the standard abbreviation for the name of the country, and character encoding information.

On some platforms, for example the Sun Solaris platform, locale is used to define a collection of files, data, and sometimes code, that contains the information needed to adapt the operating system or application to local market needs. In this context, the locale also contains all translated user interface messages and strings.

4.4 MFC Components

MFC, short for Microsoft Foundation Class library, is a set of C++ classes that contain standard resources including common dialog boxes for applications running under Windows 9x and NT. Examples of these standard resources are the Open, Print, Print

Preview, and Save As dialog boxes, and the OLE Interface. MFC components are either compiled into another application, or the MFC .dll (for example MFC42.DLL) is copied to the Windows System folder and referenced by the application at run-time. The MFC standard resource file names are afxres.rc, afxprint.rc, afxolecl.rc, afxolesv.rc, and afxdb.rc.

The MFC files are generally referenced in the .rc file that is localized. For example, an .rc file may contain the following code:

```
#include "afxres.rc"   // Standard components
#include "afxprint.rc"  // printing/print preview resources
```

This indicates that the standard resources included in the afxres.rc and afxprint.rc files are compiled into the .dll or .exe file. If you translate the resource file, but use the English versions of afxres.rc and afxprint.rc, the compiled program file will obviously be partly in English.

To create a completely localized .dll file, either translate the referenced MFC files, or use one of the pre-translated files that are included on the Visual C++ disk. By default, the compiler uses the MFC files in the \MFC\INCLUDE folder of the Visual C++ program folder. The \MFC\INCLUDE\L.* folders contain pre-translated MFC files in some languages, including German, Spanish, French, Italian, and Japanese.

For example, to use the German MFC files, copy all files from the \MFC\INCLUDE\L.DEU folder to the \MFC\INCLUDE folder, or change the include lines in the .rc files to reflect the correct path, for example:

```
#include "1.fra/afxres.rc"   // Standard components
#include "1.fra/afxprint.rc"  // printing/print preview resources
```

Make sure to provide translators with a glossary of the MFC files that are used. The MFC translations can also be found in the Microsoft glossary set that is described in the Microsoft Glossaries section on page 404. Using these glossaries will save translators unnecessary work and improve consistency.

Other standard resource files that are included with MFC are prompts.rc and indicate.rc. The indicate.rc file contains string resources for the status bar key-state indicators, such as CAP or INS. The prompts.rc file contains status bar descriptions for each of the pre-defined commands, such as "Create a new document" for the New command. Pre-translated versions of these files can be found in the \MFC\SRC\L.* folders.

4.5 Dialog Box Resizing

If localization engineers are expected to only do basic engineering and cosmetic testing, resizing the dialog boxes will probably be the most time-consuming task. Resizing can be done either in a resource editor of a development environment, e.g. Visual Studio, or in a software localization tool, such as Corel Catalyst.

For general dialog box resizing guidelines, refer to the Dialog Box Resizing section on page 108.

4.5.1   VISUAL C++ 1.X

If you are using Visual C++ version 1.x, use App Studio to open resource or program files. Note that App Studio only supports 16-bit program files, and that .rc files can only be opened when all include files are available. For more information on App Studio, refer to the Microsoft App Studio section on page 78.

4.5.2   VISUAL C++ 2.X AND LATER VERSIONS

Microsoft C++ 2.x and later versions contain an integrated resource editor, so you can simply use the Open command from the compiler's File menu to open resource files for editing.

For information on how to edit different resource types, refer to the Microsoft App Studio section on page 78.

Open each dialog box and resize items where necessary. Be careful not to overlap any hidden items, for example controls in which variables such as page numbers will be shown in the running application.

Tip: Resize a control one dialog unit at a time by holding down the Shift key and using the arrow keys.

If translated text does not fit in a control, you can choose the Size to Content option from the Layout menu. However, this is not always a good feature to use because the command will also adjust the height of the control which is not necessary.

To review the way in which a dialog box will be displayed in the running application, use the Test option of the resource editor.

To align two or more items, such as buttons, use the following commands/shortcuts:

Button	Command	Key Combination
	Make Same Height	Ctrl+\
	Make Same Width	Ctrl+-
	Make Same Size	Ctrl+=
	Align Left	Ctrl+left arrow
	Align Right	Ctrl+right arrow
	Align Top	Ctrl+up arrow
	Align Bottom	Ctrl+down arrow

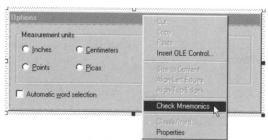	Center Vertical	Ctrl+F9
	Center Horizontal	Ctrl+Shift+F9
	Space Across	Alt+right arrow
	Space Down	Alt+up arrow

Some software localization tools, such as Corel Catalyst, contain features that automatically check for clipped text in the controls. Refer to the Software Localization Tools section on page 383 for more information.

4.6   Checking Hot Keys

Each option in a dialog box or menu must have a unique hot key, or mnemonic. In the property window of a resource item, the hot key can be changed by typing an ampersand character (&) in front of the letter representing the mnemonic.

In Visual C++ versions older than version 4.x, and in most other resource editors, the hot keys will need to be checked manually. Visual C++ 4.x and later versions contain a Check Mnemonics command that automatically identifies duplicate hot keys in dialog boxes or menus.

To run an automatic search for duplicate hot keys, follow these steps:

1.   Open a dialog box.

2.   Right-click in the dialog box and choose the Check Mnemonics command.

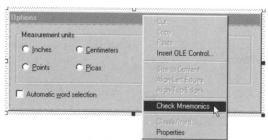

3.   When duplicates are found, a warning dialog box is displayed.

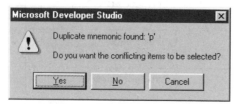

4. Click Yes to locate the duplicates and change one of the hot keys.

5. Repeat the command until all mnemonics in the dialog box are unique.

Some software localization tools, such as Corel Catalyst, contain automatic hot key checking functions. Refer to the Software Localization Tools section on page 383 for more information.

4.7 Bitmap Editing

When editing bitmaps from Windows resources with an image editor like JASC Paint Shop Pro, ascertain which font was used to create the original bitmap. On the Windows platform, the most common fonts are MS Sans Serif (Windows 9x) or Tahoma (Windows 2000). To see which font was used, place a text block containing the original text on top of the text in the original bitmap. For more information, refer to the Editing Graphics section on page 353.

Microsoft Visual Studio contains an integrated graphics editor that contains all of the basic tools needed for image editing. Bitmaps can be edited using this graphics editor, or exported using the Save As command, then edited in an image editor, and re-imported.

When working with a build environment containing .rc files, and source files for all bitmaps, icons, and cursors, it is important to locate the file containing the bitmap image to be edited, and open the file directly in an image editor. Once the bitmap file has been edited, compile the project to include the localized bitmap in the program.

4.8 Creating Installers

Although installers for Windows applications can be created in many ways, many of the Windows type installers available are based on one of two setup technologies, InstallShield or WISE. InstallShield is a Setup development system from InstallShield Software Corporation, WISE is a product developed by WISE Solutions.

With both systems, installers can be created using a combination of custom scripts and pre-translated components. The custom scripts contain installation options specific to the program installed, and the pre-translated components contain standard elements such as buttons, dialog box titles, and error messages. With both technologies the user can define folder structures, file locations for an application, as well as identify which system settings change during installation.

When engineering an installer, first check whether the pre-translated standard installer components are available in all required languages, and then locate the remaining text to be translated. These strings are normally located in script files which are very similar to standard software resource files. As stated previously, it is often not possible to resize dialog boxes, particularly when they are common dialog boxes used for all languages. It is, therefore, advisable to keep translations as short as possible.

In addition to script files that contain messages, many installers contain splash screen bitmaps that need to be localized. Locate the appropriate bitmap file in the installer build environment and localize it using an image editor.

4.8.1 INSTALLSHIELD

InstallShield International is a special version of InstallShield Professional that produces one installation to support multiple languages or combinations of localized installations and applications. Here is an example of a typical folder structure as created by InstallShield:

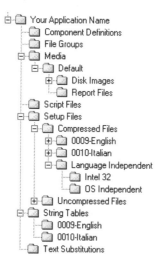

InstallShield creates separate language folders with language-specific files. This allows the user to select the language of the installer that needs to be created. These project folders will contain all application files such as executables, .dll files, sample files, and online help files.

As a rule, the entire installer interface created consists of standard InstallShield windows that are available in most languages supported by Windows.

It is important to follow these steps when creating a localized version of an installer:

- Translate the string table file with all existing string identifiers. This file is called Value.shl and can be found in the \String Tables\<language> folder. In this file, all text appearing after the equal sign (=) should be translated. If the strings have not been externalized to an .shl file, the translatable text can probably be located in the installer script file with the extension .rul.

- Include the localized application files. Ensure that all <language> equivalents of the 0009-English folder contain localized versions of .dll files or bitmaps. Include the localized readme and license files.

- Include pre-translated InstallShield files. These files include _setup.dll, _isres.dll, and IsUninst.exe. By including these files in the setup, all of InstallShield and unInstallShield dialog boxes and error messages will appear in the required language. These files will automatically be added when an installer is created using InstallShield International. These files can also be found in the \Redistributable folder in InstallShield's program folder.

- Set the File Groups to include only localized files.

To create a localized installer, click on the Media Build Wizard in the main project window. Click the Next button until the Languages dialog box is displayed.

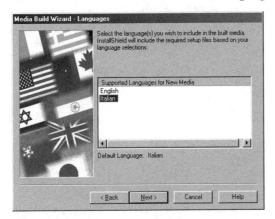

In the Languages dialog box, select the desired language, and click Next and Finish to create the installer. The localized setup will be created in the \Media folder.

For more information on InstallShield International, visit the InstallShield web site at www.installshield.com.

4.8.2 WISE INSTALLER

The WISE setup system supports multiple language installations by default. The Wise Installation System International Edition comes with an additional number of pre-translated components.

WISE language support is a component selection that must be selected when installing the WISE Installation System.

To set the installer language, follow these steps:

1. Select Installer Message from the Edit menu and select a language. If the required language is not listed, choose another language option available on the list.

2. In the Translated Name field enter the name to be displayed when an Installation Language is selected. The messages should now be translated.

3. Once all messages have been translated, go to Edit > Installation Properties on the language tab, or Advanced Configuration in the Installation Expert, and choose Installation Language. If only one language is displayed, then this will be the default language. Otherwise, WISE will check the language setting that in

the user's Windows setup. If the language code matches the code of any of the translated languages, this language will be the default language.

4. If a default language should not be selected, select Always Prompt in Installation Properties on the language tab. It is important to note that if a Language Name from one language is used for another language, and no change is made to the language code, the Language Code is still that of the original language.

WISE 5.0g and later versions support double-byte characters. For Japanese installers, the fonts needs to be changed on the font tab in Installation Properties, for example, change the message box font to M SGothic, the point size to 10, and character set to 128.

For more information on WISE, visit the WISE Solutions web site at www.wisesolutions.com.

4.9 Updating

When software is updated during the localization process, all changes in the new English resource files or program files will need to be implemented in the partly-localized files.

How these updates are processed depends entirely on how the software is translated, whether it is done in text-only resource (.rc) files, or directly in the program files. It also depends on the tools used to translate the files.

Change and file management is of critical importance when processing multiple software updates. As mentioned previously, there are two options: either create a standard folder structure in which all updated files are clearly traceable, or use a version control tracking tool such as Microsoft's Visual SourceSafe.

Resource Files

The easiest way to process small software updates of .rc files is to compare the new resource file with the old resource file, and implement all changes in the (partly) localized resource files. Good file comparison (diff) tools can be downloaded from the web.

This manual method only works, of course, when the update contains only very few or minor changes. If the updated resource files have been completely re-written or re-ordered, translating these new files is recommended.

If the resource files are translated using a translation memory tool such as Trados Translator's Workbench or IBM TranslationManager, it is relatively easy to update the new resource files using the previous translations. As a rule, this is a fairly automatic process. Load the new files in the translation memory tool, and pre-translate the file using the translation memory database. TM tools usually provide a function that allows the user to select various options in order to specify the level of leverage desired. Most software localization tools also contain leveraging (translation re-use) features. As mentioned previously, Corel Catalyst contains features that not only enable the user to re-use translations in new or updated resource files, but also leverage resizing information from dialog boxes.

Program Files

If translation is done directly in the program file, such as a .dll file, it is advisable to use a software localization tool to update files that have previous translations, because most compilers or development environments do not support this feature.

Corel Catalyst and AppLocalize are examples of tools that allow automatic leveraging of existing translations in binary software program files.

To perform the leveraging task in Corel Catalyst, insert the new file into the project, click on the file name, and select the Import Translations command from the Object menu. Selecting a localized program file will automatically import all translations for matching items. Exact matches are displayed with a check mark.

5 Mac OS

Translating Mac OS software using a resource editor, such as ResEdit or Resorcerer, requires very little programming or engineering knowledge. Nor do these tools require that the user perform compilation or post-processing tasks. For this reason, most resizing and relevant engineering information is covered in the Mac OS section of Chapter 2, Software Translation.

If software cannot be translated using a resource editor, extract all text from the binary application files to text-only format using the AppleGlot tool. For more information on extracting text for translation, refer to the AppleGlot section on page 389.

5.1 Compiling

Some Mac OS software does require compilation, for example when the publisher has used Apple's MPW or Metrowerks CodeWarrior to develop the software application or some components.

In a typical scenario, however, software developers would compile their code using MPW or CodeWarrior, and then send the resulting executable out for translation using a resource editor or software localization tool.

5.1.1 MPW

Macintosh Programmer's Workshop is a development environment for Mac OS software applications. MPW comes with a variety of compilers and assemblers that produce code for different runtime environments. These tools can vary from release to release but generally include C, C++, and assembler programs.

Programs are normally compiled using a *makefile*, which is a text file containing all commands needed to build an application. To compile an application, use the Build command in the MPW Shell utility. In MPW speak, to compile an application is called to "rez", and to decompile is called to "derez".

Software command code is located in .c files, and resources in files with the .r file extension. These .r files are comparable to Windows resource files, in that all translatable text is embedded in quotation marks (" and "). Resource files can be edited directly in MPW or using a Mac OS-based text editor or word processor.

For more information on MPW, refer to the Apple Developer Connection web site at www.apple.com/developer (search for "MPW"). MPW can be downloaded from ftp.apple.com/developer.

5.1.2 CODEWARRIOR

Another commonly used development tool on the M acOS platform is CodeWarrior from Metrowerks. CodeWarrior is a tightly integrated set of tools, which includes an editor, compiler, linker, and debugger, and also work in tandem with MPW.

The robust cross-platform functionality is one of the reasons why many software developers are moving to CodeWarrior. Applications developed on the Windows platform can be easily ported to the Macintosh and vice versa.

CodeWarrior resources, particularly Ppob resources, are edited using the Constructor resource editor, which is part of CodeWarrior Pro. The Constructor interface is similar to Resorcerer. The following images shows the SimpleText resources opened in Constructor. Please note that resizing in Constructor may be tricky because in the Windows & Views resources not the actual text is displayed, but simply item IDs.

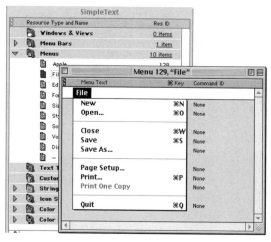

For more information on CodeWarrior and Constructor, refer to the Metrowerks web site at www.metrowerks.com.

5.2 Dialog Box Resizing

When resizing items in dialog boxes using ResEdit, Resorcerer, or another Mac OS resource editor, avoid dragging the boxes with the mouse. It is better to change the coordinates in the properties window for each control in order to ensure a consistent look and to avoid sizing errors.

When resizing or checking resized items on Mac OS systems, it is important to test the results on different versions of Mac OS. As the standards system fonts vary between different Mac OS systems, the user interface may be displayed slightly differently from one version to the next. The default Charcoal system font on Mac OS 8, for example, is smaller than Chicago, which is the system font on the older Ma cOS versions. Truncations can therefore be introduced when the application is run on a 7.x version of Mac OS. According to Apple's Mac OS 8 Human Interface Guidelines "Chicago provides the best basis for text layout; in fact, it is the metric standard upon which Charcoal is based. It is very important for you to design your dialog boxes and control panels with Chicago text, so they will look good in any System font the user selects."

For general dialog box resizing guidelines, refer to the Dialog Box Resizing section on page 108. For more information on resizing controls using ResEdit and Resorcerer, refer to the Dialog Boxes section on page 89.

5.3 Bitmap Editing

When editing bitmaps from Mac OS resources in an image editor like Adobe Photoshop, ascertain which font was used to create the original bitmap. On the Mac OS, the most common fonts are Geneva, Helvetica, Chicago, or Charcoal. To see which font was used, place a text block containing the original text on top of the text in the original bitmap. For more information, refer to the Editing Graphics section on page 353.

When a colored bitmap resource is copied via the Clipboard to Photoshop, it will default to open in RGB mode. It is important to convert the image to indexed color before pasting it back into the resource, because RGB image resources increase the size of the application and do not display correctly on some monitors.

Instead of copying and pasting a bitmap resource, try importing it into Photoshop. To import a bitmap resource, follow these steps:

1. Start Photoshop.

2. From the File menu, select Import > Pict resource.

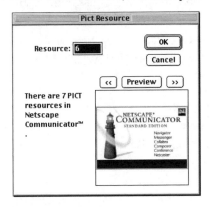

3. In the Pict Resource window, use the browse buttons to locate the bitmap to edit. Click OK to open the resource in Photoshop.

4. Use the Type tool to add translated text. Translations can be added directly; alternatively, copy and paste text from a text editor or word processor.

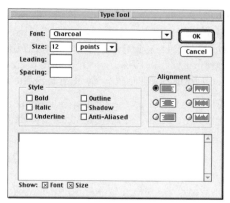

5. Choose Mode > Indexed Color from the Image menu to convert an image from RGB mode to indexed color.

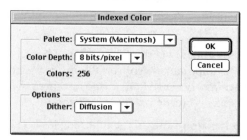

6. In the Indexed Color window, select Exact palette and Other color depth, saving only the colors that are actually used in the image.

7. Press Command-A to select the entire image, and press Command-C to copy the image.

8. Switch to the resource editor, ResEdit or Resorcerer. Next, open the resource that has been edited and press Command-V to paste the localized image into the resource.

5.4 Creating Installers

Most Installers for Mac OS applications are created using Installer VISE from Mindvision. VISE is a graphical interface tool for building master installation sets for disks, CD-ROM, or network distribution.

Installer VISE is used to create the basic components of an installer, i.e. archives and packages. The archive contains all files that may need to be installed. Packages are different combinations of files that a user can choose during a custom install.

The following section describes how to localize a sample archive called My App.cvt. File packages are defined in this archive. The Installer VISE localization features enable the user to create installers for different languages without the need to completely recreate the archive in the new language. File and package names, descriptions, and messages are translated, while package definitions, and disk information remain unchanged from the original archive. Installer VISE ships with pre-translated installer files in many languages.

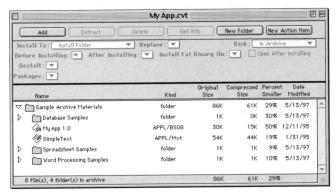

Installers can operate in single-language or multiple-language mode, which means the installer checks the language of the operating system and then runs the installer in that language.

To create a single-language installer from an archive, create and import a translator application for all items, such as files and folders, contained in the archive. The translator application can be edited by the translator if the names of the files, packages, install text, and disks need to be altered.

To create a translator application containing all localizable strings, follow these steps:

1. Start Installer VISE and open the archive to be localized.

2. From the Extras menu, select the Create Translator command.

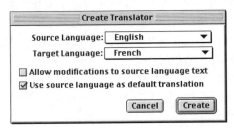

3. Select the source and target languages, and save the translator file using the default name, e.g. English to French.

For more information on translating Installer VISE translator applications, refer to the Installers section on page 94.

When the translator application has been translated, a localized installer can be created. To create a localized installer, follow these steps:

1. Run Installer VISE and select the Archive Settings command from the Archive menu.

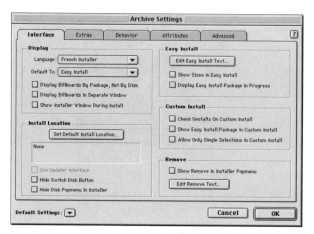

2. In the Archive Settings window, select the Advanced tab, and click the Set Language button.

3. In the Language File Setup window, click the Language File button and import the desired language file from the Installer VISE Extensions folder.

4. Next, click on the Import File button in the Language File Setup dialog box. Select the translator file, English to *language*, and click on OK. Remember to select the desired language at the bottom of the import dialog box.

Tip: To build a multilingual installer, use the Import File button to import the language files and translator applications from the languages to be supported.

5. Click OK to close the Language File Setup dialog box.

6. In the Archive Settings window, select the Interface tab and select the desired language from the Language drop-down menu.

7. Click OK to close the Archive Settings dialog box.

If an Installer contains billboards, i.e. images displayed during the installation process, these will probably need to be localized. To check whether an Installer contains billboards, check whether the Display Billboards by Package option is selected, rather than Display Billboards by Disk option in the Interface tab of the Archive Settings window.

To localize billboards, follow these steps:

1. Translate the image files that need to be used as billboards.

2. Open the image file using an image editor and copy the entire file to the clipboard.

3. Select the Edit Packages command from the Archive menu.

4. In the Packages window, select a package name and click on the Edit Package button.

5. In the Edit Package window, click on the Setup Billboard button.

6. In the Setup Billboard dialog box, select Black and White for 1-bit images, and Color for 8-bit images.

7. Press Command-V to paste the localized billboard in the Setup Billboards window.

Before the final build of the localized installer is created, assign the localized readme file and license agreement. To build the localized installer, select the Build Installer command from the File menu.

For more information on Installer VISE, visit the Mindvision web site at www.mindvision.com.

5.5 Updating Software

If the translation of a Mac OS application is well under way or completed, or there is an update or a new version of the software application, there are several tools available to facilitate an automatic pre-translation process.

If it is a small update, run a file compare on the text-only resource files, and follow the procedure described in the Processing Updates section on page 111. If a resource editor, such as Resorcerer or ResEdit, has been used to enter translations, the previous translations can be copied and pasted into the new version. For larger updates a software localization tool, such as AppleGlot or PowerGlot, would be more appropriate.

5.5.1 APPLEGLOT

To re-use previously completed translations for a new version of an application using AppleGlot, do the following:

1. Create a new AppleGlot environment.

2. Copy the old English files to the _OldUS folder, copy the new English files to the _NewUS folder and copy the old localized files to the _OldLoc folder.

3. Open the environment by choosing Open from the File menu, selecting the environment folder and clicking the Select Folder button.

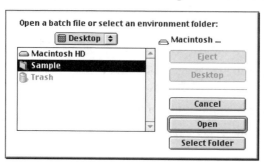

4. Choose Mark All in the Environment window and then click Translate and Verify.

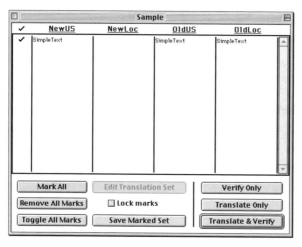

5. The updated localized files will be placed in the _NewLoc folder and the _WG folder will contain a work glossary file that needs to be translated/updated.

The work glossary file or files in the _WG folder can be translated or updated using a text editor or word processor. The tags in the work glossary will highlight to the translators the strings taken from the previous translation and the new strings. Refer to the AppleGlot section on page 389 for more information on translating work glossaries.

To update the program file with the new and updated translations, follow these steps:

1. Copy the translated work glossary files to the _WG folder. Use the original file names so that the old files can be overwritten, and ensure that the work glossary is in text-only format.

2. Run AppleGlot and open the batch file that was saved when the project was created.

3. Select the Translate & Verify button. This command will also compare and verify the resources in the original and localized files.

The localized version of the application will be placed in the _NewLoc folder.

When updating Mac OS applications, please note that all exact matches will be stored in the application database in the _AD folder, and all fuzzy matches (guesses) and new text will be stored in the work glossary. Exact matches are text items in the new application that have a matching resource type, ID, name and position as in the previously translated version.

To include all text, exact matches, new text and fuzzy matches in the work glossary, enable the All Text -> WG option in AppleGlot's Preferences window.

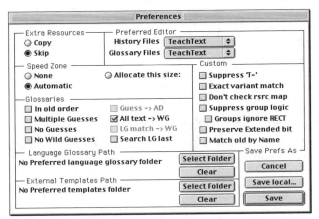

More information on the AppleGlot features can be found in the user manual, which is included in the AppleGlot application. AppleGlot can be downloaded from Apple's FTP server at ftp.apple.com/devworld/Tool_Chest/Localization_Tools.

5.5.2 POWERGLOT

PowerGlot is a software localization tool for Mac OS applications. It uses databases and glossaries to store translated strings. A database consists of a single file with references to work files, the extracted text, translations, and comments added by the translator or localization engineer.

For more information on translating software using PowerGlot, refer to the PowerGlot section on page 391.

A glossary is a file that contains a list of terms and equivalent translations. Glossaries can be used to pre-translate a project database. A glossary created from a previously translated project database, for example, can be used to automatically generate a pre-translation of a new application or an update.

To update software files using PowerGlot, follow these steps:

1. Open the project database from the previously translated application.

2. From the Database menu, choose the Build Glossary command.

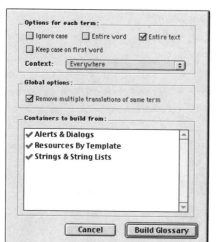

3. Select the desired options for the glossary and click the Build Glossary button.

4. Choose the Save command from the File menu to save the glossary.

5. Create a new project database and import the program file(s) to translate using the Add Work Files command from the Database menu.

6. Select the Translate Using Glossary command from the database menu, and open the glossary created in step 4 and 5.

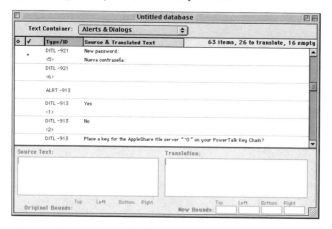

7. All translations identified in the glossary are inserted in the project database.

If the previous version of the application was not translated using PowerGlot, create a project database and glossary by merging the previous English version with the previous translated version. To do this, add the previous English version to a new project database, and select the Merge Localized Files command from the Database menu. PowerGlot will automatically insert the translations below the English strings.

For more information on PowerGlot, visit the PowerGlot web site at www.powerglot.com.

6 Other Environments

Although most software localization work is currently done in C++, many software localization vendors may have to work with products developed in other development environments, such as Java or Visual Basic. Here is some general information, which includes tools references, tips and hints on working in these environments. A section has also been included on firmware localization. Firmware localization involves the localization of strings displayed on portable devices or LED displays, such as printers or handheld devices.

6.1 Java

Java is a programming language with language features similar to C++, which was developed by Sun Microsystems in the mid-1990s. Java *applets* are small applications that are embedded in HTML code and run on an end-user's computer in a Java-enabled web browser. Java *applications* are complete stand-alone programs and do not require a web browser or HTML to run.

6.1.1 INTERNATIONALIZATION

Sun's Java Development Kit (JDK) contains all the tools needed to create and compile Java applets and applications. Since release 1.1 of the Java Development Kit, Sun Microsystems have improved and enhanced many of the internationalization and localization features of this product. To learn more about the internationalization and localization in the latest Java products, search for "internationalization" or "localization" on the Sun Java web site at java.sun.com.

JDK 1.1 and later versions enables programmers to develop truly global programs by isolating language-dependent components from the actual Java code. In addition to functionality with respect to locale support, Unicode and locale-sensitive settings, programmers can isolate all text strings and other language-dependent objects in *resource bundles*. The JDK uses resource bundles to isolate localizable elements from the rest of the application. The resource bundle contains either the resource itself or a reference to that resource.

JDK will typically provide one set of Java code or HTML files, with resource bundles in several languages. These resource bundles will have a locale extension added to the file name, so the desired language is loaded at run-time in the language of the active system locale. The locale extensions are based on the ISO639 standard for language codes, which can be found at www.unicode.org/unicode/onlinedat/languages.html, and ISO 3166 for country codes, www.unicode.org/unicode/onlinedat/countries.html. An example of a file name is *file_fr_CA* for Canadian French.

6.1.2 LOCALIZATION

In Java software projects, each file type needs to be analyzed carefully to assess whether it contains translatable text and to identify localizable components of the product. Java developers using resource bundles to isolate localizable elements, can choose to use property resource bundles or list resource bundles.

In property resource bundles, items have the format `<key><separator><value>`.

Here is an example of the contents of a property resource bundle file:

```
accesspath.writepath.text=Write:
appletviewer.menuitem.restart=Restart
confirm.overwrite.file.prompt=File already exists.\nDo you want to replace it?
```

In the above example, the text displayed after the equal sign separator should be translated. The key can provide some reference information to translators, but it is important to run a linguistic check on the translated strings in the running application. The keys are referenced in the actual Java code, and the string is loaded into the application or applet at run-time. Comment text is marked wi th# or !.

Resource bundles of the list type are more complex because where property resource bundles can only store text, list resource bundles can contain any Java object type. List resource bundles are more like C++ resource files, because they contain program code, and translatable text is enclosed in quotation marks. Comment text is marked with //.

Here is an example of a list resource bundle:

```
// MyResource.java
import java.util.ListResourceBundle;
public class MyResource extends ListResourceBundle {
public Object[][] getContents() {
return contents;
}
public static Object[][] contents = {
{ "TEXT_NOT_FOUND", "The file could not be found." },
{ "TEXT_HELLO", "Hello, world!" },
{ "TEXT_WARNING", "There are {0} warnings in the file {1}." },
{ "TEXT_INSERT_PAPER", "Please insert more paper." },
{ "TEXT_DISREGARD", "Please disregard the man behind the {0}." },
};
}
```

Java software applications, as a rule, are far more difficult to localize than a standard Windows application, one of the main reasons being that they have not always been designed with localization in mind. There is no accepted standard for localized GUI types in Java applications, so localizers are often forced to translate out of context in text files. This adds significantly to the linguistic testing effort. A layout manager may have been used to create the forms and panels in the English product. The JDK tool has some layout managers, and additional layout managers can be downloaded from the Sun web site. Where possible, use the same layout manager used by the original developer when resizing or adjusting the interface. If it is unclear which layout manager should be used, contact the Java developer.

For more information on localizing Java applets, refer to the Embedded Code section on page 209.

6.1.3 TOOLS

The Java Internationalization and Localization ToolKit was released by Sun Microsystems in 1999 to facilitate internationalization and localization of Java applications.

The toolkit contains the following components:

- The Project Manager module defines a project to manage all source files and corresponding resource bundles.

- Internationalization Verifier checks Java files for internationalization issues, and reports any errors found.

- Message Tool defines resource bundles, converts and exports message text, and generates resource bundles in different locales.

- Resource Tool merges and compares different resources, converts the resource bundle type from *list* to *property*, and converts the encoding of resource files, for example to Unicode.

- Translator is used to translate the resource bundles and to leverage existing translations.

For more information on the Java Internationalization and Localization ToolKit, visit the Sun Java web site at java.sun.com (search for "Localization Toolkit").

Here are some examples of other software localization tools that support Java internationalization and localization:

- Multilizer – more info at www.multilizer.com

- Spirus – more info at www.slangsoft.com

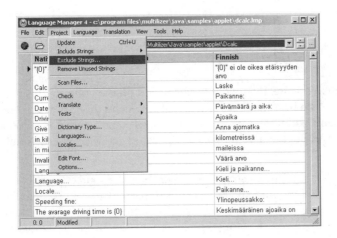

6.2 Visual Basic

Visual Basic is a programming language quite similar to Visual C++. It is included in Microsoft's Visual Studio development environment.

6.2.1 INTERNATIONALIZATION

Before version 4 of Visual Basic, all text was encoded in the files defining the forms (dialog boxes) and menus. There was no central location where translatable text could be stored.

In Visual Basic 4.0 and later versions, it is possible to add a resource (.res) file to a project that centrally stores all translatable text and bitmaps in an application. This .res file can be created from one or more resource script (.rc) files compiled using a resource compiler. An example of this can be found in the Microsoft Visual C++ product.

For more information on internationalizing Visual Basic applications, refer to the International Issues section in the Visual Basic documentation.

6.2.2 LOCALIZATION

A standard Visual Basic project file (.vbp) is a collection of forms, modules, and custom controls that comprise an application. A form (.frm) is a window or dialog box containing controls, such as text fields or buttons.

Each form, control and custom control has a set of properties that are displayed in the Properties window.

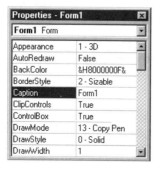

The Caption property contains the text to be displayed on the control. This is the only property that needs to be translated. A form can also contain menus, which are edited in the integrated menu editor. Similar to a control, each menu item has a property window with a Caption field, where the text is translated and the hot key is defined by an ampersand (&).

In Visual Basic projects designed using tools other than a resource (.res) file, the translation should be entered directly in the forms described above. This can be a very time-consuming process, where errors can easily be introduced. To make the process easier, several tools have been developed which enable localizers to extract the text from all forms, translate it, and re-import the translations into the forms. Visual Basic Language Manager from WhippleWare is a good example of such a tool.

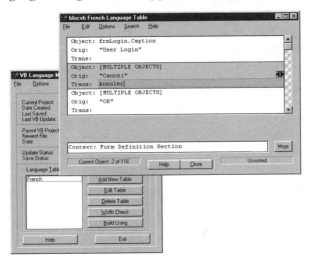

For more information on Visual Basic Language Manager, visit the WhippleWare web site at www.whippleware.com.

Here are some examples of other software localization tools that support Visual Basic internationalization and localization:

- Multilizer by Multilizer Ltd. For more information, visit the web site at www.multilizer.com.

- Localization Guru by Beta-Sigma Data Systems is a software tool designed for Visual Basic programmers working on applications that require multiple language support. For more information on Localization Guru, visit the Beta-Sigma Data Systems web site at www.beta-sigma.com.

- ResMe by Resource Mining is a stand-alone utility that makes a Visual Basic project localizable. This is done by extracting hard-coded strings and moving them to a 32-bit resource file. For more information, visit www.resourcemining.com.

If internationalization features of Visual Basic 4 or later versions are used, there is no need to use these tools. Localizers can then follow the translation instructions for standard Windows resource script (.rc) files discussed earlier in this chapter.

Some companies developing software localization tools have integrated support for Visual Basic projects. For more information on these tools, refer to the Software Localization Tools section on page 383.

6.3   Delphi

Delphi, from Inprise, is a set of visual client and server development tools. It is used to create distributed enterprise and web-enabled applications. Delphi applications are generally built from project files (.dpr) using forms (.dfm) and code (.pas) files. The forms contain all user interface components. Translatable items in .pas files are considered "hard-coded" and need to be exported.

Inprise's Delphi Translation Suite is an internationalization and localization environment that supports Delphi applications. This tool automates the process of translating Delphi applications, and includes translated versions of Delphi files for several Western European languages. The Delphi Language Pack is a modular version of the Translation Suite, and contains commonly used pre-translated forms, messages, and project templates.

The tools in the Delphi Translation Suite extract the language-dependent text prompts, captions, and other strings in a project. This text can then be included with translation tools in a Translation Kit. These files are then ready for a translator to work on. The Translation Kits created include a Form and Menu Editor specifically designed for translation.

For more information on the Delphi Translation Suite and Language Pack, visit the Inprise/Borland web site at www.inprise.com, and search for "translation".

Here are other examples of software localization tools that support Delphi internationalization and localization:

- Lingscape MultLang. For more information, visit the web site at www.lingscape.com
- Multilizer. For more information, visit the web site at www.multilizer.com
- Helicon Translator. For more information, visit the web site at www.helicon.co.at
- PolySuite. For more information, visit the web site at www.prettyobjects.com

Some companies developing software localization tools provide support for Delphi forms. For more information on these tools, refer to the Software Localization Tools section on page 383.

6.4   Firmware Localization

Firmware is the term used to describe the software stored in hardware devices. This software includes programs or data stored in the Read-Only Memory (ROM) of a device. Part of firmware is comprised of the messages displayed on LCD displays on printers, mobile phones, and other electronic devices.

There are many issues to consider when localizing text displayed on LCD screens. Translatable text is generally stored in C source code. Once the text has been translated, the source files are compiled, and the results are tested on the hardware device. The most important issues here are length restrictions and character support:

- Length restrictions. Text expansion options are quite limited on an LCD display. A comment should be added advising the translators on the maximum length of each (set of) strings.

- Character support. This depends mainly on the firmware (the engine that displays the text on the LCD) being used. If, for example, the firmware does not support Cyrillic or double-byte characters, the firmware manufacturer will need to upgrade to another firmware (version) that supports international characters.

If the publisher wants the source C firmware files compiled into binary files, instructions should be provided with the build environment. If possible, the compiling should be done by the company rather than the vendor. It is a relatively small component of the product, but it is usually quite a complex task to compile and load the software into a device.

In order to test localized firmware it is important to have a copy of the device running the firmware as well as a utility that enables the user to load compiled firmware into the device. Alternatively, the firmware company may be able create a utility that simulates the device and creates a software display of the LCD screen. Some companies develop emulators to fake the functionality of hardware and firmware during development. These emulators can be shared with localization vendors for testing.

7   Further Reading

The books listed below cover different aspects of software engineering. This list is not exhaustive and only lists books that provide a quick overview of software engineering basics relevant to software localization engineers. Most of the books dealing with specific development environments are available online.

Austraat, Bjorn. 1999. *Introduction to Software and Web Localization*. For more information, visit www.austraat.com.

Fowler, Susan and Victor Stanwick and Mark Smith. 1997. *GUI Design Handbook*. McGraw Hill Text, ISBN0-070-59274-8.

Galitz, Wilbert O. 1996. *The Essential Guide to User Interface Design*. John Wiley & Sons, ISBN 0-471-15755-4.

Chapter 5:
Software Quality Assurance

This chapter contains information on the different levels of testing performed on localized products. It also provides tips, techniques and instructions on writing problem reports. This information is particularly relevant to translators, localizers, and test engineers working specifically on software components.

This chapter includes the following sections:

1. Introduction
2. Levels of Testing
3. Preparation
4. Test Management
5. Testing Tools
6. Further Reading

Chapters related to these topics are Chapter 3, which contains information on translating software applications, and Chapter 4, which contains information on engineering localized software.

1   Introduction

Testing localized software applications is an integral part of the whole localization process. It is important to note that "testing" can have many different meanings in the context of a software localization project.

Most localization vendors only perform cosmetic, or user interface testing on localized applications. With cosmetic testing, the focus is on the appearance of the localized application. A tester would check, for example, whether all translated options fit in the dialog boxes, and whether the hot keys have unique letters, etc.

Cosmetic testing is only a very small portion of the full software quality assurance cycle. Some software developers expect a fully tested product from their localization vendors. During the project setup phase, it is essential that the vendor and publisher agree on the amount of testing to be performed on the localized versions, and on the team members responsible for implementing fixes in the localized software. Depending on the availability of test scripts or plans, and on the number of tests to be performed, the functional testing cycle can run for a few hours, or be extended to weeks or months. An application can never be tested completely, so the testing team should focus on finding problems rather than verifying whether the application works.

In summary, the vendor and publisher should agree on the following issues before the project begins:

- Who is responsible for testing?
- Who is responsible for implementing fixes?
- What level of testing needs to be performed?
- Are test scripts, tools, or other resources available?
- If no test scripts are available, who will be responsible for writing them?
- How will bugs be reported?
- Which bug tracking system will be used?
- Will automated testing tools be required?
- How many regression test cycles are required?
- What is the estimated time frame for each test cycle?

As a rule, localization vendors will perform cosmetic and basic functional testing on the software applications they have localized, while publishers take responsibility for full functional or internationalization testing. Vendors should focus on the problems that can be resolved at the vendor site, such as resizing errors. Other issues, such as source code or internationalization problems are clearly the responsibility of the publisher.

More information on software testing procedures and tools can be found on the following web sites:

- Software QA/Test Resource Center at www.softwareqatest.com
- Software Testing & Quality Magazine at www.stqemagazine.com
- Quality Assurance Institute at www.qaiusa.com
- Testing Stuff at www.testingstuff.com

When referring to quality, a distinction should be made between quality assurance (QA) and quality control (QC). Quality assurance is defined as the steps and processes used to ensure a final quality product, while quality control focuses on the quality of the products produced by the process. Localization vendors should have a QA procedure in place for any processes they perform, such as translation and engineering. Examples of QA procedures for translation and engineering are provided in the Localization Testing section of this chapter. In software quality assurance projects, the quality processes are generally defined by the publisher, for example, specific test scripts or test plans. It is then the responsibility of the localization vendor to ensure quality control with respect to the functionality of the localized product.

2 Levels of Testing

A software product should go through several testing cycles before it can be successfully localized and released. In this book, the focus is on the testing activities related to localization aspects of software projects.

The three levels of testing relevant to the software localization process are listed below:

- Internationalization testing
- Localization testing
- Functionality testing

Internationalization testing is an important testing phase and should be performed *before* a product is localized. Basically, it involves testing an English product for international support and *localizability*. Localization testing is performed after the translation cycle. Here, the translator reviews the translated software in context, an engineer then verifies the cosmetic aspects of the localized version, comparing it to the English product. Functionality testing is the final testing cycle in a localization project, where localization engineers verify that the localization process has not damaged the functionality of the product.

At the very end of the software localization process, a delivery test is usually performed as part of the functional testing cycle. This test involves installing the localized product according to installation instructions for an end user. Another way to do this is to verify and compare the final deliverables against the original product, instructions, and localization kit.

The following sections cover each level of testing and any preparation work required to test localized files.

2.1 Internationalization Testing

The purpose of internationalization testing is to ascertain how well a product has been internationalized. The types of issues that come up are, whether the localized product supports all possible locales and scripts, and whether the product is easy to localize. This type of testing should be performed on the English product during the development cycle.

Software publishers should be aware of the importance of this step. Any problems caused by poor internationalization planning will need to be fixed in all target language versions, which will have an impact on localization budgets. Furthermore, a well-internationalized product will require a minimum level of testing after localization, because language support will be fully integrated, and the language-specific resources will be separated from the application source code in order to make it easier to translate resources without corrupting the functionality of the program.

For more information on software internationalization, refer to Chapter 2, Internationalization.

2.1.1 INTERNATIONAL SUPPORT TEST

International support testing focuses on the language support integrated in the application, i.e. how well are languages, regional settings, and scripts supported?

It is advisable to perform this test prior to the localization cycle, particularly if the product is to be localized into multi-byte languages.

Here is a list of issues to consider when performing international support testing:

- Text input and handling – Does the product support all possible extended characters and text scripts, specifically in the multi-byte languages, such as Korean, Japanese, and Chinese?
- Text output and display – Does the product display and print all possible text scripts?
- Are multi-byte file and folder names, file contents, and other multi-byte data parsed, processed, viewed and saved correctly?
- Regional settings – Does the product support different regional settings, such as date/time and currency formats, calendar standards, decimal separators, paper size standards, measurements, and address and telephone formats?
- Collation – Are different sorting methods supported? For example, does the product support the Japanese Shift-JIS phonetic sorting order?
- Operating system support – Does the software run on localized versions of the target operating system. Does it use the regional settings of the operating system? Is the clipboard functionality supported?
- Third-party components – Do third-party components that are used by or integrated into the product pass all required internationalization tests?
- Hardware support – Does the software support international hardware, such as local keyboard layouts?

Internationalization testing should be an iterative process throughout the development cycle. This will result in an application that can easily be adjusted to support a certain locale.

2.1.2 LOCALIZABILITY TEST

In addition to checking support for different languages, internationalization testing should also verify whether the application is easy to localize, i.e. the extent of the adjustments required for the source code and the presence of hard-coded strings.

Here is a list of issues to consider when performing localizability testing:

- Translatables – Have all translatable components been externalized from the source code? During the internationalization cycle, any hard-coded strings should be located and externalized.
- Regional settings – Have any regional settings been hard-coded, such as time/ date formats?

- Concatenations – Are there many concatenations that may cause problems for translators? For more information on concatenation, refer to the Concatenated Strings section on page 70.

- Over-externalizing – Do the resource files containing translatable text have any non-translatable items?

- Expansion – Do dialog boxes and forms allow for text expansion?

- Bitmap text – Does the application contain many bitmaps or icons with translatable text? Images with text are time-consuming to localize, as the editing needs to be done manually using an image editor.

- Does the application contain any graphics, colors, or other components that need to be adjusted for certain target locales? Can these components be easily adapted to be more generic? This level of testing is often referred to as usability testing.

Try to involve target language native speakers in the internationalization testing cycle. They may discover issues in the application that will need to be adjusted for their languages, and it is much easier to make these adjustments at this point in the development cycle.

Pseudo-translation is an integral part of internationalization testing. During the pseudo-translation phase, each translatable text string in the software is replaced with a longer string or a series of accented characters. This exercise is performed to identify any potential problems in compiling and executing the localized files, and displaying character sets. Corel Catalyst, for example, contains a pseudo-translation feature that can be applied to Windows-based resource files.

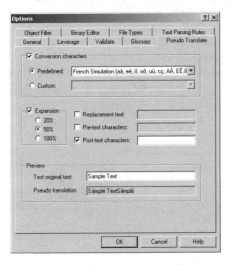

Several tools have been developed that automate certain phases of internationalization testing. I18n Expeditor from OneRealm is one example of such a tool. Examples and descriptions of such tools can be found in the Tools section on page 35.

2.2 Localization Testing

Localization testing should be performed separately on each language version of a localized software product. This type of testing is usually performed by the localization vendor using a subset of the test scripts designed for the English product. It includes a linguistic and a cosmetic verification of the localized application. The linguistic check needs to be performed on the localized application by a native speaker; cosmetic checks can be performed by localization engineers who have a working knowledge of target language characteristics.

Localization testing is particularly important on projects where many user interface components are generated "on the fly", for example, Active Server Pages, Java applications, or Perl scripts.

2.2.1 LINGUISTIC TEST

The linguistic test focusses on all language-related aspects of a localized application, i.e. linguistic verification of the running application. Linguistic testing should ideally be performed by the software translator, either with the help of a localization engineer or using test scripts.

During this testing cycle, the linguist should review each dialog box, menu and as many strings as possible in the running application. Even if the software translator has been using a WYSIWYG localization tool or resource editor to translate the resources, this is a critical step, particularly when verifying strings inserted in dialog boxes and menus at run-time. Dynamic dialog boxes, for example, only show one option when opened in a resource editor, but may contain several more or different options in the running application, depending on the situation or context. Translators should never assume that dialog boxes will display exactly as they are shown in a resource editor or software localization tool!

If there are no test scripts available, an alternative way of performing linguistic testing is to open the translated resource files, one by one, in a resource editor or text editor (depending on the format). Ensure every menu, dialog box and alert box is displayed in the running application. Then, browse through the string sections in the resources and try generating error or status messages on screen, particularly the longer ones and any concatenations. For example, type invalid entries in dialog boxes.

Here is a list of issues to consider when performing linguistic testing:

- Has all text been translated? For example, if English strings are displayed, these may originate from hard-coded text or third-party components.
- Do accented characters display and print correctly?
- Does punctuation follow the rules of the target language?
- Does localized text wrap, hyphenate, and sort correctly?
- Do dialog boxes and error messages display correctly, without truncations?
- Do menu items and dialog box titles have consistent translations?

- Have any icons, graphics or sounds been used that need to be adjusted for the target language market, such as the B icon for Bold.

- Do concatenated strings display correctly? Leading or trailing spaces are often deleted during the translation cycle, causing two strings to be merged into one word. Do the translations of various components read like a proper sentence?

- Do strings with variables display correctly in the running application?

- Are hot key or control key assignments consistent with operating system standards?

- Do translations still make sense when seen in context? For example, if the word "copy" was translated in the resource files as the noun "a copy", whereas the running application may use it as a verb, i.e. "to copy". These types of context-related issues and errors can only be identified at run-time.

An experienced software localizer should use detailed test scripts when working through the screens and user interface elements. If possible, the linguist should be assisted by a localization engineer, who is very familiar with the product and can locate and display each component quickly.

Linguistic testing is a good milestone to use for freezing the software, so that no more language changes can be made to the translations. This will help avoid last-minute terminology changes that could serious impact a schedule. Last minute software terminology changes after linguistic testing may result in additional editing in online translated help or documentation files that contain references to the software.

2.2.2 COSMETIC TEST

Cosmetic testing, or user interface (UI) testing, focusses on all visual aspects of a localized application, i.e. dialog boxes, menus, reports, and messages.

By default each localization project requires some level of cosmetic testing, unless vendors are requested to translate software strings only.

Here is a list of issues to consider when performing cosmetic testing:

- Ensure the localized versions display the same number of menus, options, and commands as the original application.

- Are dialog boxes properly resized, without truncations? Pay special attention to dynamic dialog boxes, where object overlays, such as buttons, fields, and drop-down menus, are used to change the items on a dialog box, depending on the options selected by the user.

- Do all extended characters display correctly?

- Do all menu items, status bar messages, help balloons, and dialog boxes fit on the screen in all resolutions?

- Are application aesthetics acceptable, i.e. alignment of buttons, consistent sizing of control boxes, buttons, etc.

- Are all hot keys in dialog boxes and menus unique?

- Does the tab order of the options in the localized dialog boxes match the original order?
- Do combo boxes or drop down menus display all necessary options?
- Does the main menu bar fit on the screen in any resolution?
- Do dialog boxes display correct regional settings, i.e. decimal separators, date/ time formats, etc.?

There are two levels of cosmetic testing. One is performed in the resource editor and the other in the running application. Many resource editors and software localization tools contain features that automatically run some standard tests, such as a search for clipped text or duplicate hot keys. Once all reported errors have been fixed, a full cosmetic test should be performed on the running application. At this point commands can be executed, options selected, drop-down menus checked, and error messages generated.

Once a linguistic and cosmetic test has been performed on the user interface, the UI should be frozen. This means that no more changes are permitted on the localized user interface, unless absolutely necessary. At this point, screen captures can be created for use in online help and documentation, and the functional testing cycle can begin.

2.3   Functionality Testing

This testing level focusses on the actual functionality of the localized application. Functionality testing usually mirrors the testing process that has been performed on the source language product. If the application has been well internationalized, i.e. if all language-specific elements have been separated from application code, it is unlikely that problems will be introduced during the translation cycle.

Nonetheless, even well internationalized applications require functional testing to verify how compatible they are with localized operating systems and applications, or local hardware standards.

Generally speaking, functionality testing is not a standard task in a software localization project. At this point in the test cycle, the translation should be finalized and stable, and the focus should only be on the functionality of the localized product. Software developers will often provide the localization vendor with test scripts which systematically test the function of the application. They also guide testing engineers through all features of the application, focusing on locale-specific functionality.

Here is a list of issues to consider when performing functional testing of localized applications:

- Does the functionality and feature set of the localized application mirror that of the source language? In essence, were any problems introduced during the localization cycle?
- Can documents that were saved when working in the original version be opened in the localized version, and vice versa?

- Is it possible to type accented text, use hot keys, and use control keys with international keyboards and keyboard layouts?

- For Asian languages, are all major Input Method Editors (IME) supported?

- Do regional settings, such as paper size, date/time, number and currency formats, reflect the language of the localized product by default? Does the localized application automatically default to the regional settings specified in the operating system?

- Can users copy and paste text with accented characters from the localized application to another application?

- Does the application function correctly on a localized operating environment?

- Is the localized product compatible with locally developed products that are popular in the target markets?

- Does the application link to locations on the world wide web, for example, sites containing support information in English? Are localized versions of these web pages available?

- Do language-specific add-ons, such as spelling checkers, or character conversion tables for a telecommunication product, work correctly?

Functionality testing often includes a compatibility test specifically designed to check how compatible a product is with other products available in target languages. But the main purpose of compatibility – or configuration – testing is to ensure the software runs properly in various localized hardware and software environments. Testing involves checking program execution and functionality against all relevant processors, language versions of operating systems, applications, memory configurations, video adapters and sound boards, as well as CD drives and all associated drivers. An example of compatibility testing is checking how well a localized web-based application works with numerous releases and language versions of popular web browsers, or testing localized Japanese applications on the NEC9800 series of computers, which are still used on a large scale in Japan.

Here are some other examples of levels of testing that are often included in a functional testing cycle:

- Integration testing – Testing several product components together once they have been tested individually.

- Performance testing – Testing how a product or web site performs under certain conditions, often called stress or load testing.

- Regression testing – Re-testing a new release of a product which contains previously fixed problems or other modifications. This level of testing is usually performed during the localization testing cycle.

- Acceptance testing – Formal testing to decide whether or not to accept the final product.

Publishers may ask localization vendors to perform full functionality testing and deliver a gold master of the translated software product. A gold master is the final version of the product that has passed all QA and engineering processes and is ready for manufacturing and redistribution.

2.4 Delivery Testing

The delivery test should be performed on a localized operating system using the final disk images or deliverables. The main purpose of a delivery test is to check the basic functionality of the deliverable and to verify whether all instructions were followed, all updates implemented, and the delivery meets the deliverable specifications that were outlined by the publisher at the start of the project.

With large localization projects, it is always a good idea to refer back to the original instructions or localization kit to check whether all instructions on deliverables, file formats, and folder structures have been followed.

Here is a list of issues to consider when performing delivery testing on the localized applications:

- Where disk images are part of the deliverables, do the original disks and the localized disks contain the same number of files?
- Open all program files on the installation disks using a resource editor and browse through all dialogs. Are all files and all resources in the right language?
- Does the localized version of the application install the same number as files as the original version?
- Are all installed components in the correct language? Check this by double-clicking on all executables and help files in the program folder of the installed application.
- Does the Uninstaller work correctly? Are all files removed from the system?
- Have escalated issues been resolved with the publisher? If not, report them again.
- Are any temporary or old file versions included in the final delivery?
- Are the files delivered in the same folder structure as the original files?
- Have all files in the deliverable been checked with an up-to-date virus checker?
- Do the file names match the source language file names, and do they correspond to the list of required deliverables?

In addition to checking the deliverables, verify that all requested reports and sign-off forms are included in the final deliverable.

3   Preparation

There are a number of steps to be taken when preparing for the functional testing cycle in a project. Assuming that the software publisher is providing test scripts, a testing team needs to be assigned to the project and computers need to be configured for testing localized applications.

3.1   Testing Team Setup

A testing or QA team generally consists of testing engineers and QA engineers, headed up by a team lead. Responsibility for testing and bug fixing is assigned to the various team members who are skilled to perform these tasks. These two activities, i.e. testing and fixing, should never be performed by the same person. Any problem found should be reported by a testing engineer, corrected by the QA engineer, and then regressed by the testing engineer.

Depending on the complexity of the application and the problems found, the localization engineer who has worked on the software project can act as a bug fixer. It is best for testing teams to have a good mix of people with language and technical skills.

With a dedicated testing team working on the localized software applications, testing engineers should typically have the following skill set:

- Knowledge of software quality assurance procedures and principles
- Experience using many different computer platforms and operating systems
- Knowledge of interface guidelines for each platform being used
- Product knowledge
- Working knowledge of target languages, e.g. accented characters and the look of the language(s) involved
- Experience in reporting problems or bugs, and knowledge of typical problem or bug life-cycles
- Attention to detail
- Experience using automated testing tools

Testing team managers, or QA Managers, should have the following skill sets, in addition to the list above:

- Ability to design test plans or scripts for localized software applications
- Knowledge of scheduling testing projects and managing a testing team
- Professional experience in software quality assurance
- Experience developing or customizing bug tracking databases

Skill sets for localization engineers, who will typically act as QA engineers, can be found in Chapter 4, Software Engineering. Above all, it is important for QA engineers to understand the product development process so they can easily implement changes or fix bugs found by the testing team.

If help and documentation are translated after the software application has been localized, involve translators in the testing process as much as possible. They should have access to a bug reporting database or form where they can report errors encountered while using the translated software for reference purposes. These error reports are usually an invaluable source of information for testing engineers.

3.2 Computer Configuration

The hardware setup and operating environment for localized applications is of critical importance to the testing cycle. The application should be tested on an operating system in the target language of the application. This has several advantages:

- It is very likely that end users will be running the application on a localized operating system in their own language. Bugs generated by localized operating systems will generally be identified in this way.

- All default regional settings are normally programmed on the operating system, such as time, date, separator, and currency settings. If the application is using incorrect default settings for the target language, this will become obvious, once it is tested on the localized operating system.

- It is easier to check whether all components of the application have been translated. If the application is tested on an English operating system and English messages or dialog boxes are displayed, it is not always apparent whether these should be treated as software bugs or whether they are being generated by the operating system.

Localized versions of operating systems can be found on the Microsoft MSDN or the Apple Developer Connection CDs.

Before testing an application, make sure the computer is "clean", i.e. contains no old or other language versions of the application to be tested. Testing engineers should ideally have three machines, one running the localized software on a localized operating system, one running the English software, and one machine where bugs can be entered in a bug tracking system.

Since localized applications should be tested on an operating system in the target language, it is advisable to install a new version of a localized operating system on a machine. To do this, you can either create several disk partitions with different language versions of operating systems, or use a multi-boot utility to switch between language versions. It is possible to install multiple language versions of Windows 3.x or Windows 9x on one hard drive and then switch between the different versions. To multi-boot different language versions of Windows NT or Windows 2000, partitions will need to be created on the hard drive, or a multi-boot utility used that supports Windows NT. Windows 2000 comes with locale-switching features and language packs that enable users to select the interface language and regional settings, which effectively means an engineer can test localized versions using a single installation of Windows 2000.

If a number of testing cycles are necessary, where a "clean" machine is required each time, store the entire computer configuration on another disk or on the network. The best way to save an installed version of Window s95, for example, is to use a disk-cloning application such as Ghost. For more information, visit the Ghost web site at www.ghost.com.

To create multi-boot systems where the user selects a specific language version of the operating system at start-up, follow the steps outlined in the following sections.

3.2.1 CONFIGURING WINDOWS 3.1

For Windows 3.1 applications, the best way to ensure an engineer is testing on a clean Windows version is to install Windows from the installation disks or CD in a folder called WIN*xxx*, where *xxx* is the language code. Refer to the Locale Codes and IDs section on page 118 for a list of language codes. A German version, for example, would be installed in a folder called WINDEU.

Once Windows has been installed, compress (use PKZIP) all files in the WIN*xxx* and WIN*xxx*\System folder and store them on a hard disk or on a network drive. Once the testing is completed, delete the WIN*xxx* folder. When a clean version of Windows is required again for testing, unzip the files and run the new tests. A compressed Windows 3.1 version requires about 5MB of disk space.

3.2.2 CONFIGURING WINDOWS 9X

A computer can be configured in several ways to create a multi-boot system. When using Windows 9x, edit the startup files or use a utility called WinBoot. When using other operating systems on the same computer, use a professional multi-boot utility like System Commander by V-Communications.

The following sections describe how to set up a multi-boot system.

Changing Boot Sequence

To install two or more different language versions of Windows 9x, follow these steps:

1. Install Windows 9x.

2. Restart in DOS mode and install another language version of Windows 9x. Assign this version to a folder with a different name, for example WIN*xxx*, where *xxx* is the language code. Add the language code extension to the name of the \Program Files folder, because in some languages this folder name matches the English folder name.

3. Once all required languages of Windows 9x have been installed, open Windows Explorer and locate the msdos.sys file in the root of the hard drive.

4. Open the Properties for this file, and deselect the Read Only option.

5. Open the file using Notepad, and change the path following the `WinDir=` and `WinBootDir=` options to reflect the folder of the language version to run.

6. Change the \Program Files folder for this language version to its original name.

7. Restart the machine.

Please note that this only works when the language or code page settings that are loaded from the autoexec.bat and config.sys startup files are not relevant. For most European languages this is not an issue; for multi-byte languages, always use a fully installed and loaded multi-byte operating system.

Using WinBoot

WinBoot is a multi-boot utility that enables the user to install and switch between different language versions of Window s9x. The tool can be found on the Microsoft Developer Network CDs, and downloaded from www.microsoft.com/globaldev/ gbl-gen/intlboot.htm. Please note that this utility is not a Microsoft product, and is not supported by Microsoft.

The utility stores all language-specific files (autoexec.bat, command.com, config.sys, io.sys, and msdos.sys) with an ISO language code extension in the \Winboot folder. It uses the files for the language selected by the user in the WinBoot screen.

To set up multiple language versions of Windows 9x on the computer using WinBoot, follow these steps:

1. Copy the WinBoot files (winboot.exe and winboot.hlp) to the root directory C:\ of the system boot drive.

2. Start winboot.exe from Explorer, or choose Run from the Start menu and type winboot.exe in the Run dialog box.

3. In the WinBoot dialog box, select a language in the Change Language To drop-down menu, and select the Click here to install a new language version of Windows 95 option.

4. Press OK in the Setup New Language Version message box.

5. Once the computer restarts in MS-DOS mode, install the new language version of Windows 9x. Make sure to assign the new Windows version to a folder other than the default \Windows folder. For example, install it in a \WIN*xxx* folder, where *xxx* is the language code.

6. A \Winboot folder will be created in the root of the hard drive, containing the settings files for the installed languages.

To switch between the language versions of Windows 9x, select the desired language by clicking on Change Language To. The computer will reboot and start Windows in the selected language.

Using System Commander

System Commander enables the user to install and run any combination of PC-compatible operating systems, including Windows 95/98, Windows 3.1, Windows NT, DOS, OS/2, and all of the PC compatible Unix versions.

With System Commander, it is possible to run operating systems in several different languages or versions.

For more information on System Commander, visit the V-Communications web site at www.v-com.com.

3.2.3 CONFIGURING THE MAC OS

It is possible and easy to multi-boot different language versions of the Mac OS on one machine.

To set up multiple language versions of the Mac OS, use the System Picker utility, which can be found on the Apple Developer Connection CDs. It can also be downloaded from Apple's FTP server at dev.apple.com/devworld/utilities.

To set up the computer to switch between different language versions of the Mac OS, follow these steps:

1. Locate the currently active System Folder on the hard disk where the new Mac OS is to be installed. An active System Folder has a Mac OS symbol on the folder icon.

2. Change the name of the active System Folder. For example, add the system version number or language extension to the folder name, e.g., *System Folder 8*.

3. Open this folder and drag the Finder file out of the folder window to any location.

4. Close the folder window. The folder icon no longer has the Mac OS symbol.

5. Insert the installation disk from the new operating system and double-click the Installer icon. Click OK in the first window that appears.

6. In the Easy Install window, select the hard disk that previously contained the active System Folder. Make sure the window says Click Install to Place. If it says Click Install to Update, then it is obvious that the System folder has not been de-activated. Quit and go back to step 2. Please note that in Syste m8.x and later versions, the user can choose to install a new operating system version in the Installer, so there is no need to follow steps 1 to 4.

7. Once the installation has been successfully completed and the Macintosh restarted, drag the "Finder" back into the folder it was moved from in step 3. If this is not done, the original System Folder will not show in System Picker list.

8. Repeat these steps for any additional system languages that need to be installed.

To switch between multiple installed language versions of the Mac OS, follow these steps:

1. Run the program by double-clicking on the System Picker icon.

2. In the System Picker window, select the name of the System Folder of the desired language and click Restart.

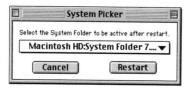

If Options > Search Depth is selected in the System Picker, the user can determine the number of folders System Picker should search on the mounted disks, in order to locate system folders.

4 Test Management

The testing process is a continuous process, which is not complete until all identified bugs have either been closed, fixed, or escalated to a third party. Testing engineers and localization engineers should work very closely; once a problem is solved or a bug fixed by a localization engineer, this should be double-checked by the testing engineer. Testing engineers should be the only people to open and close bugs! This simplifies the process and avoids unnecessary errors.

The sections below describe how a bug tracking system can be set up, and the stages a problem or bug can go through.

4.1 Bug Tracking

Bug reports, or software problem reports (SPR), are critical to localization projects and in the communication between localizers and software developers. A bug report is maintained by testing engineers and localization engineers and may cover issues in the following problem areas:

- Functionality problems in the source language application

- Internationalization problems, for example incorrect display or output of accented characters, no support for foreign keyboards, incorrect default page sizes or other default settings, no support for local hardware or software, etc.

- Localization problems, for example items displayed in English because they are hard-coded, or problems introduced during the localization cycle

- Questions to the software development department about technical issues

A typical localization problem report would contain the following fields:

- Number of the problem, and date it was reported
- Name of testing engineer opening the problem
- Product, version, build number, language, platform, and platform version
- File name, location, and cause of the problem, or product area or component
- Exact location of problem in the file or application
- Description of the problem, severity, and the steps needed to reproduce it. Examples of choices from the "severity" pick list are Cosmetic or Stop Shipment.
- Machine configuration details where the bug was found
- Workarounds suggested by engineer
- Ownership of bug-fixing; testing engineers need to determine whether the bug should be fixed by a localization engineer or by the publisher.
- Solution suggested by the engineer responsible for fixing the problem
- Status of the problem, i.e. has it been fixed? Refer to the next section for more information on the status of a problem.

Professional bug tracking databases will allow the users to include a screen capture of the window where the error occurs. Databases can often be viewed in several ways, based on the user preferences. A user can view the database by platform, severity of the problem, or by problem status. This makes it easy for an engineer to get an accurate snapshot of the number of unresolved bugs.

Bugs need to be reproducible. If a problem only occurs once and it cannot be reproduced on the same or other machines, do not report this problem. Problem reports can be created in any format, from basic word-processing documents to advanced bug tracking databases. The content of a problem report is far more important than the file format. Above all, problem reports should be simple and clear and easy to follow.

Here is an example of the layout of an online bug report.

The easiest way to keep track of bugs is to set up a file that can be viewed by the publisher and the vendor engineering team, such as a web-based database. Avoid sending problems, questions, and bugs in separate e-mails or messages; this makes it too difficult to keep track of all issues and there is a high risk of losing critical information. Tracking problems and bugs in a central database is the most efficient way to track the status of bugs and minimizes errors.

Examples of commercially available bug tracking databases are TechExcel DevTrack (www.devtrack.com) and Elsinore Visual Intercept (www.elsitech.com).

4.2 Testing Workflow

Here is a typical scenario on how a problem is identified and resolved:

1. Problem is discovered.

2. Problem is isolated, i.e. steps to reproduce it are registered.

3. All problem specifications are entered in a bug tracking database.

4. Problem is resolved by engineer, and assigned back to the testing engineer who opened the bug.

5. Bug is verified by testing engineer, who can reactivate the problem in case it was not fixed correctly.

6. Step 5 is repeated for each bug as many times as needed.

7. Bug is closed by testing engineer.

Issues found during this process are logged using a bug tracking system. These issues are then addressed by the engineer responsible. Each issue must pass through at least four levels or stages.

It is the responsibility of the testing manager or publisher to decide on the number of levels that should be used to categorize a problem. It is advisable to limit the number of options in the status field. Where possible, limit these to critical or essential categories. Here are some examples of categories that can be used to identify the severity of a problem:

1. Open – a new problem opened by the testing engineer

2. Resolved – fixed by the engineer, but not yet verified by the testing engineer

3. Fixed – fixed by the engineer, verified by the testing engineer

4. Closed – re-verified bugs fixed by the testing engineer, and closed

When an engineer resolves a problem, it does not necessarily mean the bug is fixed. Engineers may decide, for example, to ignore the bug because it occurs in the source language version. Alternatively, the engineer may decide to fix it in the next release, or include a comment on the bug in the readme file, or return the bug to the development team.

5 Testing Tools

Even though software application testing is still a highly manual process, there are now some automated testing tools available that can handle some of the more repetitive testing activities.

Even though many general-purpose testing tools are available for testing software applications or web sites, very few tools have been developed specifically for localization testing.

5.1 Automated Testing

Most automated testing tools use scripts that need to be designed by testing engineers. Many of the commercially available testing tools are very sophisticated and use existing or proprietary coding and scripting languages. The task involved in automating an existing manual testing effort is no different from having a programmer use a programming language to create applications that automate any other manual process.

Here are some examples of automated test tools:

- Segue Silk Product Family – For more information, visit the web site at www.segue.com.

- Rational Test Foundation – For more information, visit the web site at www.rational.com.

- Mercury Interactive Winrunner – For more information, visit the web site at www.winrunner.com.

- Compuware QACenter products – For more information, visit the web site at www.compuware.com.

These tools will have already been used on the English product, where scripts, for example, were created to "record" a sequence of actions, such as clicking through a user interface, opening dialog boxes, executing commands, selecting options, etc. Running these scripts on localized software will automatically indicate whether the functionality of the application differs from the original because of the localization process.

5.2 Localization Testing

Many software localization tools contain utilities that test localized resources for common errors, such as truncated text and duplicate hot keys. Most of these tools will only work with the resource files, rather than on a running application.

5.2.1 COREL CATALYST

Corel Catalyst is a software localization tool that contains a testing utility called Validate Expert. This utility checks a localized user interface for errors such as missing hot keys or missing control characters.

For more information on the Validate Expert, refer to the Compiling section on page 114. For more information on Corel Catalyst, refer to the Corel Catalyst section on page 383.

5.2.2 TOOLPROOF

ToolProof is a dynamic user interface verification tool designed to speed up and improve the quality of user interface testing performed by software developers and software localizers.

When ToolProof is run on a testing PC, it continually scans active windows, dialogs and menus and reports any user interface problems that occur.

For more information on ToolProof, visit the SDL International web site at www.sdlintl.com.

6   Further Reading

The books listed below cover different aspects of product testing and quality assurance.

Hall, P.A.V. and R. Hudson. 1997. *Software Without Frontiers: A Multi-Platform, Multi-Cultural, Multi-Nation Approach*. John Wiley & Sons, ISBN 0-471-96974-5.

Kaner, C. and J. Falk, H.Q. Nguyen. *Testing Computer Software*. International Thomson Computer Press, ISBN 1-850-32847-1.

Kit, E. 1995. *Software Testing in the Real World: Improving the Process*. Addison-Wesley, ISBN 0-201-87756-2.

Luong, Tuoc V. and James S.H. Lok, David J. Taylor. 1995. *Internationalization: Developing Software for Global Markets*. John Wiley & Sons, ISBN 0-471-07661-9.

Perry, W.E. 1995. *Effective Methods for Software Testing*. John Wiley & Sons, ISBN 0-471-06097-6.

Chapter 6:
Online Help Translation

This chapter contains information for translators of online help documents. Topics cover the fundamentals of online help and the translation approach for HTML Help, Windows Help (WinHelp), and Apple Mac OS help systems.

This chapter includes the following sections:

1. Introduction
2. Windows
3. Mac OS
4. HTML and XML
5. Readme Files
6. Further Reading

Chapters related to these topics are Chapter 6, which contains information on translating documentation files, Chapter 7, which contains information on engineering and testing localized online help files, and Chapter 12, which contains information on terminology issues.

1   Introduction

Online help is the largest translation component of most localization projects. Online help files and manuals have, to a great extent, replaced traditional printed documentation. Over the years, substantial functionality has been integrated into online help files; for example movie files, animations, and sound can now be embedded in most online help systems.

Here are some advantages to selecting online help over printed manuals:

- Context-sensitive help gives users instant access to information required. Pressing the Help button in a dialog box, for example, opens a help window which explains all options in that specific dialog box.
- Users can quickly navigate through the required information using hypertext jumps and index keywords. Online help files are called hypertext documents, meaning they contain links (*jumps*) to other topics, pop-up definition windows, and graphics.
- Most current online help systems include multimedia features such as animations, movies, or sound.

- Updates or additions to the online help files can be distributed easily through the web.

- Indexing features enable users to perform full-text searches on information in a set of online help documents.

- There are significant savings on printing costs for software publishers.

Online help systems typically contain an overview of the product, procedures, dialog box descriptions, and reference information. Help information focuses on task-based topics.

There are several different types and formats of online help used in the software industry. This chapter covers the most commonly used online help systems:

- Windows help, including WinHelp 3 and 4

- HTML-based help, including HTML Help and JavaHelp

- Mac OS Help, including Apple Guide and Apple Help

- Readme Files

Each of these help formats is created using different source files and compilers. As a result, each file type requires a different translation approach.

1.1   Translation Approach

Most online help files are created from a set of source files which are compiled into one central binary help file. Source files typically include the following:

- Files containing text and formatting information, such as RTF files for WinHelp, HTML files for HTML Help, and XML/HTML files for JavaHelp

- Image files, such as .bmp files for WinHelp, and .gif or .jpg files for HTML Help

- Multimedia files, such as movies or sound effects

- Document layout files, such as Cascading Style Sheet (CSS) files for HTML-based Help.

Compiled help files have the extensions .hlp and .cnt (Windows Help) or .chm (HTML Help) on the Windows platform. For JavaHelp and some other online help formats, no compilation is required and information can be accessed through HTML or XML files.

Online help files are typically localized by translating the source files using a translation memory tool, adapting the image files using a graphics editor, and then compiling the translated files to create a new localized online help document.

Most translation memory tools support the document file formats used for online help systems, such as RTF and HTML. These file formats are generally quite easy to process. For more information on translation memory, refer to Chapter 11, Translation Technology.

1.2 Translation Guidelines

This section provides general guidelines for translators of online help source files. Most of these guidelines also apply when using a translation memory tool.

1.2.1 GENERAL GUIDELINES

Follow the guidelines listed below, when editing online help source files:

- Hidden text – Never translate, change, or move hidden text which may appear in the document; the only exception may be where certain words or phrases linked to hidden text or tags need to be moved because grammatical rules dictate word or sentence order changes.

- Coding – Do not translate, change or delete references to screendumps, index markers, encoding, or formatting tags.

- Sorted items – Never sort (alphabetize) items when working in a translation memory tool. This should always be done after the files have been converted back to their original formats.

- Line or page breaks – Do not insert or delete line or page breaks, or hyphenate words or justify lines manually.

- Text formatting – Agree on a text format for software user interface options, for example all software references should be bolded or enclosed in quotation marks.

- Search and replace – When using global search and replace options, always confirm each change. After applying the first change, verify that it is correct before continuing. An incorrect global substitution can be very difficult to rectify; it may inadvertently replace a hidden text section with a translation.

- Document settings – Do not change any of the document settings, e.g. tabs, margins, page size, line spacing, paragraph spacing, and paragraph styles.

1.2.2 LANGUAGE GUIDELINES

It is very unlikely that users will read the complete online help documents or software manuals. Therefore, style is not the most critical issue in the translation of help and documentation. It is more important to focus on consistency, technical accuracy, use of correct references to the software user interface, and delivering clear, concise translations.

Here are some guidelines on language and style in online help translations.

Terminology

In most cases, the publisher will provide the vendor with a language style guide and terminology glossary. Always adhere to this terminology, and if there are issued with the terminology and style guide, these should be discussed with the publisher.

If no glossary is provided, create a terminology list with translations of frequently occurring terms or phrases in the source text. Ask the publisher to approve this terminology list before proceeding. For more information on terminology, refer to Chapter 12, Terminology.

If the online help describes a software application, always use a software user interface glossary, and use the running localized software as a reference when translating an online help file.

Choose terminology which is consistent with the target operating system, such as Apple Mac OS or Microsoft Windows terminology.

Adaptations

If the source text contains country-specific statements which may require adjustment for the target language, for example, "1-800 phone numbers" for the United States, AM/PM time specifications, federal law restrictions, and local support contact information, ask the publisher for the relevant information for the target language or country.

Text and examples used in online help documents and illustrations should be culturally acceptable for the target language. If the examples contain many references to common U.S. sports or holidays, suggest alternatives to the publisher that are more appropriate to the target country or language.

In case of metric or other conversions, consult the publisher on the conversion standards to be used, and whether both metric and non-metric figures should be used in the translation.

Style

Many documents originating from the United States contain significantly more jargon, slang, and humor compared to documents written for non-U.S. markets. Always keep the target audience in mind when translating technical documentation, and adjust the style to suit local conventions.

In technical translation, it is recommended to use active voice, imperative form, and active verbs. Avoid passive style or sentences with many nouns. Try to avoid following the word order or syntax of the source language too closely.

Use a consistent style for certain standard text elements, such as headings. Most online help documents contain headings such as "Printing documents", "Searching text", and "Indexing documents". Try to maintain the same level of consistency in the target language.

Agree on standards with the team of translators before the translation begins. Here are some issues that should be considered:

- Acronyms – How to deal with them, e.g. the first occurrence should always include an explanation between brackets.
- Bulleted and numbered lists – Agree on the standard to be used for capitalization of the initial letter and ending each item with a period or another punctuation mark. As a rule, all list items end with a full stop when they contain full sentences, and without a full stop when they contain phrases or single words.

- Capitalization – When and where to use capitals. Be very specific about items in search keyword lists.

- Numerals/Measurements – How to write numbers and measurements, and which conversions to include.

- Captions – Style to be used for image captions or callouts.

- Em/En Dash – In many languages, the em/en dashes are not used. Identify where they should be replaced by hyphens or commas.

- Americanisms – Avoid the use of Americanisms or Anglicisms. For example, in French use "prendre en charge" for "support" instead of "supporter". In German, use "erstellen" for "create" instead of "kreieren".

- Spelling – If a spelling reform has taken place in the target country, or if the target language is spoken in different variants in different countries, agree on a standard to be used, e.g. Iberian Spanish versus Latin American Spanish.

- Punctuation – Apply the punctuation rules of the target language. For example, if the English source files contain two spaces after each period, this should generally be replaced by one space in the target language.

Issues like these should normally be included in a style guide for each language. Most large software publishers and localization vendors have language style guides available.

Software References

Most online help files and user manuals contain several references to dialog box or menu options, prompts, and error messages in running software.

To avoid time-consuming correction work later in the process, keep the software references correct and consistent from the very beginning of the project. If the translated software is not yet finalized, it is advisable to leave all software references untranslated until a localized version of the software is available. Never translate a software reference without checking this against the actual translation used in the running software!

It is not unusual for online help files to be translated before the software. If this is the case, translate the software references in the text and create a glossary for these references. This will make it easier to translate the software. Furthermore, the software translations will probably be more accurate because the descriptive text for all options are translated. It is important to use glossaries from the target operating environment or other localized products.

Translation Order

First and foremost, never translate a table of contents before translating the help contents. Headings can only be translated accurately, when the related sections are available for reference to the translator.

It is important to decide when index entries need to be translated and who will be responsible for the translation. Some translators prefer to translate index entries while translating the topic contents; others prefer to translate all index entries once the running text has been translated. In most cases, translation memory tools are used to translate online help. Therefore, the recommended approach is to translate index entries while the running text is being translated. If index entries are segmented separately in the translation memory tools, translators working on a network will automatically choose consistent translations for all index entries. If index entries are segmented as a group of entries, this may cause problems. In either case, agree on a style for index entries before the translation cycle starts, e.g. use of upper/lower case, grammatical form, etc.

1.3   Linguistic Quality Assurance

In addition to standard quality assurance steps performed during the translation process, it is important to add an additional linguistic QA step once the online help files have been localized, assembled, and compiled.

This is particularly relevant when online help files have been translated using a translation memory tool, since certain help components can only be verified in the compiled online help systems, such as:

- Table of contents
- Keyword index
- Graphics
- Tables

Always review the running online help text fully, after files have been converted from the translation memory tool to their native file format. At this point, translators should be able to identify common errors, such as missing leading or trailing spaces, and unnecessary formatting or translation memory tool codes.

The following sections explain what translators or reviewers need to focus on when performing a linguistic QA on these components.

1.3.1   TABLE OF CONTENTS

Since the table of contents is often translated in a source file, such as a .cnt file for WinHelp or an .hhc file in HTML Help, it is not always possible to verify the tree structures of a typical table of contents.

As the table of contents is generally the first screen displayed in the online help, double-check to ensure that it contains no errors or inconsistencies.

Most importantly, translators should check that all translated items in the table of contents are consistent with the actual headings found in the online help document.

In addition, translators should check that no special characters have been corrupted in the main window title or table of contents entries. Please note that some online help systems have limited character support for table of contents entries.

1.3.2 KEYWORD INDEX

A keyword index is not unlike an index in a printed manual, i.e. it is generated from index markers located in each file. These index markers are used to compile the keyword index in the online help system.

If a translation memory tool has been used to translate the online help files, the keywords will more than likely have a high degree of consistency. Some translation memory tools, however, do not segment keyword entry lists, because they consider a set of keywords such as "localization, translation, internationalization" as a single segment. In cases like this, individual translations for each keyword will not be retrieved from translation memory, so consistent translations cannot be guaranteed.

If a keyword index is generated, translators should focus on the following:

- Consistency – Are there minor differences between two translated items and can they be merged into one entry? It does not make sense to have both "creating a report" and "creating reports" in an index. Use one rather than the two entries.

- Upper/lowercase – Some online help systems distinguish upper/lower case entries, so the index might contain both "Localization" and "localization". Decide on a standard and use only that standard.

- Sorting order – The language support in the online help system will decide the sorting order, which is set by the language setting in the compiler. Make sure the sorting order adheres to the standard for the target language.

- Usability – Are the index entries user-friendly? If an English index contains a long list of menu items, for example "File menu", "Edit menu", and in German the word order is reversed in the translation to "Menü Datei", "Menü Bearbeiten", assess whether users would search for "Datei" or "Menü" to find information on the File menu. The majority of users will probably look for "Datei" so always place the most significant word first in index entries.

- Main entries and sub entries – In many cases, main and sub entries in online help source files are separated by a semi-colon, while main entries are separated by a comma. If a translator inadvertently changes a comma to a semi-colon, an incorrect sub entry will be created under a main entry. So check that all sub entries make sense under their respective main entries.

- Completeness – In some languages, certain terms may have synonyms that do not necessarily exist in English. In such cases, it may be necessary to add these synonyms to the keyword index. By the same token, some synonyms in English may translate into a single word in the target language, so keywords can be deleted.

As many of the current keyword index lists in online help systems can be generated from several different online help files, it is important to perform a linguistic QA step on the generated file.

1.3.3 GRAPHICS

In most online help systems, graphics are linked to, rather than embedded in, online help source files. This means that the graphics are not visible to the translator, until the compiled help files are reviewed.

Graphics can be screen captures or manually edited images. In both cases, the translators do not necessarily create the localized images. Therefore, translators should review the graphics in compiled help files and pay attention to the following:

- Language – Are the graphics well localized, i.e. are they in the correct language, and has the sample text been translated?
- Callouts – If the graphics contain callouts with image descriptions, make sure these references are consistent with the localized images, and check whether they point to the right location or section in the image.
- Text references – If the text refers to the images, ensure these references are consistent with the localized images.
- Alt text – If images are linked to "Alt" text in HTML or XML files, i.e. text displayed when the image cannot be found or when the mouse pointer is placed on top of the image, ensure this text is consistent with the localized images.
- Hot spots or Image maps – If localized images contain hot spots (WinHelp) or image maps (HTML), where areas of the image contain hypertext links, make sure these areas have been resized to correspond to the localized images.

If graphics have been well prepared before project initiation, there should be no inconsistencies between graphics and running text.

1.3.4 TABLES

Translation memory tools often display tables very differently from the format displayed in the compiled help file or HTML file. To ensure high-quality translation, translators should review the localized table after the files have been converted to the original formats.

2 Windows

Help files for Windows applications normally have an .hlp or .chm file extension. Windows Help files can be opened in the application from the Help menu, directly in Windows Explorer, or from within a dialog box.

Since the introduction of Windows 3.1, Microsoft has developed the following help formats for the Windows operating system:

- WinHelp 3 – Used on Windows 3.1 and Windows NT 3.x operating systems
- WinHelp 4 – Used on Windows 9x and Windows NT 4 operating systems
- HTML Help – Introduced with Windows 98 and Windows 2000

The main difference between the WinHelp and HTML Help standards is the source files used to create the online help files. WinHelp files are created from Rich Text Format (.rtf) and bitmap (.bmp) files; HTML Help files are created from HTML and .jpg/.gif files.

For more information on online help systems, visit the following web sites:

- HTML Help by The Web Design Group – www.htmlhelp.com
- HTML Help Center – mvps.org/htmlhelpcenter
- WinWriters – www.winwriters.com
- HelpMaster – www.helpmaster.com

HTML Help and WinHelp 3 and 4 topics are discussed in the sections below.

2.1 HTML Help

Microsoft HTML Help is the next-generation online authoring system from Microsoft Corporation and is based on Microsoft WinHelp 4.

2.1.1 INTRODUCTION

HTML Help files are viewed using the HTML Help Viewer (hh.exe), which is included in all flavours of Windows since Window s98, or in a web browser. A typical HTML Help file looks like this:

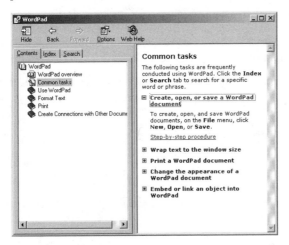

For more information on HTML Help, visit Microsoft's MSDN web site at msdn.microsoft.com (search for "HTML Help").

Navigation

Most navigation and search features in HTML Help are similar to those included in WinHelp 4, and many of these features, such as the full-text search engine, have been enhanced. Refer to the Navigation section on page 183 for more information on navigating through WinHelp 4 files.

One navigation change that was made between WinHelp 4 and HTML Help is the Table of Contents, which is always visible in the left pane when viewing an HTML Help document. The same applies to keyword index entries, i.e. the index is visible while viewing the topic associated with that index entry.

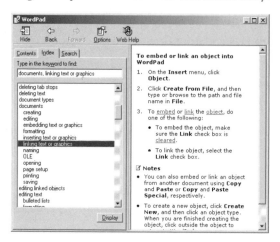

HTML Help can be accessed through the HTML Help Viewer or in a web browser using an ActiveX control.

Creation

The main difference between HTML-based Help and WinHelp is their respective source formats. WinHelp uses Rich Text Format (.rtf) files as source files, while Microsoft HTML Help uses HTML documents with advanced scripting and ActiveX features.

An HTML Help project is compiled using a project file and Microsoft's HTML Help Workshop compiler. The .hhp file is the project file containing all help settings. It is used by the help compiler to compile one or more HTML and image files into a .chm file.

The following text from an .hhp file, for example, defines that the name of the compiled online help file is wordpad.chm, the title is Wordpad, and several files are compiled, including HTML, contents (.hhc), and index (.hhk) files.

```
[OPTIONS]
Compiled file=wordpad.chm
Default topic=wripad_whatis_intro.htm
Title=WordPad
Default Window=windefault
Full-text search=Yes

[FILES]
compile_date.htm
wordpad.hhc
wordpad.hhk
wordpad_create_save_open.htm
wordpad_ct.htm
```

HTML files can be edited using any HTML editor, but it is advisable to author them using the tool that was used to create the source, or edit them as HTML code. The HTML Help Workshop application contains a basic HTML editor. For more information on translating HTML files, refer to the HTML section on page 207.

The HTML Help Workshop compiler is generally used in conjunction with a macro shell, such as Robohelp HTML or Doc-to-Help. These shells add extra authoring, conversion, or testing features to the help compiler.

The following table shows some HTML Help executables and corresponding WinHelp file formats:

WinHelp	HTML Help	Comment
.bmp	.gif and .jpg	Image files
.cnt	.hhc	Contents file
.gid	.chw and hh.dat	Merged keywords and preferences
.h	.hh	Header file
.hlp	.chm	Compiled help file
.hpj	.hhp	Project file
.rtf	.htm and .html	Source files
hcrtf.exe	hhc.exe	Help compiler
hcw.exe	hhw.exe	Help workshop
n/a	.hhk	Index file (in WinHelp integrated in RTF)
winhelp.exe	hh.exe	Help viewer

Refer to HTML Help section on page 233 for more information on compiling and testing HTML Help files.

2.1.2 TRANSLATING HTML HELP

The actual help file text is contained in HTML files. Other files that require translation in an HTML Help project are the contents (.hhc), project (.hhp), index (.hhk) files, and images (.gif or .jpg).

The "What's This?" help, which can be accessed from the application is typically included in the .chm file. The information in the text pop-ups is usually included in a separate text file (.txt) in the build environment.

HTML files are normally translated using a translation memory tool. When editing HTML files without translation memory, always use the correct editor, preferably the one used to create the source files.

The sections below discuss translation approaches for each of the translatable file types in HTML Help projects.

HTML Files

HTML files used in HTML Help projects can be edited like regular HTML files. For more information on editing HTML files, refer to the HTML section on page 207.

The following image displays an HTML Help topic, along with its HTML code:

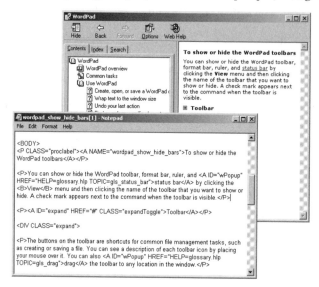

The `<A ID="wPopup" HREF="HELP=glossary.hlp TOPIC=gls_status_bar">` tag marks a hypertext popup link to a topic in a glossary help file. In most cases, these tags do not change, unless the file name `glossary.hlp` is translated.

A Related Topics item is encoded as follows:

```
<P><A ID="relTopics" HREF="CHM=windows.chm;wordpad.chm;howto.chm
META=a_wordpad_notepad_editors;a_app_wordpad;a_wordpad_create_save_o
pen">Related Topics</A></P>
```

In this example, topics from three different .chm files are referenced. The only text that requires translation is "Related Topics".

Hypertext links in HTML Help files can display a text balloon that describes the jump when the mouse pointer is located on the link. These text balloons are encoded as follows:

```
<tr><td><img alt="*" src="oBullet.gif"></td><td class="link"><a
href="MS-ITS:windows.chm::/searchhelp.htm" class="cold" title="How to
use the Search feature of Help to find specific information">Find it
fast</a></td></tr>
```

In the above example, "Find it fast" should be translated, as well as the text following the `title=` attribute.

HHP Files

HHP files contain all settings used to compile the HTML Help file. An .hhp file is a text-only file that can be edited in a text editor or Microsoft HTML Help Workshop.

The following pages list the sections in an .hhp file that may require translation.

Window Titles
The title of the HTML Help file, displayed in the title bar of the help file, is translated in the .hhp file. In a text editor, translate the words following the TITLE= line in the [OPTIONS] section.

When using Microsoft HTML Help Workshop, open the .hhp file, click on the Options button, click on the General tab and translate the title in the Title field.

HTML Help files may also contain secondary windows. Secondary windows often contain systematic instructions for tasks listed in the main help window. Titles for these windows can be translated in the [WINDOWS] section.

In Microsoft Help Workshop, click on the Modify Windows button, choose the General tab, and translate the Title bar text for each window type.

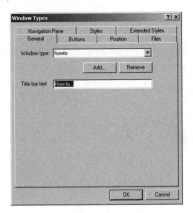

Button Names

The [WINDOWS] section in an .hhp file also defines custom buttons in the help file button bar, or customized menus in the menu bar. Glossary and Close are commonly used buttons that display a list of terms and close the help file respectively.

In addition to these custom buttons, the button bar will also contain a set of standard help buttons, i.e. Contents, Index, Find, Help Topics, Back, Options, and Print. These buttons will be displayed in the language of the operating system – or more specifically, of the HTML Help viewer – that is used.

The custom buttons are defined in the window definitions. If the [WINDOWS] section contains a line such as:

```
main="Topics","C:\HTML Help Project\sample.hhc","C:\HTML Help
Project\sample.hhk","C:\HTML Help Project\File1.htm",,,"Jump
Text",,,0x2520,,0x43006,,,,,,,0
```

A button titled Jump Text will be created on the button bar.

In Microsoft HTML Help Workshop, click on the Buttons tab in the Window Types dialog box, and translate the Jump text for each window type.

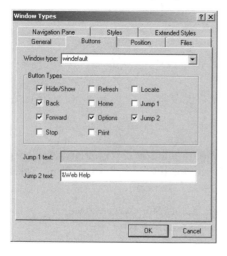

Text Pop-ups

If the HTML Help API is used to display "What's This?" text boxes in a running application, the text file containing the pop-up content is compiled into the .chm file.

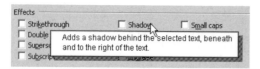

Text files used for pop-up text include the topic number and the pop-up text:

```
.topic 1069
Enter a title for the compiled help (.chm) file.
.topic 1070
Enter the file name for the topic that appears when an end user first
opens the compiled help (.chm) file.
```

The text following the topic numbers should be translated.

HHC Files

HHC files contain the Table of Contents for an HTML Help file, i.e. the entries displayed in the left pane of the viewer window. In WinHelp files, the Table of Contents is generated from a .cnt file.

An .hhc file is referred to as a sitemap file. Sitemap is a file format developed and proposed by Microsoft to the World Wide Web Consortium. Sitemap files have a `<!-- Sitemap 1.0 -->` comment line in the file header and control many navigation features, such as the table of contents and index panes.

To translate .hhc files, use a text editor or work in HTML Help Workshop. Opening an .hhc file in HTML Help Workshop displays the entry hierarchy:

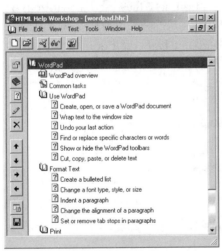

To translate the text, select an item and click the Pencil button. When editing the .hhc file in a text editor, translate only the entries following the "Name" value= attribute, as shown in the following example:

```
<LI> <OBJECT type="text/sitemap">
<param name="Name" value="Use WordPad">
</OBJECT>
<UL>
<LI> <OBJECT type="text/sitemap">
<param name="Name" value="Create, open, or save a WordPad document">
<param name="Local" value="MS-ITS:wordpad.chm::/
wordpad_create_save_open.htm">
</OBJECT>
<LI> <OBJECT type="text/sitemap">
<param name="Name" value="Wrap text to the window size">
<param name="Local" value="MS-ITS:wordpad.chm::/
wripad_word_wrap.htm">
</OBJECT>
```

Please note, these translations should correspond to the actual topic titles.

HHK Files

HHK files are comparable to the .hhc files described in the previous section. HHK files replace the K keywords and $ footnotes from RTF files used in WinHelp projects, i.e. they contain the search keywords list that is included in HTML Help files.

Like .hhc files, .hhk files can be translated in a text editor or in HTML Help Workshop. Opening an .hhk file in HTML Help Workshop displays the keyword index hierarchy:

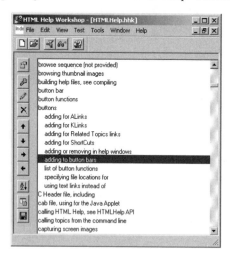

To translate the text, select an item and click the Pencil button. When editing the .hhk file in a text editor, translate only the entries following the "Name" value= attribute.

When translating .hhk files in a text editor or using a translation memory tool, the contents will be displayed as follows:

```
<LI> <OBJECT type="text/sitemap">
<param name="Name" value="documents">
<param name="Name" value="Create, open, or save a WordPad document">
<param name="See Also" value="documents">
</OBJECT>
<UL>
<LI> <OBJECT type="text/sitemap">
<param name="Name" value="creating">
<param name="Name" value="Create, open, or save a WordPad document">
<param name="Local" value="wordpad_create_save_open.htm">
</OBJECT>
<LI> <OBJECT type="text/sitemap">
<param name="Name" value="editing">
<param name="Name" value="Cut, copy, paste, or delete text">
<param name="Local" value="wripad_cut_info.htm">
<param name="Name" value="Edit linked objects">
<param name="Local" value="wripad_edit_links.htm">
<param name="Name" value="Create a bulleted list">
<param name="Local" value="wripad_insert_bullet.htm">
<param name="Name" value="Embed or link an object into WordPad">
<param name="Local" value="wripad_insert_new_object.htm">
</OBJECT>
</UL>
```

This section is displayed as follows:

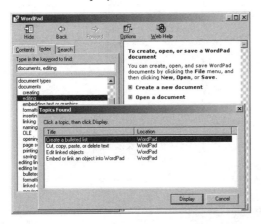

The <OBJECT> tags define a keyword entry, the <UL> tag defines the start of a subentry. Each index entry references one or more topics, which are included in each <OBJECT> section. Please note, these translations should correspond to the actual topic titles.

There is no need to sort the index entries manually in the .hhk file, as this can be done automatically using HTML Help Workshop.

Stoplist Files

Full-text search stop lists prevent common words, such as *the* and *or*, from showing up in the Search results when running the compiled HTML Help file. Including a stop list reduces the size of the full-text search index, which generates a smaller compiled file, and reduces the search time.

Stop lists are text files with the .stp file extension. They contain a list of words which can be translated using any text editor or translation memory tool. The HTML Help Workshop online help file contains a sample stop list in English.

2.2 WinHelp

Even though HTML Help has been adopted as the new standard with the arrival of Windows 98 and Windows 2000, many software publishers are still creating WinHelp files for users of older Windows versions.

2.2.1 INTRODUCTION

Here is a typical help file for Windows 3.1 (based on WinHelp 3):

Here is a typical help file for Windows 9x (based on WinHelp 4):

For more information on WinHelp, visit the HelpMaster web site at
www.helpmaster.com.

Navigation

There are several ways to navigate through Windows Help files. The Contents tab
displays the help file table of contents. Clicking on a topic title will automatically open
the associated topic.

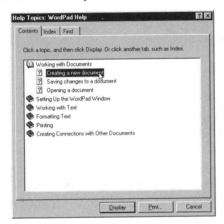

Click the Search or Index button or tab to display a keyword index. The keyword index
helps the user to find specific information. Either select an entry from the list or type
(part of) a word and press Enter.

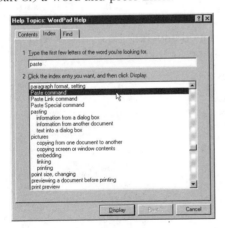

Click the Find button for a full-text search index of all words in the help file (WinHelp 4 help only).

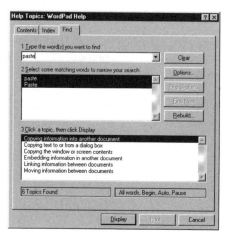

In a help topic, click a jump to open the help information for that topic. Jumps can be text, graphics or parts of a graphic. Jumps in graphics are called hotspots. The Back button on the help navigation bar returns the user to the page where the jump was located.

Click a definition pop-up, an item with dotted underline, to display a window with the definition or explanation of the word, string, or graphic.

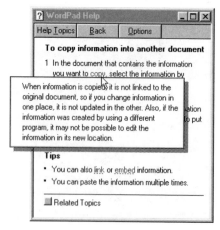

Use the browse buttons (<< and >>) on the help navigation bar to browse through predefined sequences in the help file page-by-page.

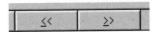

Press the Help button or F1 key in a dialog box or screen to display help information on that dialog box. This function is called context-sensitive help. In WinHelp 4, click the small question mark symbol at the top of a dialog box, and then click the item about which information is required. This help type is called "What's This" help.

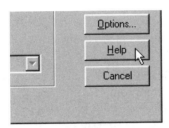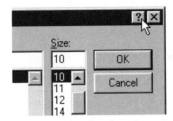

The mouse pointer changes shape when it is placed on a jump or hotspot. The Back and History buttons are additional navigation tools. Refer to How to Use Help in the Help menu of Program Manager (Windows 3.1) or Start > Help > How to > Use Help (Windows 9x/NT) for more information on navigating through online help files.

Creation

A Windows Help project is compiled using a project file with the extension .hpj and the Microsoft Help Compiler. The .hpj file is a text-only file used by the help compiler to compile one or more RTF (Rich Text Format) files and image files into an .hlp file, and to define all help file settings.

For example, the following text from an .hpj file defines that the online help file is English, a compilation report should be created, the bitmaps can be found in the Images folder, the compiled help file is called Sample.hlp, and the three RTF files that are compiled are called File1.rtf, File2.rtf, and File3.rtf.

```
[OPTIONS]
LCID=0x409 0x0 0x0 ; English (United States)
REPORT=Yes
BMROOT=IMAGES
HLP=Sample.hlp
[FILES]
File1.rtf
File2.rtf
File3.rtf
```

RTF files can be edited using Microsoft Word or other word processors. Each topic (page) in an RTF file has a unique ID, and represents one screen in the compiled online help file. Footnotes in the RTF files define the index keywords and search topic headings linked to each topic. The Microsoft Help Compiler automatically converts these footnotes to index or topic entries. The Help Compiler is shipped with most Windows software development environments, and can be downloaded from the Microsoft web site.

The Microsoft Help Compiler is generally used in conjunction with a Word macro shell, such as Robohelp, Doc-To-Help, Help Magician or ForeHelp. These shells add extra authoring, conversion, or testing features to the help compiler.

Refer to the WinHelp section on page 239 for more information on compiling and testing Windows Help files.

2.2.2 TRANSLATING WINHELP

The help file text is stored as RTF files. Other translatable files from a WinHelp project include the contents (.cnt), project (.hpj) files, and images (usually .bmp).

RTF files are generally translated in a translation memory tool. However, the guidelines below assume the translator is working directly in the RTF files. Even when translating RTF files in a translation memory tool, it is important to understand the internal structure of RTF files. This is mainly because final edits will often have to be made directly in the RTF files after they have been converted back from the TM tool.

Before editing RTF files, ensure the correct word processor is being used. The RTF output from different versions of word processors may differ. This could create compilation problems. Some older versions of the Microsoft Help Compiler, for example, are not compatible with RTF files saved in Microsoft Word 8 and later versions. If it is not clear which word processor should be used, ask the publisher which version was used to create the RTFs.

When a help shell like Robohelp is used, translation is usually performed in Word (DOC) documents. These Word files are automatically saved as RTF by Robohelp before being compiled into a help file.

RTF Files

RTF files are usually edited with Microsoft Word. Here is a sample RTF page in Word:

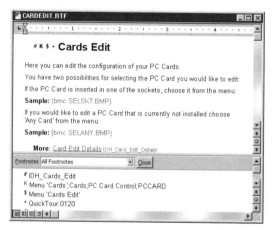

Here are some tips on working with RTF files:

- Set the page view to display hidden text. To enable this option in Microsoft Word, choose Options in the Tools menu and select Hidden Text in the View tab, or activate the ¶ button on the toolbar.

- Disable the Replace Straight Quote with Smart Quotes option of the AutoCorrect feature from the Tools menu.

- Disable all other AutoFormat and AutoCorrect features from the Tools menu.

- Avoid using the Autoformat command from the Format menu. This overwrites the styles in the attached template.

- Always save the file in RTF format.

- Disable the Automatic Word Selection and the Use Smart Cut and Paste options in Word's Options > Edit.

- Disable all revision marks in Word.

- Disable the Allow Fast Saves option in Word.

- Avoid inserting or deleting manual page breaks, paragraph marks, or hyphens in the text, because all lines in a help file are wrapped by the help system. Text wrapping is automatically adjusted to the size of the help window in which the information is displayed.

- Pay special attention to periods and commas preceding or following a link. To avoid corrupting the link, periods and commas should not become part of the hidden text.

By following these guidelines character corruptions or other problems can be avoided when compiling the online help file.

Jumps And Popups

In RTF files, items with single green underlines, such as desktopdesktop@glossary.hlp, become definition popups in the compiled help file. Items with double green underlines (Changing Existing Color SchemesChanging_Existing_Color_Schemes) become jumps. Text with dotted underline following these items is hidden text. This text contains the topic ID related to the link. Topic IDs are defined by the footnotes, which are linked to every topic title. Refer to the Pound '#' character section on page 188 for more information on topic IDs.

Note that the hidden code text is only visible when the View Hidden Text option is enabled in the word processor. Never translate or change hidden jump text in help source files! When these codes are changed or deleted, the jump will not work in the compiled help file.

Because help files contain many jumps and references to other topics within the help file, consistency in translation is very important. If, for example, the help file contains the sentence "See also: Using Jumps and Popups for more information", the translation of "Using Jumps and Popups for more information" should match the corresponding topic title exactly.

When using a translation memory tool, such as IBM TranslationManager or Trados Translator's Workbench, the correct translation will automatically be retrieved from memory once it has been entered in the system. Most help files are very repetitive, so it is advisable to use a translation memory tool for these files. Refer to Chapte r11, Translation Technology, for more information on translation memory.

If no translation memory is used, use global search and replace functions for the topic titles in RTF files to save time.

Translate topic titles in a consistent and systematic manner. This is particularly important for help topics describing menu items or dialog box titles. It is advisable to translate topic titles in the same way that index entries are translated, i.e. keyword first. Refer to the Translating Indexes section on page 307 for more information.

Footnotes
In RTF files, topic titles are usually preceded by the #, $, K and + symbols, which are linked to footnotes in the document. Footnotes determine how individual topics should be accessed and linked by the help compiler.

To display the footnotes in Microsoft Word, select the Footnotes command from the View menu, or double-click on a footnote symbol, such as the $ symbol, to jump directly to the footnote linked to the symbol.

Here are examples of the type of footnotes contained in RTF files:

```
#  IDH_CONTENTS
$  Contents
K  Contents;Index
+  main:000
```

Pound '#' character
The string following the pound (#) character is the context string that uniquely identifies each topic in the help system. It can be compared to an address, which is a required element. All items in .cnt files and all links in a help file refer to this topic ID.

This footnote text **should not** be translated.

Dollar sign '$' character
The string following the dollar sign ($) character is the title string which is displayed when the reader uses the search feature in WinHelp. It is displayed in the Go To box (WinHelp 3) or Topics Found box (WinHelp 4), the Bookmark dialog box, and the History window.

This string is usually identical to the topic title. Copying the topic title and pasting it in this footnotes field is the fastest way to translate the footnote. This also helps maintain consistency throughout the file. Scroll through the footnote field using the arrow key to automatically display the topic related to the footnote.

This footnote text **should** be translated.

Letter 'K' character

The string following the letter 'K' character contains search keywords for the topic, separated by semi-colons (without spaces). The keywords are displayed in the index list of the Search dialog box or Index tab of a WinHelp file. First and second level entries are separated by commas or colons.

Here is an example of how a ^{K} keyword entry in an RTF file is displayed in the search index of a compiled online help file. The following ^{K} keyword text results in the index entries listed below it, with main entries separated by semi-colons, and sub-entries separated by a comma:

```
K first;second, third;fourth
```

```
first
second
   third
fourth
```

Help keywords are comparable to index entries in a printed manual, and should be translated as such. Refer to the Translating Indexes section on page 307 for more information. Add or delete entries from the keyword footnote section, if necessary.

Please note that no more than 255 characters should be used per keyword entry. This footnote text **should** be translated.

Plus '+' character

The string following the plus (+) character is the browse sequence string used by WinHelp to provide a browsing order accessible using the left and right browse buttons on the WinHelp button bar.

This footnote text **should not** be translated. Help engineers may, however, want to change the browse sequence for sorted help topics, such as glossaries. Refer to the Browse Sequence section on page 243 for more information.

Letter 'A' character

This type of footnote functions like the 'K' character except that it is never visible to the user and is not included in the Index. The items in this footnote are hidden search phrases that are used mainly to activate Alink macros.

This footnote text **should not** be translated.

The @ sign

This footnote is used to add comments to a footnote section. The author of the help file, for example, may use this to include comments for the localizer.

This footnote text **should not** be translated.

The document may contain other footnote types, but these are irrelevant to the translation. Refer to the help compiler documentation for more information on additional footnote types.

Graphics

Most WinHelp files contain graphic images, such as screen captures of the running software. These images are not embedded or pasted in the RTF files, but linked or referenced.

Strings like {bmc GFXFILE.BMP} in an RTF file indicate that a bitmap with the name GFXFILE.BMP is inserted during the compilation process. The compiler searches for this file in the path specified in the BMROOT= option in the .hpj file.

Never change bitmap names or links to the bitmaps. In bitmap links, bmc indicates that the bitmap is aligned as a text character, or treated as regular paragraph text. If bml or bmr is used, the bitmap is aligned with the respective left or right margin of the help topic.

In addition to bitmaps with the extension .bmp, there are various types of graphics that can be included in help files, for example, Windows metafiles (.wmf), Windows Help multiple-hotspot (SHED) bitmaps (.shg), and Windows Help multi-resolution bitmaps (.mrb). Refer to the Graphics section on page 245 for more information on these graphic types.

.HPJ Files

.HPJ files contain all settings used to compile the help file. An .hpj file is a text-only file that can be edited in a text editor or Microsoft Help Workshop (WinHelp 4 only).

The following pages list the sections in an .hpj file that may need to be translated.

Window Titles

The help file title, displayed in the title bar of the help file, should be translated in the .hpj file. In WinHelp 3 projects, open the .hpj file as text-only and translate the text displayed after the TITLE= line in the [OPTIONS] section.

In Microsoft Help Workshop, open the .hpj file, click on the Options button, click on the General tab and translate the title in the Help title field.

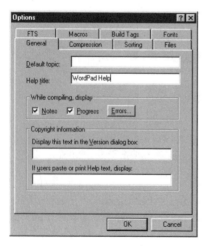

Help files may also display secondary windows. Secondary windows often contain systematic instructions for tasks mentioned in the main help window. Titles for these windows can be translated in the [WINDOWS] section.

In Microsoft Help Workshop, click on the Windows button, choose the General tab and translate the Title bar text for each window type.

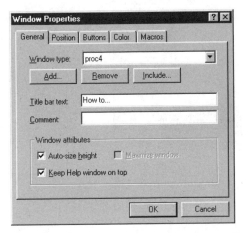

Button Names
The [CONFIG] section in an .hpj file contains commands that activate macros to insert buttons in the help file button bar, or customized menus in the menu bar. The Glossary and Close buttons are commonly used buttons that display a list of terms and close the help file, respectively.

In addition to these custom buttons, the button bar also contains a set of standard help buttons, i.e. Contents, Index, Find, Help Topics, Back, Options, and Print. These buttons are displayed in the operating system – or rather, WinHelp viewer – language that is used.

The custom buttons are defined by the CreateButton macro. The [CONFIG] section may contain a macro line such as the following:

```
CreateButton("Glossary_Btn","&Glossary","JI
(`bubble.hlp>Gloss',`IDH_Glossary')")
```

If this is the case, a button titled *Glossary* will be created on the button bar. In this statement, the word &*Glossary* should be translated, with the ampersand (&) character followed by the letter that defines the accelerator key. This should be a unique accelerator key on the button bar in a localized help viewer.

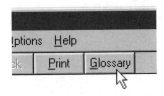

In Microsoft Help Workshop, click on the Config button, select the line with the button macro, click on Edit and translate the button title.

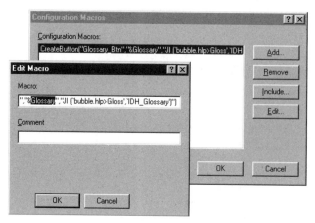

If the [CONFIG] section contains a statement such as:

```
ExtInsertItem(mnu_file,itm_wpad,&Launch Wordpad,
ExecFile(wordpad.exe),3)
```

a menu item labeled Launch Wordpad is inserted on the WinHelp File menu.

Copyright Info
If an .hpj file contains a COPYRIGHT= option, the text following the equal symbol is displayed if a user selects the Version command in the Help menu. To translate copyright info in Microsoft Help Workshop, click the Options button, select the General tab, and translate the text in the "Display this text in the Version dialog box" field.

The CITATION= option defines text that is appended if users copy and paste or print text from the help file. To translate citation text in Microsoft Help Workshop, click the

Options button, select the General tab, and translate the text in the "If users paste or print Help text, display:" field.

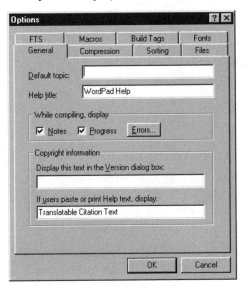

CNT Files

The contents (.cnt) file is a text-only file that provides all information displayed when the Contents tab in the Help Topics dialog box is selected. The .cnt file also determines from which help files the keywords are displayed on the Index and Find tabs. Only WinHelp 4 help files support .cnt files.

CNT files can be translated in a Windows-based text editor or in Microsoft Help Workshop. However, be careful when using Microsoft Help Workshop to translate .cnt files. Some versions of the Help Workshop corrupt .cnt files by deleting @help_file_name.hlp references.

Titles

The string following the :Title marker in the beginning of the .cnt file can be translated. The title shows up in the title bar of the Help Topics window. Text that is preceded by a semi-colon is comment text and should not be translated.

Please note that the first lines of a .cnt file may contain markers that should not be translated, for example :Base, :Index, and :Link.

In Microsoft Help Workshop, open the .cnt file and translate the Default Title box text.

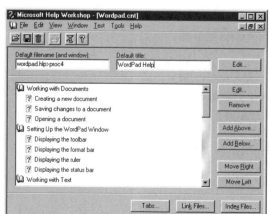

Contents

Each line in a .cnt file starts with the level number. When translating a .cnt file in a text editor, only the text preceding the equal symbol (=) should be translated. Be careful not to delete any codes. The codes following the equal symbol are help topic IDs.

```
1 Working with Documents
2 Creating a new document=WRIPAD_CREATE_DOCUMENT
2 Saving changes to a document=WRIPAD_SAVE_FILE
2 Opening a document=WRIPAD_OPEN_DOC
1 Setting Up the WordPad Window
2 Displaying the toolbar=COMMON_TOOLBAR_ON_OFF@common.hlp>proc4
```

To translate a .cnt file in Microsoft Help Workshop, open the file and activate the Translation option in the File menu. This option ensures that only visible text is translated. Topic IDs, help file names, or window names cannot be modified.

To translate an entry in a .cnt file, double-click on the entry and type the translation in the Title field of the Edit Contents Tab Entry dialog box.

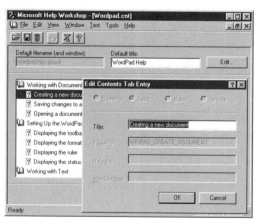

When the entire .cnt file has been translated, test it using Help Workshop. Refer to the Contents File Test (WinHelp 4 only) section on page 249 for more information.

If all the RTF files have been translated and compiled into an .hlp file, the .cnt file is the last component to be translated, and no translation memory has been used, follow these steps to ensure the translations in the .cnt file correspond to the help topic titles:

1. Open the folder containing the .hlp and corresponding .cnt file.
2. Make a copy of the .cnt file, and give it a .txt extension.
3. Double-click on the .hlp file to display the Contents window with the information from the .cnt file.
4. Open the .txt file using Notepad or any other Windows-based text editor.
5. Open the first topic in the Contents window, and double-click on the first topic (with a question mark).
6. In the translated topic window, select the title and press Ctrl+C to copy the title.
7. Switch to Notepad and replace the original topic title preceding the equals symbol (=) with the copied translated title.
8. Switch to the help window, and click the Help Topics button to display the Contents window and copy the next topic title.

When all titles in the .txt file have been translated, delete the original .cnt file. Change the .txt extension to .cnt and double-click on the .hlp file to open the translated Contents window.

3   Mac OS

There are several online help systems available on the Mac OS platform. The most important ones include:

- Apple Help
- Apple Guide
- QuickHelp

Apple Guide Help is a procedural help system, which is compiled from guide script files, which are based on AppleScript, the standard Apple user scripting language. QuickHelp is the Mac OS equivalent of WinHelp, described in the previous sections. Apple Help is the new HTML-based online help system from Apple, is becoming the standard over other help formats used, including Apple Guide.

A third online help format, balloon help, is considered as a component of the software, rather than a standard help format. For more information on balloon help, refer to the Balloon Help section on page 92.

3.1   Apple Help

Apple Help is the new help technology used in Mac OS 8.6 and later versions. It can display HTML content along with utilities allowing developers to integrate instructional media, such as QuickTime movies or Apple Guide files, into the Apple Help Viewer.

3.1.1   INTRODUCTION

Apple Help includes the Help Viewer application, which reads HTML-based help files, connects to other help sites on the Internet, and provides links that automatically open files and perform tasks.

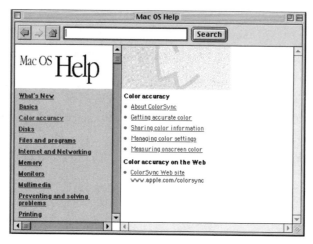

Sets of Apple Help HTML documents, also called "books", can be indexed, so users can perform full-text searches.

More information on Apple Help can be found on the Apple Developer Connection web site at www.apple.com/developer (search for "Apple Help").

Navigation

The Apple Help Viewer is a lightweight browser, optimized for using AppleScript and Sherlock, the Apple search engine.

Apple Help files typically have a contents page and a table of contents in the left window pane. The Previous, Next, and Home buttons enable users to browse through the files.

AppleScripts or Apple Guide files can be launched from the HTML files in Apple Help.

Creation

Creating an Apple Help file is a relatively simple task. Developers first need to create and organize the HTML content, using standard HTML editors. Then, a title page for the "book" is created which is displayed in the Mac OS Help Center.

The HTML pages can be indexed for full-text searching, but no compilation is required. To index a folder containing HTML files, the folder is dragged to the Indexing Tool icon. Index files have the .idx file extension.

The Apple Help SDK, which can be downloaded from the Apple FTP site, contains a style guide and standard HTML templates to allow the user to create a consistent look and feel to the Apple Help documents.

Most Apple Help projects have different folders for each chapter. Each chapter folder contains a contents HTML files and a subfolder containing separate HTML files for each topic. Graphics are usually centralized in one folder.

For more information on Apple Help engineering, refer to the Apple Help section on page 252.

3.1.2 TRANSLATING APPLE HELP

The HTML files included in Apple Help projects can be translated using any text-based HTML editor or translation memory tool.

Please note that contents files for books not only have the `<TITLE>` metatag defining the HTML file title, but also the "AppleTitle" metaname, which defines the header of the title page file in the Apple Help Viewer.

For example, in the following HTML header, both `<TITLE>` and the `DESCRIPTION` and `AppleTitle` meta tags need to be translated:

```
<HEAD>
<META HTTP-EQUIV="content-type" CONTENT="text/html;charset=iso-8859-
1">
<META NAME="generator" CONTENT="GoLive CyberStudio">
<TITLE>Apple Help Style Guide</TITLE>
<META NAME="DESCRIPTION" CONTENT="This section describes how to create
Apple Help projects.">
<META NAME="AppleTitle" CONTENT="Apple Help Style Guide">
<META NAME="ROBOTS" CONTENT="NOINDEX">
</HEAD>
```

Apple Help HTML files may also contain keywords in the header, describing the file content. The following example shows some translatable keywords:

```
<META NAME ="KEYWORDS"CONTENT ="delete,erase,throw away,discard">
```

Sometimes keywords are placed in comment lines with the `AppleKeyWords` tag. These keywords only apply to a particular file segment and also must be translated because the Apple Help Indexing tool recognizes them. These file segments can also be returned themselves as a separate "hit" in a search. Therefore, segments may contain a title and a short description, which both need to be translated. The following example includes a segment definition.

```
<!--AppleSegStart ="Locking A Disk"-->
<A NAME="Locking A Disk"></A>
<!--AppleKeywords ="lock,floppy disk,unlock"-->
<!--AppleSegDescription ="This section describes how to lock and
unlock a floppy disk."-->
...content of segment...
<!--AppleSegEnd -->
```

The <A NAME> anchor tag links the search result to the right segment in the HTML file
and does not need to be translated.

For more information on translating HTML files, refer to the Translation Approach
section on page 213.

3.2   Apple Guide

Apple Guide is an online help system for Mac OS computers that can be accessed using
the Help command in an application. The Apple Guide help system was introduced
with System 7.5 in 1994. Apple Guide files typically comprise a general help, tutorial,
or shortcut overview.

3.2.1   INTRODUCTION

An Apple Guide help system consists of one or more guide file databases, which are
created using a word processor or text editor in conjunction with a help authoring tool,
such as Guide Maker.

Apple Guide files can contain text, sound, graphics and movies. A typical Apple Guide
help file contains an access window with Topics overview, a keyword index, and
search screen. An Apple Guide file contains a *sequence* of *panels*.

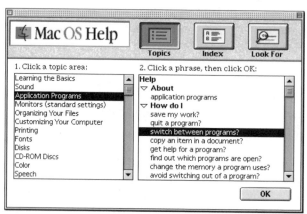

In addition to index, search, and hypertext capabilities common to most help systems,
Apple Guide offers the following options:

- Context checking – Apple Guide offers the ability to split out and present
  different instructions, depending on the computer configuration or user
  keystrokes. For example, if the guide instructs the user to open a control panel,

it will check to ensure the control panel has been opened before proceeding to the next step.

- Coaching – Apple Guide files can draw arrows and circles on the screen to highlight buttons, menus, and other user interface elements in an application or operating system.

- Scripting – Apple Guide files can launch an AppleScript to perform certain automated tasks when the user clicks on a button or help item.

Apple Guide is an interactive tool and is used mostly to guide users through certain features in an application.

For more information on Apple Guide, refer to the Apple Guide Complete book, which can be accessed and downloaded from the Apple Developer Connection web site at www.apple.com/developer (search for "Apple Guide Complete").

Navigation

Apple Guide consists of a sequence of different panel types, such as introductory panels, decision panels, action panels, tip panels, definition panels, and Oops panels. Each panel presents a different type of help instruction, for example an Oops panel tells the user that a condition specified on a previous panel (for example, opening a control panel) was not met. The following image displays an elementary information panel.

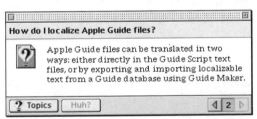

Apple has designed a standard layout for each panel type. Apple Guide authors normally create a roadmap which defines when panel types or sequences of panels should be used. Without this roadmap, it would be very difficult to navigate sequentially through the topics of a complete Apple Guide file, unless an Apple Guide authoring system or compiler is used.

Creation

Apple Guide files are based on Guide Script, which is a mark-up language that identifies Apple Guide elements. It also controls content layout and sequence panels. The language is a combination of definitions, content layout, and panel sequencing. Apple Guide files are compiled versions of text files containing Guide Script tags and instructions written by the developer. These text files can be edited using a word processor or text editor. A Guide database is a compiled set of instructions or information that works with the Apple Guide extension. The tool used to compile Apple Guide files is called Guide Maker.

Guide Maker only compiles word processor documents containing Apple Script and instructions. There are, however, several Apple Guide authoring tools available that provide a what-you-see-is-what-you-get (WYSIWYG) content entry.

The most commonly used tool is Guide Maker, which is now part of the Apple Guide Software Development Kit (www.apple.com/developer – search for "Apple Guide SDK"). Other commonly used tools are the Apple Guide Starter Kit (www.dannyg.com) and AG Author (www.lakewoodsoftware.com).

3.2.2 TRANSLATING APPLE GUIDE

Apple Guide files can be translated in two ways:

- Directly in the Guide Script text files, which are normally in Word 5 or Write II format.

- By exporting and importing localizable text from Apple Guide source files using Guide Maker.

Character style information, including the blue color and underlining from links, is generally lost when exporting text from an Apple Guide database using Guide Maker's Localize utility. It is, therefore, advisable to translate directly in the Guide Script resources if the Apple Guide file contains font and style information that is embedded in the source files.

If the source files contain style information defined using the `<Define Format>` commands as opposed to being formatting in the source files, it is safe to use the Localize feature in Guide Maker.

Translating Guide Script Files

A Guide Script file typically contains information with the following structure:

```
<Define Panel> "How do I localize Apple Guide files?"
<Format> "Tag"
<PICT> 9457, RIGHT
<Format> "Body"
Apple Guide files can be translated in two ways: either directly in
the Guide Script text files, or by exporting and importing localizable
text from a Guide database using Guide Maker.
<End Panel>
```

Here is an example of this panel definition compiled using Guide Maker:

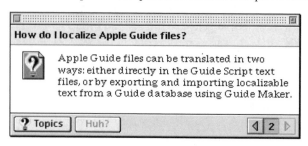

Follow these instructions when translating a Guide Script file:

1. In Guide Script, tags are enclosed in angled brackets (< and >). These tags should not be changed or translated.

2. Comments (or remarks) are preceded by a # character. These usually keep a record of the code. These comments should not be translated.

3. Keep the translations short. Even though panels resize automatically, the translation should remain as short and concise as possible.

In Apple Guide, all sections and elements are intrinsically related, so consistent translation of topics, panel and sequence names is very important. Apple Guide files often contain coach marks, which are indicators that point a user to a specific element. A coach mark will draw a colored circle around a software menu or dialog box option. Coach marks require special attention during translation, because translated coach marks only work when they exactly match the translated software option.

If it is not clear whether a string needs to be translated, locate the screen in the running Apple Guide file, and compare it with the Guide Script document. A list of tag meanings and tags followed by translatable text can be found in the *Apple Guide Complete* manual, for example: "<Header> – Specifies a header associated with a particular topic area or index term."

Using Guide Maker

Guide Maker provides a Localize utility to help translate all elements of an Apple Guide file, such as topic areas, topics, panel titles, text in panels, coach marks, button labels, index terms, and any other content. The advantage to using the above method is that there is no need to work in scripted text files. The Guide Maker Localize utility enables the users to translate all text strings in ResEdit.

Follow these steps to localize an Apple Guide file using Guide Maker:

1. Start Guide Maker. Select the Localize command from the Utilities menu.

2. Click in the Script Source File area of the Localize window to select the source Guide Script file, where the text strings should be extracted.

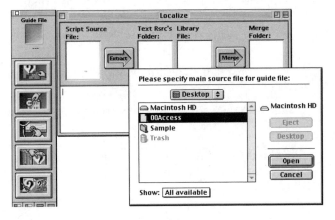

3. Click in the Text Rsrc's Folder field to select the folder where the files containing the extracted strings should be placed.

4. Click in the Library File area of the Localize window to create a localization library file. The localization library file contains information on the location of the extracted text strings in the source files.

5. Click the Extract arrow in the Localize window to extract the text strings. A text file is created for each source file, with the RSRC extension added to the file name.

6. Use a resource editor such as ResEdit or Resorcerer to translate the extracted strings. All translatable text can be found in the TEXT resource. Guide Maker stores the extracted text strings as TEXT resources with resource names that provide information on the text string. By looking at a resource name, it is possible to identify the Guide Script command associated with the text string. This information makes it easy to ascertain the structure of the text string. Refer to the Translatable Resources section on page 203 for a description of these resources.

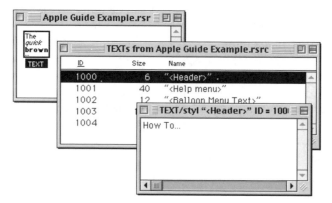

7. In addition to the translatable TEXT resources in the extracted Guide Script files, a Standard Resource file is included with the build environment. This resource file contains image (PICT) resources. For more information on translating these resources, refer to the Image Resources section on page 203. It is important to check whether any other art resource files included in the file need to be localized.

8. Click the Merge Folder area of the Localize window to select the folder that will store the localized files.

9. Click the Merge arrow to merge the translated strings from the RSRC files and localization library.

Now build a Guide file with the localized source files. Refer to the Compiling Apple Guide section on page 257 for more information.

Translatable Resources

A list of translatable TEXT resource names (Apple Script tags) can be found in Chapter 7 of the *Apple Guide Complete* manual. This book can be accessed and downloaded from the Apple Developer Connection web site at www.apple.com/developer (search for "Apple Guide Complete").

Image Resources

Images that are used in the Apple Guide file, such as the common Oops and Huh? buttons, are stored as individual PICT resources in the Standard Resources file. This resource file is compiled into the Apple Guide file. To edit an interface button, copy it from the resource file and edit it in Photoshop (or another image editing program). For more information on translating PICT resources, refer to the Images section on page 92.

These are common translations of Apple Guide terms:

English	Oops	Huh?	Tip	Do This
French	Attention	Infos	Conseil	Action
German	Hinweis	Noch Fragen?	Tip	Aktion
Italian	Ops	Come?	Consigli	Fai così
Spanish	¡Ojo!	?Qué?	Consejo	Haga esto

Translations for other languages can be found in Chapter 2 of the *Apple Guide Complete* manual, which can be downloaded from the Apple Developer Connection web site at www.apple.com/developer (search for "Apple Guide Complete").

If localized versions of the Apple Guide extension or the Macintosh Guide file are installed, most of these standard localized buttons can be copied from these files to the Standard Resources file. The PICT resources contain different color versions of buttons.

3.3 QuickHelp

Many Mac OS applications include a help system comparable to the WinHelp file system. This help system is called QuickHelp and has been developed by Altura Software (www.altura.com).

3.3.1 INTRODUCTION

Like WinHelp, a QuickHelp project is composed of RTF files and images which are compiled into an online help file using a project file. This project file can be edited and compiled on a Mac OS with the QuickHelp compiler. QuickHelp files are fully compatible with WinHelp 4, which means it is possible to perform full-text searches, use contents (.cnt) files, and include secondary windows. For more information on Windows Help and translating RTF files, refer to the WinHelp section on page 182.

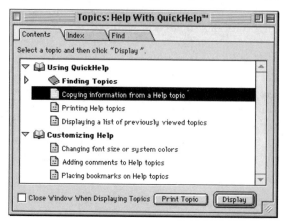

For more information on navigation and other online help features, refer to the Introduction section on page 182.

Because of the compatibility with WinHelp, QuickHelp is often used for cross-platform products. The QuickHelp Viewer is available in most European languages.

Navigation

Navigating through QuickHelp files is identical to navigating through WinHelp 4 files. Refer to the Navigation section on page 183 for more information.

Creation

Creating QuickHelp files is identical to creating WinHelp 4 files. However, a different compiler will need to be used. QuickHelp files are compiled on the Mac OS using the QuickHelp Compiler by Altura.

Refer to the Compiling QuickHelp section on page 261 for more information on compiling and testing QuickHelp files.

3.3.2 TRANSLATING QUICKHELP

RTF files for Mac OS QuickHelp projects are translated using the same tools and approach as RTF files from WinHelp projects. In fact, the RTF files are usually translated using Microsoft Word for Windows, transferred to the Mac OS, and then compiled.

The use of conditional text in the Mac RTF file may, however, be different from standard Windows RTF files. The QuickHelp compiler can use hidden phrases preceded by two "|" characters and hidden text instead of regular text to create a Mac-specific version of an online help file. Refer to the QuickHelp manual for more information on conditional text in RTF files.

The QuickHelp compiler contains some features which automatically change all Windows-specific file contents to Mac OS standards, such as font mappings.

4 HTML and XML

Markup is defined as everything in a document other than content, i.e. everything which is not part of written text or graphics. There are two basic types of markup: procedural and descriptive:

- Procedural markup mainly defines the layout of a text, for example the font, font size, and color of each heading style in a document.
- Descriptive markup, also known as generic markup, defines the purpose and content structure of a document, i.e. it defines what each element in a text is, rather than how it is displayed.

The key issue with descriptive markup is separating content from presentation. For example, descriptive markup states that each chapter of a manual starts with a title and an introduction, followed by an overview of the topics discussed in the chapter.

Examples of markup languages are SGML, HTML, and XML.

4.1 Introduction

SGML, or Standard Generalized Markup Language, is an international standard for information exchange that was adopted as a standard by the International Organization for Standardization (ISO 8879) in 1986. It prescribes a standard format for using descriptive markup within a document, defining three document layers: structure, content, and style. Each SGML document has an associated document type definition (DTD) that specifies the rules for the structure of the document.

HTML, or HyperText Markup Language, is a procedural tagged document type written in SGML. In fact, each HTML version, 3.2 or 4 for example, has its own DTD defining all tags that can be used in HTML documents for that version. HTML has become the standard file format for displaying pages on the World Wide Web. In the future, most online help will be published in HTML or related markup languages such as XML.

An emerging new standard is XML, or eXtensible Markup Language, which is an initiative proposed by the World Wide Web Consortium (www.w3c.org) as an alternative to HTML. It has been developed because SGML proved too complex for the web, while HTML is not sophisticated enough for the creation of complex, interactive web sites or web-based applications. XML is a "metalanguage" that enables users to create their own markup, both procedural and descriptive, optimized for web use.

XML will not replace HTML. XML provides an alternative for web developers in designing their own HTML DTDs, or customized versions of HTML. HTML is layout-oriented tagging, while XML is a content-oriented.

For more information on SGML and XML, visit the following web sites:

- SGML Source – www.sgmlsource.com
- The SGML/XML Web Page – www.oasis-open.org/cover
- The XML Industry Portal – www.xml.org

- The XML.commune web site – www.xml.com
- XMLInfo – www.xmlinfo.com
- World Wide Web Consortium – w3c.org/XML

SGML has been a standard in the automotive and aerospace industries for many years, to cite only a few major applications. As software and web publishers have focused more on HTML and XML applications, the following sections will concentrate specifically on these two file formats.

The HTML or XML file format can be used in online help formats in different ways:

- Plain HTML or XML files with images: these files are viewed with a web browser or viewer. Examples are JavaHelp and Apple Help.
- Compiled HTML or XML files: these files, for example HTML Help files, are compiled sets of HTML files.

In both formats, the files that need to be translated are HTML or XML files, and image or multimedia files, such as .jpg and .gif graphics, and movies or sounds.

The HTML language defines thousands of HTML tags, and each new HTML version introduces new tags. HTML tags are defined by the World Wide Web Consortium (W3C). Since very few tags are relevant to the translation task, the following sections will focus on a general outline of the HTML format and language-dependent tags. Tags normally do not need to be changed. However, it is sometimes necessary to change text *within* a tag.

4.2   Tagged File Formats

HTML and XML files are text files with tags that allow structuring of the content, page layout, text formatting, insertion of images, generation of forms, etc. Tags are typically enclosed in angled brackets (< and >). HTML and XML files can be viewed using browsers, such as Microsoft Internet Explorer or Netscape Navigator, or other viewers.

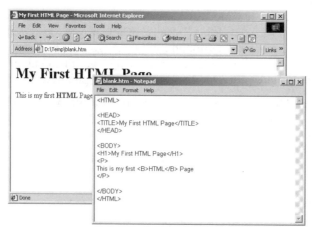

HTML or XML files are usually edited either in WYSIWYG mode, where the document layout is visible, or in source mode, where only text and tags are visible. Since translators will most likely be working in source mode, for example in translation memory tools or tag editors, it is important to know the general file components and tag types before starting to translate tagged files.

Note that there are two types of tags: internal and external. Internal tags are embedded in sentences, such as the `<B>` and `</B>` tags that mark the start and end of bold text. External tags are outside translatable segments and are used to mark paragraph content or formatting.

Translators should be able to edit internal tags, for example to change the formatting of words within a translated sentence from bold to italic, or to change English quotation marks to quotation marks which are standard in the target language. External tags, however, usually do not change between different language versions, so some editors or translation memory tools either hide or extract these external tags before translation.

The following example contains an English sentence with the Swedish translation. Note that the external tags (`<P>` and `</P>`) remain unchanged, but the internal tags (`<I>` and `</I>`) have been changed by the translator:

```
<P>Do you want the <I>Design Checker</I> to test whether your
publication will download quickly?</P>
<P>Vill du att <B>Layoutkontrollen</B> ska testa om publikationen
kommer att läsas in snabbt?</P>
```

Unlike XML, the HTML format has a specific number of pre-defined tags. Since XML is a metalanguage, an unlimited number of tags can be defined in a DTD using XML. Another difference is that HTML tags are mainly procedural, i.e. defining layout, and XML tags can be both procedural and descriptive.

4.3 HTML

HTML files can only contain tags which are defined in the DTDs for each HTML version; the HTML standard does not allow the user to create customized tags or markup. Most translation memory tools have integrated support for these standard HTML versions in their filtering process, so tags are automatically recognized, externalized, or made available for editing.

Each HTML file starts with the `<HTML>` tag and ends with `</HTML>`. HTML files consist of two sections, the header (HEAD tag) and the contents (BODY tag). The body of most HTML files contains text, images, comments, and JavaScript.

4.3.1 HEADER

The HEAD section contains the title and META tags, which describe the document properties. Here are some examples of elements included in the HEAD section:

- Title of the page, for example `<title>About converting existing help projects</title>`

- Style sheet definition, for example `<LINK REL="STYLESHEET" HREF="ota.css">`

- Character set used in the document, for example
  `<meta http-equiv="Content-Type" content="text/html; charset=iso-8859-1">`

- Application that was used to create the HTML file, for example `<meta name="GENERATOR" content="Microsoft HTML Help Workshop 4.0">`

- Keywords for search engines, for example `<META NAME="keywords" CONTENT="localization, translation, globalization">`

- Name of the document's author, for example `<META NAME="author" CONTENT="Bert Esselink">`

- Document descriptions for search engines, for example `<META NAME="description" CONTENT="This chapter deals with localization of online help documents.">`

The `<TITLE>` tag is the only mandatory element within an HTML header.

The other elements described are optional and can be used where appropriate. The header of the HTML file may also contain META tags which are not directly visible, but do require translation, such as the keywords and description keywords shown in the example.

4.3.2 BODY TEXT

The BODY section contains everything that appears on the page, including text, images, tables, and embedded JavaScript. The BODY tag can assume attributes that indicate to the browser how the HTML page should be displayed, e.g. which color the text should have, what background color should be used, and how links should appear.

Paragraphs within the BODY section can have styles, such as `<H1>` for Heading 1 or `<OL>` for ordered lists. Standard paragraphs are often enclosed in `<P>` and `</P>` tags. These are examples of external tags.

Within a paragraph, internal tags can be used to change the character formatting of a word or string. If a word is enclosed between `<B>` and `</B>` tags, for example, it is displayed in boldface type.

Hypertext links are inserted in text using the anchor tag (`<A>`). In the sentence "... is a `<A HREF="http://www.lisa.org">` LISA`</A>` member.", for example, the acronym LISA is hyperlinked to the URL for the LISA web site.

4.3.3 GRAPHICS

Most HTML pages contain links to images. Images are linked to HTML documents using the `<IMG>` tag. Graphics linked to HTML pages are usually in .gif or .jpg format. For example `<IMG SRC="Pebbles.gif">` inserts an image called pebbles.gif into the HTML document.

Links to graphics also define an alternative text that is displayed when the image is loading, or when the image is unavailable. This text is also displayed in a text balloon when the mouse pointer is placed on the image.

In the following example, an image called home.gif is inserted in the HTML file, and the alternative, translatable text is "Anteprima sito Web".

```
<img src="home.gif" alt="Anteprima sito Web" border="0">
```

Because graphics are often used to create banners with special fonts, colors and backgrounds, they pose the most challenges for translators. Ask the publisher for font information, layered graphic files with a separate text layer, or blank background images. For more information on graphics editing, refer to the Editing Graphics section on page 353.

4.3.4 COMMENTS

Comment text in HTML files is enclosed in `<!--` and `-->` tags.
For example:

```
<!-- This is comment text -->.
```

Please note that if an HTML file contains JavaScript, the JavaScript section may contain comment text which is preceded by two slashes (`//`).

Comment text is usually not translated.

4.3.5 EMBEDDED CODE

Many web technologies can be included in HTML pages, such as JavaScript, Java applets, VBScript, ASP, CGI, DHTML, ActiveX, Perl, ShockWave, Flash, and VRML. Scripting elements in HTML pages usually trigger an event on the server, for example a query in a database, or verification of data entered by a user in an HTML form. Others, such as DHTML, Flash, and VRML merely enhance web sites by adding multimedia features. Web server applications such as ASP or CGI are typically used to generate HTML pages on-the-fly from information stored in databases. To localize ASP or CGI applications, translators need access to the program's resources, comparable to regular software applications.

Tip: Never just download ASP or CGI pages from a web site and localize the text in these pages, as they may contain variable text retrieved from a database or separate *include* file. Publishers should provide localizers with the source ASP or CGI templates, containing only the static text that needs to be translated. All variable content strings should be translated in the database or *include* file which publishes to the ASP or CGI files on a live web site.

Most of these elements are created using a software development environment such as Microsoft Visual Studio or Java, and are comparable to programming code. It is, therefore, essential for translators working on embedded elements to have programming skills or knowledge of coding basics. Translatable text is in most cases enclosed in quotation marks (" and ").

The `<SCRIPT LANGUAGE="JavaScript">` tag indicates that a JavaScript component is included in the section following the tag. Many HTML pages on the Internet contain Java applets, which are Java applications that do not run stand-alone, but can only be run from an HTML page within a Java-compatible browser. Java applets are marked with the `<APPLET>` tag. The following HTML example describes a Java applet, with an ALT tag defining text that will be displayed when users are using a web browser that does not support Java:

```
<applet
    name="Blink"
    code="Blink.class"
    codebase="/<i>your_home_directory</i>/jws/Blink"
    width="500"
    height="600"
    align="Top"
    alt="If you had a java-enabled browser, you would see an applet
here."
</applet>
```

The following example contains a text overlay applet, where text is placed on top of an image. Only the text following `text value` would require translation. The applet box can be resized using the coordinates in the first line, which should match the sizes of the `AdminBanner.gif` image used. For information on translating embedded code in HTML files, refer to Chapter 3, Software Translation.

```
<APPLET codebase="../Home" code="SATextOverlay.class" width=534
height=49>
<param name=image value="./images/AdminBanner.gif">
<param name=text value="Text Overlay Applet Example">
<param name=font value="SansSerif-plain-28">
<param name=posx value="68">
<param name=posy value="center">
</APPLET>
```

Text used in applets can also be stored in resource bundles. For more information on resource bundles, refer to the Java section on page 137.

The best way to ensure that everything has been translated is to open the HTML file in a browser while translating it in a text editor. Save the HTML source and click the Refresh button in the browser to see the changes.

4.3.6 STATUS BAR TEXT

One tag which may be easily overlooked is the `onmouseover=window.status` tag. The text following this tag is displayed in the browser status bar, when the mouse pointer is placed on a link.

```
<a href="edit.htm" onmouseover="window.status='Copying and pasting
text';    return true">Copy and Paste</a>
```

This line displays "Copying and pasting text" in the status bar, when the mouse is on the link "Copy and Paste".

4.4 XML

Unlike HTML, XML files can contain tags which are defined in a customized DTD. Therefore, in order to correctly identify and translate text in XML files, it is important to obtain the DTD associated with to the XML file.

According to the W3C Recommendation for XML, "each XML document has both a logical and a physical structure. Physically, the document is composed of units called entities. An entity may refer to other entities to cause their inclusion in the document. A document begins in a "root" or document entity. Logically, the document is composed of declarations, elements, comments, character references, and processing instructions, all of which are indicated in the document by explicit markup."

In most cases, all translatable text is included in the XML files, but it is possible for entity labels or status descriptions to be externalized to DTDs. Always check the DTD files for translatables.

The Netscape code (Mozilla) is a useful resource for information on translating XML files, and it is publicly available on the web. It was translated by a large number of volunteers into many different languages. It can be accessed by visiting the Mozilla Localization Project area on the Mozilla web site at www.mozilla.org.

4.4.1 HEADER

The header, or prolog, of each XML document starts with an `<XNL>` declaration, such as `<?xml version="1.0" encoding="shift_jis"?>`.

The `<?` and `?>` delimiters indicate a processing instruction for an XML parser. For XML documents that do not use a DTD, the `<XML>` declaration will include a standalone statement, as in `<?xml version="1.0" standalone="yes"?>`. However, most XML documents will contain a DTD specification, as in:

```
<!DOCTYPE advert SYSTEM "http://www.foo.org/ad.dtd">.
```

A DTD is a file (or group of files), written in XML, which contains a formal definition of a particular type of document. DTD files can be stored locally or on a remote web server. XML files containing a DTD specification are called "valid" XML files. DTD files typically contain no localizable text or settings, unless the text defines a content structure which needs to be adjusted for another country, such as an address format.

4.4.2   BODY TEXT

In XML files, paragraphs are usually enclosed in markup that describes the content of the paragraph, not just the formatting, for example:

```
<Member>
  <First Name>John</First Name>
  <Second Name>Waters</Second Name>
  <Address>7 Highway Drive</Address>
  <City>San Diego</City>
  <Zip>80231</Zip>
</Member>
```

These tags are defined in the DTD, which is specified in the header of the XML file.

4.4.3   GRAPHICS

In XML files, graphics are treated as any other document link, which can be represented in a number of ways, for example:

```
<LOGO HREF="logo_big.gif" STYLE="IMAGE-WIDE"/>
<LOGO HREF="logo_med.gif" STYLE="IMAGE"/>
```

or

```
<IMAGE_URL>http://myweb.com/shared/image.gif</IMAGE_URL>.
```

Compared to HTML, the linking specifications provide much better control over the display and behavior of links, so a web author can specify, for example, whether or not to have an image appear when the page is loaded.

In many cases, however, the regular HTML `<img src=` tag is used to load images for regular display.

4.4.4   COMMENTS

As in HTML, comment text is enclosed in `<!--` and `-->` tags.
For example:

```
<!-- This is comment text -->.
```

Please note that if an XML file contains JavaScript, the JavaScript section may contain comment text which is preceded by two slashes (`//`).

Comment text is usually not translated.

4.4.5   EMBEDDED CODE

For more information on embedded code in XML or HTML files, such as JavaScript, refer to the Embedded Code section on page 209.

The `<SCRIPT LANGUAGE="JavaScript">` tag indicates that a JavaScript component is defined in the section following the tag. It is also possible that JavaScripts have been externalized to files with the .js extension. The XML file will then only contain a reference or link to this script file, such as `<html:script src="run.js" encoding="UTF-8"/>`.

4.5 Translation Approach

Many tools have been developed for creating and editing HTML and XML files, by many companies and individuals. Translators can choose to work with a combination of tools, depending on the project size, specifics, and client requirements. Here are some examples of tools that can be used by translators:

- WYSIWYG editors
- Text editors (directly in the source code)
- Protected tag editors
- Translation memory tools

The following sections discuss the advantages and disadvantages of working with each of these tool types.

4.5.1 WYSIWYG EDITORS

WYSIWYG HTML or XML editors are applications that enable the user to create pages, where all page and text layout is visible and the markup is not displayed. Most current word processors and desktop publishing programs have HTML editing features. There are also many other commercially available HTML editors available, and some developers even offer their tools for free.

Here are some examples of commonly used HTML editors:

- Microsoft FrontPage – www.microsoft.com
- Adobe PageMill – www.adobe.com
- NetObjects Fusion – www.netobjects.com
- Sausage Software Hotdog Pro – www.sausage.com
- SoftQuad HotMetal Pro – www.softquad.com
- Netscape Communicator – www.netscape.com

For a complete list of HTML editors and related web site authoring applications, refer to the Tools section on the World Wide Web Consortium web site at www.w3c.org/Tools.

The following image shows the editing windows of Microsoft Frontpage.

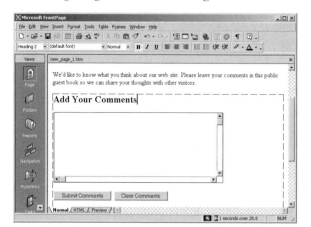

The main advantage of translating files in a WYSIWYG HTML editor is that the translator can view and edit the text, while displaying all layout and graphical information. Furthermore, it is more difficult to corrupt or delete tags from the HTML code.

A major disadvantage is that HTML editors tend to re-write HTML code to reflect their proprietary default standards. This often means that HTML markup is changed, deleted or added automatically, simply by opening and saving a file in a WYIWYG HTML editor. If the HTML file contains embedded code, such as JavaScript, the editor may completely change or delete various sections, depending on the level of support for JavaScript or the version of the editor.

HTML files should be translated in the same version of the editor that was used to create the files, to avoid such problems. To find out which editor was used to create an HTML file, view the HTML source and check whether the HEAD section contains a line such as:

```
<meta name="GENERATOR" content="Microsoft FrontPage 4.0">
```

The GENERATOR meta tag describes which editor was used to create the file. Nevertheless, the web developer may have added some content in the raw HTML code after these files were created using the HTML editor, so in virtually all cases it is recommended not to use WYSIWYG HTML editors for translation purposes.

As an alternative, use one of the tool types described in the following sections. With these tools, users work directly in the HTML markup, but a browser or viewer window enables them to preview the translations in layout mode.

There are few WYSIWYG editors are available for XML; this is because XML files, as a rule, do not store layout information. All layout information in XML files is stored in Cascading Style Sheets (CSS) or XML Stylesheet Language (XSL).

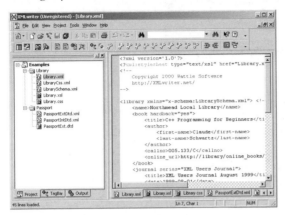

Here are some examples of commonly used XML editors:

- XMetal – www.softquad.com
- XMLwriter – www.xmlwriter.net
- XML Spy – www.xmlspy.com

A comprehensive list of available XML editors can be found at www.xmlsoftware.com.

4.5.2 TEXT EDITORS

For reasons explained in the previous section, translators, in most cases, edit HTML or XML documents as text files, where they need to locate the translatable text between the HTML tags.

The Source command from the View menu in Microsoft Internet Explorer, for example, displays the HTML source code in a Notepad window. Another option is to right-click on the HTML page or frame and select the View Source command. Any change entered and saved in Notepad is displayed in the browser when the Refresh button is selected.

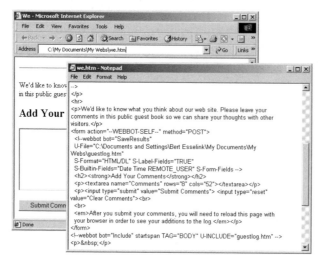

There are a number of disadvantages to translating HTML files directly in the source, including the following:

- The layout of the HTML file is not visible; only a preview can be seen in a browser window.

- It is relatively easy to corrupt the HTML code, for example by inadvertently deleting < markers.

- There is a risk that translatable text will be overlooked. Text may be located within tags, or not directly recognizable as translatable text.

- Translators may translate text that should not be changed, for example comment text or variables.

- Very few text editors have spell checking tools. Furthermore, spell-checking is virtually impossible, because all markup will be considered as spelling errors.

- Special and accented characters or tabs are often represented by named or numeric character entity references, which define replacement text for escape sequences. For example, the © character is displayed in HTML code as © and the é character as é.

By using named or numeric entities in HTML, the user can rely on the correct display of extended characters on all platforms and browsers, although different HTML versions define different entities and not all browsers support all entries.

Here is the recommended approach to specifying character encoding for HTML files:

- Make sure that the web server hosting the HTML pages provides the charset parameter correctly in the Content-Type: header, or/and add the correct <META> element. This is very important even for iso-8859-1 (Latin-1). Even though the HTTP specification identifies this as the default, browsers outside the United States and Europe do not recognize it as the default; otherwise the majority of the documents displayed to a reader would look garbled.

- Use the byte codes for all characters covered by the encoding.

- Use decimal numeric character references for characters outside the specified encoding, for example Ä for Ä.

- Use named character entities only in cases where no editor is appropriate for these characters, and where it is difficult to handle numbers.

A complete list of entity references for HTML can be found at www.hexadyne.com/ entities.htm or www.htmlhelp.com (search for "entities").

A good alternative to translating HTML or XML files in basic text editors, such as Notepad, is to use a text-based HTML editor. These types of editors enable users to edit the HTML code in text-mode with all tags and HTML markup displayed in different colors. An example of a text-based HTML editor is Allaire HomeSite.

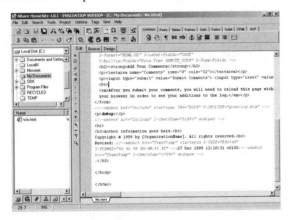

Some HTML editors, such as HomeSite, contain tools that automatically search and replace extended characters with HTML equivalents. When using a text-based HTML editor to translate HTML files, check that this feature is present, otherwise the user will be forced to enter an ampersand code for every accented character.

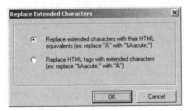

HomeSite not only enables users to edit HTML pages, but also to view pages in an external or internal browser, check the spelling of pages, search and replace strings, and verify links. For more information on HomeSite, visit the Allaire web site at www.allaire.com.

4.5.3 TRANSLATION MEMORY TOOLS

In addition to using HTML editors or text editors to translate HTML or XML files, translation memory tools can also be used very effectively. Most translation memory tools have standard filters for HTML files. HTML files usually contain very repetitive text, so it is worthwhile using translation memory, because of the substantial time and cost savings. Furthermore, translating updates of web sites is much easier and quicker if a translation memory of the previous version exists.

Examples of translation memory tools that support the HTML format are Trados Translator's Workbench, IBM TranslationManager, STAR Transit, SDLX, and Atril Déjà Vu. For more information on translation memory tools, refer to Chapte r11, Translation Technology.

HTML filters in translation memory tools either externalize all markup and only display the translatable text to the translator, or mark all markup using different colors or text styles. The following image shows both methods, using the same HTML file.

The filters used to import the HTML files in these translation memory tools need to support all the HTML tags in the translatable files. It is important to run some tests with the HTML files before starting translation. Problems can be expected when the HTML files contain embedded code, such as JavaScript, because not all translation memory tools can distinguish translatable text strings. The best way to check whether filters in an HTML tool find all translatable text is to compare word count statistics between different tools.

Considering the fact that XML files usually contain customized markup, translation memory tools need to be able to separate tags from translatable text. Basically, this means that a separate filter is required for each XML file. Most translation memory tools read the DTD file, which defines the tags in the XML files in order to identify the tags and tag types.

4.5.4 PROTECTED TAG EDITORS

A new generation of editors for HTML, XML or even SGML documents are the tag editors, equipped with translation memory functionality. These tools enable translators to work in the HTML source, with only the relevant markup visible to translators. A translation memory engine keeps track of all translations, while they are being inserted.

Some translation memory tools have integrated tag editors, others distribute them as stand-alone tools. Trados Translator's Workbench, for example, now contains an add-on called Tag Editor which can be used to translate SGML, XML, Workbench RTF, and HTML documents in a semi-WYSIWYG environment.

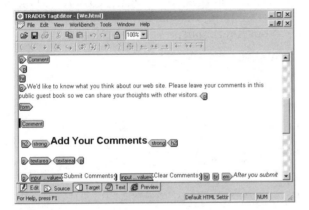

TagEditor protects all tags in the file, and enables users to specify markup settings or to import DTD files for XML and SGML files.

A comparable tool is SDL's Html-CAT, which contains an HTML4.0 parser, file management, and translation memory features.

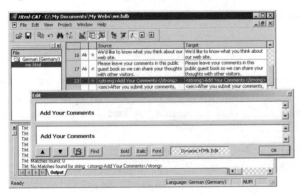

For more information on translation memory and other computer aided translation tools, refer to Chapter 11.

4.6   JavaHelp

JavaHelp is a platform-independent system for application help and online documentation. It is written in Java and provides capabilities for navigating, searching, and displaying information.

4.6.1   INTRODUCTION

JavaHelp is an on-screen help system used for Java applications, applets, and JavaBeans components. JavaHelp includes a help viewer, and works with both plain HTML files and with compressed HTML files. The .JAR format is used to encapsulate help information, i.e. HTML files and images, into a single, compressed file which is comparable to the Windows HTML Help .chm file format. Compression and encapsulation is not required but is recommended.

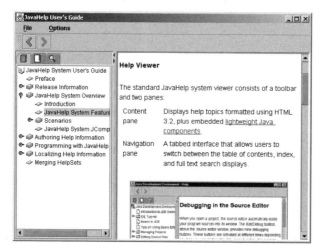

More information on JavaHelp can be found on the Sun Java web site at java.sun.com (search for "JavaHelp").

Navigation

The main navigational features in the JavaHelp viewer are the table of contents, keyword index, and full-text search feature. Each of these navigators comes with a metadata file in XML format that contains navigational data. These files are comparable to the HTML Help .hhc and .hhk files.

Most of the navigation and search features included in JavaHelp are similar to those included in HTML Help, i.e. the left pane displays the table of contents, index or full-text search feature, and the help contents are displayed on the right.

JavaHelp windows can also be embedded in application user interfaces or browsers.

Creation

JavaHelp uses HTML documents and .gif/.jpg images as source files. A JavaHelp project is compiled using a project file (called HelpSet) with the extension .hs by running the Jar command which is included in the Java Development Kit (JDK). The .hs file is an XML file containing all help file settings and defining all components. It defines the title of the JavaHelp file, the navigators (table of contents, index, full-text search), and map file containing a list of included files.

HTML files used for JavaHelp can be edited using any HTML editor, but it is recommended to edit them using the tool used to create them, or to edit them as HTML code. The JavaHelp web site contains a list of help authoring tools for JavaHelp, such as the ForeFront ForeHTML Pro (www.ff.com).

The compiler is generally used in conjunction with a macro shell, such as Robohelp HTML or Doc-to-Help. These shells add extra authoring, conversion, and testing features to the help compiler.

Refer to Chapter 7, Online Help Engineering and Testing, for more information on compiling and testing JavaHelp files.

4.6.2 TRANSLATING JAVAHELP

The actual help file text is contained in HTML files. Other files that require translation in a JavaHelp project are the table of contents, HelpSet (.hs), keyword index files, and images (.gif or .jpg).

HTML files are generally translated using a translation memory tool. When editing HTML files without translation memory, use the appropriate editor, preferably the one used to create the source files. In addition to HTML files containing the actual help content, JavaHelp projects include XML files containing the project settings, table of contents, index, and file mappings. For each of these XML files, a DTD describing the markup and the structure is included in the JavaHelp development environment, in \doc\spec\dtd.

The sections below discuss translation approaches for each of the translatable file types in HTML Help projects.

HTML Files

HTML files used in JavaHelp projects can be edited as regular HTML files. For more information on editing HTML files, refer to the HTML section on page 207.

The following image displays a JavaHelp topic, along with its HTML code:

HS Files

HelpSet (.hs) files contain all settings used to compile the JavaHelp file. The HelpSet file also contains all the information needed to run the help system. An .hs file is an XML file that can be edited in a text or XML editor.

This section lists the sections in an .hs file that may require translation.

The title of the JavaHelp file, which is displayed in the title bar of the help file, is translated in the .hs file. In a text editor, translate the words following the <TITLE> tag. For example:

```
<helpset version="1.0">
  <!-- title -->
  <title>Java Development Environment - Hilfe</title>
```

The view definitions may also contain translatable text, such as the table of contents definition below.

```
  <!-- views -->
  <view>
    <name>TOC</name>
    <label>Das Inhaltsverzeichnis</label>
    <type>javax.help.TOCView</type>
    <data>IdeHelpTOC.xml</data>
  </view>
```

The .hs file in most cases also contains labels for the index and full-text search views.

Table of Contents and Index Files

In JavaHelp projects, two XML files define the table of contents and index of a JavaHelp file, i.e. the entries displayed in the left pane of the viewer window.

These files have names like IdeHelpIndex.xml and IdeHelpTOC.xml. Here is an example of a section from a table of contents file:

```
<tocitem text="Menüs">
    <tocitem text="Menü &quot;Datei&quot;" target="menus.file"/>
   <tocitem text="Menü &quot;Bearbeiten&quot;" target="menus.edit"/>
     <tocitem text="Menü &quot;Erstellen&quot;"
target="menus.windows"/>
     <tocitem text="Menü &quot;Hilfe&quot;" target="menus.help"/>
   </tocitem>
```

Here is an example of a section from an index file:

```
<indexitem text="breakpoints">
    <indexitem text="advanced functions" target="debug.breakpoint"/>
    <indexitem text="conditional" target="debug.conditional"/>
    <indexitem text="list of" target="debug.breakpoint"/>
    <indexitem text="location" target="debug.breakpoint"/>
    <indexitem text="window" target="debug.breakpoint"/>
  </indexitem>
```

It is important to note that only the text following `text=` attribute should be translated.

5   Readme Files

Readme files are included with application setup disks to provide users with last-minute information that was probably not available when the manuals were printed or online help files finalized. Furthermore, corrections and additions to the manual or online help, platform-specific compatibility information, and any additional setup instructions can be placed in a readme file.

5.1   Introduction

Readme files usually are text files and usually have a .txt extension. As a rule, they do not contain any character or paragraph formatting. Translation can be performed in a text editor running on the target platform.

Readme files for the Windows platform can be edited using Notepad or any other Windows-based text editor or word processor. Mac OS readme files can be translated using SimpleText or any other Mac OS text editor or word processor.

On the Windows platform, readme files may also be in Windows 3.1 Write (.wri), Windows 9x Wordpad (.doc) or HTML (.html) format. Wordpad files, with the .doc extension, are, in fact, Microsoft Word 6 documents. It is possible to translate them using Word, but the final layout should be done in Wordpad.

The original English readme file may often contain carriage returns at the end of each line. If this is the case, use regular paragraphs for translation and, after proofreading and QA, save the file as "text only with line breaks".

5.2 Translation Approach

Since the English readme file is often finalized before the localization project is completed, it is possible that much of the information contained in the readme can be corrected in the localized documentation or online help. For example, if corrections to the English user guide are described in the readme file, there may still be time to implement these changes in the localized user guide. This can reduce the size of the readme file considerably. Check with the publisher to ascertain whether they prefer a fully translated readme file, or corrections applied to the translated material.

6 Further Reading

The books listed below all cover various topics on technical translation.

Newmark, Peter. 1998. *More Paragraphs on Translation*. Multilingual Matters, ISBN 1-853-59402-4.

Samuelsson-Brown, Geoffrey. 1998. *A Practical Guide for Translators*. Multilingual Matters, ISBN 1-853-59428-8.

Sofer, Morry. 2000. *The Translator's Handbook*. Schreiber Publishing, ISBN 1-887-56348-2.

Chapter 7:
Online Help Engineering and Testing

This chapter contains information on engineering and testing localized online help files on standard operating systems. Topics include compiling, engineering, and testing commonly used help systems, such as HTML Help, JavaHelp and Apple Help.

This chapter includes the following sections:

1. Introduction
2. Evaluation and Preparation
3. Windows
4. Mac OS
5. HTML and XML
6. Testing Localized Online Help
7. Further Reading

Related chapters are Chapter6, which contains information for translators, and Chapter 10, which contains a section on creating and editing graphics.

1 Introduction

Online help engineering is a central component of the whole localization process, and it is often underestimated. Engineers usually have a wide range of tasks and responsibilities, which will vary from one company to another, including:

- Project evaluation and setup
- Compilation and testing
- Processing updates
- Editing graphics

Because software localization vendors usually work with a broad portfolio of clients, online help engineers need to familiarize themselves with a large number of different online help systems, platforms, tools, and file formats.

This chapter covers the basic tasks involved in engineering localized online help projects, and includes specific information on commonly used help formats on the Windows and Mac OS platforms. Chapter 4, Software Engineering, contains information on engineering activities related to localized software. Chapte r10,

Graphics Localization, contains information on editing graphics and creating screen captures.

As mentioned above, localization engineers require an in-depth knowledge of many different operating systems, utilities, translation tools, development environments, and localization models. Most localization vendors expect, as a minimum, that their engineers have the following skills:

- Working knowledge of installation and configuration management of the most common operating systems and platforms

- Experience with industry-standard online help development environments, e.g. Microsoft HTML Help Workshop, Microsoft Help Workshop, RoboHELP, Doc-to-Help, Apple Help

- In-depth knowledge of markup languages, such as HTML and XML, and commonly used editors

- Knowledge of international layout issues and desktop publishing basics, such as graphics, style sheets, and templates

- Understanding of language and character set issues in online help systems

- Experience using macro and scripting languages, such as Visual Basic for Applications, Perl, and JavaScript

- Professional and creative approach to problem-solving and bug-fixing

- Awareness of localization models and workflows, and project scheduling issues

- Experience selecting and using computer aided translation (CAT) tools

- Knowledge of Internet technology and communication software and protocols

- Excellent communication skills, both written and oral

- Foreign language skills (preferred)

Online help localization engineers need to have wide range of software applications at their disposal in order to produce the highest quality localized online help. In addition to the standard Office and Internet applications, a localization engineering "toolkit" will most likely include the following:

- Industry-standard online help compilers, such as Microsoft HTML Help Workshop or the Microsoft Help Compiler

- An advanced text editor, such as TextPad or Programmer's File Editor

- An image editor, such as Paint Shop Pro or Adobe Photoshop

- A screen capture utility, such as Collage Complete

- File management utilities, such as diff tools and file synchronizers

- Online help testing tools, such as HelpQA and HtmlQA

- HTML validation tools

- (Evaluation versions of) all commonly used translation memory tools, such as Trados Translator's Workbench, Atril Déjà Vu, and STAR Transit

Depending on the projects, development tools such as Java Development Kit (JDK) or scripting tools such as Perl or Awk will be required.

2 Evaluation and Preparation

When working with software products or online help files, it is important to fully and thoroughly evaluate and prepare the source materials. The consequences of not checking can be quite significant, for example, if files that contain errors are sent out for translation into four languages, any errors originating in the source files will need to be fixed four times!.

The purpose of project evaluation is to try to spot potential problems with source materials before the translation cycle. Apart from evaluating and checking the source files, all material needs to be prepared for translation in the most efficient and cost-effective way.

At this point in the project, localization engineers should focus on the following tasks:

- Checking source material
- Test-compiling
- Preparing for translation

The end of this section provides a check list that may help determine whether the source material is complete and ready for translation.

2.1 Checking Source Material

In the online help localization kit, locate the files necessary to compile the online help file and check whether all source material is valid and complete. The source material must be checked in several stages:

1. Is the localization kit complete, i.e. does it contain all files that were expected?
2. Does it contain extraneous files?
3. Were instructions or guidelines included?
4. Are all files valid and virus-free?
5. Does the localization kit include file types that are unknown or unreadable?
6. Are duplicate files included? Are there any files with identical names but with different dates or properties?
7. Does the localization kit include information for the project manager, such as schedules or word counts? These files should be given to the project manager for evaluation.

8. Does the kit include information for linguists, such as previously localized versions, translation memories, or glossaries. These files should be given to the translators.

It is advisable to copy all contents of a localization kit to the hard drive and browse through the folders and files. Also, carefully read the guidelines provided to check whether any special hardware or software is required to build or test the online help, for example, an online help shell such as RoboHELP or Doc-to-Help.

2.2   Test-Compiling

Test-compiling an online help project before it is translated will automatically show whether all required files have been included. Missing source or image files will be reported by the compiler. If the compiler reports many errors, report the results to the publisher, and ascertain whether the files are complete and ready for translation.

Here are some advantages to be gained from running the test-compilation on the source material:

- Compilation problems are identified early in the process.
- Missing files are identified.
- Configuration issues are flagged at an early stage.
- The validity of the compiled online help file can be addressed.

If there are problems compiling the English product, these problems should be resolved before the translation cycle.

It is important to use the right compiler for the online help file. Refer to the Compiling sections in this chapter for information on the compilers to be used.

Once the online help file compiles with no errors, check whether the compiled file, such as a .chm or .hlp file, is the same size as the original help file. If there is a substantial file size difference, ask the publisher whether the increase in file size will cause any problems. It may be useful to open the compiled file and compare the layout with the original version. If the layout is entirely different, something may be wrong with the style sheet information.

It is advisable to use an online help testing or validation tool to verify the validity of the source files, in particular, the hypertext links. Examples of such tools are HelpQA for WinHelp projects and HtmlQA or Trans Web Express for HTML projects. In the case of HTML or XML projects, run a tag validation tool on the source files. For more information on these testing tools, refer to the Testing Localized Online Help section on page 278.

2.3   Single Source Publishing

Software publishers are now using the "single-source-multiple-output" method more frequently to create the source as well as translated documents. When a printed manual has been translated, for example, the online help for the same application is not translated, but converted from the translated manual, or vice versa. Or, when one set of source files has been translated, these files are used to generate different online help formats, online documentation in PDF format, and printed manuals.

Because of the array of online help and online documentation formats, online help engineers are often asked to convert translated files from one format to another. Usually, help authoring tools, such as eHelp RoboHELP or Wextech Doc-to-Help, are used to automate this task.

During evaluation and preparation, it is important to know if documents need to be converted or translated!

2.3.1 USING ROBOHELP

RoboHELP is a help authoring tool that offers a fast and easy way to create help systems. RoboHELP Office 2000 will allow the user to use a single project to generate any standard Help format, whether it be JavaHelp, Microsoft WinHelp, Microsoft HTML Help, printed documentation, or other formats. The RoboHELP Office includes RoboHELP for WinHelp, RoboHELP for Microsoft HTML Help, RoboHELP for JavaHelp, eHelp's single-source technology and a collection of help utilities.

For translation purposes, the RoboHELP toolkit does not need to be installed, since the translation will be done in the source files, which are in standard HTML or RTF format. For compilation and page layout purposes, however, the RoboHELP tools and templates should be installed. Opening project files will display a set of Robohelp tools used to configure the help project, and to compile and run the help file.

For more information on RoboHELP, visit the eHelp web site at www.ehelp.com.

2.3.2 USING DOC-TO-HELP

Doc-to-Help is an application that enables publishers to create printed documentation and online Help in several formats, including WinHelp, HTML Help, and JavaHelp, and from a single source using different templates for Word or RTF files and cascading style sheets for HTML files.

The Doc-to-Help true single-source approach enables the user to create and maintain online help and printed documentation from one source document. For example, Doc-to-Help automatically converts index markers to help keyword entries, titles to help page topic titles, and it automatically generates pop-up definitions, hypertext links, and content files.

Doc-to-Help Professional 2000 also contains the AnswerWorks technology, which includes natural language processing in online help files. Users simply type in questions using their own words, and AnswerWorks analyzes each question in the background and lists the most pertinent Help topics. Please note that AnswerWorks only supports a limited number of foreign languages.

For more information on Doc-to-Help, visit the Wextech web site at www.wextech.com.

2.4 Preparing for Translation

Once all source material is complete and compiles without problems, check the following:

- Which files need to be translated?
- How much of the existing translations can be re-used or leveraged?
- What is the most efficient translation method or approach?

A thorough preparation of the source material should provide a translation kit that makes it easy for translators to start working directly on the files, and avoids re-translation of text that has already been translated before.

2.4.1 TEXT FEATURES

If online help files are to be translated in a translation memory tool, it is advisable to scan the source files for formatting and other issues that may cause problems.

For more information on translation memory tool segmentation, refer to the Segmentation section on page 362.

2.4.2 TRANSLATABLE FILES

If the online help localization kit does not contain a list of files that need to be translated, they can be located in the build environment. In WinHelp projects, translatable text is usually included in RTF, .cnt, .hpj and .bmp files, in HTML-based projects in HTML or XML files and .gif/.jpg. Refer to the File Types sections in this chapter for more information on translatable files in localization kits. If it is not clear which files should be translated, create a list of translatable files and ask the publisher for confirmation.

In addition to identifying translatable text in the source files, it is important to identify any image files that may require localization, such as screen captures or other graphics. Most current online help systems also support embedded sound, movie or animation files, so check these components for translatable items.

If HTML or XML files contain a lot of embedded code or scripting, it is advisable to process these as software rather than online help files. For more information on these file types, refer to the Embedded Code section on page 209.

2.4.3 LEVERAGE

With most online help localization projects, it is possible to re-use existing translations from the following sources:

- Previously localized versions of the online help
- Localized versions of other online help files from the same publisher
- Localized versions of other documentation types from the same publisher, for example printed documentation
- Terminology from software user interface glossaries

Re-using existing translations will not only reduce the word counts and therefore increase translation speed, it will also improve terminology consistency. For example, when translating version 4 of an online help file, it may be possible to automatically pre-translate 90% of the file if a localized version 3 exists.

The way in which existing translations can be leveraged depends entirely on the file format and the translation approach. The following table shows some typical scenarios, where the first column indicates whether a text has been previously translated, the second column indicates whether a translation memory tool was used, and the third column shows a typical localization approach in each of the cases.

Translated?	TM used?	Approach
no	no	Translate from scratch using TM
yes	no	Align previous translations to create TM
yes	yes	Use existing translation memory

Depending on the quality and the one-to-one correspondence of the previous translations, alignment can be a relatively easy task. For more information on alignment and translation memory, refer to Chapter 11, Translation Technology.

2.4.4 TRANSLATION TOOL SELECTION

The selected translation approach depends largely on the tools strategy adopted by the localization vendor, whether they have developed their own tool set, or elected to use the standard commercial tools?

Either way, the vendor will need to decide, if the publisher has not already decided, how to send the files out for translation.

The choice of tool should be based on the criteria listed below:

- Publisher instructs the vendor to use a specific industry standard tool.
- Publisher instructs the vendor to use a proprietary tool. Some software publishers have developed their own localization tools, which have to be used on all projects.
- Are the investments for developing or purchasing a translation memory tool justifiable? For example, a 3000 word online help project may not justify the costs of a professional tool like Trados Translator's Workbench.
- Which method is safest, i.e. how can we minimize or reduce the risk of translators damaging or altering the online help markup or embedded codes? For example, if HTML files are translated using a text editor, it is very easy to inadvertently alter the markup surrounding translatable strings.
- Is the file format supported by the tool? Some translation memory tools, for example, do not support XML files.

- Is it possible or easy to re-use translations if updates need to be processed during the project?

- Does the tool support all target languages, especially double-byte or bi-directional languages?

In the case of custom online help file types, a text filter or parser will need to be created, using regular expressions in scripting languages, such as Perl or Awk. Regular expressions are patterns used for searching text in data. Not all translation memory tools are equipped with customized filters utilities. For more information on filters, refer to the Translation Memory tools section in Chapter 11, Translation Technology.

2.5   Check List

If the publisher has not supplied the vendor with detailed guidelines or instructions, ask the following questions to get a complete overview of the work to be done and the services expected.

2.5.1   ONLINE HELP COMPILATION

Here is a list of questions on compilation issues for an online help project. If these issues are unclear from the localization kit, they should be discussed with the publisher:

- ✓ Which compiler and which version should be used?
- ✓ What is the name of the online help file that is being compiled?
- ✓ Are specific tools required for compiling the online help?
- ✓ Should *locale* information be changed in the resource files?

2.5.2   SOURCE MATERIAL

Here is a list of questions on the source material for an online help project:

- ✓ Which online help source files need to be translated?
- ✓ Which editor should be used to edit the source files?
- ✓ Which graphics need to be translated?
- ✓ Are blank or layered versions and font information for the images available?
- ✓ Do the files contain country-specific information to be changed, such as default page sizes, currency symbols, etc?
- ✓ Are previously translated versions of the source files or translation memories available?

2.5.3   TESTING

Here is a list of questions on testing an online help project:

- ✓ On which platforms should the online help be tested?
- ✓ On which viewers or web browsers should the localized online help be tested?
- ✓ Which help testing tools are preferred?

A well-constructed localization kit should address most of these issues. Refer to the Creating Localization Kits section on page 48 for more information on localization kit contents.

3 Windows

The most commonly used online help systems on the Windows platform are the Microsoft HTML Help and WinHelp. For a general introduction and more information on these help formats, refer to the Windows section in Chapter 6, Online Help Translation. Chapter 6 contains information on the file types to be translated and the recommended approach, whereas this chapter focuses on compiling online help files, and specifying language and character settings.

3.1 HTML Help

HTML Help is a help system that enables the user to create help files or web pages in HTML format. Like WinHelp, HTML Help uses a project file to combine help topic, contents, index, image, and other source files into one file.

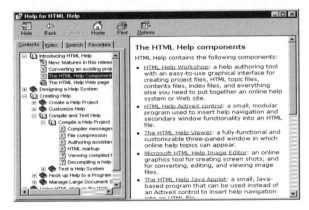

Sets of HTML source files and .jpg or .gif images are compiled into a single, compressed file with the .chm extension.

Refer to the HTML Help section on page 173 for more information on HTML Help.

3.1.1 INTRODUCTION

HTML Help projects require localization engineers to have extensive knowledge of the HTML language, because most of the content is in HTML format.

The following sections will discuss all engineering tasks involved in localizing HTML Help files, i.e. compiling, engineering, and testing.

3.1.2 FILE TYPES

When evaluating an online help build environment, it is important to first identify the translatable files.

The following table lists the different file types that are likely to be included in an HTML Help localization kit. It also indicates whether the file may contain localizable text or settings.

Extension	File Type	Localizable?
.ali	alias file	no
.chi	index file for CD-ROM use	no
.chk	index file for MSDN help system	no
.chm	compiled HTML Help file	no
.chq	full-text search file of combined CHMs	no
.chw	merged keywords file (temporary)	no
.css	cascading style sheet	yes
.dat (hh.dat)	favorites file	no
.gif	graphic	yes
.hh	header file for context-sensitive help	no
.hhc	sitemap file with table of contents	yes
.hhk	sitemap file with index entries	yes
.hhp	project file	yes
.htm or .html	HTML file	yes
.jpg	graphic	yes
.js	JavaScript file	no
.log	HTML Help compiler log file	no
.ocx	ActiveX control	no
.png	graphic (portable network graphic)	yes
.stp	stop list	yes
.txt	text pop-ups file	yes
.wav	sound file	yes
.xml	XML file	yes
.zip	compressed file	no

To identify the translatable files in the build environment, first check which files are included in the compilation. In HTML Help projects, this information is stored in the [FILES] section of the .hhp file. Compare the file list in this file with the files included in the build environment. The build environment may contain extra files or images which may not require localization.

3.1.3 COMPILING HTML HELP

To compile or edit HTML Help projects, use Microsoft HTML Help Workshop, which includes the compiler. This tool can be downloaded from the Microsoft MSDN web site at msdn.microsoft.com (search for "HTML Help Workshop"), or from one of the web sites listed in the Windows section on page 172.

A typical HTML Help project consists of a help project (.hhp) file, a contents (.hhc) file, an index (.hhk) file, and folders containing the topic files (\HTML) and graphics (\Images). Refer to the Creation section on page 174 for more information on these files and how they relate to traditional WinHelp project files.

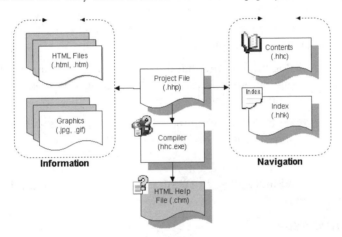

To compile an HTML Help project, follow these steps:

1. Create a new folder with a language code in the name, for example \Help_DE, and copy all English source files to this folder.

2. Make sure all translated HTML files and graphics have replaced or overwritten the original English files. To check that no old, untranslated files remain in the folders, display the file list sorted by Date.

3. Start HTML Help Workshop and open the project file (.hhp) using the Open command from the File menu. The project settings are displayed in the left window pane.

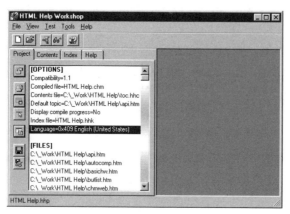

4. Click the Change Project Options button, or double click on the [OPTIONS] line. The Options dialog box is displayed.

5. In the Options dialog box, ensure that the Title is translated, and set the language of the help file. Also check the [WINDOWS] section to see whether all window titles have been translated.

6. Choose the Compile command from the File menu to compile the help project. Before clicking Compile, check the Save All Files Before Compiling option.

The compiler processes all the files listed in the [FILES] section of the .hhp file, including the contents and index files, all HTML topic files, and images. All files are compiled into one .chm file.

3.1.4 ENGINEERING HTML HELP

Since the topic files in HTML Help projects are all in HTML format, most of the information provided in the HTML section on page 264 can be applied. The following sections cover the most important engineering tasks related to HTML Help.

Layout

Check all individual HTML files in a browser or in an HTML testing tool, such as HtmlQA, to verify that everything has been translated and images display properly, etc. In many cases, the layout of HTML files will be determined by Cascading Style Sheets. These CSS files are referenced in the headers from the HTML files, for example:

```
<HEAD>
<Title>Menus</Title>
<LINK rel="StyleSheet" href="ottawa.css">
</HEAD>
```

In this example, the ottawa.css file will be included in the compilation, and referenced in the [FILES] section of the .hhp project file.

HTML files sometimes refer to style sheets located somewhere on the web, or in another compiled HTML Help file. It is, therefore, important to ensure that the computer can access this web location or .chm file, before compiling the HTML Help project. For example, if the HTML files contain the following information:

```
<LINK REL="stylesheet" MEDIA="screen" TYPE="text/css" HREF="MS-
ITS:ntshared.chm::/coUA.css">
```

Make sure the ntshared.chm file containing the coUA.css style sheet is present on the compiler machine.

For more information on checking HTML layout and adapting CSS files to support other languages, refer to the Engineering HTML section on page 264.

Character Encoding Definition

In HTML Help projects, the character encoding needs to be specified in the header for each HTML file using the `charset=` meta tag. The character encoding used for the .hhk and .hhc files will be determined by the compiler language setting (see next section), so there is no need to include a charset specification in these files.

For more information on specifying character encoding in HTML files, refer to the Engineering HTML section on page 264.

Language Setting

The language setting in an HTML Help project (.hhp) file defines the character encoding used in the navigation files, i.e. the contents (.hhc) and index (.hhk) files.

To specify the language of an HTML Help project using HTML Help Workshop, open the Options dialog box.

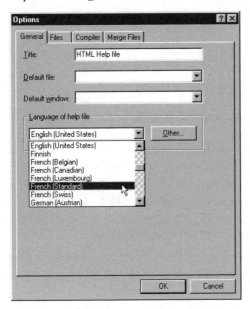

To change the language setting directly in the .hhp file, locate the LANGUAGE= setting in the [OPTIONS] section.

```
Language=0x411 Japanese
```

In this line the Locale ID and Locale name are defined. For a complete list of locale IDs and names, refer to the Microsoft MSDN web site at msdn.microsoft.com (search for "locale IDs").

3.1.5 TESTING HTML HELP

Testing localized HTML Help files is comparable to a translation quality assurance task in that the localized version first needs to be compared with the source and then a final review of the local version is done.

To compare localized HTML Help files with source files, use a tool such as HtmlQA or Berlitz Trans Web Express. These tools are designed to compare the layout and functionality of two different language versions of HTML or HTML Help projects. For more information on these tools refer to the Testing Localized HTML section on page 268.

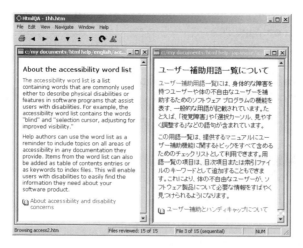

As a final QA step, review the localized online help file in the environment that will be used by the end-user, i.e. a localized operating system or localized help viewer. To avoid having to install the localized operating system for testing purposes, download the help viewer redistribution files from the Microsoft MSDN web site at msdn.microsoft.com (search for "HTML Help German" or another language name).

Unlike WinHelp, the HTML Help viewer does not contain a feature that allows the user to browse through the help topics in sequential order. To do this, use a third-party tool, such as KeyTools by KeyWorks Software (www.keyworks.net).

HTML Help Workshop contains a Test menu that enables the user to test pop-up attributes, keywords and the HTML Help API. Refer to the HTML Help Workshop online help for more information on testing HTML Help projects.

For general online help testing procedures, refer to the Testing Localized Online Help section on page 278.

3.2   WinHelp

Windows Help (WinHelp) is a help system that enables the user to create help files in .hlp format, using a project file that combines help topic, contents, index, image, and other source files into one file.

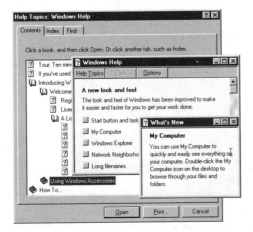

Sets of RTF source files and .bmp images are compiled into a single, compressed file with the .hlp extension.

Refer to the WinHelp section on page 182 for more information on Windows Help.

3.2.1   INTRODUCTION

WinHelp projects require localization engineers to have extensive knowledge of RTF file structure and Microsoft Word style sheets, because most of the content is in RTF format.

The following sections will discuss all engineering tasks associated with localizing WinHelp files, i.e. compiling, engineering, and testing.

3.2.2   FILE TYPES

The following table lists different file types that could be included in an online help localization kit. It also indicates whether the file should be localized or translated:

Extension	File Type	Localizable?
.ali	alias file	no
.ann	annotation file	no
.avi	movie file	yes
.bmk	bookmark file	no

.bmp	image file	yes
.cnt	contents file	yes
.dib	device-independent bitmap	yes
.doc	source text file (Robohelp)	yes
.dot	template file	no
.fts	full-text search database	no
.gid	merged keywords file (temporary)	no
.h	header file	no
.hlp	compiled help file	no
.hpj	project file	yes
.log	log file	no
.map	mapping file	no
.mrb	multi-resolution bitmap	yes
.rtf	source text file	yes
.shg	hypergraphic file (bitmap with hot spots)	yes
.txt	include or log file	no
.vcp	project configuration file	no
.ver	version information header file	no
.wav	sound file	no
.wmf	Windows meta file	yes
.zip	compressed file	no

3.2.3 COMPILING WINHELP

Before compiling, check whether the help file should be compiled using the HCP (Windows 3.1) or HCW (Windows 9x) help compiler. If a help project contains a .cnt file and the .hpj file starts with `"This file is maintained by HCW. Do not modify this file directly."`, use the HCW.EXE WinHelp 4 compiler.

To compile a Windows help file, use the Microsoft Help Compiler. For Windows 3.0 and 3.1 help (WinHelp 3) files, use the HC.EXE/HC30.EXE or HC31.EXE compiler respectively. The HCP.EXE is the protected-mode version of the Windows3.1 help compiler, i.e. it supports extended memory usage. HCRTF.EXE is the Windows 9x help compiler, for WinHelp 4 projects. This compiler is activated from within the Microsoft Help Workshop shell, HCW.EXE.

Help compilers are included with most programming languages, and can be downloaded from the Microsoft FTP server at ftp.microsoft.com/softlib/mslfiles. The HC505.EXE file contains all Windows 3.1 help compilers. The HCWSETUP.EXE installer contains Microsoft Help Workshop version 4.03, which is compatible with Word 97 RTF files. Help compilers can also be found on the Microsoft Developer Network CDs, and on the Help Master web site at www.helpmaster.com, or the WinWriters web site at www.winwriters.com.

Please note that RTF files saved in Word for Windows 8 (Microsoft Offic e97) or later versions contain new tokens that are incompatible with help compilers older than HCRTF 4.02.

A typical WinHelp project consists of a help project (.hpj), a contents file (.cnt), and folders containing the topic files (\RTF) and graphics (\Images). Refer to the Creation section on page 185 for more information on these files.

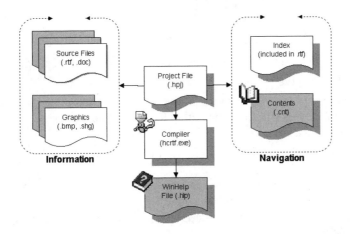

To compile a WinHelp 3 project, go to the DOS prompt and type:

```
HCP help_project_filename.hpj
```

Before compilation, translate all RTF files and appropriate items in the .hpj file, as described in the .HPJ Files section on page 190.

If error messages are displayed, refer to the HC31.HLP file for a possible solution. During compilation, a *help_project_filename*.hlp file will be created in the folder where the command has been issued.

To compile a WinHelp 4 project, follow these steps:

1. Create a new folder with a language code in the name, for example Help_DE, and copy all English source files to this folder.

2. Make sure all translated RTF files and graphics have replaced or overwritten the original English files. To check that no old, untranslated files remain in the folders, display the file list sorted by Date.

3. Start Microsoft Help Workshop (HCW.EXE), open the project file (.hpj) using the Open command from the File menu. The project settings are displayed.

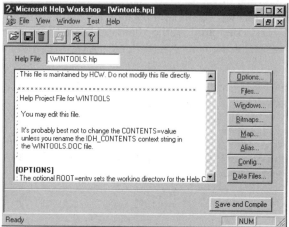

4. Change the project settings according to the instructions in the Engineering WinHelp section on page 242.

5. In the Options dialog box, ensure that the Title is translated, and set the language of the help file. Also check the [WINDOWS] section to see whether all window titles have been translated.

6. Click the Save and Compile button to compile the help project.

The [FILES] section in the .hpj file defines which RTF files will be included in the help file. Do not change the order of the files listed in this section.If the names of the localized RTF files have been changed, change the file names in this section accordingly. Please note that file names should normally not be changed.

Tip: If the compression option is enabled in the .hpj file (COMPRESS=TRUE), compilation time will be considerably longer. For this reason, consider disabling compression until the final release build.

3.2.4   ENGINEERING WINHELP

Since the topic files in WinHelp projects are all in RTF format, most of the engineering work should be done in Microsoft Word. The following sections cover the most important engineering tasks related to WinHelp projects.

Layout

Check all RTF files in Microsoft Word, or the compiled online help file in a WinHelp testing tool, such as HelpQA, to verify that everything has been translated and images display properly, etc.

In many cases, the layout of RTF files used in WinHelp will be determined by Microsoft Word templates. These templates are attached to the RTF. Always check whether the correct templates are attached to the translated files.

There may be problems with character formatting, when compiling a help file using the WinHelp 3 help compiler, particularly with curly (or "smart") quotes, emdash, endash, and bullet symbols. These symbols can be searched and replaced with equivalent, supported symbols in the word processor. The tool that automates this task is called Rich Text Format Modifier and is available from the Microsoft FTP server at ftp.microsoft.com/developr/drg/Multimedia/RTFMod.

In the WinHelp 4 help compiler, most of these issues have been addressed. In this version of the help compiler, it is even possible to automatically localize quotation marks. If the RTF files contain the string "sample", for example, and the help file is compiled using the French language setting, this string will be displayed in the compiled help file as «sample», or in German as „sample".

When experiencing problems displaying bulleted or numbered lists or square bullets, change the compression settings in the project file to the Zeck compression option.

Browse Sequence

A browse sequence is the order in which help topics are displayed when the user clicks on the browse buttons (<< and >>) in the compiled help file. A help file can have one browse sequence, which means the user can browse from the first to the last page of the help file, or several smaller browse sequences, for example, one per subject section. Browse sequences are mostly used in WinHelp 3 help projects.

Help files often contain glossaries, which are alphabetically sorted. When the glossary text is translated, the sorting order changes. Instead of manually sorting all glossary entry pages in the RTF file, it is also possible to change the browse sequence of every topic.

The footnote mark for browse sequences is the plus sign (+). The footnote itself consists of a code string and a number, with the number indicating the order in which the topic will be called.

To change the browse sequence of a subset of topics, follow these steps:

1. Open the RTF file containing the topics in a word processor.
2. Open the footnote section and go to the first topic in the sequence.
3. Go to the lowest number for that sequence, which is not necessarily number 1.
4. Change the sequence numbers following the + footnote symbol to the correct alphabetical order.

The translated text that should be on top of the list will have the lowest number.

Character Encoding Definition

The character encoding used in a localized help file can be specified using the CHARSET= option in the [OPTIONS] section of the .hpj file. When the RTF files have been edited using Microsoft Word 6.0 or later versions, there is no need to include this statement, because Word specifies the character encoding. If an earlier version of Word or an RTF editor has bee used that does not specify the character encoding, specify it in the .hpj file.

To change the default character set, open the .hpj file using Microsoft Help Workshop, click the Options button, select the Fonts tab and select an option from the Character Set list.

The DBCS= option in the [OPTIONS] section of the .hpj file specifies whether the files to be compiled use a double-byte character set (DBCS). Setting the language setting to a DBCS language, such as Japanese or Chinese, will automatically force the DBCS= option to YES.

Language Setting

Specifying the language of the help file in the .hpj file will adjust the sorting order of the keywords in the search index. For example, in Scandinavian languages, words starting with **ä**, **å**, or **ö** are sorted at the end of the alphabet, and not under the **A** section.

WinHelp 3 only supports English and Scandinavian sorting. If the help file is translated into a Scandinavian language, add the following option to the [OPTIONS] section of the .hpj file:

LANGUAGE=scandinavian

In WinHelp 4, the LCID= option (Locale ID) defines the language of the help file. The LCID= option is followed by a language code, such as 0x409 for American English. This option will also automatically determine whether topic files use a double-byte character set (DBCS).

To change the language identifier using Microsoft Help Workshop, click the Options button, select the Sorting tab, and choose a language from the Language of Help file drop-down list.

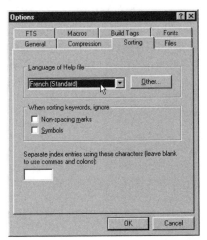

By default, Help Workshop uses a language based on the regional settings specified in the Windows Control Panel. In order for language settings to work and sort index keywords properly, set the Windows regional settings to the language of the localized help file.

Graphics

WinHelp files may contain the following types of graphics:

- Windows bitmaps (.bmp or .dib)
- Windows metafiles (.wmf)
- Windows Help multiple-hotspot (SHED) bitmaps (.shg)
- Windows Help multi-resolution bitmaps (.mrb).

WinHelp 3 supports only 16-color bitmaps, whereas more recent versions support 256-color bitmaps. WinHelp 4 supports any number of colors. The color depth of bitmaps is automatically reduced if the display driver does not support more colors, which does not always generate the best results. A solution is to use multi-resolution bitmaps, which are compiled by the Multi-Resolution Bitmap Compiler (MRBC.EXE), included in the Help Workshop compiler. Refer to the help compiler's documentation for more information on graphics in help files.

In the .hpj file, the location of the graphics is set by the BMROOT= option in the [OPTIONS] section. When this option is not specified, the compiler will only search in the help project folder for referenced graphics.

Bitmaps are inserted in help files through bmc, bml, or bmr statements between curly brackets in the RTF files. A bmc statement, such as {bmc bitmap.bmp}, inserts a bitmap in the text as if it were a character. The bml and bmr statements place the bitmap in the left or right margin of the help window, with the text wrapping around the bitmap. In the localized RTF files, make sure these bitmap references have not been changed.

WinHelp files often contain graphics with hotspots, or *hypergraphics*. These hypergraphics allow the user to click on bitmaps, such as buttons or graphics, and jump to other topics. Hypergraphics are similar to hyperlinks in a text. When a user places the pointer cursor on a hotspot, the cursor changes to a hand with pointing index finger, indicating that the user may click to activate a link. One bitmap can contain several hotspots. For example, a screen capture of a dialog box can contain a number of hotspots that take the user to related help information.

These hotspot graphics, with the .shg extension, are created with the Microsoft Hotspot Editor (SHED.EXE). The SHED.EXE utility is available from the Microsoft FTP server at ftp.microsoft.com/softlib/mslfiles and is also included in the Help Workshop compiler installation folder. Another .shg editor is included in the HelpScribble shareware application, which is available from www.jgsoft.com.

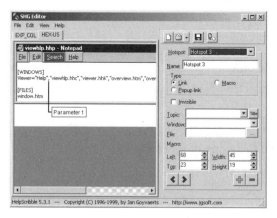

Several versions of SHED Hotspot Editor are available. It is advisable to get version 2, which can be downloaded from www.helpmaster.com (search for "shed").

To create a localized .shg file using SHED 2, follow these steps:

1. Open the English .shg file in SHED. The hot spots are displayed with red borders.

2. Choose the Import Graphic command from the File menu, and select the localized .bmp file.

3. Adjust the hotspot areas to match the localized image.

Please note that earlier versions of SHED do not include the Import command.

3.2.5 TESTING WINHELP

Testing localized WinHelp files is comparable to a translation quality assurance task in that the localized version needs to be checked against the source, followed by a last review of the finalized local version.

To compare localized WinHelp files with source files, use a tool such as HelpQA. This tool is designed to compare the layout and functionality of two different language versions of a WinHelp project.

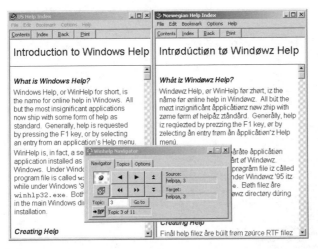

As a final QA step, review the localized online help file in the environment that will be used by the end-user, i.e. a localized operating system or localized help viewer.

For general online help testing procedures, refer to the Testing Localized Online Help section on page 278.

Using HelpQA

HelpQA by Translation Craft (acquired by SDL International in July 2000) is a utility designed specifically for the localization industry, technical translators and particularly localization engineers. It manages all aspects of the quality assurance process for multiple language Windows help files.

HelpQA compares localized help projects or help source files against the original ones. It not only generates a full report of the help file, i.e. word counts, graphic references, and .cnt file analysis, it also checks whether the localized file mirrors the functionality of the original help file. The HelpQA tool eliminates the need to click manually on every link in a help file to verify that the link has been preserved.

To test a help project using HelpQA, follow these steps:

1. Open the source and target project files (.hpj) using the Source and Target tabs.

2. Click on the Project Compare tab to test the number of topics, links, footnotes, commands, formatting, graphics and .cnt file.

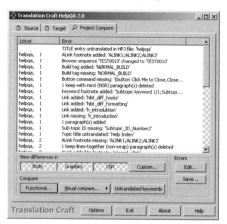

3. Click on the Visual button in the Project Compare tab window to view the source and target help files side-by-side.

For more information on HelpQA, visit the SDL International web site at www.sdlintl.com.

Localized Viewer

To avoid having to install the localized operating system for testing purposes, copy the help viewers from the operating system setup .cab files. The help viewer is called winhelp.exe or winhlp32.exe.

If a French version of the help viewer files are required, for example, open the folder containing the setup disks for the French version of Windows 9x. Localized versions of Windows 9x can be found on the Microsoft Developer Network CDs. The Setup disks are compressed .cab files, and can be extracted using current compression tools.

Follows these steps to extract the files:

1. Locate the help viewer files in the .cab files on the setup disks

2. Right-click on the file names, and choose Extract to copy the files to a folder on the hard drive.

3. Open the localized help file with the help viewer of the same language.

Contents File Test (WinHelp 4 only)

The .cnt contents file contains the text displayed when the Contents tab is selected in a WinHelp 4 help file.

To check the integrity of help topic links in a localized contents file, follow these steps:

1. Start Microsoft Help Workshop.

2. From the Test menu, choose Contents File.

3. Select the .cnt file to be tested. This file should be in the same folder as the corresponding .hlp file(s).

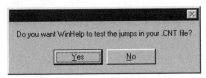

Microsoft Help Workshop will verify that all the jumps in the contents file work. If errors are reported, open the .cnt file and correct the link to math the related topic ID in the RTF file.

Visual Test

HelpQA will enable the user to browse through all topics of an online help file side-by-side with the source files, but it is advisable to also browse through all localized help topics using a localized viewer.

Using the browse buttons (<< and >>) is not the ideal way to do this, because browse sequences often contain only part of the help file. Refer to the Browse Sequence section on page 243 for more information.

However, WinHelp 3 and 4 do enable the user to browse through a compiled help file, page-by-page, in another way. The following sections describe which settings should be changed to enable this feature.

To configure the Windows 3.x operating system for WinHelp 3 help file testing, follow these steps:

1. Open the WIN.INI file in the Windows folder with a text editor.

2. In the WIN.INI file, go to the `[Windows Help]` section, or create this section if it does not exist.

3. Enter the following line: `seqtopickeys=1`.

4. Save the changes, and restart Windows.

5. Open the .hlp file to be viewed.

6. Press Ctrl+Shift+Home to jump to the first topic of the help file.

7. Press Ctrl+Shift+right-arrow to browse through the help file page-by-page.

To configure the Windows 9x operating system for WinHelp 4 help file testing, follow these steps:

1. Install Microsoft Help Workshop (HCW.EXE).

2. Start Microsoft Help Workshop, and make sure the Help Author option in the File menu is enabled.

3. Exit Microsoft Help Workshop.

4. Open the help file to be tested.

5. Press Ctrl+Shift+Home to jump to the first topic of the help file.

6. Press Ctrl+Shift+right-arrow to browse through the help file page-by-page.

The topic number is displayed in the title bar, the Help Author is displayed as *active*. After disabling the Help Author function, the help window titles will be displayed again.

It is possible to browse backward using the Ctrl+Shift+left-arrow key combination. Press Ctrl+Shift+End to jump to the last page of the help file. Press Ctrl+Shift+J to enter the number of the required topic.

To view topic information, right-click in a help topic window, and select Topic Information. In the Topic Information window, the Help File field will display the name of the .hlp file and its version, i.e. 3.1 or 4.x.

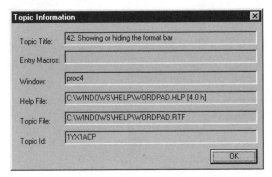

If a correction needs to be entered in this specific topic, open the relevant RTF file and search for the string displayed in the Topic Id field. By default, the Topic File name and Topic Id fields will not be displayed. To ensure this information is included in the .hlp file, compile the help file with the "Include RTF filename and topic ID in Help file compilation" setting enabled.

4   Mac OS

Apple Help and Apple Guide are the most commonly used online help systems on the Mac OS platform. For a general introduction and information on these help types, refer to the Mac OS section in Chapter 6, Online Help Translation.

4.1   Apple Help

Apple Help is a help system used to create help files or web pages in HTML format. Unlike most other online help types discussed in this chapter, Apple Help does not require compilation.

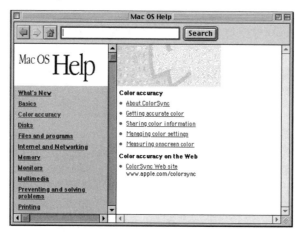

Sets of HTML files and .jpg or .gif images are placed in a folder structure called an "Apple Help book". The help viewer displays a table of contents, but Apple Help does not contain a keyword index. However, HTML files in an Apple Help system use special tags that will enable users to quickly locate information using the Sherlock search engine on a Mac OS.

Refer to the Apple Help section on page 196 for more information on Apple Help.

4.1.1   INTRODUCTION

Apple Help projects require localization engineers to have extensive knowledge of the HTML language, because most of the content is in HTML format.

The following sections will discuss all engineering tasks associated with localizing Apple Help files, i.e. engineering, and testing.

4.1.2 FILE TYPES

When evaluating an online help build environment, it is important to first identify the translatable files.

The following table lists the different file types that are likely to be included in an Apple Help localization kit. It also indicates whether the file may contain localizable items.

Extension	File Type	Localizable?
.css	cascading style sheet	yes
.gif	graphic	yes
.hqx	compressed, binhexed file	no
.htm or .html	HTML file	yes
.idx	full-text search index file	no
.jpg	graphic	yes
.sit or .sea	compressed file	no
.xml	XML file	yes
n/a	AppleGuide file	yes
n/a	AppleScript file	no
n/a	QuickTime movie	yes

As the Apple Help online help system is enhanced and developed further, the developers may add other file types, depending on user requirements.

4.1.3 ENGINEERING APPLE HELP

Since Apple Help topic files are usually in a standard HTML format, the information provided in the HTML section on page 264 can be applied. The following sections cover the most important engineering tasks related to Apple Help.

Layout

Check all individual HTML files in a browser or in a Windows-based HTML testing tool, such as HtmlQA, to verify that everything has been translated and images display properly, etc. Fix any errors found by these tools in the HTML files on the Mac OS.

For more information on checking HTML layout, refer to the Engineering HTML section on page 264.

Character Encoding Definition

In Apple Help projects, the character encoding should be specified in the header for each HTML file using the `charset=` meta tag. For more information on specifying character encoding in HTML files, refer to the Engineering HTML section on page 264.

A font can be specified for the title of the help book. This can be done by including the optional `AppleFont` meta tag in the header of the HTML file containing the main table of contents. For example, the following line specifies the Japanese Osaka font.

```
<META NAME ="AppleFont"CONTENT ="Osaka">
```

This is only relevant when the Apple Help file has been localized into a language with a non-Roman scripting system which may not be directly supported by a non-localized version of the Help Viewer. When indexing the localized Apple Help book, check that a font is specified for displaying search results, using the `AppleSearchResultsFont` meta tag in the header of the title page file.

Language Setting

Since Apple Help is not compiled, the only relevant language settings are those specified in the localized HTML files. Refer to the Engineering HTML section on page 264 for more information.

Indexing Apple Help

Once all HTML files in an Apple Help book have been localized and tested, the localized book should be indexed using the Apple Help Indexing Tool. This tool is included in the Apple Help SDK. Indexing means that all content can be searched using the Apple Help search engine.

Before creating an index from a set of localized HTML files, copy all help files to their final folder locations.

To create an index using the Apple Help Indexing Tool, follow these steps:

1. Start the Apple Help Indexing Tool.

2. Select the Preferences menu and set the correct language in the Preferences dialog box.

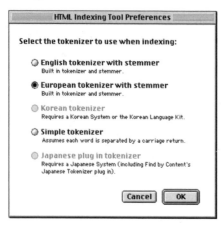

3. Drag and drop the folder containing the localized Apple Help project onto the Indexing Tool. The index file is created and then saved inside this folder.

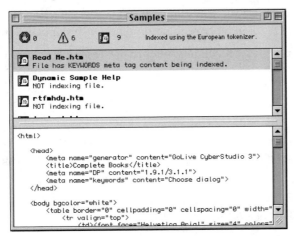

Please note that to index Kanji text, the Indexing Tool should be run on a Japanese Mac OS.

4.1.4 TESTING APPLE HELP

Testing localized Apple Help files is comparable to a translation quality assurance task in that the localized version needs to be checked against the source, followed by a last review of the finalized local version.

To compare localized Apple Help files with source files, use a Windows-based tool, such as HtmlQA or Berlitz Trans Web Express. These tools are designed to compare the layout and functionality of two different language versions of an HTML project. For more information on these tools refer to the Testing Localized HTML section on page 268.

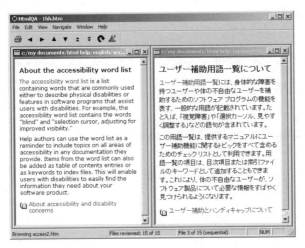

As a final QA step, review the localized online help file in the environment that will be used by the end-user, i.e. a localized operating system or localized help viewer.

Especially when testing the HTML files using a Windows-based tool, view the entire help content on a Mac OS, preferably running on different system versions.

For general online help testing procedures, refer to the Testing Localized Online Help section on page 278.

4.2 Apple Guide

Apple Guide is a help system that enables the user to create online help files using Guide Script, a mark-up language that identifies Apple Guide elements, controls content layout, and sequences panels. Apple Guide files are viewed using the Apple Guide system extension.

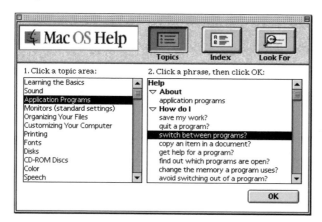

Sets of Guide Script source files and resource files containing pictures are compiled into a single, compressed file using Guide Maker.

Refer to the Apple Guide section on page 198 for more information on Apple Guide.

4.2.1 INTRODUCTION

Guide Maker projects require localization engineers to have extensive knowledge of the Guide Script language, plus experience using Guide Maker and Mac OS resource editors, such as ResEdit.

The following sections will discuss all engineering tasks associated with localizing Apple Guide files, i.e. compiling, engineering, and testing.

4.2.2 FILE TYPES

When evaluating an online help build environment, it is important to first identify the translatable files.

The following table lists the different file types that are likely to be included in an Apple Guide localization kit. It also indicates whether the file may contain localizable items.

Extension	File Type	Localizable?
.gs	Guide Script files	yes
.hqx	compressed, binhexed file	no
.mcw	source file	yes
.pict	image file	yes
.r	text-only resource file	yes
.rsrc	binary resource file	yes
.sit or .sea	compressed file	no
.src	source file	yes
.SYM	symbols file for testing	no
n/a	Apple Guide file	no

4.2.3 COMPILING APPLE GUIDE

Apple Guide files can only be compiled with Guide Maker or Guide Maker Lite. Guide Maker Lite is a leaner, faster version of Guide Maker that only compiles files. It does not contain the Localize, Import/Export, Diagnose, and Conversion features from Guide Maker.

The Guide Maker compilers can be downloaded from the following web sites:

- Apple Developer Connection web site – www.apple.com/developer (search for "Apple Guide SDK")
- Danny Goodman's web site – www.dannyg.com
- Step Up Software web site – www.stepupsoftware.com

Before compiling the Apple Guide files, make sure that:

- The Apple Guide fonts are installed on the Mac OS. These fonts, Espy Sans and Espy Serif, are included with most Apple Guide authoring kits, such as the Apple Guide Starter Kit, which is available from www.dannyg.com.
- All Apple Script source files are in a format compatible with Guide Maker. The best format to use is MacWrite II or Word 5. When converting files to MacWrite II format from the word processor, make sure the XTND Power Enabler is in the Extensions folder.

An Apple Guide project includes a build file, which is a Guide Script file containing only <Include> and <Resource> commands. This file identifies the source files to be compiled. When building an Apple Guide file, all source files that are referenced in the build file must be placed in the same folder as the build file. To compile an Apple Guide file using Guide Maker, follow these steps:

1. Start Guide Maker and select the Build command from the Utilities menu.

2. Click on the Source file area in the Build window, and select the build file from the Apple Guide project.

3. Click in the Guide file area of the Build window to specify the Apple Guide file to be built. Open an existing file or create a new file. To create a new guide file, specify a name.

4. Click the Compile button to start building the Apple Guide file.

5. When compilation is complete, save the Apple Guide file.

When compiling a large Apple Guide file, use Guide Maker Lite to reduce the compilation time.

4.2.4 ENGINEERING APPLE GUIDE

Since Apple Guide topic files are all in Guide Script format, most of the engineering work will be done on these source files. The following sections cover the most important engineering tasks related to Apple Guide.

Layout

Apple Guide projects consist of a number of panels all describing a single, self-contained step. Therefore, most panels contain no more than a few sentences. Panels automatically resize vertically. Guide Script files define column coordinates for the top, left, and right coordinates of a panel, using the <Define Format>, <Define Transparent Format> commands.

These commands have the following syntax: <define format> *formatName, columnCoords [, txFnt] [, txSize] [, txStyle] [, txColor] [, txAlign] [, alignPrompt]*.

The following example defines the text regions for all panels in an Apple Guide file:

```
<define format> "Tag", Column(6,0,54),"Espy Sans Bold",10, , black,
right,false
<define format> "Body", Column(6,65,330), ,10, ,black,left,true
<define format> "Full", Column(6,11,330), , 10, ,black,left,false
<define format> "ResetZero",Column(0,0,330), , , , black, , false
```

Refer to the *Apple Guide Complete* manual for more information on specifying formatting in Apple Guide files.

Character Encoding Definition

If no special fonts are specified using the <Define Format> command, Guide Maker uses the default text attributes: Espy Serif, 10-point, plain, and black. If the language character set is not supported by this Apple Guide font, consider changing the font attributes to a font supported by the target language, such as the Mac OS system font.

For example, to change the font to the Japanese font Osaka in the first line of the previous example, use this command:

```
<define format> "Tag", Column(6,0,54),"Osaka",10, , black,
right,false
```

Buttons will automatically be displayed using the system font.

Language Setting

The Apple Guide source files or compiler do not include a language setting feature. By default, a large number of languages are supported by Apple Guide. For non-Roman languages, however, Apple Guide engineering and compilation needs to be done on a localized Mac OS.

4.2.5 TESTING APPLE GUIDE

There are several items that need to be tested in Apple Guide files, such as:

- Interface
- Coachmarks
- Context checks

Remember to test the search feature ("Look For"), because Apple Guide does not support advanced language-specific search features and there may be some problems with this feature in some languages.

For general online help testing procedures, refer to the Testing Localized Online Help section on page 278.

Interface Test

The interface test indicates whether the order of the panels is correct, the graphics display well, all text fits in the space available, etc.

To test the guide file interface using Guide Maker, follow these steps:

1. Choose the Diagnose command from the Utilities menu.

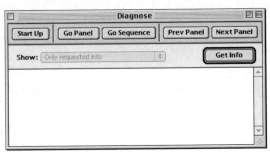

2. Use the Start Up button to display the startup window in the guide file. If the Apple Guide file does not display, open the guide file from within the corresponding application, and open the same guide file using Guide Maker's Open command.

3. Use the Go Panel and Go Sequence buttons to jump to a specific panel or sequence in the guide file.

4. Use the Prev Panel and Next Panel buttons to browse through the panels of the localized guide file.

5. Use the Get Info button to see information on the current panel, such as the sequence it belongs to, the ID number, and the panel name.

Please pay special attention to the Topics list. The text needs to fit in the available space. If the topic titles are longer, they will be truncated, rather than wrapped!

Coachmarks Test

There are five coachmark types: menu, item, object, window and AppleScript. Coachmarks highlight items in the user interface, using red circles or underlining. The coachmark items in the source files need to be translated exactly as the translated items in the related application, otherwise they will generate error messages. Coachmarks need to be tested by opening each panel with the application running in the background.

Here is an example of a menu coachmark command in a Guide Script source file:

```
<Define Menu Coach> "FileSaveCoach", 'WAVE', REDCIRCLE, "Datei",
"Sichern", RED, UNDERLINE
<Coach Mark>  "FileSaveCoach"
```

In this line, the German translations for the File and Save As menu should match the menu translations in the localized application.

Context Check Test

A context check determines that certain conditions are appropriate to the user environment. For example, some panels will only be displayed when the Date & Time control panel is opened.

These context checks need to be carefully tested in a localized environment.

4.3   QuickHelp

Mac OS QuickHelp is a help system that enables the user to create help files in a WinHelp 4 compatible format, using a project file that combines help topic, contents, index, image, and other source files into one file.

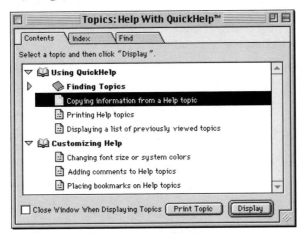

Sets of RTF source files and .bmp images are compiled into a single, compressed help file, using the Altura QuickHelp compiler (www.altura.com).

Refer to the QuickHelp section on page 203 for more information on QuickHelp.

4.3.1   INTRODUCTION

QuickHelp projects require localization engineers to have extensive knowledge of the RTF file structure, the WinHelp 4 standard, and Microsoft Word style sheets, because most of the content is in RTF format.

QuickHelp is very similar to WinHelp, so please refer to the instructions in the WinHelp section on page 239. The following sections only cover Mac-specific issues. For information on compatibility between WinHelp and QuickHelp, refer to the Altura web site at www.altura.com.

4.3.2   FILE TYPES

Please refer to the File Types section on page 239 for information on file types.

The only file type added on the Mac OS is the temporary .qh file, which contains all help file settings. This file is not localizable.

4.3.3   COMPILING QUICKHELP

The QuickHelp Compiler is very similar to the Windows help compiler. It does, however, contain additional options that must be set to resolve platform differences between Windows and Mac OS.

To compile a QuickHelp file using the QuickHelp Compiler, follow these steps:

1. Launch the compiler and open the help project .hpj file. The compiler will create a settings file with the same name as the project file plus the .qh file extension.

2. Set the desired options using the commands in the Project menu. As a rule, the only settings that may need to be changed are the paths where the compiler will search for files specified in the RTF and .hpj files.

3. In case the source RTF files contain conditional text, select the Use Hidden Macintosh Text from the Project menu.

4. Select the Compile command from the Project menu.

The compiler will ask for a location and name for the compiled help file.

4.3.4 ENGINEERING QUICKHELP

For engineering procedures, refer to the Engineering WinHelp section on page 242.

Layout

For layout procedures, refer to the Layout section on page 242.

Character Encoding Definition

While the ASCII format is standard across the Mac OS and Windows platforms, upper-ASCII characters are not. This is why the QuickHelp Compiler maps characters from all RTF files created on Windows to appropriate Mac characters, so accented characters are transferred correctly.

For Latin-character languages, leave the font mapping settings as they are in the source. This may, however, cause problems for Asian languages. Check the Don't Map Windows RTF Characters option in the Options menu to turn off the mapping for those languages.

Language Setting

The LANGUAGE= command in the .hpj file is not processed when the QuickHelp compiler compiles a set of source files. All sorting algorithms are retrieved from the language of the MacOS.

4.3.5 TESTING QUICKHELP

To test localized QuickHelp files, which typically will be translated on the Windows platform anyway, follow all Windows testing procedures and tools as described in the Testing WinHelp section on page 247.

To test localized online help and contents files on the Mac OS, copy them into the same folder on the local Macintosh hard disk and open the help file with the QuickHelp viewer. Localized viewers are available in numerous languages from Altura.

For general online help testing procedures, refer to the Testing Localized Online Help section on page 278.

5   HTML and XML

Most current online help systems and web sites are built using a combination of HTML and XML files. In this chapter we will focus on the associated engineering issues.

5.1   Introduction

For a general introduction about markup languages, such as SGML, HTML, and XML, refer to the HTML and XML section on page 205. Chapter 6 provides information on translatable files and the translation approach.

In localization projects handled by localization vendors, markup languages are typically found in the following files and formats:

* Online help systems, such as Apple Help
* Compiled online help files, such as HTML Help and JavaHelp
* Web sites
* Web-based software applications

Regardless of how HTML or XML pages are applied, they all have common engineering challenges. As a rule, the layout needs to be adapted for localized pages, language and character encoding need to be specified, and localized files need to be tested. Please note that this chapter only deals with the front-end elements of localized web sites, i.e. the pages containing content. For information on web globalization issues, such as server platform or multilingual web strategy, refer to the Web Sites and HTML section on page 36.

Tip: When localizing a web site, always ask the publisher for the complete set of source files, rather than downloading the source language files from the web. The web pages may contain content, such as server-side scripts or other generated content, which may not be accessible unless the entire web site structure is made available.

5.2   File Types

The following table lists the different file types that are likely to be included in an HTML or XML-based online help or web site localization kit. It also indicates whether the file may contain localizable text or settings:

Extension	File Type	Localizable?
.asp	active server page file	yes
.css	Cascading Style Sheet	yes
.gif	image file	yes
.html	HTML file	yes
.jpg	image file	yes

.js	JavaScript file	yes
.xml	XML file	yes
.xsl	XML stylesheet	yes
.zip	compressed file	no

5.3 HTML

HTML has become the standard file format for web pages and many online help systems.

5.3.1 ENGINEERING HTML

The following sections cover the most important engineering tasks related to HTML files.

Layout

The layout of HTML files can be defined separately in each HTML file, or Cascading Style Sheets can be used to define the layout globally for a group of HTML pages. The layout of HTML pages is determined by the HTML tags, supported by the browser or viewer, and by the installed fonts and window size. In running text, lines of text wrap automatically to fit the browser or viewer window. If there are images on a page, the browser window will automatically display scroll bars in cases where an image does not fit in the browser window.

In many cases, the layout of HTML files will be determined by Cascading Style Sheets. Cascading Style Sheets (CSS) files are files containing layout properties that can be applied to HTML files by reference. They can be used to define all layout properties, such as font properties, tables, colors and backgrounds, and even generated content and automatic list numbering. Web sites generally load different style sheets to display HTML pages, to match the user's browser, platform, or language.

For localized HTML pages, engineers should focus on the following layout issues:

- Text formatting, with particular emphasis on fonts
- Page formatting, with particular emphasis on tables
- Images, with particular emphasis on image maps

Text formatting focuses mainly on font usage. All other text formatting, such as bold or italic words, should be handled during the translation cycle. As a rule, Western languages require no changes, unless HTML authors have used the <FONT> or <STYLE> tags to hard-code certain font sets that do not support accented characters.

For non-Western languages, font specifications will need to be adjusted, either in the HTML file or the CSS file. The font information will need to be changed, as well as the font size and text direction settings. The font information can usually be removed. As long as the language and character code specifications are adjusted, the browser will use the default system font for the specified language.

The following image shows an example from the Microsoft MSDN web site with a font specification from a CSS file, in English and adjusted for Japanese:

The specified fonts should be installed on the machine where the pages are viewed. Most operating system developers distribute language packs which will install fonts and keyboard mappings for foreign language display and input. The latest browser versions support font embedding in HTML pages. These font definition files are usually included in style sheets. Ascertain whether localized font definition files are available.

Irrespective of the font used, special characters in localized HTML files should be represented, if possible, using named or numeric character entities, rather than the actual accented characters. For more information on using character entities, refer to the Text Editors section on page 215.

Page formatting can be more complex, particularly with Asian or bi-directional languages. Page formatting in localized HTML pages can be altered by using the LANG language specification attribute. Refer to the following sections for more information. The HTML 4 specification and CSS2 contain special bi-direction features. In HTML files, for example, the <DIR> tag can be used with the values LTR (left to right) and RTL (right to left) to distinguish text direction. To change the text direction in tables, the DIR attribute must be used in the <TABLE> tag. In CSS files, the text direction is specified using the direction:ltr|rtl|inherit property.

If the localized HTML pages contain tables, make sure table widths have not been hard-coded, for example, the <TD WIDTH="23"> tag. Tables should accommodate the localized strings, and resize dynamically when the browser window size changes.

If the <q> element is used to define quotation marks in the HTML pages, the quoting style is defined by the CSS. HTML text, such as <q>Language<q>, would display as „Sprache" in German, and « Langue » in French.

If the HTML pages contain images with clickable image maps, these may need to be adjusted. For more information on editing image maps, refer to the Image Maps section on page 357.

Character Encoding Definition

HTML was designed around the ISO 8859-1 character set, also known as ISO Latin-1, which only supports Western European languages, such as French, German, Italian, Spanish, Swedish, Portuguese, Finnish, and Danish. For Asian, Cyrillic or bi-directional languages, different character sets and encodings must be specified so the browser can identify and display the appropriate font. HTML authors can choose from a wide range of standard code sets, for example:

- ISO series (ISO-8859-1 to ISO-8859-9)

- Windows single-byte (`windows-1250` to `windows-1257`)
- Windows multi-byte (`Shift-JIS`, `Big-5`, `gb2312`)
- DOS code pages
- EBCDIC encodings for IBM mainframes
- UNIX encodings (`EUC-JP`, `EUC-CH`, `EUC-TW`)

The HTTP content-type returned by the server hosting the HTML pages should ideally determine the character encoding. Always consult the publisher on the server content-type, and see if it is possible for the publisher to set this. If this is not possible, specify the encoding in each of the localized files, using the content-type `META` tag.

Based on the encoding included in the source files, choose an equivalent scheme for the localized versions. For example, when the source HTML files contain the 8859-1 character set specification, add the following line to the localized HTML documents, just below the `<HEAD>` tag, to indicate to browsers the encoding format used in the file:

```
<META HTTP-EQUIV="Content-Type"
CONTENT="text/html;charset=ISO-8859-x">
```

where *x* is replaced with the MIME name of the character set used in the localized file:

- *x*=1 for Western European
- *x*=2 for Central/Eastern European
- *x*=3 for Other Latin Script Languages
- *x*=4 for Northern European/Baltic
- *x*=5 for Cyrillic
- *x*=6 for Arabic
- *x*=7 for Greek
- *x*=8 for Hebrew
- *x*=9 for Turkish

If the source files contain a standard `windows-1252` Western European code page specification, change this in the localized versions to one of the following settings:

- `windows-1250` for Eastern European
- `windows-1251` for Cyrillic
- `windows-1253` for Greek
- `windows-1254` for Turkish
- `windows-1257` for Baltic

Here is a list of the most commonly used character sets for Asian languages:

- Traditional Chinese – `charset=big5`

- Simplified Chinese – `charset=GB-2312`
- Thai – `charset=Windows-874`
- Japanese – `charset=Shift_JIS` or `charset=iso-2022-jp`
- Korean – `charset=ks_c_5601-1987`

Most browsers contain features that automatically detect the character encoding, or let users select the correct character set or encoding. Nonetheless, by including the correct `charset=` specification in the HTML pages, the browser will automatically switch to the correct one, if supported.

Note that a Cascading Style Sheet may also contain a character encoding specification which needs to be changed, for example:

```
@charset "ISO-8859-1";
```

More and more HTML files or style sheets contain the following character encoding specification:

```
<meta http-equiv="Content-Type" content="text/html; charset=utf-8">
```

UTF-8, 8-bit Unicode Transfer Format, is an encoding form of Unicode. It is a multi-byte format that supports ASCII for backward compatibility and covers the characters for most languages. If UTF-8 is specified in the source files, this does not need to be changed in the localized versions. When implementing UTF-8 in web pages that only currently support one encoding, such as 8859-1, the publisher should be consulted.

For more information on character sets and code pages, refer to the following web sites:

- Unicode Consortium – www.unicode.org
- World Wide Web Consortium – www.w3c.org
- Microsoft's GlobalDev – www.microsoft.com/globaldev

Nadine Kano's book *Developing International Software for Windows 95 and Windows NT* also contains a lot of useful information on code pages and character sets.

Language Setting

Language identification is a feature that has been introduced with HTML 4. Many aspects of document presentation depend not only on the character set, but also on the language of the text. It influences text display aspects, such as quotation marks, hyphenation, ligatures, and spacing.

Set the language of an entire document, using a META tag, or set the language for individual page elements, using the LANG attribute. The LANG attribute overrides the language setting defined in the META tag.

For example, to set the language of an entire HTML document to French, include the following line in the HEAD of the HTML file:

```
<META HTTP-EQUIV=Content-Language CONTENT=fr>
```

To set the language of one paragraph in an HTML file using the LANG attribute, which can be used with most HTML elements, create a section like this:

```
<P LANG="fr">Feuilles de présentation alphabétique</P>
```

The language META tag and LANG attribute assign a two-letter abbreviated language tag as a value. A list of these codes is defined by the ISO 639 standard, and can be found on the Unicode web site at www.unicode.org. Extended identifiers can be used to identify the region, or locale, where the language is spoken, for example fr-CA for Canadian French. These locale identifiers are based on the ISO3166 standard, which can also be found on the Unicode web site.

Language identifiers can also be used in other formats, for example in HTML files indexed by Microsoft's Index Server:

```
<META NAME="MS.LOCALE" CONTENT="EN-US">
```

In most cases, these codes will also be based on the ISO standards, but check with the publisher before changing the code.

5.3.2   TESTING LOCALIZED HTML

When HTML files are localized, there are two different types of tools required to run the tests:

- Generic HTML validation tools
- Testing tools for localized HTML

The generic testing tools will analyze one set of (localized) HTML files and verify that all internal and external links are valid. These tools will check that all images are present and there are no corrupt HTML tags. Most HTML editors offer verification features for web sites or batches of HTML files. Here are some examples of HTML validation tools:

- HTML Validator – www.htmlvalidator.com
- LinkBot – www.linkbot.com

For general online help testing procedures, refer to the Testing Localized Online Help section on page 278.

The other tools, mentioned above, will compare a localized set of HTML files with the original files. This is a worthwhile test to run, as it will allow the user to check that no text or tags were corrupted or lost during translation. It is advisable to run both tests on localized HTML.

There are two commercial tools currently available, that are used to compare a localized set of HTML files with the original source files. These tools are HtmlQA from SDL International and Trans Web Express from Berlitz.

Using HtmlQA

HtmlQA is an analysis and quality assurance tool that is used to check whether two HTML-based files or groups of files are still functionally identical. These two files would typically be an untranslated source project and a translated target project.

HtmlQA is not only useful for engineers, for testing localized web sites or HTML-based online help projects, it is also an invaluable tool for project managers, because they can create detailed reports on HTML files, containing word counts, number of files and images, problems in source material, and other data.

To test localized HTML files using HtmlQA, follow these steps:

1. Load the source and target HTML files using the Source and Target tabs.

2. Save the file list in a project file by selecting the Save Project command from the File button menu.

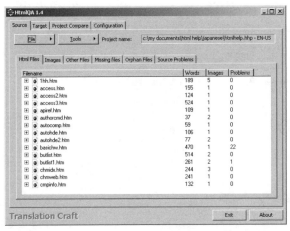

3. Check the project statistics. Switching between the Source and Target tab will display all source and target statistics.

4. Click on the Project Compare tab in the main window to run a detailed comparison between the source and target files. Run a specific comparison by

clicking on the appropriate button on the left of the page, or execute all the checks by clicking the Group Verify button.

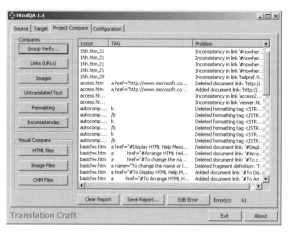

5. Click one of the buttons in the Visual Compare field to run a visual comparison of the source and target HTML, image or .chm files side-by-side.

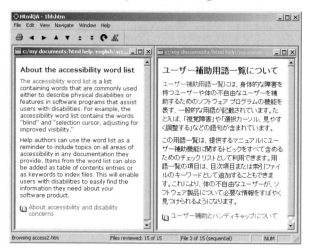

HtmlQA uses Internet Explorer or Netscape Navigator for the visual comparison.

For more information on HtmlQA, visit the SDL International web site at www.sdlintl.com.

Using Trans Web Express

Berlitz Trans Web Express has been designed specifically for the localization of web pages and HTML help files. It includes a comprehensive set of utilities, which handle translation, engineering, and testing. It also has a feature for resource planning, which is located in the Project Management component.

With Trans Web Express, it is possible to navigate through an entire HTML project viewing files as HTML code or as web pages. The navigator can view one window or two windows side-by-side. Trans Web Express can be used on any HTML project and is particularly suited to web projects and HTML help.

To test localized HTML files using Trans Web Express, follow these steps:

1. Open the source and target files using the Open command from the File menu or the Source and Target buttons. The HTML file that is selected first will be displayed in the Source and Target tab windows.

2. Choose the Project Analysis tab and click on Compare to run a functional comparison of the source and target tags.

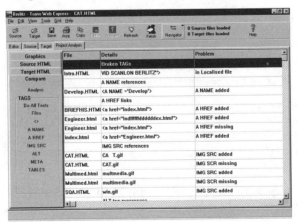

3. Fix errors by double-clicking on an error in the Compare window and editing the HTML code in the internal editor.

4. Click on the Navigator button to run a visual comparison on the files.

Trans Web Express has a Project Analysis function which can provide a detailed analysis of HTML files for project management and scheduling purposes. It not only counts the words and images, but also calculates the complexity factor for the project, indicating how complex the files will be for translation.

For more information on Trans Web Express and to download a fully functional version, visit the Berlitz Trans Web Express web site at www.berlitz.ie/twe.

5.4 XML

XML is a new markup language standard, used mainly for web pages and web-based applications.

5.4.1 ENGINEERING XML

The following sections cover the most important engineering tasks related to XML files.

Layout

Since SGML and XML are both descriptive markup languages as opposed to HTML, which is procedural, all layout information is stored externally in style sheets.

The Cascading Stylesheet Specification (CSS) provides a simple syntax for assigning styles to document elements. A new Extensible Style Language (XSL) has been drafted by the World Wide Web Consortium for use specifically with XML. The XSL standard uses XML syntax, but combines formatting features from both DSSSL (SGML) and CSS (HTML and XML).

Unlike HTML, which only supports CSS, XML supports both CSS and XSL. Both style sheet types may contain information that needs to be changed, so that localized XML pages, and more specifically, font information, are correctly displayed. For more information on CSS, refer to Layout section on page 264.

Depending on how it will be implemented and supported, XSL will also include features that control language-specific sorting, spacing, wrapping, numbering, hyphenation, and font settings.

For more information on style sheets and new developments in the CSS and XSL standards, refer to the World Wide Web Consortium Style Sheet pages at www.w3c.org/Style.

XML is not restricted in its use of graphic formats; it is the browsers that dictate which file formats can be read. Graphics are inserted as links, and they are linked to image files rather than text.

Character Encoding Definition

In XML files, the character encoding is specified in the header, or prolog. Here is an example of an XML prolog that specifies the Unicode character set used in the document:

```
<?xml version="1.0" encoding="UTF-8"?>
```

Because the XML standard is based on Unicode (ISO 10646), it is no longer necessary to separate character set codes. Unicode's UTF-8 is the default encoding applied to all XML documents. Most recent browsers support the Unicode standard. This allows all language character sets to be transmitted electronically without being corrupted.

Language Setting

A special attribute, xml:lang, can be inserted in XML files to specify the language to be used in the contents and attribute values of any element, for example:

```
<tocitem xml:lang="de">Online-Hilfe</tocitem>
```

According to the World Wide Web Consortium's XML 1.0 recommendation (www.w3c.org/XML), possible values of the xml:lang attribute are a two letter code as defined by the ISO 639 standard, or a language identifier registered with the Internet Assigned Numbers Authority (www.iana.org), or a language identifier assigned by the user.

Similar to HTML, extended identifiers based on the ISO 3166 standard can be used to identify the region, or locale, where the language is spoken, for example fr-CA for Canadian French.

5.4.2 TESTING LOCALIZED XML

XML files can be tested using syntax checkers that verify the tagging syntax of XML files to ensure they are valid and well-formed. Validity refers to the logical structure of the XML tagging, well-formedness to the physical structure.

Many of these tools can only be used online, over the web. Refer to the web sites listed on page 205 for more information on these tools.

A comprehensive list of available XML parsers can be found at www.xmlsoftware.com.

5.5 JavaHelp

JavaHelp is a platform-independent help system that enables the user to create help files in HTML format. Like HTML Help, JavaHelp uses a project file called HelpSet to combine help topic, contents, index, image, and other source files into a single file.

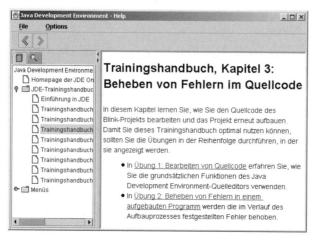

Sets of HTML and XML source files and .jpg or .gif images are packaged into a single, compressed file with the .jar extension.

Refer to the JavaHelp section on page 220 for more information on JavaHelp.

5.5.1 INTRODUCTION

JavaHelp projects require localization engineers to have extensive knowledge of the HTML language, because most of the content is in HTML format. It is also important to have a in-depth knowledge of the XML standard, since the contents and index files are in XML format.

The following sections will cover all engineering tasks related to JavaHelp files, i.e. compiling, engineering, and testing.

5.5.2 FILE TYPES

The following table lists the different file types that are likely to be included in a JavaHelp localization kit. It also indicates whether the file may contain localizable text or settings:

Extension	File Type	Localizable?
.css	Cascading Style Sheet	yes
.gif	image file	yes
.hs	JavaHelp HelpSet file	yes

.hsw	JavaHelp window definition (Robohelp)	yes
.html	HTML file	yes
.jar	compiled JavaHelp document	no
.java	Java file	yes
.jhm	map file	no
.jpg	image file	yes
.js	JavaScript file	yes
.map	map file	no
.properties	properties file	yes
.shar or .tar	compressed file (Unix)	no
.xml	XML file	yes
.xsl	XML stylesheet	yes
.z or .gz	compressed file (Unix)	no
.zip	compressed file	no

To identify the translatable files in the build environment, first check which files are actually included in the compilation. In JavaHelp projects, this information is stored in the map file with the .jhm extension. Compare the file list in this file with the files included in the build environment. The build environment may contain extra files or images which may not require localization.

5.5.3 PACKAGING JAVAHELP

To compress or "package" (JavaHelp terminology) JavaHelp projects into .jar files, the Java Development Kit is required. The `jar` command can be found in the \Bin folder. JAR files are ZIP files with an optional manifest file, describing the .jar contents. The Java Development Kit (JDK) can be downloaded from the Sun Java web site at java.sun.com (search for "JDK").

To create the full-text search index and view the HelpSet files, the JavaHelp development kit needs to be installed. It can be downloaded from the Sun Java web site at java.sun.com (search for "JavaHelp").

A typical JavaHelp project consists of a help project or HelpSet (.hs), a contents file (TocXML), an index (IndexXML) file, and folders containing the topic files (\HTML) and graphics (\Images). Refer to the Creation section on page 221 for more information on these files.

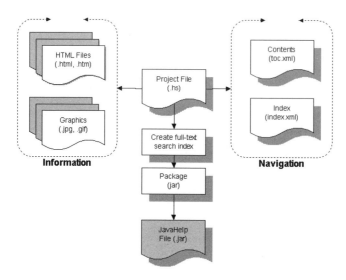

To create a localized JavaHelp project, follow these steps:

1. Make sure all translated HTML, XML files, and graphics have replaced or overwritten the original English files. To check that no old, untranslated files remain in the folders, display the file list sorted by Date.

2. Create a full-text search database of all localized help files using the `jhindexer` command, which is included with the JavaHelp development kit. Refer to the JavaHelp user guide for more information. Please note that a stop word list may be included, which should also be localized.

3. Package all files into a .jar file using the `jar` command.

All files listed in the map file, including the contents and index XML files, all HTML topic files, and images are packaged into one .jar file.

5.5.4 ENGINEERING JAVAHELP

Since JavaHelp topic files are all in HTML format, most of the information provided in the HTML section on page 264 can be applied. The following sections cover the most important engineering tasks related to JavaHelp.

Layout

Check all individual HTML files in a browser or HTML testing tool, such as HtmlQA, to check that all text has been translated and images display properly, etc.

As a rule, the layout of HTML files will be determined by the Cascading Style Sheets. These CSS files are referenced in the headers from the HTML files, for example:

```
<HEAD>
<Title>Menus</Title>
<LINK rel="StyleSheet" href="ottawa.css">
</HEAD>
```

In this example, the ottawa.css file will determine the layout in the HTML file. HTML files often refer to style sheets that are located on a live web site. If this is the case, ensure that the computer can access this web site before packaging the JavaHelp project.

For more information on testing HTML layout and adapting CSS files for language support, refer to the Engineering HTML section on page 264.

Character Encoding Definition

In JavaHelp projects, the character encoding should be specified in the header for each HTML file using the `charset=` meta tag. For more information on specifying character encodings in HTML files, refer to the Engineering HTML section on page 264.

In the headers of the HelpSet, contents, and index XML files, include the encoding definition in the `<?xml>` tag. For more information on specifying character encoding in XML files, refer to the Character Encoding Definition section on page 273.

Language Setting

In JavaHelp projects, the language should be specified in the header for each HTML file using the `lang` attribute. For more information on specifying languages in HTML files, refer to the Engineering HTML section on page 264.

In the headers of the HelpSet, contents, and index XML files, include the language definition in the tag describing the file contents, for example:

```
<helpset xml:lang="fr"> or <toc xml:lang="ja">
```

For more information on specifying character encoding in XML files, refer to the Character Encoding Definition section on page 273.

5.5.5 TESTING JAVAHELP

Testing localized JavaHelp files is comparable to a translation quality assurance task in that the localized version needs to be checked against the source, followed by a final review of the local version.

To compare localized HTML files with source files, use a tool such as HtmlQA or Berlitz Trans Web Express. These tools are designed to compare the layout and functionality of two different language versions of an HTML project. For more information on these tools refer to the Testing Localized HTML section on page 268.

As a final QA step, review the localized online help file in the environment that will be used by the end-user, i.e. a localized operating system or localized help viewer. The JavaHelp system viewer inherits its locale from the application being tested. For information on localized viewers, refer to the Sun Java web site at java.sun.com (search for "JavaHelp").

Unlike WinHelp, the JavaHelp viewer does not contain a feature that allows the user to browse through the help topics in sequential order. For general online help testing procedures, refer to the next section.

6   Testing Localized Online Help

Once the online help file has been translated, reviewed, proofread, formatted and compiled, it should be tested, firstly for linguistic issues and then for functionality issues. For more information on linguistic testing of online help files, refer to the Linguistic Quality Assurance section on page 170.

Before testing online help files, check that all files have been translated and reviewed, including images. It is important to compile the file using the language settings for the target language.

Always test localized help files using a viewer for the target language, preferably running on an operating system for that same language. Because many items in an online help system originate from the standard help viewers, it will be difficult to perform a reliable help file test using a viewer in another language.

In each online help project, several components need to be tested or checked:

- Project statistics
- Layout
- Navigation
- Context help

The following sections provide detailed information on each of these tests.

6.1   Project Statistics

When a help file is compiled, the generated error or log file will contain project statistics, such as the number of topics, jumps, keywords, and images involved. Information will also be provided on the file size of the compiled help file and compression ratio.

For example, the WinHelp compiler log file will contain the following information:

```
Resolving keywords...
Adding bitmaps
52 Topics
2 Jumps
279 Keywords
3 Bitmaps
Created C:\My Documents\Help\WordPad.hlp, 28.616 bytes
Bitmaps: 213 bytes
Hall+Zeck compression decreased help file by 7.257 bytes.
Compile time: 0 minutes, 0 seconds
0 notes, 0 warnings
```

The HTML Help compiler log file will contain the following information:

```
Compile time: 0 minutes, 4 seconds
38 Topics
412 Local links
0 Internet links
0 Graphics
Created c:\My Documents\Help\wordpad.chm, 30,949 bytes
Compression decreased file by 94,400 bytes.
```

Once the localized help file has been compiled, check to ensure that the number of topics, jumps, keywords, and images match the numbers in the source project. In some cases, the number of index keywords will have changed. This will depend on how the search index entries have been translated. It is not unusual for two English synonyms to have only one translation, or for the target language to require the documentation of a synonym where none exists in English.

Also check that there is no significant change in file size or compression ratio. If file sizes are very different, it is possible that the localized version contains images with a different resolution from that of the source files.

Automated testing tools for WinHelp and HTML, such as HelpQA and HtmlQA, will automatically check project statistics.

6.2 Page Layout

The most important aspect of online help files is probably the layout of the help topics. Online help engineers should focus on the following items, when performing a layout check in online help documents:

- Page and text formatting
- Window titles
- Graphics

The best way to ensure that all topics have been checked is to browse through every page of the compiled help file. In some online help systems this can be done easily, by setting some environment variables. For other help systems, third-party tools may be necessary in order to browse through each page in a more structured manner. HelpQA and HtmlQA, for example, enable the user to view localized help topics side-by-side with the source topics so differences can be spotted quickly.

6.2.1 PAGE AND TEXT FORMATTING

As a rule, help file formatting should mirror the format in the original files. It may, however, be necessary to change the column width of tables, or tab settings. In general, though, all text wrapping and page layout will be adjusted automatically in the compiled help file. Therefore, line or page breaks should never be inserted in translated source files.

When performing a layout check of a localized online help system, pay attention to the following issues:

- Missing or untranslated text
- Missing leading or trailing spaces, following punctuation symbols or hypertext links
- Incorrect paragraph indentation
- Incorrect font type and size
- Incorrect or missing formatting of software references
- Garbled display of accented characters
- Inconsistent line spacing
- Incorrect numbered and bulleted lists
- Incorrect wrapping and resizing of text and tables when viewer or browser window is resized
- Extraneous tags or codes from translation memory tools
- Unsorted lists, such as glossaries
- Incorrect or garbled quotation marks

When handling HTML-based online help projects, check the layout in several browsers or on several platforms. Run the tests on the most popular web browser for each target platform, e.g. Internet Explorer or Netscape Navigator.

6.2.2 WINDOW TITLES

Window titles can easily be overlooked in online help systems, and are often translated in project files instead of regular HTML or RTF documents. Special attention should be paid to all window titles in a localized help project to ensure that they are translated and displayed correctly.

When performing a check on window titles in a localized online help system, pay attention to the following issues:

- Untranslated window titles
- Insufficient space to fit translated title in default window title bar
- Garbled display of accented characters

Check all titles, including the secondary window titles. The window definitions can be found in the project files of most online help systems.

6.2.3 GRAPHICS

Most current online help systems can handle fairly sophisticated graphics, which can be anything from screen captures to toolbar icons. Graphics are usually included in build environments as image files which are linked to the source files containing text.

During compilation, the images are inserted in the running text and displayed in the compiled help file.

When performing a check on the graphics in a localized online help system, pay attention to the following issues:

- Untranslated or missing graphics
- Resolution problems
- Un-adjusted image maps or hotspots
- Distorted images

In early WinHelp systems, only 16 colors were supported in graphics. Any graphics with higher resolutions caused display problems. This is no longer an issue, as the current systems now support 256-color graphics.

Where localized images contain hypertext jumps, such as image maps in HTML files and hotspots in WinHelp, these elements should be adjusted for localized images. A screen capture of a dialog box where each button is linked to a help topic explaining that button, for example, will probably need to change in a localized version. If the dialog box is resized, the hotspot areas and image maps need to be adjusted to the new button coordinates and positions.

6.3 Navigation

In addition to the visual aspects of a localized online help system, check the navigation features. Online help engineers should focus on the following items when performing a navigation check in online help documents:

- Table of contents
- Keywords index
- Full-text search index
- Hypertext jumps
- Custom buttons or menu items

These items dictate how the users will navigate through the online help file.

6.3.1 TABLE OF CONTENTS

The table of contents in an online help file is usually the first file displayed to the user. Each item in a table of contents is linked to a topic ID in the help file.

It is important to ensure that all the table of contents entries work and whether they jump to the right location in the help file. The text in the table of contents does not necessarily match the header for the related topic. For example, a table of contents entry such as "Create a bulleted list" can jump to a topic with the header "To create a bulleted list". Unless the topic and header are identical in the source, there may be discrepancies in the translations.

Some compilers or third-party tools will automatically check the links in the table of contents. In WinHelp projects, for example, Microsoft Help Workshop contains a feature that automatically checks all links in a .cnt file. Test the links manually, where there is no tool or feature available.

6.3.2 KEYWORDS INDEX

Most online help systems contain an index with keywords, comparable to an index in a printed book. In most help viewers, the Index tab is located next to the Table of Contents tab, for example in the following German online help file.

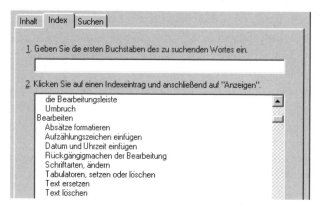

When performing a keyword index check in a localized online help system, pay attention to the following issues:

- Untranslated entries
- Truncated items created by window size limitations
- Duplicate entries caused by leading or trailing spaces or mismatched upper/lower cases
- No support for typing accented characters in keyword field
- Extraneous entries
- Target language sorting rules not applied
- Errors in headings hierarchy

When completed, the search index should look like an index in a printed manual. For more information and general guidelines, refer to the Translating Indexes section on page 307.

6.3.3 FULL-TEXT SEARCH INDEX

Most compiled online help systems contain a full-text search feature which enables users to query the entire contents of an online help file for certain keywords or phrases. Some help systems support the use of boolean, wildcard, and nested expressions in search queries.

Full-text search engines index all words in the online help text. The results of a search are usually sorted based on the number of "hits" found in each topic, and the individual hits are highlighted within the selected topic.

To test the full-text search index feature in a localized online help file, follow these steps:

1. Compile the localized online help file.

2. Delete all temporary files from the build environment.

3. Type some words or phrases in the target language and check the results.

4. Identify some key terms in the localized help contents and check whether the search engine can locate them.

5. Type some common English words like "the" or "at" to check whether the localized help file contains untranslated sentences.

6. If supported, enter some queries using boolean operators or wildcards.

Please note that some full-text search engines do not fully support all languages. Asian languages can be particularly problematic for some engines, so run the tests carefully, and if there are problems, decide with the publisher whether the full-text feature should be disabled for some languages.

6.3.4 HYPERTEXT JUMPS

Most online help files will contain hypertext links to internal or external information. Internal jumps will open topics within the online help file, while external jumps will open topics in remote help files or web site pages. Both types need to be carefully tested.

Depending on the size of the help file, it may not be feasible to run a manual check on all links in the file. When running tests on the links, many authoring tools can generate reports on all the links, with both the source and the destination topics listed. Online help testing tools, such as HelpQA and HtmlQA, can compare all links in the localized version to the links in the source version, as well as test any links that have external destinations, such as web sites.

When performing a links check in a localized online help system, pay attention to the following issues:

- Broken or unresolved links, jumps or pop-ups
- Broken "See Also" or "Related Topics" links
- Working links, but incorrect destinations
- Jumps to remote non-localized online help files
- Jumps to non-localized web sites

Online help is becoming more integrated with information on the web, so it is important to check whether external links to web sites can be "localized". For example, if a link jumps to a company's .com web address check whether this company has a local web address or a localized section on their web site.

Remember to test the hotspots or image maps included in graphics. For more information on hotspots, refer to the Graphics section on page 280.

6.3.5 CUSTOM BUTTONS OR MENUS

If custom buttons or menu items have been added to the localized help viewer, check whether hot keys used in these buttons or menu items function properly and do not conflict with the hot keys in the default localized help viewer.

For example, when a Glossary button has been added to the WinHelp button bar in the help file, make sure that the hot key used for the translation of Glossary does not conflict with any of the hot keys used in the default menu or button bar in the localized viewer window.

In the following example of a localized Italian help viewer button bar, there is a hot key conflict between *Sommario, Opzioni* and *Glossario*.

The first two are errors in the default WinHelp viewer localization, the second is an error introduced by the "Glossario" translation, taken from the localized .hpj file in the tested help.

6.4 Context-Sensitive Help

Context-sensitive help is information that can be accessed from within the application, for example by clicking a Help button, pressing F1, or requesting "What's This?" help. The help information displayed is only relevant to the active or open location in the application. Most online help systems include an Application Programming Interface (API), which enables software developers to add context-sensitive help to their applications.

Context-sensitive help is usually integrated using a map file which maps topic IDs in the online help file to resource IDs in the software application. Testing context-sensitive help is also referred to as integration testing.

To test the functionality of a localized context-sensitive help file, copy the localized help file to the folder containing the localized application. Run the application, and choose the commands in the Help menu.

Press the F1 key or Help button in the dialog boxes. Many Windows 9x applications also offer "What's This?" help. To check the help text, click on the question mark button in the upper right corner of a dialog box, and click on a field or option. Alternatively, right-click an option or field and choose the What's This? command. Menu items can also contain context-sensitive help. To access these help items, highlight a menu command and press F1.

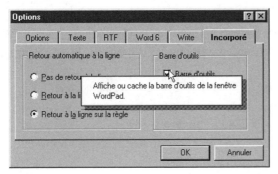

6.5 Check List

The following checklist can be used to check whether all items have been tested in a localized online help project.

6.5.1 PROJECT STATISTICS

First of all, examine the integrity of the localized online help files in relation to the source files, using the following list as a guideline:

✓ The number of translated files should match the number of original files.

✓ No errors are reported when compiling the online help file.

✓ The number of topics, jumps, links, and bitmaps match the source project statistics (the number of keywords may differ slightly).

✓ The file sizes for source and compiled files do not deviate substantially from the original files.

✓ The compression algorithm for the source project is used on the localized files.

✓ The file syntax should match the original files exactly. No tags should be added or deleted, unless added intentionally, i.e. formatting tags surrounding software references in some languages.

6.5.2 PAGE LAYOUT

When the project statistics on the online help file have been validated, check the layout, using the following list as a guideline:

✓ Fonts, colors and styles used in headings and text match the source.

✓ The main help file title and all window titles should be translated and fit in the viewer or browser title bars.

✓ Accented characters and quotation marks display correctly in the window title bars and running text.

✓ All meta-information, such as keywords and titles in the headers of the HTML files should be translated.

✓ All encoding and language specification settings have been changed to reflect the target language.

✓ The sorting language is set correctly for the online help file.

✓ Numbered and bulleted lists display and wrap correctly.

✓ Paragraph formatting, including indentation, alignment, line spacing, matches the source.

✓ Tables display translated text, wrap, scroll, and resize correctly.

✓ All custom viewer buttons or menu items have been translated and do not cause hot key conflicts with localized help viewer.

✓ Text displayed in the status bar and pop-up text has been translated.

✓ All indexes and glossaries are sorted according to target language standards; extended characters are sorted according to language defaults.

✓ No translation memory tags or codes remain in the text.

✓ All graphics are in the correct language, display correctly, and image placeholders have been translated. Image placeholders will show up in HTML files when images are not available.

✓ Image maps or hot spots have been adjusted for the localized images.

✓ Images match the source files in terms of transparency, resolution, or animation.

6.5.3 NAVIGATION

When the page layout in the online help file has been validated, concentrate on the navigation features, i.e. table of contents, keyword index, and full-text search, using the list below as a guideline:

✓ All topic names in the table of contents should be translated.

✓ All links in the table of contents work.

✓ All keyword index entries should be translated.

✓ Keyword index entries fit in the localized help viewer box.

✓ Keyword index entries are sorted according to the target language conventions.

✓ There are no extraneous or duplicate entries in the keyword index.

✓ Main and sub entries in the keyword index are organized correctly.

✓ Input boxes in the keyword index and full-text search field support the entering of accented characters.

✓ The full-text search engine generates results in the target language.

✓ The full-text search engine does not generate results when common English words like "the" or "at" are entered.

✓ Boolean operators and wildcards are supported in the full-text search.

6.5.4 CONTEXT-SENSITIVE HELP

✓ The localized online help file can be accessed from within the localized application, for example by using the Help menu items, or pressing F1 in a dialog box.

✓ The What's This? help can be accessed from within the localized application.

7 Further Reading

The books listed below cover different aspects of online help authoring and engineering.

This list is not exhaustive, but provides an overview of the most relevant and recent books on online help engineering technologies.

Boggan, Scott, Dave Farkas, and Joe Welinske. 1996. *Developing Online Help for Windows 95*. International Thomson Computer Press, ISBN-1-850-32211-2.

Goldfarb, Charles F. and Paul Prescod. 1999. *The XML Handbook*. Prentice Hall, ISBN 0-130-14714-1.

Hackos, Joann T. and Dawn M. Stevens. 1997. *Standards for Online Communication: Publishing Information for the Internet/World Wide Web/Help Systems/Corporate Intranets*. John Wiley & Sons, ISBN 0-471-15695-7.

Hickman, Nancy. 1996. *Building Windows 95 Help*. M&T Books, ISBN 1-558-51477-5.

Microsoft Manual of Style for Technical Publications. 1998. Microsoft Press, ISBN 1-572-31890-2.

Musciano, Chuck and Bill Kennedy. 1998. *HTML: The Definitive Guide*. O'Reilly & Associates, ISBN 1-565-92235-2.

Sun Technical Publications. 1996. *Read Me First! A Style Guide for the Computer Industry*. Prentice Hall, ISBN 0-134-55347-0.

Wexler, Steve. 1998. *Official Microsoft HTML Help Authoring Kit*. Microsoft Press, ISBN 1-572-31603-9.

Wium Lie, Hakon and Bert Bos. 1999. *Cascading Style Sheets: Designing for the Web*. Addison-Wesley, ISBN 0-201-59625-3.

Wilimek, Debbie. 1995. *Mastering Windows 95 Help: The Official Book for Help*. Blue Sky Corp, ISBN 0-964-72361-1.

Chapter 8:
Documentation Translation

This chapter contains information on translating printed and online manuals, and collateral materials. Topics include file setup, translating index markers, spell-checking, and editing and proofreading translations.

This chapter includes the following sections:

1. Introduction
2. Translating Manuals
3. Translating Collateral Material
4. Reviewing Documentation
5. Further Reading

Chapters related to these topics are Chapter 9, which contains information on desktop publishing localized documentation, and Chapter 6, which contains information on translating online help files.

1   Introduction

As mentioned in the Introduction of this book, most localization projects contain some user documentation. Here are some examples of documents often included with software applications:

- Installation Guide
- Getting Started Guide
- Online manuals
- Collateral material

Most of the instructional text will be included in the online documentation. It is now quite common to have reference or administrative guides that are published in online format. The only printed books generally provided with the software are the Installation or the Getting Started guides. Software products also contain collateral material that is translated. Standard items include quick reference cards, marketing pieces, disk labels, and the product box.

Printed manuals are typically created using applications such as Microsoft Word or Adobe FrameMaker. Online manuals are either created in Word or FrameMaker, or converted from some online help format. Collateral materials are usually created with layout applications such as QuarkXPress or Adobe PageMaker and Illustrator.

This chapter outlines some of the issues that translators face when translating any of these document types. Please note that Chapte r9 contains information on desktop publishing translated documentation.

Most software localization vendors now use translation memory tools for virtually all translation work. Translators in localization, as a rule, do not work within the application used to create the original documents, such as Adobe FrameMaker. Last-minute corrections or changes do, however, need to be implemented in the translated files that have been converted back into their original formats. So it is important for translators to have a basic knowledge of these applications. There are still translators who may not be using translation memory tools and who prefer to work directly in the source files. And even when translation memory is used, translators need to be able to recognize certain application features which will most likely appear as codes in the translation memory tool document, such as index markers or cross-references.

Translation memory tools support most of the commonly used document formats, such as FrameMaker, Word, and SGML. For documentation types not supported, the source text should be exported from the application, imported in the translation memory tool, translated, exported from TM, and re-imported into the original application. It may still be necessary to fix some aspects of the layout after files have been translated in a translation memory tool.

For more information on processing documentation files using translation memory tool filters, refer to the Translation Memory Tools section on page 362.

1.1 Translation Approach

Documentation files typically comprise front matter, text divided into chapters and appendices, and generated components such as the table of contents and index. The front matter contains the manual cover and small pieces of text, such as copyright, trademarks, and disclaimers. The table of contents is generated from the headings in every chapter, for example by including the first two heading levels and automatically adding the actual page numbers where the headings are located. An index is generated based on the index markers that are inserted throughout the body of the text. Index markers are usually inserted right next to the word or sentence they are referring to. When an index is generated, all index markers are merged and sorted in a separate file at the end of the document.

Documentation files can also contain all sorts of other generated components, such as image lists, internal cross-references, and chapter content overviews.

In a documentation project, the following components should be translated:

- Body text
- Index markers
- Screen captures and other graphics
- Callout text

Body text in technical documentation consists of headings, standard paragraphs, numbered or bulleted lists, tables, and special notices. Index entries can be placed throughout the text, in headings or in running text. Depending on the format, they are inserted as hidden text (in Word) or markers (in FrameMaker).

Graphics are inserted to show readers key components of a software product, and often contain illustrations of key actions that users must perform. Software manuals, in particular, will contain many screen captures. These are normally made up of images showing elements of the user interface, such as dialog boxes or menus. Screen captures and other graphics will usually contain callout text. Call-out text is normally found in a box, explaining or describing the contents of the image. In most cases, the callout text will be part of the body text, not of the image itself. Refer to the Editing Graphics section on page 353 for more information.

When using a translation memory tool to translate documentation files, it is important to have a printed or online version of the original document, including layout and graphics. Here are some of the key reasons:

- Printed layout will give translators a much better overview of the structure and feel of the source document.
- Items such as tables and callout text will be displayed out of context in a translation memory tool.
- In order to translate image callout text, it is important to see the related graphics in context.
- In certain tagged formats, it is not always clear what the tags represent. A printed copy of the layout will make this much easier for the translator.
- In the source text, items are often separated by carriage returns to place them on two lines. When the text is imported into a translation memory tool, the text "Image Size", for example, will be separated into two different segments. Translating the words Image and Size independently will more than likely produce an inaccurate translation, because it is not translated as a phrase.

The following example shows a table displayed in a documentation file in its native format, and how it is displayed as tagged text in a translation memory tool. This particular example contains a table from a FrameMaker file converted by TRADOS S-Tagger to RTF format.

Extension	File Type	Localizable?
.ali	alias file	no

```
<ps "table head" 3><:cs "Default Paragraph Font" 2>Extension<:/cs>
</ct>
<ct 1>
<ps "" 4><:cs "Default Paragraph Font" 1>File Type<:/cs>
</ct>
<ct 1>
<ps "" 4><:cs "Default Paragraph Font" 1>Localizable?<:/cs>
</ct>
</row>
<row 1>
<ct 1>
<ps "table in list" 5><:cs "Default Paragraph Font" 1>.ali<:/cs>
</ct>
<ct 1>
<ps "" 4><:cs "Default Paragraph Font" 1>alias file<:/cs>
</ct>
<ct 1>
<ps "" 4><:cs "Default Paragraph Font" 1>no<:/cs>
```

It is very important to review or proofread translation documentation once it has been converted back to the original file format and layout. For more information, refer to the Reviewing Documentation section on page 315.

1.2 Translation Guidelines

Software documentation files and online help files have much in common and may even contain the same text. Refer to the Translation Guidelines section on page 167 for more information on translating online help files.

One important difference between online help files and printed documentation files are the generated components. Printed manuals often contain more generated components than online help files, including the table of contents, and internal cross references. In online help files, the table of contents is typically included in a separate translatable file. In documentation files, this file should not be translated, because it is automatically generated from the headings in the document. Another difference is the use of page numbers; in printed documents, page numbers are used in the table of contents, index, and cross-references. In online help documents, page numbers are usually omitted and replaced by hypertext links.

As a general rule, never translate generated files, such as table of contents or index files! The table of contents is automatically generated, and the index is generated from index markers that are translated as part of the body text.

Tip: Even though the text in the table of contents and index files is automatically generated, the titles or heading of these files should be translated.

It is important to preserve all layout, typographic conventions and styles from the source text, unless instructed otherwise. Avoid removing any markers, such as index markers and conditional text markers, or changing any of the document properties.

2 Translating Manuals

Manuals are generally created and translated in an application like Word or FrameMaker. Chapter are usually arranged into single files, and then added to a book or master file. The master file is used to automatically generate a table of contents, index, and internal cross references.

2.1 Adobe FrameMaker

Adobe FrameMaker is an application that combines core word processing, desktop publishing (DTP), and graphics features in one software package. It is available on several platforms and in numerous language versions. The latest versions of FrameMaker have integrated support for Asian languages, and ship with a large number of language dictionaries.

For more information on Adobe FrameMaker, refer to the Products section on the Adobe web site at www.adobe.com.

Information can also be obtained from the FrameMaker newsgroup comp.text.frame or the Worldwide Online FrameMaker User Network at www.frameusers.com.

2.1.1 FILE SETUP

A typical FrameMaker manual setup consists of a book file, linked to a table of contents file, several chapter files, appendices, and an index file. The book file typically has a .bk extension and can be recognized by the book icon.

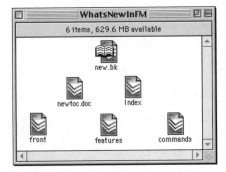

The book file is used to generate the table of contents, index and all internal and external cross-references. When opening a book file, a window is displayed with a list of the file names. Double-click on the listed file name to open a chapter. Avoid changing the order of the files in a book file, as this will change the page numbering.

2.1.2 OPENING FILES IN FRAMEMAKER

When opening a file, FrameMaker may ask where "missing" screen captures or other graphic files are located. A Missing File screen will be displayed:

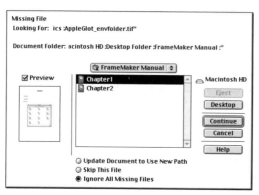

Select the Ignore All Missing Files option and confirm this option by clicking on the Continue button. When selecting the Update Document to Use New Path option without pointing to the correct folder, all links to the images may be lost. This may mean that all images need to be manually re-imported.

If a message reports that the document is using unavailable fonts, install the missing fonts before continuing. Otherwise, FrameMaker substitutes available fonts for the missing ones. In FrameMaker 5.5 and later versions, choose Preferences from the File menu and activate the Remember Missing Font Names option before opening any files. If this setting is enabled, FrameMaker will not permanently substitute fonts.

2.1.3 COUNTING WORDS

To count the words in a FrameMaker document, follow these steps:

1. From the File menu, select the Utilities command.

2. In the Document Reports dialog box, select Word Count.

3. Click the Run button to count the words in the FrameMaker document.

4. A window will then display the word count.

Please note that the FrameMaker word count utility does not include index markers, so the word count report should also be run on the generated index file. For a more accurate word count, generate an index markers list for each chapter, because the same index markers may appear in different locations. Translation memory systems will automatically deal with these internal matches, so once a marker has been translated, equivalent entries in other locations will be automatically translated. Please note that this will only be the case if each index entry is processed as a separate segment. Some translation memory tools import all index entries and sub-entries in a marker as one segment, which will result in fewer full matches.

The table of contents should not be included in the word count, because the contents are automatically generated from the translated chapter headings.

To generate page and word counts from entire book files with just one command, use the BookInfo plug-in. The tool can be downloaded from www.frameusers.com.

2.1.4 TRANSLATING FRAMEMAKER FILES

To avoid deleting index or other markers when translating text in FrameMaker or inserting edits in translated FrameMaker files, it is important to select the Text Symbols option in the View menu. Enabling this option will display markers as **T** symbols in the text.

Use the Delete or Backspace keys to delete the source text once the translation has been entered. When overtyping highlighted text, there is a risk of deleting the index markers in the text block!

In FrameMaker, the following components require special attention: headers and footers, index markers, cross-references, and conditional text.

Translation Memory

To translate FrameMaker files using a translation memory tool, the files first need to be saved to .mif format, as this is the file format that is supported by most TM tools. Trados has released a special translation memory filter application for FrameMaker files called S-Tagger. Trados S-Tagger converts .mif files to a file format which can be opened and edited using Microsoft Word.

Tip: There are several tools available that batch-convert FrameMaker files to .mif format, such as Bruce Foster's MifSave plug-in, which can be downloaded from www.frameusers.com.

Here are some important issues to consider before importing FrameMaker files in a translation memory tool:

- Make sure there are no missing fonts or images. Check this by opening the FrameMaker files or book file. FrameMaker should not display any error dialog boxes or a console window.
- Make sure the table of contents and index generate correctly, and that there are no unresolved cross-references.
- Make sure change bars are switched off. To do this, select Format > Document > Change Bars, and choose the Clear all Change Bars option.

Also refer to the general segmentation guidelines in the Segmentation section on page 362.

Headers and Footers

To translate headers or footers, choose Master Pages in the View menu. In the master pages, the user can edit the header or footer displayed on every page. Master pages typically contain default page settings, including header or footer text, for left (even) pages, right (odd) pages, and starting pages for chapters or sections.

Tip: Please note that headers and footers in FrameMaker often contain variables that automatically insert chapter or section titles and do not require translation.

Once the header or footer text has been translated, choose Body Pages in the View menu and select the Keep Overrides option and the Continue button to apply the translated text to the body pages.

Headers or chapter titles are often included in markers. To translate these, choose the Find/Change command in the Edit menu and select Marker of Type in the Find drop down list. Type *header/footer* in the Find text box to search for header or footer markers. To open and edit a marker, choose Marker in the Special menu. If the marker belongs to the header, the type box will say Header/Footer.

```
┌────────────────────────── Marker ──────────────────────────┐
│                                                            │
│ Marker Type: │ Header/Footer $1 ▼ │                        │
│ Marker Text:                                               │
│ ┌────────────────────────────────────────────────────┐ ▲  │
│ │ This is a header marker│                            │ █  │
│ │                                                    │    │
│ │                                                    │ ▼  │
│ └────────────────────────────────────────────────────┘    │
│ ┌──────────────┐                                           │
│ │ Edit Marker  │                                           │
│ └──────────────┘                                           │
└────────────────────────────────────────────────────────────┘
```

Index Markers

In FrameMaker, index entries are inserted in the main text using markers, not fields. These markers need to be opened in order to access and edit the text of an index entry. Index markers are indicated with **T** symbols, and are only visible when the Text Symbols option in the View menu is enabled.

To translate index markers, follow these steps:

1. Open the first chapter of the document, go to the beginning of the text, and search for the first index entry. To do this, choose the Find/Change command from the Edit menu or press Ctrl+F or Command-F.

```
┌────────────────────────── Find/Change ──────────────────────────┐
│                                                                 │
│ Find │ Marker of Type:     ▼ │ │ index                      │   │
│                                                                 │
│ ☐ Consider Case   ☐ Whole Word   ☐ Use Wildcards   ☐ Find Backward │
│                                                                 │
│ Change │ To Text:           ▼ │ │                            │   │
│                                                                 │
│ ☐ Clone Case                                                    │
│                                                   ● Document    │
│ ┌──────┐ ┌────────┐ ┌──────────────┐ ┌──────────────┐ ○ Selection │
│ │ Find │ │ Change │ │ Change & Find│ │ Change All In:│           │
│ └──────┘ └────────┘ └──────────────┘ └──────────────┘           │
└─────────────────────────────────────────────────────────────────┘
```

2. In the Find list menu, select Marker of Type. In the Find text box, type *index*.

3. Click on the Find button to jump to the first index marker in the chapter.

4. When the first index marker is found and selected, choose Marker from the Special menu.

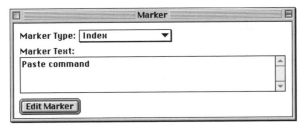

5. Translate the index marker, and press Return or click the Edit Marker button. Do not close the Marker window.

6. Press Ctrl+Shift+F or Command-G to automatically open the next index marker, and repeat step 5.

Within the marker window, a colon separates levels in an entry, a semi-colon separates entries in a marker, angled brackets ([and]) specify a special sorting order for the entry, <$startrange> and <$endrange> indicate a page range, and <$nopage> suppresses the page number.

After translating all index markers, generate the index. For information on generating an index, refer to the Generating Book Files section on page 301.

Check the generated index for consistency or other errors. To correct an index entry, hold Ctrl+Alt or Ctrl+Option and click on the index entry. The chapter containing the index marker will automatically be opened, with the index marker selected. To edit the marker, choose Marker from the Special menu.

For more information on translating indexes, refer to the Translating Indexes section on page 307.

Cross-references

Cross-references are references to other sections in the manual. An example of a cross-reference is "For more information refer to Copying Files on page 3". The section "Copying Files on page 3" is a cross-reference. The title of the paragraph that the cross-reference refers to is "Copying Files", the page where that paragraph can be found is page 3.

When clicking on a cross-reference in FrameMaker, a block of text is selected. Text within a cross-reference cannot be edited directly by the user. If the cross-reference is selected and the translator starts typing, the cross-reference will be deleted!

For more information please refer to Copying Files on page 3.

When the actual paragraph heading "Copying Files" on page 3 is translated, the cross-reference will automatically reflect the translated text and page number when the book file is generated. For more information on generating book files, refer to the Generating Book Files section on page 301.

Although cross-references are automatically updated, the text between the paragraph title and the page number is part of the cross-reference definition, and must be translated. In the above example, the words "on page" need to be translated. Cross-reference format text only needs to be translated once.

To translate the cross-reference format, follow these steps:

1. Double-click on a cross-reference to open the Cross-Reference dialog box.

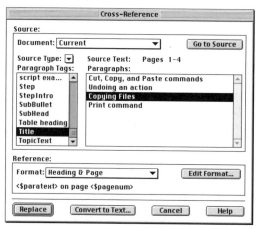

2. In the Cross-Reference dialog box, click the Edit Format button to open the Edit Cross-Reference Format dialog box.

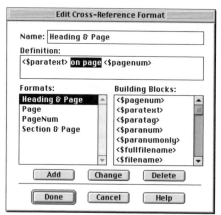

3. In the Definition field, translate the words "on page". Do not change any other items in the Definition field.

4. Click on the items in the Formats box to display other format definitions that may need to be translated.

5. Click the Change button to store the new cross-reference format definitions.

6. Click the Done button to close the dialog box.

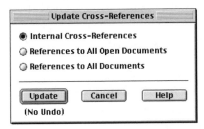

7. In the Update Cross-References dialog box, select the files to which the new format definition must be applied.

Conditional Text

Conditional text is text that is displayed or hidden, based on certain options being selected. Software manuals often contain conditional text, for example, to mark sections relevant to certain platform versions of an application. Paragraphs related to Mac OS features will be marked with a Macintosh only condition tag, and paragraphs related to Windows features will be marked with a Windows only tag. Before publishing, the author can then decide to publish or print a Mac version of the manual, or a Windows version.

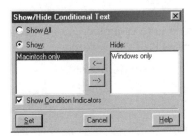

Translators need to be aware of these options, and should probably translate all text included in the document. For more information on how to display or hide conditional text, refer to the FrameMaker documentation. Always verify with the publisher, what conditional text should be shown and what text should be hidden. It is important to confirm whether hidden conditional text should also be translated. Most translation memory tools only process the text included in the Show field.

2.1.5 SPELL CHECKING TRANSLATIONS

Prior to running the spelling checker, a language must be applied to the document. The language must also be applied so that the hyphenation rules for the target language can be used.

Users can only change language settings if the appropriate language dictionaries have been installed with the FrameMaker application. If the dictionary for the target language is not installed, copy it from the FrameMaker CD-ROM, or re-install the application with the language dictionaries selected. All dictionary files need to be copied to the Dictionaries (dict) folder inside the FrameMaker application folder. For more information on installing additional dictionaries, refer to the FrameMaker documentation.

To apply a language to a document, follow these steps:

1. Click any paragraph in the translated text.

2. Open the Paragraph Designer (Ctrl+M or Command-M) and choose Default Font from the Properties menu.

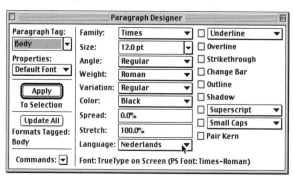

3. Choose Commands and select the Set Window to As Is option.

4. Choose Default Font from the Properties menu and change the language in the Language pop-up menu. Note that, in earlier versions of FrameMaker, the language choice is made in the Advanced Properties window.

5. Confirm the new setting by clicking the Update All button.

6. Select the Advanced Properties Only and All Paragraphs and Catalog Entries. Confirm this by clicking on the Update button.

If FrameMaker has completed the process, close the window (Ctrl+W or Command-W) and start the Spelling Checker by choosing Spelling Checker from the Edit menu.

2.1.6 GENERATING BOOK FILES

Once all chapters have been translated and re-converted to FrameMaker format, overwrite the source chapter files with the localized ones, with the exception of the book, table of contents, and index files. To update the table of contents, index, and cross-references to display the translated text taken from the localized chapters, re-generate the book file.

To generate a book file, follow these steps:

1. Open the book file and choose the Generate/Update command from the File menu.

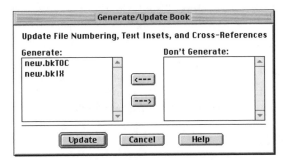

2. In the Generate/Update Book dialog box, select the appropriate option in order to generate the table of contents, index, or both.

3. Click the Update button to update the book file.

The sorting order of the generated index is specified on the reference pages by changing the building blocks. The reference pages will normally contain lines defining the index headers and sorting order, for example:

```
<$symbols><$numerics><$alphabetics>
Symbols[\];Numerics[0];A;B;C;D;E;F;G;H;I;J;K;L;M;N;O;P;Q;R;S;T;U;V;W
;X;Y;Z <$pagenum>
```

The first line contains the sorting order for the index entries, i.e. first symbols, then numerics, and then the standard English alphabet. For languages using other alphabets, replace the <$alphabetics> section with the appropriate sorting order. In some languages, such as Finnish and Swedish, accented letters are added at the end of the English alphabet, so the sorting order line changes as follows:

```
<$symbols><$numerics><$alphabetics>Åå Ää Öö
```

The line starting with Symbols [\] defines the index headers, including their formatting. Modify the line to reflect the appropriate headings for the target language. For more information on changing index specifications, refer to the FrameMaker documentation.

2.2   Microsoft Word

Many publishers use Microsoft Word to create small to medium sized manuals. Word is available on several platforms and in numerous language versions.

For more information on Microsoft Word, refer to the Microsoft web site at www.microsoft.com. Another interesting source of information is the Word newsgroup at microsoft.public.word.

2.2.1   FILE SETUP

Manuals that have been written using Microsoft Word often consist of one master document and several subdocuments. A master document is comparable to a book file in FrameMaker, and can be used to generate a table of contents, index, and cross-references for a set of subdocuments.

Microsoft Word 8 and later versions provide a master document view, which enables the user to view an outline of the master document and all its subdocuments. When working with a master and subdocuments, always open subdocuments from within the master, otherwise cross-references to other subdocuments will not be recognized and updated.

2.2.2   OPENING WORD FILES

Microsoft Word handles both embedded and linked graphic files. Embedded files have been inserted into a document and are now part of that document. Linked graphic files are only referenced in the document, and are stored in another location.

If the Word file contains embedded files, translated files should be re-embedded or copied into the document manually. Linked files can be replaced just by overwriting the source language image files with the localized versions. When opening a file, Word will not notify the user of missing screen captures or other graphic files. If images are not found by Word, a replacement box for missing linked graphic files will be displayed. However, the link information is preserved.

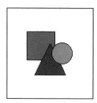

Browse through the Word document to check whether any linked files are missing.

When opening documents containing fonts that are unavailable on the operating system, Word will not display a warning message. Go to the Font Substitution button in the Compatibility section of the Options dialog box to check whether font substitution is necessary.

2.2.3 COUNTING WORDS

To count words in a Word document, select the Word Counts command from the Tools menu.

Please note that different versions of Word generate different word counts. This is because word-clusters, such as "web-based" are sometimes as single words. Some versions of Word do and others do not include numbers in the word counts. Always verify the word counts using another tool, such as a translation memory tool.

Word counts generated in Microsoft Word do not include the index markers, so remember to run the word count on the generated index. This will still not give a very accurate result, because identical index entries that occur on several pages will be counted only once.

2.2.4 TRANSLATING FILES

When translating text in Microsoft Word or inserting edits in translated Word files, it is important to have the View All Formatting Marks option selected in the Options dialog box, to avoid deleting index or other markers. To open this dialog box, select Options from the Tools menu.

In Microsoft Word, the following components require special attention: headers and footers, index markers, and cross-references.

Translation Memory

Most translation memory tools support Microsoft Word by default. Some TM tools even use Word as the translation editor interface.

Here are some important issues to consider before importing Word files in a translation memory tool:

- Make sure the styles are setup properly in the Word document and no manual style overrides or definitions exist. After using a translation memory tool, it may be necessary to re-attach the original style sheet.

- Make sure the Word files do not contain any revision marks. Check with the publisher whether the revision marks can be removed from the document by selecting the Accept or Reject Changes > Accept All command from the Track Changes menu.

Also refer to the general segmentation guidelines in the Segmentation section on page 362.

Headers and Footers

Switch to Page Layout view or Print Layout mode to check whether the document contains a header of footer. Headers and footers are repeated throughout the entire document or document section.

To translate headers or footers, choose Header and Footer in the View menu. Please note that headers and footers do not display in Normal view.

Index Markers

To translate index entries in Microsoft Word, set the Page View to show hidden text. To enable this option in Microsoft Word, choose Options in the Tools menu and select Hidden Text in the View tab. Another option is to click on the ¶ button on the toolbar.

Index entries in Word are fields with the XE (Index Entry) field code. An index entry in Word is displayed as { XE "Print to File" } or { XE "Printing";"Print to File" } or { XE "Print to File"\t "See Printing" }.

In the index fields, a colon (:) separates main entries from sub entries. If the \t instruction is used, the text following \t will be inserted in place of a page number. In the above example, the field will generate the "Print to File, *See* Printing" entry in the index.

To translate index entries using Microsoft Word, follow these steps:

1. Open the first chapter of the document and search for the first index entry by choosing the Find command from the Edit menu and typing ^d XE in the Find what: box.

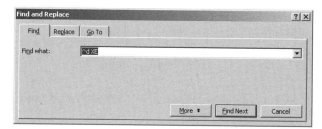

2. When the first index entry is found, leave the Find and Replace dialog box open and click in the index entry field.

3. Translate the index entry by replacing the text between quotation marks.

4. Click on the Find Next button to jump to the next index entry, and repeat step 3.

For more information on generating or updating indexes, refer to the Generating a TOC and Index section on page 305.

Cross-references

In Word documents, cross-references are updated automatically, when the index or table of contents is generated. Cross-references in Word only contain the relevant heading text for the paragraph, and the page number. All text within the cross-reference, such as "on page", needs to be translated manually.

A cross-reference can be displayed as a field code {REF_Ref401222306 \h}. To display the actual text in the cross-reference, right-click on the field code and select the Toggle Field Codes command.

2.2.5 SPELL CHECKING TRANSLATIONS

To run the spelling checker on a document, first apply a language to the document. In order to do this, the spelling and grammar files must be installed for the required target language.

Setting the correct language for a document is always useful, because some text features, such as quotation mark styles, are language-dependent and adjusted automatically by Word.

To apply a language to a document, follow these steps:

1. Select the text that a language must be applied to.

2. Choose Language and Set Language from the Tools menu.

3. Select a language.

4. Click OK to close the Language dialog box.

Now start the Spelling Checker by choosing Spelling and Grammar from the Tools menu or pressin gF7.

2.2.6 GENERATING A TOC AND INDEX

After the entire document has been translated, including all chapter and heading titles, run an automatic update on the table of contents to display the translated headings. Make sure all hidden text and field codes are turned off before generating a table of contents or index, otherwise the pagination will be incorrect.

To update a table of contents, right-click on the table, and choose the Update Field command or press F9. The index can also be generated by right-clicking and choosing the Update Field command.

To update the table of contents, index and cross-references simultaneously, select all text within the document using the Select All command from the Edit menu, right-click on the table of contents, and select the Update Fields command. The table of contents and index can be found in the master document or in the translated document. The sorting order of the index is determined by the language setting in the document.

2.3 SGML

An introduction to SGML and other markup languages such as XML and HTML can be found in the HTML and XML section on page 205. While XML and HTML has been used mainly to create online documents, such as online help or web pages, SGML has traditionally been used for large volume documentation projects.

SGML has been a standard format in the automotive and aerospace industries for years, for example, and is now gaining popularity among software publishers who recognize the merits of SGML. Many software publishers, however, prefer to work with XML, which is a less complicated subset of SGML.

One of biggest advantages of SGML is single-source publishing. Documentation written in SGML typically consists of a structured information repository which can be output to a variety of formats, such as HTML for on-screen display, PDF for online distribution, or PostScript for printing. This is possible because formatting information is strictly separated from content. SGML databases only contain information and the structure in which the information is written. All information is stored separately from any encoding that will be used to determined its final printed or displayed form.

In SGML projects, translatable text is stored in SGML files, formatting and layout information in DSSSL files, Document Style Semantics and Specification Language. Document Type Definition (DTD) files describe the structure of the SGML documents and define the tags used in the SGML code.

To translate an SGML project, follow these guidelines:

- Text should be exported from the SGML authoring tool, such as Arbortext Epic Editor or Adobe FrameMaker+SGML. This tool is often integrated in a content or document management system.

- Text should be imported into a translation memory (TM) tool, where the DTD will indicate to the TM tool which markup tags contain translatable text.

- After translation, the translated text should be re-imported into the SGML authoring environment.

- Localized graphics should be stored in the document management system.

- The DSSSL file may require some adjustments for non-Roman languages.

- The translated text is output to the required format.

Once the text is output, some additional desktop publishing or layout work may be necessary, depending on the output format and language.

Since there is no real standard authoring environment for SGML, and it is unlikely that translators will ever work directly in an SGML environment because of its complexity, no tools are discussed in this section. For more information on how text in markup languages are translated, refer to the HTML and XML section on page 205.

2.4 Translating Indexes

In most documentation formats, indexes are generated from index entries or markers, which have been inserted in the running text of a manual.

If a manual contains an automatically generated index, never translate the generated index file. If the source entries are translated in the generated index file, all translations will be overwritten with the English index entries as soon as the index is generated! Locate the index entries or markers in the running text instead, and translate the index entries in a consistent way.

For more information on how index entries are translated, refer to the Index Markers section on page 296 (Adobe FrameMaker), and Index Markers section on page 304 (Microsoft Word). When using another word processor or application, refer to the online help or documentation for more information.

2.4.1 TRANSLATING INDEX ENTRIES

Indexes can pose many problems for the translator, particularly if the index is large, or the source text has been poorly written or constructed. Several issues need to be considered by translators working with index entries. Once the index has been generated after the translation, it should be checked carefully against the running text.

Keywords

Index entries should always start with the keyword that refers to the topic or subject. Always consider how a user will search for an index entry. If the English index is correctly written, stay as close to the original word order as possible because significant words will be listed first in each entry.

For example, if the "File menu" index entry is translated into German as "Menü Datei", the German entry will be alphabetized under "M". If the index contains entries for all other menus used in the application, they will all be sorted under "M". It is highly probable that a user will look for the word "Datei", so it is advisable to reverse the word order, and use a comma or another separator to create an entry like "Datei, Menü".

Other examples of commonly used index entries that need to be reordered in the translation are entries such as "HTML file" and "Copy Command". Readers will search for the words "HTML" and "Copy", not "file" or "command".

Duplicate Entries

Try to avoid duplicate entries. English synonyms often translate into a single word in other languages. On the other hand, it may be necessary to create two entries in the target languages when an English term can be translated in various ways.

When entries appear in both singular and plural form, combine the two, for example add an "s" in parentheses. Before translating an index file, make a rule to follow one format for all entries. Then follow this rule as much as possible. For example, the entries for "Printers" and "Printer" can be merged into a single entry, unless they are specific options or commands in the software.

Another typical error occurs where two separate English entries translate into a term which is sorted under the same letter. For example:

```
English
D
Default Window....5
W
Window, default....5

Italian
F
Finestra principale....5
Finestra, principale....5
```

Some index generators, such as the one included in Adobe FrameMaker, distinguish between upper case and lower case entries; be consistent in the use of upper and lower case in the translations. If the index markers contain the same entries with a different case, duplicate entries will be included in the generated index file.

2.4.2 PLANNING INDEX TRANSLATION

Translate the index entries *while* translating the running text, *or* leave all index entries to be translated after the entire manual has been translated.

If there is only one translator working on a document or if a translation memory tool is used, the index markers should be translated while the translator is working on the running text. When multiple translators are working on a single manual, however, there are two options. Either have all team members translate the index entries included in their sections, or ask one of the translators to translate all index entries when all text has been translated.

Many translators prefer to translate the index entries for a chapter, once they have finished translating each chapter. With projects involving multiple translators, this will make it more difficult to maintain consistency in index markers, used throughout the entire manual. One way to maintain consistency within a group of translators working on the same index is to create a keyword style sheet, and include information on grammatical form for index entries, word order, and capitalization.

The best approach is, of course, to have all translators translate the index entries in their sections of the manual, and assign one translator to review and edit the generated translated index. The index editor should pay particular attention to the following:

- Translation consistency – Check to ensure that similar terms are phrased consistently. For example, all nouns should be either in the singular or plural form.
- Duplicate entries – Check for duplicate entries because of slight phrasing differences or capitalization.
- Extraneous entries – Check for keywords that are more specific than a general keyword, but appear close to the general keywords. For example, if "printing status reports" appears immediately after "printing reports", combine the two entries.

Please note that for Asian languages major adjustments may be required, because of the different sorting options. In Japanese, for example, automatic phonetic sorting is not possible without manual input from a translator.

3 Translating Collateral Material

Collateral material includes small documents such as quick reference cards, packaging, CD labels, promotional materials, and registration cards. Collaterals do not normally contain much text, but they do contain many high-quality graphics and a complicated page layout; these are usually produced on computers running Apple Ma cOS.

The text on collaterals is often very marketing-oriented. Promotional material and packaging are used to create a first impression of a localized product among the users. Therefore, translation quality and language use is far more critical here than in online help or documentation translation.

It is important that translators working on collateral material combine good product knowledge with a commercial translation style. For this type of material, it is advisable to ask the publisher to include a review cycle, to be conducted by their local marketing or sales staff. These are the people who sell the localized product, so it is important to gain their support for the translations produced.

It is very impractical to use translation memory tools for collateral material, because of the size and nature of the materials. The effort involved in importing the text into the translation memory tools would not warrant it. Translators should also be able see the text in context to ensure that the text fits, for example on the product box. Often the text on collaterals such as marketing material requires a considerable amount of rewriting, which is difficult to do in a translation memory tool.

Typically, one- or two-page reference cards, promotional materials, and packaging will be created and translated using QuarkXPress. Multi-page leaflets or small installation guides are often created and translated using Adobe PageMaker. CD or disk labels will typically be in Adobe Illustrator format. The following sections provide a quick introduction to these packages, specifically for translators.

3.1 QuarkXPress

QuarkXPress by Quark is an application that combines advanced graphics handling with precise typographic controls and sophisticated printing and color separation functions. QuarkXPress is available in compatible versions for Windows and MacOS .

QuarkXPress Passport is the multi-language version of QuarkXPress, which enables the user to run the interface of QuarkXPress in different languages. It also enables the user to hyphenate and spell check documents in different languages. For translation of QuarkXPress files, it is advisable to use the Passport version.

For more information on QuarkXPress, refer to the Quark web site at www.quark.com.

3.1.1 FILE SETUP

Since the release of version 4 of QuarkXPress, it is possible to create chapters in book files, and generate table of contents and index components. A book is a collection of documents that share the same style sheets, colors, lists, and other settings.

QuarkXPress 4 and later versions also let the user save files in multilingual format, which means that the document contains sections with different language and hyphenation settings. This format is only compatible with QuarkXPress Passport.

3.1.2 OPENING QUARKXPRESS FILES

In QuarkXPress files, it is possible to save a preview of an image when saving a document, which will display the image in the document even when the original image file is not present. This means that no message will be displayed reporting that a graphic is missing.

The original image is required, however, when printing the document or creating a PostScript file for final output.

3.1.3 COUNTING WORDS

To count words in a QuarkXPress document, follow these steps:

1. From the Utilities menu, select the Check Spelling command.

2. Select the Document or Story option.

3. A word count window will be displayed. Clicking OK will start the spell check.

Please note that the word count does not include the index markers, so run the word count report on the generated index.

3.1.4 TRANSLATING FILES

First of all, enable the Show Invisibles option in the View menu to avoid deleting layout markers.

In QuarkXPress, all text and images are contained in boxes. Because translated text usually is longer than the original, the text will move down in the box, often making it invisible on the screen. If a box contains "hidden" text, a check mark is displayed in the lower right corner of the text box.

To ensure all text is translated, overwrite the original text instead of inserting it, and ask the publisher whether the text boxes can be resized to allow for text expansion. If boxes cannot be resized or if they are locked, adjust the translations to make them fit.

It is also possible for text to flow into another text box. This means the text in the two boxes belong to one "story". Check the following boxes in a text flow, to see if they can handle text expansion.

QuarkXPress documents are usually created when complex layouts are combined with text. Special attention should be paid when translating Quark documents. For example, do not move boxes, change color information or paragraph and character settings!

In QuarkXPress 4 and later versions, text can be saved as outlines by choosing the Text to Box command. This outline text cannot be edited or restored, so avoid using this command.

Translation Memory

QuarkXPress and translation memory tools have always had compatibility problems. There are many reasons for this, but the main reason is because the typical content of QuarkXPress files includes marketing material and brochures, which does not lend itself well to translation memory tools. Source text often needs to be partly re-written and adjusted for the target market, which may include changing the order or overall content of the files.

Another reason is due to the difficulty in exporting and importing text from Quark to another file format; it is not a fully automated process. Quark files typically exist of many small text blocks, which need to be exported and imported manually, unless a third-party extension such as CopyFlow (www.napsys.com) is used.

Index Markers

Indexing was introduced with QuarkXPress version 4. Index entries are enclosed in red brackets, and can be located by opening the Index palette and clicking on the Find Next button.

To translate the index entry, click the Edit button, and edit the text in the Text box of the Entry field. Then, click Next to locate the next index entry. It is also possible to translate the index directly in the Index palette, but this will not provide reference or context information.

Use the Build Index command from the Utilities menu to generate the localized index.

3.1.5 SPELL CHECKING TRANSLATIONS

In order to run the spelling checker on a document, first apply a language to a paragraph or range of paragraphs.

To apply a language and spell-check a document, follow these steps:

1. Select the text and the desired language in the Language pop-up menu of the Formats tab in the Paragraph Attributes dialog box.

2. Now run the Spelling Checker by choosing Check Spelling from the Utilities menu. Make sure the QuarkXPress Dictionary file for the desired language is installed in the QuarkXPress folder.

Check the spelling of the selected word, story, or the entire document.

3.2 Adobe PageMaker

Adobe PageMaker is a page layout tool for business publishing. It contains many standard templates and sample illustrations, and is used mainly for medium-sized documents.

For more information on PageMaker, refer to the Products section of the Adobe web site at www.adobe.com.

3.2.1 FILE SETUP

Recent versions of PageMaker have a new feature called book lists, that include all elements contained in a book, for example separate chapters.

A book list enables the user to generate a table of contents or index for multiple publications.

3.2.2 OPENING PAGEMAKER FILES

If a publication contains graphics that cannot be located, a "Cannot find" window will be displayed. A preview of the image will still be visible, and information on the missing linked image can be displayed by clicking on the image and choosing the Link Info command from the Element menu.

Jump to the desired page by clicking on the page number icon in the lower left corner of the screen. Clicking on the L or R icon will show the left and right master page, which may also contain translatable text such as headers.

3.2.3 COUNTING WORDS

To count words in a PageMaker document (version 6.5 or later), follow these steps:

1. From the Utilities menu, select the Plug-ins command.

2. Select the Word Counter plug-in.

Count the entire document or just the selected text. Please note that the word count does not include the index markers, so remember to run the word count on the generated index.

3.2.4 TRANSLATING FILES

In PageMaker, text can be contained in text blocks. All text is part of a PageMaker story, which can comprise numerous text objects or just one. Use the Type tool (T) on the toolbar to type translations over the original text.

Translate in page layout view or in the story editor. To switch between the two views, choose the Edit Story and Edit Layout commands from the Edit menu. In the story editor, users can search and replace text, check spelling, and translate index markers. It is advisable to translate PageMaker files in the story editor, because there is a risk of deleting index markers by working in layout mode.

Avoid altering the size or position of text boxes when translating. Translate all stories in the publication. Use the Word Counter plug-in to verify how many stories the publication contains.

Translation Memory

To translate PageMaker files using a translation memory tool, all translatable text should be exported first.

Here are some important issues to consider before importing PageMaker files into a translation memory tool:

- All stories in the document should ideally be contained in one single text flow.
- All paragraphs should have a tag.

For more information on using translation memory tools, refer to the general segmentation guidelines in the Segmentation section on page 362.

Index Markers

Index markers in PageMaker can be translated in two ways: by opening the index marker in the story editor, or by using the Show Index command. Translate the markers in the story editor first, and then preview the results using the Show Index command.

To translate index markers in PageMaker, follow these steps:

1. Switch to the story editor.

2. Select the first index marker. Index markers are included in black squares with ? symbols.

3. Select the Index Entry command from the Utilities menu.

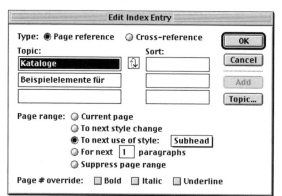

4. Type the translations in the Topic fields. It is possible to use up to three index entry levels.

5. Click OK to close the Edit Index Entry dialog box, and continue with the next index marker.

6. When all markers are translated, select the Show Index command from the Utilities menu to view the translated index entries under each letter. To change an entry, click the Edit button.

Indexes can be generated using the Create Index command from the Utilities menu. For more information on indexes in PageMaker, refer to the PageMaker documentation.

3.2.5   SPELL CHECKING TRANSLATIONS

To check the spelling of translations in PageMaker, follow these steps:

1. Switch to the story editor.

2. Set the language of the text by selecting one or more paragraphs, and choosing the Paragraph command from the Type menu.

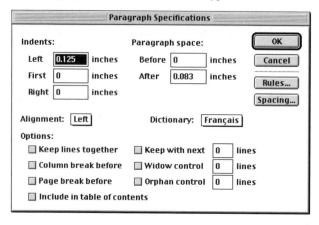

3. In the Paragraph Specifications dialog box, select the desired language.

4. Choose the Spelling command from the Utilities menu to start the spelling checker.

The languages available depend on the dictionaries selected when PageMaker was installed.

4 Reviewing Documentation

In a typical translation or localization project, the source material is translated in a translation memory or other computer aided translation tool. Translations are then edited by a senior translator/editor who also works in the translation memory tool and is responsible for the *translation* quality.

Once the page layout has been finalized and screen captures and other graphics have been inserted, the final document is proofread by a reviewer responsible for the final *linguistic* quality and accuracy of the deliverable.

Most localization and translation vendors have translation teams consisting of translators, editors/senior translators, and proofreaders. Depending on local habits and company preferences, a number of roles can be assigned to the same people within a team, or each individual can be given a specific role. Localization vendors will typically outsource translation to freelance translators or translation agencies, edit the translations in-house, and then send the files out for proofreading as the last step in a project.

4.1 Introduction

Since editing and proofreading of translated material are two distinct activities, the following sections provide separate and general guidelines for both.

4.1.1 EDITING TRANSLATIONS

Editors are usually senior translators who lead a team of translators working on a project. They are mainly responsible for ensuring consistency in terminology and style, as well as linguistic and technical accuracy, and should have a thorough understanding of both the project subject matter and fluency in the source and target language. On average, editors process two to four times the number of words translators produce, depending on the quality of the translations and complexity of the subject matter. For example, if a translator needed two days to translate a text, an editor would generally need between a half and a full day to review the translations and enter corrections.

In most cases, editors enter their corrections directly in the tool used for the translation, such as a translation memory tool. Serious or consistent errors are normally communicated to the translator responsible for the translation, so that any further errors can be avoided.

When editing translated documentation, follow these general guidelines:

- Prior to editing, ensure that translators have performed all standard quality assurance steps, such as reviewing their own translations and running a spell-check on their translations.

- Check whether the latest files are present, and verify that everything has been translated.

- Where there are a high number of mistakes in the first few pages, contact the translator, identify possible reasons, and request additional editing time from the translator. Meanwhile, discontinue the editing. Resume the editing on the revised text.

- Keep a copy of the translated files before editing. These may be needed to resolve quality issues at a later stage, or to identify the source of errors discovered by proofreaders or publishers.

- Always keep the target audience and document purpose in mind. Rephrasing perfectly clear sentences for purely stylistic reasons is a waste of time and may even damage the consistency instead of improving it.

- Eliminate wordiness or redundancy in the translated text.

- Never enter editing comments or marks in the translated text! Note them in a separate file.

- Ask engineers or desktop publishers to convert the initial translations back to their original formats, in order to generate a first version of an index or table of contents. Correct any errors in the translation memory tool to keep the memory database up-to-date.

- Use the search and replace feature with caution. Avoid using global search and replace and always confirm every instance of a replace command.

After editing, notify translators of serious mistakes, or provide them with an edited version of their translations. This will give them a chance to understand the linguistic quality expected of them. Providing constructive feedback is the best way to help a translator improve the standard of their work for the next project.

4.1.2 PROOFREADING TRANSLATIONS

A proofreader is normally not heavily involved in the localization project. Vendors will often hire freelance language specialist to perform the linguistic quality check on the translated documents. A proofreader can proof text at a rate of about 2000 words (approximately 10 pages) per hour, depending on the quality of the translation.

When proofreading translated documentation, follow these general guidelines:

- Never proofread documents on-screen. Always proofread on a clean printout of the final translated file.

- If the quality of the translations is poor, with errors on every page, discontinue proofreading and inform the project manager that a previous quality step may need to be repeated.

- Use standard proofreading marks, such as those listed in the Chicago Manual of Style. Search the internet for "proofreading marks" to get an indication of the different standards used.

- Avoid highlighting issues such as word choice, sentence structure, and organization. It is much more productive to focus on obvious errors and inconsistencies in style, spelling, punctuation, and format.

- Ensure a hard copy or PDF file of the latest version of the source document is available, with any updates or last-minute changes marked.

- If an error is repeated throughout the document, flag the first instance and write a comment instead of marking all occurrences.

- Check running headers, footers and page numbering before proofreading the running text and graphics.

- Spot-check the table of contents and index as a separate task.

Where editors focus on translation issues, such as accuracy and style, proofreaders should only do a linguistic quality check on the final product. Proofreaders need to read translated documents from an end-user perspective.

4.2   Check Lists

The following check lists contain some of the issues relevant to editors and proofreaders. The list is by no means exhaustive, but it does serve as a starting point for performing QA on documentation.

4.2.1   EDITING CHECK LIST

It is important to check the following:

- ✓ Terminology and style are consistent and appropriate throughout the translated documentation.

- ✓ Translations contain no spelling or grammar mistakes.

- ✓ Standard or recurring phrases, e.g. Note, Warning, Click on, Related Topics, and Important, have been translated consistently throughout the documentation.

- ✓ Chapter names, titles, and headings have been translated in a similar style, for example starting with a verb.

- ✓ Instructions, style guides, reference material, or glossaries provided by the publisher were used and followed.

- ✓ Comments from the publisher's language reviewer have been incorporated correctly.

- ✓ Company names, street address, zip code, telephone and fax numbers, including the area code, have been adjusted according to instructions.

✓ Metric or currency conversions are consistent and correct.

✓ Capitalization and punctuation, particularly in numbered and bulleted lists, was applied consistently.

✓ No leading or trailing spaces have been deleted, for example in tagged file formats.

✓ Any reference formatting, for example bolding of software references, has been applied correctly.

✓ Software references in localized manuals or online help files are accurate, and match these components exactly.

✓ References to titles or headings from other localized components, such as online help files or sample files, are accurate.

✓ Cultural references or examples have been adapted to the target language or country.

✓ The overall meaning of the source text is rendered accurately.

✓ Translations of headings and image captions are not too long.

✓ Translations are technically accurate and clear.

Editors also need to make sure a spell-check is run on the files before the final DTP and proofreading cycle. Remember, most typos are made when entering corrections in translated material!

4.2.2 PROOFREADING CHECK LIST

If the proofreaders are also responsible for checking layout and formatting, refer to the Do not reduce graphics by more than 15%, and when scaling a graphic, reduce any graphics on the same page to the same degree. section on page 338.

It is important to check the following:

✓ All text has been translated, and no text is missing.

✓ Translations do not contain any grammar, typing, or spelling mistakes.

✓ All special characters, such as ® registered trademark and © copyright symbols, are present and print properly. This is particularly important for the title page and first few pages of a document.

✓ Company names, street address, zip code, telephone and fax numbers, including the area code, have been adjusted to suit local conventions.

✓ The copyright and warranty pages display the proper date, version, and part number of the product. These items in localized versions usually differ from the source files!

✓ Any sorted components, such as a glossary appendix, are alphabetized according to target language standards.

✓ Quotation marks are formatted according to the target language standards.

✓ No editing or review marks remain in the translated text.

✓ All updates and last-minute changes were incorporated correctly.

- ✓ Punctuation is applied consistently, especially in numbered or bulleted lists.
- ✓ Hyphenation, if any, conforms to the target language standards.
- ✓ Screens and other graphics are displayed correctly.
- ✓ Screen captions appear correctly and point to the right place. Ideally, an illustration should appear on the same or next page on which it is mentioned.
- ✓ The examples and screen captures match the surrounding text.
- ✓ Manually edited graphics contain correct translations.
- ✓ The heading entries and page numbers in the table of contents are accurate.
- ✓ The entries and page numbers in the index are correct, and the index does not contain duplicate or extraneous entries.
- ✓ Cross-references in the body text refer to the correct page numbers.

Once proofreading has been completed, corrections should be implemented by the editor or translator responsible for the translations. All corrections need to be double-checked and signed-off by the proofreader *before* the final document is delivered to the publisher.

4.3   Review with Adobe Acrobat

Once the translated documents have been converted from a translation memory tool back to their original file formats, localized screen captures have been inserted, and table of contents and index have been generated, return the document to a reviewer or proofreader for a final review.

Sending the files in their native file format, such as Adobe FrameMaker, may cause problems, because the reviewers or proofreaders may not have the right version of the application, or may not have the application at all. If they are not proficient in using this application, there is also the danger of changing or corrupting the formatting, thus causing additional DTP work. The files including linked images may be too large to quickly transfer via e-mail or FTP. Mailing or faxing printed versions is time-consuming and can be costly when files need to be sent back and forth several times.

In this scenario, consider converting the translated files to Acrobat PDF files, and asking reviewers to use the notes feature in Adobe Acrobat. Notes enable the user to add annotations to PDF documents which are comparable to "sticky notes" on paper documents.

If, for example, a set of FrameMaker documents have been translated into German and the reviewer does not own a copy of (the same version of) FrameMaker, convert the translated FrameMaker files to PDF and send the PDF file to the reviewer. Images will be compressed and the layout will be preserved, so the reviewer will see the contents as they are displayed in FrameMaker.

The reviewer can then open the file using Acrobat Exchange (with Acrobat Reader notes can be read, but not created!), and add notes next to or below the paragraphs that require changes. Proofreaders should print the PDF file, read the text on paper, and then add notes with corrections to the PDF version.

After reviewing the document and adding all necessary notes, the reviewer or proofreader can export the notes from the PDF file by choosing the Export Notes command from the File menu. The reviewer will only need to return the resulting export file, because the notes can be imported in the original PDF file using the Import Notes command from the File menu. Using the Import and Export commands will drastically reduce the size of the files and allow them to be sent quickly via e-mail.

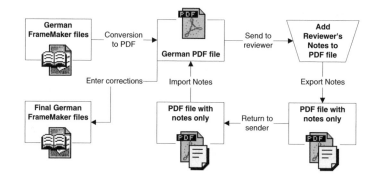

When files are returned or notes have been imported, search for the first note in the document by pressing Ctrl-T (Windows) or Command-T (Mac OS). It is possible to generate a summary of all the notes, using the Summarize Notes command from the Tools menu. The comments from the reviewer can now be incorporated in the translated FrameMaker documents. It is, of course, advisable to then create a new PDF version of the corrected document and send this off to the reviewer for a final sign-off.

Please note that Adobe Acrobat 4.0 and later versions provide more advanced features for document review. For example, reviewers can now manually highlight, underline, and circle text and mark files as "Approved" or "Confidential", directly in the PDF file. It is now also possible to sign off on PDF files electronically, using digital signatures.

For more information on Acrobat's document review features, refer to the Products section of the Adobe web site at www.adobe.com.

5   Further Reading

The books listed below all cover different aspects of editing and proofreading. Refer to the Further Reading section on page 224 for general books on technical translation.

The Chicago Manual of Style. 1993. University of Chicago Press, ISBN 0-226-10388-9.

Killen Anderson, Laura. 1990. *Handbook for Proofreading.* Vgm Career Horizons, ISBN 0-844-23266-1.

Smith, Peggy. 1997. *Mark My Words: Instruction and Practice in Proofreading.* Editorial Experts, ISBN 0-935-01223-0.

Sullivan, K.D. 1996. *Go Ahead, Proof It!* Barrons Educational Series, ISBN 0-812-09744-0.

Chapter 9:
Desktop Publishing

This chapter contains information on desktop publishing for localized documentation. Topics include computer setup, source file testing, multilingual page layout issues, format checking, and creating PDF files.

This chapter includes the following sections:

1. Introduction
2. Evaluation and Preparation
3. Formatting and Page Layout
4. Documentation Output
5. Further Reading

Chapters related to these topics are Chapter 8, which contains procedures for working with multiple desktop publishing tools and word processors, and Chapter 10, which contains a section on creating and editing graphics.

1   Introduction

As a rule, desktop publishing specialists working for localization vendors will not have the responsibility of creating material or designs on a localized manual or document. They are mainly responsible for reproducing a layout in multiple languages, with all technical and cultural adaptations necessary. DTP operators working in localization have a wide range of tasks and responsibilities, including:

- Evaluating and setting up the documentation project
- Generating books in multiple languages
- Fixing the layout of translated material
- Editing graphics
- Converting or generating output of translated material in multiple formats
- Performing quality checks on finalized translated material

DTP operators generally need to have a knowledge of multiple operating systems, utilities, translation tools, publishing applications, and localization models. Most localization vendors expect DTP operators to have some if not all of the following skills:

- Working knowledge of installation and configuration management of common operating systems and platforms, specifically MacOS and Windows
- Experience with industry-standard desktop publishing and graphics applications, e.g. Adobe FrameMaker, Adobe PageMaker, QuarkXPress, Adobe Type Manager, Adobe Illustrator, Adobe InDesign, and Interleaf
- In-depth knowledge of international layout issues, typographical conventions, and desktop publishing fundamentals, such as graphics, style sheets, and templates
- Understanding of language and character set issues in multilingual documentation
- Working knowledge of markup languages such as HTML, which is commonly used in online help systems
- Working knowledge of online documentation formats, such as Acrobat PDF
- Awareness of localization models and workflows, and project scheduling issues
- Experience selecting and using computer aided translation (CAT) tools
- Knowledge of Internet technology and communication software and protocols
- Excellent communication skills, both written and oral
- Foreign language skills (preferred)

DTP operators need a wide range of software applications to perform the DTP tasks correctly and efficiently. In addition to the standard Office and Internet applications, a DTP "toolkit" will more than likely include the following packages and tools:

- Industry-standard desktop publishing and graphics applications, such as Adobe FrameMaker and QuarkXPress, for Mac OS and Windows
- Font management application, such as Adobe Type Manager, for Mac OS and Windows
- All common printer driver versions and printer description files for Mac OS and Windows
- Adobe Acrobat family of tools
- Bitmap image editor, such as Paint Shop Pro or Adobe Photoshop
- Line art editor, such as Adobe Illustrator or CorelDraw
- Screen capture utility, such as Collage Complete
- Professional PostScript printer
- (Evaluation versions of) all commonly used translation memory tools, such as Trados Translator's Workbench, Atril Déjà Vu and STAR Transit

As a rule, where there is a multilingual translation requirement, manuals are prepared centrally by DPT operators. Once this has been done, source files are then imported in translation memory tools and translated. After the translation and editing cycle, files are converted back to their original formats, and DTP operators incorporate localized components for all languages. These normally include the translated text, a generated table of contents, and localized graphics. Once these components have been integrated, the layout is fixed, and the translated files are generated or converted to the required formats or hardcopy.

For more information on desktop publishing or pre-press publishing, refer to one of the following web sites:

- www.desktoppublishing.com
- www.dtp.com
- www.publish.com

Questions on DTP related issues can be posted to the comp.text.desktop newsgroup on the web.

2 Evaluation and Preparation

Before documentation files are translated, it is advisable to do some preparation work. This will help avoid many problems, including manual editing, once the files have been translated. It is important to verify that the source material is correct before the translation cycle begins. If a file is to be translated into four languages, it is easier to fix any problem identified in the source file rather than fix it later in four translated files.

The purpose of project evaluation is to highlight potential problems in source materials prior to the translation phase of the project. In addition to evaluating and checking the source files, all material should be prepared for translation in the most efficient and cost-effective way.

At this stage in the project, desktop publishers should focus on the following issues:

- Computer configuration
- Integrity of source material
- File preparation for translation

A check list has been provided at the end of this section to help a DTP operator determine whether the source material is complete and ready for translation.

2.1 Configuring Computers

The layout of a document can be seriously affected by the configuration of a computer. Changing printer drivers or font type, for example, will completely rearrange the page layout and text flow. Try using a computer configuration that matches the one used by the publisher to create the source files.

When performing desktop publishing tasks, such as page layout and output, it is very important to ensure that the computer is configured correctly. Before beginning any DTP work, configure the operating system and the application.

Unless Asian language documents are being localized, in which case an Asian operating system may be required, always use an English operating system instead of a localized version. Localized operating systems may not necessarily support certain printer driver or font settings.

2.1.1   OPERATING SYSTEM

If no specific instructions have been provided on the operating system or versions required for the DTP tasks, consult the publisher in order to avoid any problems down the line.

Different operating systems, and even different versions of operating systems, for example, Windows 98 versus Windows 2000, have different ways of handling fonts and generating printer output. If the publisher has generated PostScript files on a Windows 95 machine using specific printer drivers and settings, it may not be possible to duplicate these settings on a Windows 2000 machine. If all layout work has been performed and the operator switches to another operating system afterwards, a certain amount of rework may be necessary because text flows will change.

Avoid these problems by working on the same operating system version used to create and generate the source material.

2.1.2   SOFTWARE APPLICATION

Always use the English language versions of desktop publishing applications or word processors. Document files edited in localized applications may contain field codes that will not re-convert correctly when files are opened in the English version by a publisher or a printing house. In some cases, for example with Asian languages, localized versions must be used because the English versions may contain limited or no support for these languages. Before starting the DTP work, analyze and ascertain the most effective way to work. It could mean working in the English version of an application, working in the English application on a localized platform, or working in a localized version of the application on an English platform.

Never edit or save documents in an application other than the version used to create the source files. If files are edited using a more recent version of an application than the version used to create the files, for example, the new features may introduce unnecessary changes to the page layout. Furthermore, a software publisher may not be able to open the files if the new file format is not *backwards-compatible*. A backwards-compatible file is a file created in a newer version of an application that can be opened by older versions of the same product.

Always avoid converting documents into formats for translation purposes, unless this is required by translation memory tools. Never import and translate WordPerfect documents in Word, for examples, unless this has been agreed with the software publisher. The same thing applies to cross-platform products. Even though these applications claim to be 100% compatible, display discrepancies can be generated by the differences in the operating system, i.e. different font types or font rendering.

Before working with translated files, install all dictionaries or language modules for the target languages.

2.1.3 FONTS

Make sure all fonts used in the source files are installed correctly; these should be the exact font types and versions used in the source files. Most applications display a warning dialog box when files are opened and fonts are missing. Missing fonts are often automatically replaced by the default fonts installed on the system.

Even if the required fonts are installed and no font messages are displayed when files are opened, it is advisable to ask for specifics of the fonts that were used to create the original documents. Standard fonts like Arial and Garamond, for example, exist in many versions and formats. These versions can vary in width, so text flow may change depending on the font version used. If proprietary fonts are used that were created by the publisher, ensure these fonts are provided and correctly installed.

Because many fonts are produced in TrueType or Type 1 versions, verify with the publisher which font type should be used. Use a font management application, such as Adobe Type Manager, to activate or disable certain font sets or types.

In case the fonts need to be changed because the target languages are not supported by the fonts used in the source files, send a first draft of the text to the publisher and resolve any issues this way. For more information on changing fonts, refer to the Check List section on page 333.

Depending on the publisher's license agreements for fonts, localization vendors may need to purchase fonts used in localized documentation files themselves. This is particularly relevant when acquiring fonts for non-Latin languages and could be a significant cost factor which needs to be budgeted for.

2.1.4 PRINTER DRIVER

Changing printer drivers changes layout, fonts, and page flow. To avoid any desktop publishing re-work, ensure that the correct printer driver and driver settings are used from the outset. The following message is displayed by FrameMaker when printers are changed while editing a FrameMaker document:

If print-ready PostScript documents are to be delivered to the publisher, i.e. all page formatting is being done by the vendor, check whether the correct printer driver is being used; this should be the driver that will be used to print the document. In most cases, a PostScript driver will need to be installed, such as the Adobe PostScript Printer Driver, which can be downloaded from Adobe's web site at www.adobe.com.

Once the printer driver is installed, select the appropriate PostScript Printer Description (PPD) file. PPD files contain all specifications and settings for printers. Please note that several versions of PPDs may be available for one printer. Always use the same version that was used with the source files. PPDs can be obtained from the printer manufacturer or from Adobe's web site.

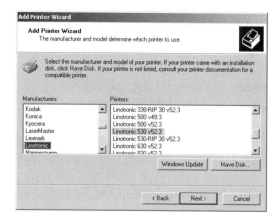

Image writer drivers, such as Linotronic drivers, are generally used for most high-end printing, with color separations and high-resolution graphics. The vendor and publisher should agree on settings that need to be used, such as PostScript level and output format, page size, scaling, font embedding or substitution, graphics resolution, halftoning, and crop marks.

It is always advisable to run a print test at the very beginning of the project. Use the first translated chapter that is available, for this purpose. When working on files, always ensure that the correct printer driver is installed and the appropriate printer selected.

2.1.5   FILE MANAGEMENT

In documentation projects, create subfolders for each language folder containing exactly the same contents as the source files. This will usually be a folder containing the documents and/or style sheets, with a subfolder containing the image files. It is very important that file names not be changed, unless specifically requested by the publisher. Changing file names will cause problems generating book files or linking images.

To prepare files for localization, isolate the documents that require translation into a separate folder. This folder can then be used to import document files into a translation memory tool. Translatable files will not include files containing automatically generated components, such as the table of contents and the index. Isolate the images that require translation from images that do not need to be changed.

Once all files have been localized, overwrite the source files with the localized files, and generate the table of contents and index files.

Different source and target files will need to be created where documents are output in several formats. A set of documents output in both printed and online format, for example, may require two sets of source and target files. One set would be needed with greyscale images for printing, and another set with color images for output to PDF.

2.2 Checking Source Material

Source materials for documentation projects should be carefully checked before the translation starts. In general, procedures for this check are identical to those described for online help in the Checking Source Material section on page 227. The only difference is that instead of test-compiling online help files, you will need to test-generate the table of contents and the index file.

As well as verifying whether all required files are included in the localization kit, DTP operators should also check to ensure that the source material is error-free.

Here is a list of issues to consider when checking the source files:

- Are the table of contents and index generated correctly in the source files?
- Is the document template or style sheet included, and should it be adjusted for the localized versions?
- How should text expansion be handled in the localized versions?
- Are all graphic files included, and how should they be localized?
- Is it clear what the required deliverables are?

Evaluating documentation source files for pre-press or printing output is referred to as a preflight check. Preflight checks are also very useful in evaluating the files from a localization perspective. There are some tools available on the market which automatically run a preflight check on files, such as Markzware's FlightCheck (www.markzware.com) or Extensis Preflight Pro (www.extensis.com). These tools analyze files and generate a report with specific details on pages, fonts, colors, images, resolution, and file lists. By generating a report on the source files, and after translation on the target files, it is easy to identify any discrepancies that may have been introduced during the localization process.

Always use a hard copy or PDF version of the source document for reference purposes.

2.2.1 TABLE OF CONTENTS AND INDEX

If the source document contains a generated table of contents and index, check whether they generate correctly and ensure that no manual editing has been performed on the English files.

Technical authors often implement last-minute changes or enhancements to the generated file rather than in the index entries. To compare generated files with the original hand-offs from the publisher, make a copy of these files and re-generate the TOC and index. Then compare the generated files with the hand-offs. If differences are found, these changes will need to be implemented in the index entries before the translation cycle.

By generating the index in the source document, it will be easy to highlight index problems before the translation starts. Fixing translated indexes is a time-consuming and tedious job. If differences between the index markers and index file are found, verify with the publisher which version should be used as a basis for the translated files.

In addition to checking the content of the generated components, ensure that the layout mirrors the source text hard copy or PDF files. No significant changes should need to be made to the layout of generated table of contents or index.

2.2.2 DELIVERABLES

If specific instructions have not been provided, ask the publisher about deliverables for the "paper" or online documentation. As a rule, the translated versions of the source files should be delivered in their original formats, such as FrameMaker files, along with a hard copy of the translated manuals. It is increasingly common, however, for localization vendors to deliver PostScript files, film or online versions of the translated documents.

For PostScript deliverables, check which settings should be used to create the Postscript files. Here are some examples of settings or other issues impacting PostScript output:

- Operating system
- Printer driver and PostScript printer description file (PPD)
- PostScript settings, such as level, data format, font inclusion and color separations

When creating hard copy versions of translated files which have been printed to PostScript files, never change printer drivers as this will change the page layout and text flow. If PostScript files have been created from the translated documentation using a Linotronic printer driver, print the generated PostScript files, not the translated documentation files, to a laser printer. To print PostScript files to a laser printer, either first convert to PDF or use a PostScript viewer.

When requested to deliver film or resin-coated paper, ask about issues such as page size, color separations, emulsion side, positive/negative film, left/right reading, lines per inch (lpi) or dots per inch (dpi).

For information on creating online manuals, refer to the Portable Document Format (PDF) section on page 342.

2.2.3 STYLE SHEET

Check which style sheet or template is attached to the document. A style-sheet is a blueprint for text, graphics, and formatting in a document. Pre-formatted documents usually contain style sheets that are either embedded or attached to the document and define its layout.

If this style sheet has not been included in the original documents, contact the publisher. Using an incorrect style sheet will alter the document layout in the translated documents. In some applications, such as FrameMaker, style sheets are embedded in the document files, whereas, in Microsoft Word, style sheets are external files.

Ask the publisher if the page size needs to be changed for the localized documentation files. Special templates for localized documents are often provided by the publisher. These templates would typically have different page sizes, and language settings. They maybe even have smaller font size definitions or line spacing to allow for text expansion. Some language-specific templates will contain translatable text. Any format definition (with the word "Note") preceding any paragraph that is formatted as a note should be translated.

In Word, check the style sheet by choosing the Templates command from the File menu (Word 7), or Templates and Add-ins from the Tools menu (Word 8). In FrameMaker, template information is stored within the FrameMaker file. Use the Import Formats command from the File menu to import the template information from another document or template.

Remember to check the source documents for format overrides, i.e. changes in styles, which are applied in the documents and which do not match the styles defined in the style sheets.

2.2.4 TEXT EXPANSION

Most languages require space for text expansion when translated from English. Text expansion in languages such as French or German accounts for a 20 to 30% increase on the text length.

There are several ways to handle text expansion in translated texts. Some suggestions are provided below:

- Add pages to the translated versions
- Decrease overall font size
- Change leading or paragraph spacing
- Change page margins
- Instruct translators to maintain a one-to-one page correspondence

In most cases, it is possible to allow for additional pages of extra text in the localized versions. Unlike online help files, there may be some restrictions on the level of expansion allowed in the documentation files. Small booklets or product sheets, for example, may only have a limited number of pages available.

Always consult the publisher when adding pages to the localized versions. If there is a requirement to maintain a one-to-one page correspondence between the original and the translated document, use the options listed above to qualify the preferred strategy. In most cases, a combination of the options will be chosen, which means the vendor or the publisher will need to create language-specific templates. In addition to different spacing, font, and margin settings, multilingual templates may also be used to define the language settings, including hyphenation settings.

It is a good idea to instruct translators on the length restrictions for the target text. This will help avoid any unnecessary post-editing later in the localization process. Although it may be difficult for translators working in a non-WYSIWYG translation memory environment, an effort should be made to adhere to the length restrictions.

2.2.5 GRAPHICS

It is possible to embed or link graphics and screen captures in pre-formatted documents. If graphics are linked, most word processors will automatically search for picture files when a document is opened. Embedded files are usually integrated in the document.

If the graphics folder is selected and the application is still unable to locate some graphics, follow the steps below:

1. Run a file search to check whether the file is located in another folder.

2. Check whether there is a file with a similar name, and verify whether this is the missing file.

3. Notify the publisher of the missing files and request the files.

It is important to know which computer configuration and software should be used to create the screen captures and other graphics in the document. More information on creating screen captures can be found in the Creating Screen Captures section on page 349.

2.3 Preparing for Translation

In the early days of localization, documentation used to be translated by overwriting source text in a document created in applications such as Word, FrameMaker, and PageMaker. Nowadays text is usually imported into a translation memory tool, and exported to its original format after translation. For more information on translation memory tools, refer to Chapter 11.

Collateral material, such as marketing material or quick reference cards is typically translated in a desktop publishing application, such as QuarkXPress. Translation memory tools are of little use for these types of documents as they contain so little repetitive text, and the content often requires heavy adaptation.

2.3.1 TEXT FEATURES

If documentation files are to be translated in a translation memory tool, scan the source files for formatting, and identify any problems that may interfere with the text segmentation process.

For more information on translation memory tool segmentation, refer to the Segmentation section on page 362.

2.3.2 TRANSLATABLE FILES

If the documentation files are to be translated in a translation memory tool, only the chapter files should be processed. Do not preprocess any generated files such as the table of contents or the index.

The table of contents file will be generated from the translated headings, and the index file will be generated from the translated index markers in each chapter. If the generated index file is translated instead of the index markers, all translations will be overwritten with the English text when you run the file generation program.

For more information on translation memory tools, refer to Chapter 11, Translation Technology.

2.3.3 GRAPHICS

To prepare graphics for translation, categorize the graphics and create a list of translatable text items. Graphics often contain examples or captions. To ensure consistency, this text should be translated by the same translator who is working on the main body of the document.

For more information on preparing graphics files for translation, refer to the Introduction section on page 347.

2.4 Check List

If the publisher has not supplied the vendor with detailed guidelines or instructions, use the list below to gain a complete overview of the services expected.

2.4.1 APPLICATION AND CONFIGURATION

Here is a list of questions the vendor should ask the publisher about the application and required computer configuration:

- ✓ Which operating system (version) should be used?
- ✓ Which application (version) should be used?
- ✓ Which fonts and font types are required?
- ✓ Which printer driver should be used, with which printer description file?
- ✓ Are specific tools required for this documentation project?

2.4.2 SOURCE MATERIAL

Here is a list of questions the vendor should ask the publisher about the source material of a documentation project:

✓ Which documentation source files and which graphics need to be translated?

✓ How should the source files be translated?

✓ Which language modifications should be made to the style information?

✓ Is a layout style guide available for the source material?

✓ Can pages be added for text expansion?

✓ Are hard copies or PDF versions of the source material available?

✓ Are blank or layered versions and font information for the images available?

✓ Are previously translated versions of the files, or translation memories available?

2.4.3 DELIVERABLES

Here is a list of questions the vendor should ask the publisher about the deliverables:

✓ What are the required deliverables, e.g. electronic files, printed copies, or film?

✓ What settings should be used to create the deliverable files?

✓ Is a test-run required for the printed manuals?

A well-constructed localization kit should address answer most of these questions. Refer to the Creating Localization Kits section on page 48 for more information on localization kit contents.

3   Formatting and Page Layout

As a rule, unless specific language modifications are absolutely necessary or have been requested by the publisher, all layout, typographic conventions and styles should match the source files. The best way to ensure this is to attach (or import) the source file templates or style sheets to the target files after translation. Never import variable definitions or other specifications which may contain translatable text.

In FrameMaker, for example, open each source and target chapter and choose Import > Formats from the File menu to import and apply all text and paragraph styles.

If the vendor has been supplied with language-specific templates or style sheets, import the styles from these documents. It may sometimes be necessary to create language-specific templates, such as in cases where a one-to-one page match needs to be maintained between the source and the translated documents.

Once the original styles have been imported, generate the table of contents, index, cross-references and other automatically generated components in the manual.

3.1 Content Check

When documentation files are returned from translation, DTP operators should first assemble all translated files, such as chapters and graphics, and replace a copy of the source files with the localized ones. In a typical setup, the source chapter files and graphics will be replaced with the localized versions, and the source book file is used to generate a localized table of contents and index.

First, check whether all content is complete and translated. Pay special attention to headers or footers, index entries, graphics, and captions. This is particularly important when a translation memory tool is used to translate the files. It is not unusual for some elements to be left untranslated.

Always check to ensure that any text printed on pages between the title and the table of contents, contains the correct information for each localized version. Here is an example of text that is often found on these pages:

- Copyright date
- Part numbers
- "Printed in" statements
- Trademark information

Fix the layout of the translated documents once the text has been checked for completeness and all the necessary information has been adjusted.

3.2 Page and Paragraph Formatting

Page layout and paragraph formatting should always match the source files, unless otherwise requested by the publisher. Here is a list of items to check when finalizing page and paragraph formatting:

- Page numbering - Each chapter begins on an odd (right) page, and ends on an even (left) page. In most cases, the book file setup and templates will automatically do this, but sometimes it is necessary to add blank pages at the end of chapters.
- Widows and orphans, i.e. single lines or words isolated from the rest of a paragraph or sentence. This is seldom an issue, as document paragraph definitions usually handle the problem. If not, check all pages for occurrences, and fix them manually or by adjusting the paragraph style definition. Notify the publisher when changing any style properties in the localized documentation.

- Language settings – Setting the language of all text will influence word breaking, hyphenation and alphabetizing. For more information on language settings in word processors or DTP applications, refer to the previous chapter.

- Sorted elements – If manuals contain sorted elements, such as a glossary of terms, the items need to be sorted, either automatically or manually, depending on the application used.

- Table definitions – If localized text is much longer than the source text, the table definition and cell spacing may need to be changed throughout the text. This may apply to one or all of the tables in the document.

- Callouts – Callouts referring to or included in images may need to be resized or replaced where image dimensions or contents have changed.

- Note, Warning, etc. – Tab spacing and indents may need to be adjusted for translations of Notes, Warning, and Tip entries.

Make sure there are no page breaks after sentences punctuated with a colon. Check that there are no images or indented paragraphs at the top of any pages. Check headers and footers for correct placement, spacing, and style.

Pay special attention to the layout of generated components, such as tables of contents and indexes. Page breaks should never separate main entries from sub entries, so it may be necessary to manually format main entries so that they begin on the next page. Remember to do these types of edits at the very end of the DTP process, because any manual changes made to table of contents and index will be lost once these components are re-generated.

Tip: Pay special attention to the sorting order of localized index files. For information on changing the sort settings in page layout application or word processors, refer to Chapter 8, Documentation Translation.

If a one-to-one page correspondence between the source files and localized versions is required, increase the number of pages or reduce the type size consistently throughout the document. Make sure that any change made to style properties is communicated to the publisher.

3.3 Text Formatting

In addition to checking the page and paragraph layout, DTP operators should also validate the localized documents on a text level. Here is a list of elements to consider:

- Font specifications, i.e. type and size

- Character spacing, kerning, and tracking

- Special attributes, such as bold and italic software references

- Language-specific quotation marks, for example „Beispiel" in German, and « Exemple » in French.

- Punctuation

Always use pre-defined paragraph and character style tags for components such as bold or italic text. Avoid applying fonts or styles locally from the format menu to the text.

Text formatting for Cyrillic or Asian languages can pose problems for DTP operators who have only handled Roman languages. The fonts used in the source documents may not necessarily support all target languages. If font substitution is required, consult the publisher on the replacement fonts that should be used. Most font types will support Roman languages. However, different fonts may be required for Cyrillic or Asian languages.

Here is a list of typical font substitutions for standard serif font types, such as Times New Roman and sans-serif fonts like Arial:

Language	Serif	Sans-Serif
English, French, German	Times New Roman	Arial
Cyrillic languages	Times New Roman CYR	Arial CYR
Japanese	Mincho	Gothic
Korean	Batang	Gulim
Simplified Chinese	Song	Hei, Kai
Traditional Chinese	Ming	Hei, Kai

In some applications, such as Adobe FrameMaker, it is possible to create combined fonts. These are combinations of Western and Japanese font families that allow the user to use Roman and Asian fonts in the same paragraph, retaining a consistent look and proper proportions.

Tip: When processing body text in Asian languages, as a rule, font sizes need to be increased to improve readability.

In addition to checking or changing font attributes, DTP operators should also check all characters that deviate from the default font, such as screen fonts, bold or italic. These special attributes should be created with character tags rather than character attributes. This will make it easier to change these attributes if necessary. In Asian languages, bold and italics are seldom used, so in most cases these attributes can be changed to the default font. Also note that fonts are available in high- and low-resolution versions. This means several versions may be needed, depending on the quality of the output requested.

In most Asian or Middle-Eastern languages, there are many text characteristics that differ from Western languages, for example:

- Text direction – Some languages are displayed vertically, some bidirectional, i.e. left-to-right and right-to-left.
- Case – Some languages, such as Hebrew, have no upper or lower case.

- Spacing – Some languages, such as Chinese or Korean, have no spaces between words (characters).
- Sorting – Most Asian languages have several different sorting orders.
- Punctuation – Some languages, such as Thai, have no punctuation marks.

It is important to be aware of the specifics of the target languages. A final but vital part of the quality check is to schedule a final review or check by native speaker.

3.4 Graphics

If the graphics are localized using the same image settings, such as resolution, color depth, but the image size remains unchanged, very little needs to be done with the localized graphics in documentation files. If the images are linked, they will be inserted automatically in the localized documents, in the right location, with the correct scaling and settings, when the localized documents are opened.

If the image size or dimensions have changed, however, DTP operators need to ensure the graphic is displayed fully and printed correctly. This can be done by enlarging the image bounding box or scaling down the image. The bounding box is called an anchored frame in FrameMaker. In most cases, graphics will be scaled down to avoid changing the original layout. Pay special attention when scaling graphics for books, published in PDF format for on-screen use. Scaled graphics may become distorted in the generated PDF file. Test this before scaling all images.

Do not reduce graphics by more than 15%, and when scaling a graphic, reduce any graphics on the same page to the same degree.

3.5 Format Check

Once every page has been checked, and the table of contents and index have been generated, check the layout of the final document against the source files. The format check refers to the process of proofing the target-language version for correct page layout, character formatting, and graphics. As with proofreading, a format check should be carried out by comparing printed versions of localized documents with the original versions.

Use the following check lists for the format check of localized documents.

In the front matter, check to ensure that:

- ✓ The correct product version number is included.
- ✓ Copyright information and date are correct.
- ✓ Part or item numbers are correct for each localized document.
- ✓ Publication date and "printed in" information are correct.
- ✓ U.S. specific statements or contact information have either been deleted or adjusted.
- ✓ All copyright and trademark symbols, such as ® and ©, are present and printed properly.

In the table of contents and index, check to ensure that:

✓ The localized version contains the same number of entries as the source.

✓ All entries are translated. This should also be checked by a proofreader before starting DTP.

✓ Titles of generated document components, such as a list of graphics or the index, are included in the table of contents and translated.

✓ No pages begin with sub entries.

✓ The index does not contain duplicate items that only differ in capitalization.

✓ Page numbers are correct.

In the document chapters, check to ensure that:

✓ Page numbering sequences are correct.

✓ Headers and footers correspond with the chapter titles and are placed correctly.

✓ All translator or reviewer comments have been removed from the translated text.

✓ Page layout matches the source, unless otherwise requested.

✓ Spacing between titles, headings, and paragraphs is consistent.

✓ For glossaries or other sorted lists, the sorting of both main and sub-entries corresponds to the target language rules.

✓ Final page count is a multiple of four, and the last page of the manual is an even page.

✓ All internal cross-references were updated and formatted correctly and reference definitions have been translated.

✓ References to the running software have been formatted consistently, for example in italics or boldface.

✓ Punctuation follows the target language rules, especially quotation marks and spacing. In French colons are preceded by a space, for example, and in French and German different quotation marks are used.

✓ Bulleted lists are aligned correctly, and numbered lists are arranged correctly.

✓ Conditional text settings are correct.

✓ Target language conventions for capitalization or other callout stylistic features are observed.

✓ Cross-references and variables are still generated, not converted to text.

In the graphics, check to ensure that:

✓ Graphics are sized correctly, and not truncated or distorted.

✓ All graphics are in the right position. Where documents contain many similar screen captures, there is a risk that images may be switched or named incorrectly.

✓ Resolution and color settings match the source.

✓ Image borders match the source.

✓ Sizing and placement of callout text, lines, or circles is correct, and text in callouts is aligned properly.

Some localization vendors combine format checking with proofreading. For more information on proofreading, refer to the Proofreading Translations section on page 316.

4 Documentation Output

Because direct computer-to-plate printing is common practice for most professional printing houses nowadays, localization vendors are usually requested to deliver PostScript or PDF files for printing, instead of film or RC paper.

PostScript files were originally intended for paper output purposes, and PDF files for onscreen display. Recent versions of the PDF file format, however, can also be used for professional printing purposes without loss of quality.

In the following sections, we will discuss settings that need to be verified with the publisher or printing house for output of these file types, and ways in which localized files can be tested.

4.1 PostScript

When PostScript files are listed as deliverables in the statement of work, it is advisable to do a test-run with the printing house to check whether the generated PostScript files can be printed. This is particularly important when localizing into multi-byte languages. Do not skip this test, as it will help prevent problems at a later stage.

For more information on PostScript, refer to one of the following web sites:

- Adobe's web site at www.adobe.com (search for "PostScript")
- Quite Software web site at www.quite.com/ps.

Questions can be posted in the PostScript newsgroup at comp.lang.postscript.

4.1.1 CREATING POSTSCRIPT FILES

PostScript files can be created from any application by choosing the Print to File or Destination: File option. This option can usually be found in the Print dialog box. PostScript files can be created using a PostScript printer driver which must be configured with the PostScript printer description (PPD) file for the printer used to output the files. Add this printer driver to the list of printers and set it as the default printer, before finalizing the document page layout.

In many cases, the vendor will be using a high-resolution Linotronic imagesetter printer driver. The following settings must be specified for this printer:

- Resolution – For high-resolution output, use a resolution of approximately 2400 dpi

- PostScript level, Level I, II or higher
- Output Protocol, ASCII or binary
- Font embedding or substitution
- Paper size, typically US Letter or A4
- Scaling, typically 100%
- PostScript Output option, typically Optimize for portability
- Color settings

The following image shows a settings screen of a Linotronic printer configuration in the Adobe PostScript printer driver.

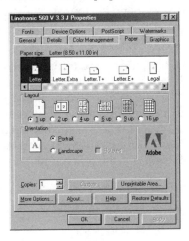

In addition to configuring the printer driver, options may need to be set in the software application, such as collation, and crop or registration marks. When all settings are correct, choose the Print command and select the Print to File or Destination: File option in the application. The name of this command may vary depending on the application. It may be necessary to enter a file name or specify font inclusion settings. Instead of printing to a printer, the application will create a PostScript file, normally with the .ps extension.

Tip: Please note that where the printer driver has been assigned to a FILE: instead of a printer port, a PostScript file will be generated automatically.

4.1.2 TESTING POSTSCRIPT FILES

Once PostScript files for localized documentation have been created, it is important to check whether they are correct. Focus on issues such as page size, crop marks, and accented characters. To test PostScript files, print the PostScript file to PDF using Acrobat Distiller (see below), or use a PostScript viewer to display or print the PostScript file contents.

On a Windows platform, another option is to send PostScript files to the PostScript printer using the COPY command, for example:

```
COPY *.ps lpt1
```

Please note that the lpt1 specification may need to be replaced with a printer network address.

Examples of tools that enable the user to view and print PostScript files are GoScript (www.lasergo.com) or GhostScript (www.ghostscript.com).

4.2 Portable Document Format (PDF)

Software publishers are shipping more and more online manuals with their products instead of printed documentation. From numerous online file formats, the Adobe PDF format has become the de-facto industry-standard. It is also used extensively on the web.

Adobe's Portable Document Format (PDF) is a file format used to distribute online documents across platforms and operating systems without losing any of the original layout or characteristics. Adobe Acrobat is a set of programs used to create, enhance, and read PDF documents. Like PostScript, PDF documents can be created from any application, and hypertext links, forms, movies, sounds, and bookmarks can be added automatically or manually. PDF files can be viewed on any platform using Acrobat viewers, such as Acrobat Reader, or on web browsers using Acrobat plug-ins.

For more information on Acrobat and PDF, refer to the following web sites:

- The Adobe web site at www.adobe.com (search for "Acrobat" or "PDF")
- PDF Zone at www.pdfzone.com
- Planet PDF at www.planetpdf.com

Questions can be posted in the Portable Document Format newsgroup at comp.text.pdf.

4.2.1 CREATING PDF FILES

If a document has been translated in a word processor or document processing application, such as Word or FrameMaker, it can be converted to PDF format in using two options. The first is the "print to PDF" option using the PDF Writer printer driver. The second option is to create a PostScript file which is then "distilled" to PDF using Acrobat Distiller. The first option is mainly used for simple documents without special fonts, formatting or graphics. The second option should be used for complex page layout documents, or documents that contain high quality images. For most localization projects, Acrobat Distiller is used.

Tip: When creating PDF files from localized versions of manuals, open the original, English PDF file in Adobe Acrobat and check File > Document Properties > General to see which application was used to create the English PDF file. The Producer field will show which version of PDF Writer or Distiller was used, and the PDF version will be displayed at the bottom of the window. Refer to the English PDF file for additional PDF settings, such as inclusion of bookmarks, thumbnails, article threads, notes, etc. The localized version should have the same specifications as the source file.

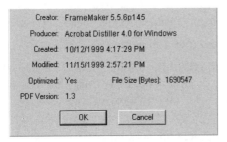

Please note that separate PostScript files may need to be created for printed and online versions of the same manual. PostScript files for printed software manuals seldom contain colors, whereas PDF files not only contain colored graphics, but also colored hypertext links.

Using Acrobat PDF Writer

To create a PDF file from a document using PDF Writer, follow these steps:

1. Open the document to be converted to a PDF file.

2. Choose the Print command from the File menu.

3. From the Printer Name drop down box, choose PDF Writer (Windows) or open the Chooser and select the PDF Writer printer driver (MacOS).

4. Enter the Acrobat document information. The information entered here will be displayed in the Info box for the PDF file.

5. Name the file with a .pdf extension and click OK (Windows) or Save (Mac OS).

PDF Writer enables the user to set several options, such as page size and orientation, font embedding and subsetting, and image compression.

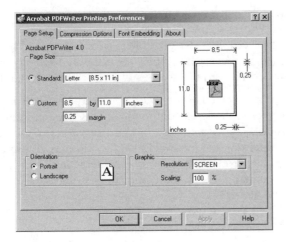

For more information on Acrobat PDF Writer, refer to the online documentation that is installed with Adobe Acrobat.

Using Acrobat Distiller

To create a PDF file from a document using Distiller, follow these steps:

1. Open the document to be converted to a PDF file.

2. Create a PostScript file by choosing the Print command from the File menu, and selecting Print to File (Windows) or Destination: File (Mac OS). Use the correct printer driver and PostScript settings (see previous sections).

3. When the PostScript file (.ps) is created, run Acrobat Distiller and open the PostScript file using the Open command from the File menu.

4. Select the required Distiller settings, name the file with a .pdf extension and click OK (Windows) or Save (Mac OS).

In some applications, such as Adobe FrameMaker 5.x and later versions, the user can set Acrobat options when creating a PostScript file. Distiller enables the user to set several advanced options, such as page size and orientation, compatibility, resolution, font embedding and subsetting, color settings, and image compression and conversion.

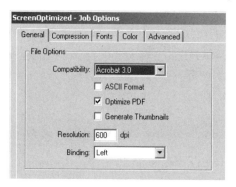

Recent versions of Acrobat Distiller have pre-configured settings for PDF documents intended for standard printing (PrintOptimized), pre-press purposes (PressOptimized), and on-screen use (ScreenOptimized). It is also possible to save customized settings to Job Option Files. Consider creating these settings files for each publisher or target language, e.g. Japanese PDF files may require settings different from German files.

If the PDF file is to be used for on-screen use, it may be necessary to add PDF features such as bookmarks, web links, or multimedia components. This depends entirely on the source format of the localized files. It may also be necessary to crop the pages to set the correct margins. After finalizing the localized PDF files, instead of using the regular Save command (which has probably been used repeatedly in the course of the project) choose the Save As command, check the Optimize box, and save the file in this mode in order to minimize file size.

Tip: In some applications, article threads are automatically included in PDF files when generated. If the source files do not contain article threads, delete them from the localized files by selecting the Article tool, clicking on the first page of the PDF file and pressing Delete.

For more information on Distiller, refer to the online documentation installed with Adobe Acrobat.

4.2.2   TESTING PDF DOCUMENTS

Because PDF documents can be created in several ways, using different options, it is advisable to compare translated PDF documents with source files to check whether any file characteristics have changed.

First of all check whether all pages have been converted and whether the page numbering is correct. Then verify that any obvious PDF features present in the source files are also present in the target files, for example bookmarks, thumbnails, annotations, hypertext links, and web links. Spot-check bookmarks and hypertext links.

To test a PDF document created from localized source material, focus on the following issues:

- File Size – Make sure that the size of the localized file does not differ substantially (no more than 10%) from the original file. If it does, use different image compression or font embedding options.
- Graphics – The quality of the graphics should reflect the quality of the original files. If the quality differs considerably, use different image compression types or image scaling.
- Page Size – Localized PDF files for European markets use A4 paper when they are intended as print-on-demand documents. Otherwise, the file size indication in the status bar of the viewer window should match the source file.
- View on Open – Make sure the localized file has the same default view on opening as the original. To check this, select Document Info from the File menu in Adobe Acrobat and choose Open.
- Document Info – Check whether the document information, such as the title, has been translated by selecting Document Info from the File menu and

choosing General. Also check that any additional information in the window matches the source file.

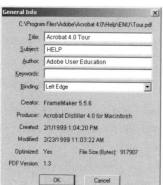

- Font Embedding – Compare the font embedding information by selecting Document Info from the File menu and choosing Fonts.

Do not forget to open and view PDF files using a localized version of a PDF viewer on a localized operating system, and always ensure that the PDF file prints without problems or quality loss on different printers, using different resolution settings. Focus on font quality, because loss of font quality in localized files may indicate unnecessary font substitution.

5   Further Reading

The books listed below cover different aspects of desktop publishing and typography.

When selecting these books, pay special attention to the publication date, when looking for the most recent information on DTP technology.

Bayroff, Andrew I. 1999. *The Stuff Type Is Made Of.* Prentice Hall, ISBN 0-13-022004-3.

Brier, David. *International Typographic Design.* Madison Square Press/North Light Books, ISBN 0-94260-439-3.

Cohen, Sandy and Robin Williams. 1999. *The Non-Designer's Scan and Print Book.* Peachpit Press, ISBN 0-201-35394-6.

Green, Chuck. 1997. *The Desktop Publisher's Idea.* Random House, ISBN 0-679-78006-8.

Lentz Devall, Sandra and Esther Kibby. 1998. *Desktop Publishing Styleguide.* Delmar Publishing, ISBN 0-827-37900-5.

Williams, Robin. 1994. *How To Boss Your Fonts Around.* Peachpit Press, ISBN 0-201-69640-1.

Chapter 10:
Graphics Localization

This chapter contains information on localizing graphics and creating screen captures of localized software applications.

This chapter includes the following sections:

1. Introduction
2. Creating Screen Captures
3. Editing Graphics

Related chapters are Chapter4, which contains information on engineering localized software applications, Chapter 7, which contains information on engineering localized online help, and Chapter 9 which contains information on desktop publishing.

1   Introduction

Most online help systems, web sites or manuals contain one or more of the following image types:

- Generic graphics
- Screen captures
- Screen captures with translatable content
- Illustrations

Generic graphics are pictures which contain translatable text on a background that needs to be re-created. A web page containing a logo with text in GIF format, for example, is a generic graphic. Generic graphics are bitmapped images which need to be edited using a graphics editor such as Adobe Photoshop or JASC Paint Shop Pro.

Screen captures are pictures of interface components of the localized software application, for example a dialog box or menu item. These can easily be re-created using a screen capture application. Refer to the following section for more information on creating screen captures.

Screen captures may contain additional translatable text, for example when a document window is displayed with a dialog box and sample text. The options in the dialog box will be localized in the localized application, but the localized content will need to be simulated in the localized application before the capture is created, or added after the screen capture has been created.

Illustrations are line-art images, which need to be edited in applications such as Adobe Illustrator or Macromedia Freehand. In line-art, text can typically be edited on a separate layer or as a separate object, so no additional image editing is required. If text in line-art images has been saved as or converted to outlines, the text needs to be re-created because text outlines cannot be edited.

Always verify with the publisher which file format is required. If original image files are available, use exactly the same format and image settings as the original files. The following table shows commonly used file formats and the documents in which they are used:

Document Type	File Format
Collateral (QuarkXPress)	.ai (Adobe Illustrator) or .eps (Encapsulated PostScript)
HTML or HTML Help (.HTML)	.gif (Graphics Interchange Format) or .jpg (Joint Photographic Experts Group)
Printed Document	.bmp (Bitmap) or .tiff (Tagged Image File format)
WinHelp (.hlp)	.bmp (Bitmap), .shg (Shed Graphic), or .wmf (Windows Meta File)

Remember to check the settings or sub-types for the file formats used. .Gif files can have different transparency settings or sub-types: version 87a Interlaced or Non-interlaced, or version 89a Interlaced or Non-interlaced. For .jpg files, the encoding and compression level to be saved can be specified.

Most graphics applications, such as Adobe Photoshop and JASC Paint Shop Pro will display detailed information on an active image, as can be seen in the following example:

Image Information   [x]

Image
Width:	500
Height:	500
Bits Per Pixel:	8
Max # of Colors:	256

Source File
File Name:	C:\Temp\Image1.gif
File Type:	Compuserve GIF
Sub Type:	Version 89a - Noninterlaced
Transparent Index:	20

When localizing graphics, always compare the image information for the localized images with the source file information.

2   Creating Screen Captures

Screen captures are images containing user interface components of an application or operating system, such as dialog boxes or menus. They are usually embedded in or linked to documentation and online help files.

In order to create a screen capture, first find out how the interface element can be accessed. As a rule, this will be straightforward, for example the Page Setup dialog box can be accessed by choosing the Page Setup command from the File menu. For more complicated applications, however, it is advisable to create screen capture scripts that explain how certain dialog boxes or options can be accessed, whether any special conditions are required in the application, or any special hardware needs to be installed, etc. When handling multiple target languages, it is possible to save time by creating these scripts after the first language has been completed. These scripts are often included in the localization kits from the publisher.

When creating screen captures of localized software applications, follow these guidelines:

- Check whether it is necessary to create the screen captures on a localized operating system. This will be required when certain options or standard buttons are retrieved from the operating system.

- Set the operating system display and appearance default settings.

- Check whether the most recent version of the localized application is installed before creating screen captures.

- Check which options or settings are specified in the original image. Text in online help or documentation often refers to particular settings in a dialog box.

- Check whether the source image contains text or other content which is not automatically displayed in the localized application. This will need to be localized separately.

- Verify that no manual editing has been done on the source language images. In some cases, even the source images may have been *faked*.

- Check whether the original screen captures contain cursors or pointers. If so, a cursor should be placed on the same spot in the localized screen capture. Most screen capture utilities have an option to include or exclude cursors in a screen capture.

Before creating any screen captures, test some of the localized images in the documentation or help files, where they are to be inserted, either in a manual or online help file. When images are linked to a document, replace the original image with the localized screen capture and print the page containing the image. Compare the test page with the original printout to check whether the screen capture scales and prints correctly. Compare the file sizes of the localized images with the file sizes of the source images. If the sizes differ considerably, it is possible that incorrect compression or resolution settings have been used for the localized images.

2.1   Windows

In the Windows operating system, screen captures can be created by pressing the Print Screen key on the keyboard, switching to a graphics editor, and choosing the Paste command. The Print Screen key will by default create a screen capture of the entire screen. Pressing Alt-Print Screen will capture the active window only.

There are numerous utilities available on the web that can be used to capture sections of a screen, such as a dialog box or a menu. Refer to the Screen Capture Utilities section on page 351 for more information on some of these utilities.

2.1.1   DISPLAY CONFIGURATION

Before creating screen captures, verify that the computer configuration and software settings reflect the original images as closely as possible. Settings include factors such as color depth (black and white, grayscale, color, 8-bit, 16-bit, etc.), font size, and screen resolution. If it is not clear which settings should be used, ask the publisher.

In Windows 3.x, the screen resolution can be set by opening Windows Setup from the Main program group, and selecting the desired resolution and color depth from the System Settings dialog box.

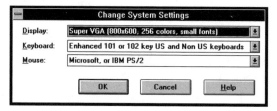

In Windows 9x and later versions, specify the screen resolution in the Display control panel. The Settings tab contains options for color palette and desktop area. A typical configuration for Windows screen captures is 256 colors and a desktop area (resolution) of 800x600 pixels.

In addition to setting the resolution and desktop area in the Display control panel, it may be necessary to change the Windows Appearance settings. The appearance should normally be set to default.

The best way to verify whether the correct settings are used, is to open the original image and the localized image side by side, and compare image size, image information, and printout.

2.1.2 SCREEN CAPTURE UTILITIES

Paint Shop Pro and Collage Complete are examples of applications and utilities that may be used to create screen captures on a Windows platform.

Paint Shop Pro is a bitmapped image editing application developed by JASC. For more information on Paint Shop Pro and a demo version, visit the JASC web site at www.jasc.com.

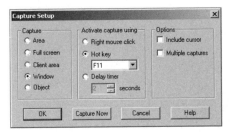

Collage Complete is a Windows and DOS screen capture and image handling utility developed by Inner Media. For more information on Collage Complete and a demo version, visit the Inner Media web site at www.innermedia.com.

Here are some more examples of screen capture utilities for the Windows platform:

- Hijaak Pro – www.imsisoft.com
- SnagIt – www.techsmith.com
- Capture Professional – www.creativesoftworx.com
- Print Screen – www.powware.com
- HyperSnap – www.hyperionics.com

2.2 Mac OS

The Macintosh operating system enables the user to create screen captures of the entire screen by default. When pressing Command-Shift-3, a screen capture of the entire screen is created and stored in a file called Picture 1 in the root of the hard drive. Additional screen captures are called Picture 2, Picture 3, etc.

Mac OS 7.6 and later versions contain more advanced screen capture features:

- Command-Shift-3 to save a capture of the entire screen in a file.
- Command-Shift-Control-3 to copy a capture of the screen to the clipboard.
- Command-Shift-4 and drag the mouse to save a part of the screen in a file. To confine the section to a square, hold the Shift key while dragging.
- Command-Shift-Control-3 and drag to copy a part of the screen.
- Command-Shift-4 with Caps Lock on, and click on a window to save a capture of the window in a file.
- Command-Shift-Control-4 with Caps Lock on, and click on a window to copy a capture of the window to the clipboard.

There are numerous utilities available on the web that can be used to capture sections of a screen, such as a dialog box or a menu. Refer to the Screen Capture Utilities section on page 352 for more information on some of these utilities.

2.2.1 DISPLAY CONFIGURATION

Before creating screen captures, verify that the software settings reflect the original images as closely as possible. Settings include factors such as color depth (black and white, grayscale, color, 8-bit, 16-bit, etc.) and screen resolution.

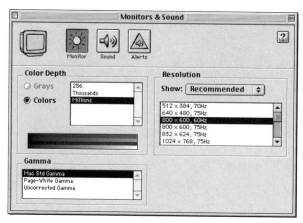

A typical configuration for Mac OS screen captures is 24-bit color (Millions of colors), and a 800x600 resolution.

2.2.2 SCREEN CAPTURE UTILITIES

Flash-It and Captivate are examples of applications that may be used to create screen captures on a Mac OS platform.

Flash-it is a freeware utility that can be downloaded from www.shareware.com.

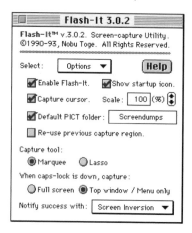

Captivate is a screen capture utility that has been developed by Mainstay. For more information on Captivate and a demo version, visit the Mainstay web site at www.mstay.com.

Captivate Select can be used to capture any portion of the screen. A pull-down menu, pop-up list, or dialog box can be captured with or without the pointer, scaled, and converted to black and white, as desired. A captured image can be placed on the Clipboard or the Scrapbook, or saved in a desired folder using one of five file formats: GIF, TIFF 5.0, TIFF 4.0, PICT, and MacPaint.

Other screen capture applications for use on the Mac OS are:

- Snapz – www.ambrosiasw.com
- Screen Catcher – www.stclairsoft.com
- Exposure Pro or ScreenShot – www.beale.com

3 Editing Graphics

It is sometimes necessary to *fake* screen captures or to manually edit graphics containing text. This often happens while waiting for the software translation to be completed, when a screen capture is needed for a marketing brochure. Another example is when the original screen capture contains a scenario or error that is difficult or impossible to reproduce in the running application.

Ms Sans Serif size 8 is the standard font used for most Windows applications, when manually entering or editing text in a user interface screen capture. Other commonly used fonts are Arial or Tahoma (Windows 2000). To check the font and font size used in error messages or menu items, open the Appearance tab of the Windows Display Properties control panel, and click on an item to see its font characteristics.

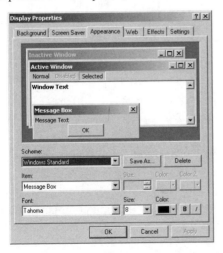

Helvetica size 10 is the standard font used for most Mac OS applications, when manually entering or editing text in a screen capture on a Macintosh, the font that is used for most Mac OS applications is Helvetica size 10. Other commonly used fonts are Geneva, Chicago, and Charcoal. A spacing of 0.5 is often applied to text in dialog boxes or folders. To check the font used in the Mac OS interface, open the Appearance control panel.

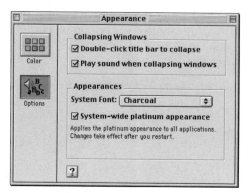

To edit screen captures or other graphics manually, follow these steps:

1. Start a graphics application, such as Paint Shop Pro or Adobe Photoshop.

1. Open the graphic to be edited. In this example, we will edit a screen capture from Windows 9x Wordpad.

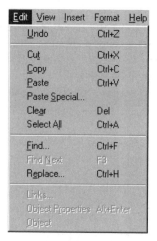

2. Use the eyedropper tool to set the background color to gray and foreground color to black.

3. Identify the font to be used. To do this, use the *type* tool to insert one of the English menu items and place it on top of the existing command. If it matches

the item exactly in size and parameters, it is the correct font. In this case, Ms Sans Serif size 8 is used.

4. Now, use the *type* tool to insert the translation next to the original item or in a separate file.

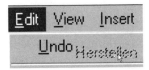

5. Draw a marquee around the translated string using the selection tool, and place the translation on top of the original item.

The English text will often need to be deleted in order to paste the translation next to it. In such cases, leave one dot of the original text to ensure the translation is pasted on the correct location.

If translations do not fit in the image, abbreviate the translation or choose shorter synonyms, and use a smaller font size or different spacing values, or modify the image size. In most cases, the first approach is recommended, because changing text attributes or image size may impact legibility of the image.

3.1 Layered Graphics

For graphics with complex backgrounds, such as photographs, it is advisable to use layered graphics. If the graphic artist has created the images using text on a separate layer, it will be much easier to localize the graphic, because there will be no need to re-create the background.

The ideal way to create localized images is to maintain one layered file containing all languages. A Photoshop image file, for example, contains the background layer and separate text layers with the translations for each target language. To save the Danish image to .gif format, activate and merge the background layer and the Danish text layer and save the file as flattened .gif.

Where no layered source files have been provided, it is advisable to create layered files containing the localized text. This means that the background needs to be re-created only once for all target languages, and keeping the localized text on separate layers makes it easier to make quick last-minute changes if necessary.

3.2 Blank Images

Where no layered images are available, check whether the publisher can provide blank versions of the images to be localized. When localizing a bitmapped image of a product box with the text "Update" on top of it, The English word "Update" needs to be removed and the picture of the box re-created, before the translation of "Update" can be pasted on the image.

When a text-free image is provided, paste the translation on the image, once the font, size, color, and type effect have been checked.

3.3 Web-based Images

When creating .gif files for use in HTML pages, consider file format variants such as subtype, transparency, and animation. It is also important to verify whether image maps are used with the image on the HTML pages.

3.3.1 SUBTYPE

In most graphics applications, subtypes can be specified for .gif files. It is important to use the same version and interlacing as in the source image files.

Using subtypes that are different from the source files can result in significant display differences.

3.3.2 TRANSPARENCY

If an image is transparent, one of the colors in the color palette for the image is selected as the transparent color, which allows the background color or background graphic of the HTML file to show through. If a .gif image has a white background with red text, for example, selecting the white color index number from the color palette as the transparent color will only display the red text on the HTML page. The white background will be replaced by the color defined in the HTML page.

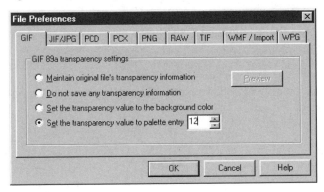

Ensure the image editor supports transparency in .gif files, and do not change transparency settings for the localized versions of the images. Always check whether the translated .gif files display correctly on the HTML page.

3.3.3 ANIMATED GIF

Animated GIF files consist of a sequence of separate images, called frames, which need to be edited. Use an animated GIF utility to separate the images first, then edit the images and paste the localized versions back in the sequence.

There are many different editors available to copy and paste frames from sequences in animated GIF files, for example the Animation Shop included in recent versions of Paint Shop Pro (www.jasc.com).

Localizing animated GIF can be a time-consuming task, depending on the number of frames in the animation, and the complexity of the background image and text effects.

Many web site developers have started using Java applets to overlay text on images because images take much longer to load into web browsers than text. For more information on translating Java applets, refer to the Embedded Code section on page 209.

3.3.4 IMAGE MAPS

HTML files often contain image maps, which are areas on an image that link to other HTML pages. If the layout or size of the localized image has changed, the image map needs to be adjusted accordingly. Depending on the editor used to edit the HTML files, it can be easy or difficult to change the coordinates. The safest way to change the coordinates is to open a copy of the HTML file in a WYSIWYG HTML editor, such as

Microsoft FrontPage. Adjust the coordinates to match the localized image, and save the file. Next, open the edited file with the original localized image, and manually change the coordinates using a text editor.

The following lines contain a sample image map:

```
<area href="h1.htm" shape="rect" coords="186, 55, 348, 119">
<area href="h2.htm" shape="rect" coords="188, 130, 346, 196">
```

The coordinates define the upper left corner (186, 55) and lower right corner (348, 119) of each image map area.

Chapter 11:
Translation Technology

This chapter contains information on the use of computer aided translation tools in the localization process. The information in this chapter will be of interest to project managers, software localization engineers, and translators.

This chapter includes the following sections:

1. Introduction
2. Translation Memory Tools
3. Terminology Tools
4. Software Localization Tools
5. Machine Translation Tools
6. Word Counting Tools

1   Introduction

Since the beginning of the 1990s, computer aided translation (CAT) tools has become common place within the localization industry. Translation memory (TM) tools have proven to be particularly valuable to companies working on large volume localization projects, or projects containing updates of previously translated material.

In addition to CAT tools, which include translation memory, terminology, and software localization tools, some companies also use machine translation and dedicated word counting tools on projects.

Most of the commercial tools discussed in this chapter have similar features. Every tool has its strengths and weaknesses. This chapter will not prescribe the best tool, it will merely introduce some of the tools currently available, and describe the key features in each tool. To learn more about specific differences between the tools, refer to the LISA web site or specialized localization and translation technology magazines, such as MultiLingual Computing & Technology and Language International.

1.1   Translation Tool Types

It is important to make a distinction between machine translation (MT) tools and computer aided translation (CAT) tools. Where the purpose of a machine translation tool is to assume and perform many of the tasks normally completed by a translator, computer aided translation tools are used to support the translator, by eliminating repetitive work, automating terminology lookup activities, and recycling previously translated texts. Machine translation has not been widely implemented in the software localization industry and this is largely due to the way in which software publishers develop their documentation; unlike in the automotive and aerospace industries, software publishers have never really created their documentation in a structured way that would facilitate efficient and cost-effective use of machine translation. This situation is changing; many software publishers are working hard to find ways to reduce their multilingual publishing costs.

Computer aided translation tools, also called computer assisted translation tools, can be categorized as follows:

- Translation memory tools
- Terminology tools
- Software localization tools

As a rule, the first two, translation memory and terminology tools, are generally combined in a tool set for the translation of documentation, online help, or HTML text. Software localization tools are used to translate and test software user interfaces, i.e. dialog boxes, menus, and messages. For more information on each of these tool types, refer to the respective sections in this chapter.

1.2 Tools Selection

Most localization vendors use several translation tools and often add custom features or enhancements. The choice of a specific tool usually depends on one or more of the following criteria:

- Client requirements – Which deliverables are required by the publisher? What is the format of existing translation memories? If the publisher is to supply the localization vendor with translation memories in Trados Translator's Workbench format, for example, the vendor will most likely prefer to use Trados.

- Supported languages – Each tool supports different feature sets and language sets. Make sure all target languages for current and possible future projects are supported by the tool chosen by the vendor.

- Source file format – Each tool has different filter sets and parsers for supported file formats; ensure that the source file format used in the project is supported. When translating SGML files, for example, ascertain whether the translation memory tool used supports SGML.

- Support – How much support will be required for the translators using the tool? Will it be possible to support them fully? If the translators are proficient users of Atril Déjà Vu, it may be advisable to use this tool, as no additional training or support would be required.

- Costs – How many product licenses are needed? Are they available, and if not, how much will the additional licenses cost?

- Alignment – If previous translations do exist, but no translation memories, the translated files need to be aligned in order to create a translation memory. Check whether the tool contains an alignment feature.

- Network support – Does the tool allow translation memories to be shared over a network? Which network protocols are supported?

- Customization – Does the tool contain features that enable the user to customize standard filters quickly or create filters for custom file formats?

To select the appropriate translation tool for a project, follow the basic guidelines in the table below:

File Type	Translation Tool	Comment
Collateral or marketing material	Native creation tool	Marketing material often needs to be rewritten; examples: QuarkXPress, Illustrator
Database exports	Translation memory tool	Create filter using Perl or other scripting language; examples: Oracle, SQL
Online help, HTML, or documentation	Translation memory tool	Examples: Trados, Déjà Vu, or SDLX
Online help, HTML, or documentation written with structured authoring	Translation memory tool combined with machine translation	Examples: Logos, Systran
Software binary files – .exe or .dll (standard)	Software localization tool	Examples: Corel Catalyst, RC-WinTrans
Software binary files (non-standard)	Native development environment	Examples: CodeWarrior
Software text-only resource files (standard)	Software localization tool, or native development environment	Examples: Corel Catalyst, Visual C++, Visual Basic
Software text-only resource files (non-standard)	Translation memory tool, or native development environment	Create filter using Perl or other scripting language; examples: Java, CGI
Terminology database or glossary	Terminology tool	Examples: MultiTerm or Excel

In some cases, the vendor will need to agree with the publisher on the tool to be used for the project, particularly when a translation memory database or other tool-generated output is part of the deliverable.

Note that some localization vendors have developed proprietary tools, which they may prefer to use. Some vendors have designed workflows and processes based on one standard tool, so additional preparation or training time may be required were they to use another tool.

2   Translation Memory Tools

Translation memory tools have always been very popular in the software localization industry, because of the short life cycle of software products and web sites. Most software products are updated at least once a year, and web sites often on a daily basis. Re-using translations from previous versions will significantly reduce the time to market for localized versions. Translation memory tools are specifically designed to recycle previously created translations as much as possible.

2.1   Introduction

Translation memory is a technology that enables the user to store translated phrases or sentences in a special database for local re-use or shared use over a network. Translation memory systems work by matching terms and sentences in the database with those in the source text. If a match is found, the system proposes the ready-made translation in the target language.

2.1.1   FILTERS

It is essential that file format filters are included in a translation memory system. A filter converts the source material from its proprietary format to a format that can be read by the TM system. In some TM tools, filters are embedded in Import and Export features. In others, applying filters is called pre-processing, when converting from native to TM format, and post-processing, when converting from TM to native format.

Most TM systems come with filters for the market standard file formats, such as HTML/ SGML/XML, RC, RTF, Word, and FrameMaker. Each tool has its own way of interpreting the source material. The frequency with which filters are updated depends largely on the tool developer and it does differ from one TM tool to another. For a recent listing of supported file formats, visit the web sites for each tool developer.

Some TM tools include filter customization features that enable the user to create import and export filters to proprietary or non-standard file formats. If the TM tool does not include these features, develop text extraction scripts, using a scripting language such as Perl. For more information on using Perl, refer to www.perl.org or www.perl.com.

Before using a TM tool for translation work, ensure that the filters support all required file formats.

2.1.2   SEGMENTATION

A translation memory system is based on *segmentation* of the source text. A segment is a text element, which is considered by the application as the smallest translatable unit, defined by periods, semi-colons, and hard returns. These are usually sentences, but can also be chapter headings or items in a list. A translation memory database is a repository of all these segments, in one or more languages. While translating a text, the TM system searches for each segment in the memory database to retrieve any existing translations. Depending on the TM tool that is used, each segment will be labeled or numbered.

Most TM tools segment units when one of the following text elements is encountered:

- Paragraph mark
- Sentence end (period followed by space)
- Cell end (within a table)
- List item end (tagged file formats)

Translation memory tools usually allow the user to change and customize segmentation rules; it is possible, for example, to change from sentence to paragraph-based segmentation only or to add additional segment separators. It is also possible to create files containing words which should not be segmented, such as "Mr. ", "e.g. " or similar abbreviations.

For a source text to be segmented correctly, check that the text does not contain any of the following items:

- Revision marks
- Conditional text
- Carriage returns within sentences
- (Index) markers in middle of words or sentences
- Change bars (FrameMaker only)
- Forced hyphenations
- Tables with tabs

Elements which are not recognized by TM tools and therefore not included in the segmentation process are text in images and embedded objects such as equations or organizational charts created in external editors.

Remember to refer to sections on file preparation in the documentation provided with the TM tool. A good overview on how to prepare different file formats for translation in a translation memory environment can be found in the Trados Workflow Manual, which can be downloaded from www.trados.com.

Some publishers have switched from sentence-based segmentation to paragraph-based segmentation. Segmenting sentences will result in a higher number of full (or exact) matches, but these must always be verified because they may need to be changed because of contextual reasons, i.e. preceding or following sentence. When using paragraph-based segmentation, the number of matches decreases, but full paragraph matches typically require no additional review or proofreading.

2.1.3 STATISTICS

All translation memory tools contain statistics utilities that enable the user to count the number of words in a document or set of documents, and determine the number of internal and external matches. Internal matches (or repetitions) are segments which are repeated within a project. External matches are segments which correspond to segments found in previously created translation memory databases.

The Analyze Files command in Trados Translator's Workbench, for example, will generate the following information:

- Number of segments
- Total number of words
- Internal matches (repetitions)
- Full matches (100%)
- Several levels of fuzzy matches (50-99%)
- No matches (new words)

These statistics are very important both to the publisher and the localization vendor, from a cost perspective. As mentioned in the Word Counts section on page 418 it is important not to rely on just one tool for word counting. Always check the results using another tool, for example the tool that was used to create the source files, such as Word or FrameMaker.

2.1.4 FUZZY MATCHING

Most translation memory systems support *fuzzy* matching, where translations are also retrieved from memory where the match between the previously stored segment and the new source segment is below 100%. A translation memory database contains the translation for the sentence "To search for text", for example, and a new sentence like "To search for and replace text" needs to be translated. The translation will be retrieved as a fuzzy match from the memory with a highlight on "and replace" indicating the difference.

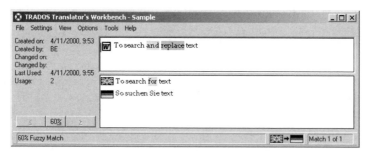

The degree of matching is measured in percentages. In the example above, the fuzzy match is 60%. Most TM systems with fuzzy matching capabilities allow the user to set a threshold where similar segments are retrieved as fuzzy matches. Fuzzy and full matches are typically priced at reduced rates, for example at 60% and 30% of the full word rate respectively.

When a fuzzy match is retrieved, it should be edited to correctly reflect the source text, the tool will then store the new segment pair in the translation memory.

2.1.5 ALIGNMENT

Alignment is a feature provided with most translation memory systems, where the user can match previously created translations. Alignment is used to enable translators to re-use translations that were previously created without using a translation memory tool. When existing translations are aligned, the source and target text are imported and matched to create a translation memory.

If a set of English HTML documents is available with Finnish translated versions, for example, and the plan is to use translation memory to translate a new version of the documents, create a translation memory by aligning the English and Finnish HTML files.

The time it takes to align translated documents depends entirely on how the translation was produced previously. If the translation was produced using a TM tool, but alignment needs to be done due to the a large number of last-minute changes in the translated, post-processed files, the alignment process will not take very long because all segments already have a one-to-one correspondence. If text needs to be aligned, where sections or sentences have been moved around by a translator, alignment will be very time-consuming, because for each source segment, a target segment needs to be located manually.

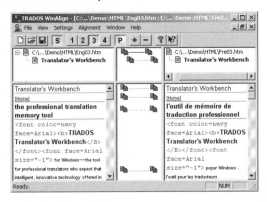

Most alignment tools contain features that enable the manual joining or splitting of segments. Where two English sentences were translated as one German sentence in previously translated material, for example, the two English sentences can be joined to make segments match again.

Examples of alignment tools are WinAlign by Trados (www.trados.com) or SDL Align by SDL (www.sdlintl.com).

2.1.6 BENEFITS IN LOCALIZATION

Using translation memory in localization projects has many benefits for localization vendors. Some examples are listed below:

* Software documentation tends to be repetitive. When a sentence has been translated once, the translation will automatically be inserted, when a translator reaches the next occurrence of that sentence.

* Software applications are regularly updated. Existing translations can be re-used in new versions of help files or manuals. These re-used sentences are called *external matches*. This also means that translation can begin before the source text has been completely finalized, or while the software or web site is still under development.

* Existing translation memories can be used when translating new or similar products.

* Most translation memory tools are integrated with a terminology management application that automatically displays key terms that occur in the source sentence. This will guarantee consistency in terminology.

* Utilities designed to report detailed statistics on word counts and the number of internal and external repetitions provide valuable information to project managers scheduling localization projects.

* Several translators can work on one project to speed up translation. Consistency in translation is guaranteed by networked use of translation memories.

* There is no need to train translators in complex word processing applications or document creation tools. Most of the translation work is performed in standard word processors or integrated text editors. In addition, encoding is protected in tagged file formats such as HTML and XML.

* On average, productivity levels can be improved by approximately 30%, or even 50%. Total translation costs can be reduced by 15% to 30%.

Most of the advantages listed above also apply to web site translations. Translation memory is an essential tool for processing the "streaming" and regular updates carried out on the content of most web sites. The best results from translation memory can be achieved when the source material is created in a structured way, avoiding wordiness and the use of ambiguity and synonyms. For more information on controlled authoring, refer to the Controlled Language section on page 29.

Translation memory is mainly suitable for technical documentation or content. It is best to avoid translating marketing material or small collateral documents using translation memory, because in many cases translators will want to restructure the text or rewrite sentences. With these types of documents, it is important for translators to have an overview of the document layout, the level of text expansion permitted, and a general idea on how the final text will be displayed.

2.1.7 DISADVANTAGES OF TRANSLATION MEMORY

Even though the benefits and advantages of translation memory systems are obvious, here are some disadvantages in using translation memory:

- Most TM tools do not display the format and layout of the document, which makes it difficult to see how translated text will be displayed in the final layout. A proofreading check is therefore required once the translated files have been converted back to their original formats.

- Translation memory management often poses problems to vendors, especially when working with several (teams of) translators in different locations.

- Since many last-minute language or translation changes are implemented in the translated files once they have been re-converted to their original formats, changes are not always inserted in translation memory; this makes it difficult to keep the TM databases up-to-date.

- Preparing source files for translation in translation memory tools and converting files back adds additional, often time-consuming, steps to the translation process.

- Translation memory filters have not always been updated to support new versions of the file formats they process. As a result, translatable text is either not recognized, or markup is presented as translatable text.

- Translators do not have the opportunity to change the overall structure of the text, i.e. to change the sequence of sentences within a paragraph.

- Creating filters for custom file formats, i.e. file formats that are not supported by default, can be a complicated and time-consuming programming task.

Always consider the points highlighted above, and review all source material before deciding whether to use translation memory. In some cases, for example small documents with virtually no external or internal matches and no future updates, it is better to translate the text directly in the source file.

2.1.8 TRANSLATION MEMORY EXCHANGE

Ever since development began on CAT tools, many different file and database formats have been used to store translated segments in translation memory. This has been causing and still causes problems for both software developers and translation service providers alike, therefore a special interest group was formed in 1997 by LISA, the Localisation Industry Standards Association.

This group of translation providers, tools vendors and customers of translation services, called OSCAR, has developed a file format specification called TMX, short for Translation Memory Exchange. The purpose of TMX is to facilitate the exchange of translation memory data between tools and/or translation vendors. For more information on OSCAR and TMX, visit the LISA web site at www.lisa.org.

OpenTag is another exchange standard that has been developed. It is a single common mark-up format, used to encode text extracted from documents of varying and arbitrary formats, designed specifically for translation and natural language processing tools. The OpenTag format is a markup format based on XML that can be used to encode text extracted from documents in various formats.

2.2 Trados Translator's Workbench

Translator's Workbench is a translation memory application developed by Trados. It can be used to translate any kind of document that can be opened by Microsoft Word. Trados Translator's Workbench generates a statistical overview of the number of internal repetitions, and fuzzy or exact matches found in the translation memory. The Translate command in the Tools menu of Translator's Workbench enables the user to segment and pre-translate files with translations retrieved from a translation memory database.

Translator's Workbench is closely integrated with MultiTerm, a terminology management application that interacts with Workbench. For more information on MultiTerm, refer to the Trados MultiTerm section on page 380.

A tool which has recently been added to Translator's Workbench is the TagEditor. The TagEditor provides direct support for HTML and other markup languages. There is no longer a need to convert from HTML to other file formats, before importing them into Trados. This can now be done in a single step.

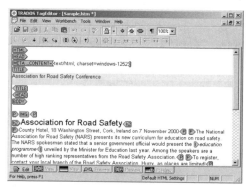

An additional Trados product is WinAlign, a tool that can be used to *align* a translated text with the source text in order to create a translation memory.

Trados Translator's Workbench supports RTF and DOC file formats by default, HTML/SGML/XML are supported by TagEditor. To import other file formats, additional Trados technology is required, such as:

- S-Tagger for Interleaf or FrameMaker files
- Story Collector for PageMaker files
- T-Window for PowerPoint files
- ITP Filter Pack for QuarkXPress and Ventura files

These tools convert native file formats to RTF for translation in Microsoft Word, using Trados Translator's Workbench.

To translate an RTF file using Translator's Workbench, follow these steps:

1. Start Translator's Workbench, create a new project or open an existing translation memory project (.tmw file).

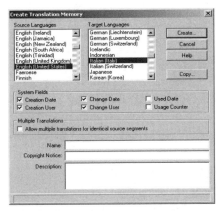

2. Start a word processor and open the translatable file. The standard file format used by Trados is RTF.

3. Attach the appropriate Trados template to the document. Templates for different Word versions can be found in the folder where Translator's Workbench has been installed.

4. Click on the first translatable string, and select Open/Get from the Trados menu in Word, or press Alt-Home. Type the translation in the field directly below the source text. If the source text is stored in the translation memory, the translation will automatically be inserted.

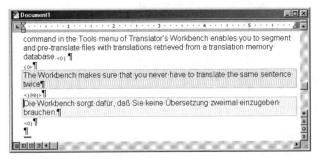

5. In the Translator's Workbench window, the string or word will be displayed in the top window, with the fully matching translation or a fuzzy match displaying in the bottom window.

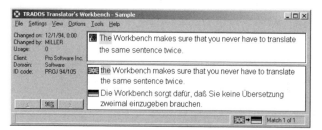

6. Select the Set/Close Next Open/Get command from the Trados menu, or press Alt-+. This will store the translation in translation memory and take the cursor to the next translatable segment. The source text from the previously translated segment will remain in the file as hidden text.

7. After the file has been translated, save and close the file.

8. Switch to Translator's Workbench and select the Clean Up command from the Tools menu. In the Clean Up window, add the files that have been translated. Cleaning up a translated RTF file means that the hidden source text is removed from the document and only translations remain.

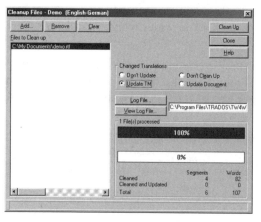

9. Click on the Clean Up button to remove all hidden source text from the file.

After cleaning up the RTF file, convert it to its original format using one of the filters listed above. If the translated file has been edited without running Translator's Workbench, you can enter the changes automatically into translation memory by selecting the Update TM option in the Changed Translations field of the Cleanup Files dialog box. It is advisable to keep copies of the *uncleaned* files, in case the translation memory databases need to be updated at a later time.

For more information on Translator's Workbench and an up-to-date list of supported file formats, visit the Trados web site at www.trados.com.

2.3 STAR Transit

Transit is a translation memory system developed by STAR. Transit contains an integrated translation editor that can emulate the Microsoft Word menu navigation and can open multiple files simultaneously. It is linked to a terminology management application, called TermStar.

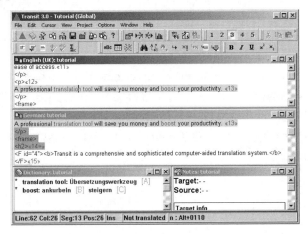

File format filters in Transit are highly customizable and support of custom file formats is possible by submitting a request order to STAR.

Follow these steps to translate files using STAR Transit:

1. Create a project, selecting target language(s), files to be imported, file types, segmentation rules, reference material, and dictionaries.

2. Import the translatable files into the project. Select the pre-translation option when importing or filtering.

3. Select the Open Language Pair command from the File menu and select the language pair.

4. Translate the text by entering translations in the target language window.

5. Once the text is translated, export the files back to the original format.

Transit is available in a Professional and a Workstation version. The Workstation version does not contain the import or export features. STAR also offers Transit Workflow Automation, which is an automated, web-based translation management system.

For more information on STAR Transit and an up-to-date list of supported file formats, visit the STAR web site at www.star-group.net.

2.4   Atril Déjà Vu

Déjà Vu by Atril is a translation memory tool that can be used for documentation, online help, and software resource files. It has been developed by Atril, and has the following components:

- Déjà Vu Interactive – a tool used to create projects, import files for translation, and to enter the translations.

- Database Maintenance – used to maintain translation memory databases, e.g. importing, exporting, aligning, and editing.

- Terminology Maintenance – used to maintain terminology databases.

- Database Conversion Wizard – used to convert Déjà Vu memory databases from an older format to the current version format.

- TermWatch – memory-resident utility that allows the user to access terminology databases from any other Windows application, using custom key combinations. For more information on TermWatch, refer to the Atril TermWatch section on page 381.

To translate files using Déjà Vu, follow these steps:

1. Start Déjà Vu Interactive.

2. To create a new project, select the Create Project command from the File menu. In the Create Project submenu, select the native file format of the files being translated.

3. Specify the name of the work file and click OK.

4. Select the Configure Current Project command from the Tools menu.

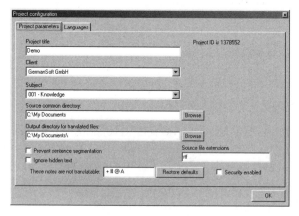

5. In the Project Configuration dialog box, specify the settings for the project.

6. Select the Import Files command from the File menu. In the Import Files dialog box, select the files to be translated, and click on the Go button.

7. In the main translation window, select the string to be translated, and type the text in the box in the lower right corner. To enter the translation in the active file, choose the Propagate in Current File command from the Edit menu.

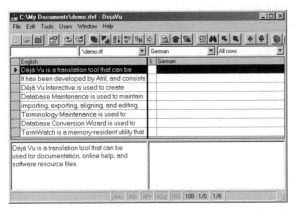

8. After the file has been translated, choose the Export Finished Translations command from the File menu.

For more information on Déjà Vu and an up-to-date list of supported file formats, visit the Atril web site at www.atril.com.

2.5 SDLX

SDLX is a suite of tools developed by SDL International including the following key components:

- SDL Align is used to align existing translations
- SDL Edit provides editing capabilities
- SDL Glossary is used to import text files into glossaries
- SDL Translate translates a set of files using one or more translation memory databases
- SDL TMX imports and exports translation databases
- SDL Analyse compares files against translation databases

The SDLX suite also contains several file validation and conversion tools, such as HTML utilities and DOC to RTF conversion.

To translate files using SDLX, follow these steps:

1. Use SDL Convert to convert the source files to SDL Edit files.

2. Start SDL Edit and open the project file and translation memory database.

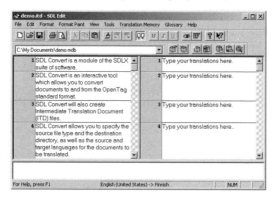

3. After the file has been translated, save the file and use the Merge feature of SDL Convert to convert the translated file back to its native format.

Recent versions of SDLX contain additional features such as a project wizard, which automatically detects and converts files in different formats and languages, and advanced project wizards and analyze features.

SDL has also developed a tool which detects changed or updated content on web sites and routes the text trough all the required steps, e.g. translation, review, and publish. This tool is called SDLWebFlow and is tightly integrated with the SDLX translation memory technology.

For more information on WebFlow, SDLX, and an up-to-date list of supported file formats, visit the SDL International web site at www.sdlintl.com.

2.6 IBM TranslationManager

IBM TranslationManager is a computer aided translation system that combines translation memory features with dictionary lookup. TranslationManager comes with an integrated word processor and alignment tool.

To translate files using IBM TranslationManager, follow these steps:

1. Start IBM TranslationManager and click on the Folder List window.

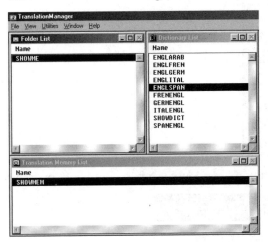

2. Select New from the File menu and enter the project properties in the New Folder dialog box. Specify a name for the new project folder, the source and target language, translation memory and dictionary to be used, and the markup (filter) method.

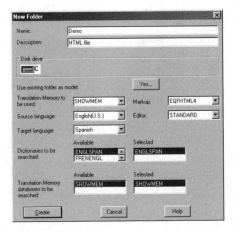

3. Click the Create button to create the new project.

4. Activate the Document List window and choose Import from the File menu. In the Import Documents dialog box, select the file(s) to be translated.

5. Click the Import button. In the Document Properties dialog box, specify the settings to be used for this file, if alternative, file-specific settings are required. To use the project settings, simply click the Cancel button.

6. In the Document List window, double-click on the file to be translated.

7. In the Translation window, replace the English text with the translations by typing over the source text. To jump to the next untranslated segment, press Ctrl+Enter. If matches are found in the translation memory or dictionary, they will be displayed in the Translation Memory or Dictionary window. To automatically insert translations, press Ctrl-n, where n is the number of the suggested translation or fuzzy match.

8. Edit the translated segment, if necessary, and confirm by pressing Ctrl+Enter.

9. To save the translated file, select Save from the File menu or press F2.

10. To export the translated file from the project folder, select the file in the Document List window and select Export from the File menu. Specify the export options and file locations in the Export Documents dialog box.

11. Click the Export button. The translated and/or source files will be exported to the folders specified. The default folders are \Source and \Target.

For more information on IBM TranslationManager and an up-to-date list of supported file formats, visit the IBM TranslationManager web site at www.ibm.com/software/ad/translat.

2.7 Other TM Tools

The tools listed in the previous sections are the most commonly used TM tools in the software localization industry. Many other translation tools are available, however, including proprietary tools developed by software localization vendors such as ALPNET and Lionbridge.

Some companies offer total solutions to publishers, integrating translation workflow automation with translation memory and machine translation systems. Considering the fact that web content is continuously being updated and published in multiple languages, automating this process can be a huge time and money saver in the long term.

2.7.1 ALPNET TECHNOLOGY

ALPNET Technology products and services provide an end-to-end solution for multilingual information publishing and integration processes, based on a client/server architecture for central management of translation and terminology resources. The software contains a web-based translation editor, and projects are routed either through real-time tcp/ip connections or via e-mail.

The ALPNET Technology software can be integrated with the standard translation memory, terminology, and machine translation tools and linked to content management and document workflow systems. In 1999 ALPNET established a "community source" program with Sun Microsystems and Novell to enable companies to participate in the development of the technology and, as members of the community, customize the technology and implement it in their organizations.

For more information on ALPNET Technology, visit the ALPNET web site at www.alpnet.com.

2.7.2 LIONBRIDGE FOREIGNDESK

ForeignDesk is a client/server based translation memory tool originally developed by International Communications. Since the acquisition of IC by Lionbridge in 2000 the tool has been integrated with Lionbridge's LionTrack translation workflow system, to create a translation management system which is fully web enabled.

The technology includes agents that automatically track changes or updates in content databases, and extract the text for translation. After translation, review, and validation, the translations are re-inserted into the content databases.

For more information on ForeignDesk and LionTrack, visit the Lionbridge web site at www.lionbridge.com.

2.7.3 TRANS SUITE 2000

Trans Suite is a relatively young translation memory application, developed by translation technology specialists in Belgium. The Trans Suite 2000 supports TMX and OpenTag and comes with a free alignment tool.

For more information on Trans Suite 2000, visit the Cypresoft web site at www.cypresoft.com.

2.7.4 HTML-CAT

Html-CAT is a localization environment for HTML projects, developed by Translation Craft, a company which was acquired by SDL International in July 2000. It includes features such as built-in translation memory, project management tools, and support for HTML script elements.

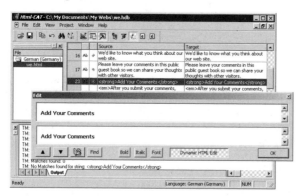

For more information on Html-CAT, visit the SDL International web site at www.sdlintl.com.

2.7.5 EUROLANG OPTIMIZER

Eurolang Optimizer is a translation memory tool which is currently marketed, supported and maintained by LANT. Optimizer integrates with word processors and can be used to pre-translate new documents using existing translation memories on a server. The text can then be edited locally in the word processor and translations added. The newly translated sentences are then stored in the translation memory on the server.

For more information on Eurolang Optimizer, visit the LANT web site at www.lant.com.

3   Terminology Tools

Terminology lookup features are optimized when used in conjunction with translation memory tools. Many TM systems are now available with integrated terminology management utilities. The following sections provide some examples of terminology management applications used, some of which are integrated in TM systems.

In the case of some TM systems, such as Trados Translator's Workbench and Star Termstar, the terminology application can be used separately from the translation memory tool. In others, such as IBM TranslationManager and SDLX, the two are tightly integrated.

In addition to terminology management systems, many translators use glossary or dictionary managers, which typically contain limited functionality, but do offer significant advantages over maintaining glossaries in a spreadsheet or word processor.

3.1   Introduction

As discussed in Chapter 12 of this book, terminology management is much more than just creating and maintaining bilingual lists of translated terms. A terminology management tool enables terminologists, technical authors, and translators to maintain term databases that include additional information such as definitions, context, gender, source, synonyms, etc.

Most publishers and professional software localization vendors will maintain core terminology databases containing multiple language versions of basic terms for particular products with additional information. Translators will typically refer to both databases and bilingual glossary lists for key terms encountered during translation. These glossaries can be any combination of operating system glossaries, user interface glossaries, and project glossaries.

A glossary tool may be the best option for maintaining large, bilingual glossaries with no other terminology information.

A third type of terminology tool that is often used in localization is the electronic dictionary. Most industry-standard monolingual or bilingual dictionaries have been released on CD-ROM. These tools often only interact with word processors, and not necessarily with translation memory tools. An example of a dictionary tool is Trados MultiTerm Dictionary. A detailed discussion on dictionary tools goes beyond the scope of this book.

3.2   Terminology Management Tools

The following tools are professional terminology management applications which are integrated with translation memory systems. Not only can they be used to create bilingual glossaries, but also to develop advanced multilingual terminology databases containing concept information such as translations, grammatical categories, definitions, and context.

Before committing to a terminology management system (TMS), consider the following work scenarios. Database concepts are never static, and it is not uncommon for certain database setups to be restructured, e.g. data has to be moved from one field to another, and extensive find and replace actions have to take place. Databases containing large amounts of data must be sustainable and very few commercial tools offer robust data manipulation features.

Please note that the tools mentioned here can also be used independently of the translation memory application.

3.2.1 TRADOS MULTITERM

MultiTerm is a database application that allows the user to create, manage and present terminology. For each source term, or concept, add equivalents in a large number of languages. The database can be queried in any language direction, and search options support wildcards and fuzzy matching.

In addition to entering equivalents, a user can enter a variety of user-defined text and attribute fields or graphics in the records, such as definitions, context, grammatical information, and images. Records can be cross-referenced, imported and exported, and shared over a network or via the web using MultiTerm Web Interface.

MultiTerm can be used in conjunction with Trados Translator's Workbench. It will automatically display translations of words found in source text segments. For more information on Translator's Workbench, refer to the Trados Translator's Workbench section on page 368.

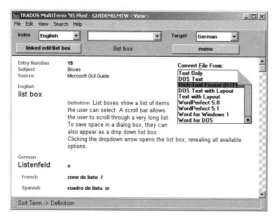

For more information on MultiTerm, visit the Trados web site at www.trados.com.

3.2.2 STAR TERMSTAR

TermStar is a multilingual Terminology Management System that is linked to the Transit translation memory system, which is discussed in the STAR Transit section on page 371. TermStar is a customizable terminology tool based on ODBC standards. This means terminology can be stored in powerful database engines, such as SQL Server or Oracle.

TermStar works with projects that consist of one or more dictionaries, which can be activated or de-activated separately and searched in a specified order.

Search queries in TermStar use regular expressions and users can process terminology by adding, duplicating and merging concepts.

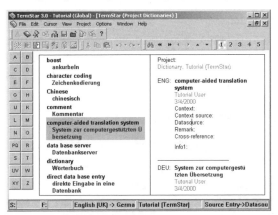

A web-based version of TermStar, called WebTerm, is also available from STAR. It enables the user to share and access terminology databases through the internet.

For more information on TermStar, visit the STAR web site at www.star-group.net.

3.2.3   ATRIL TERMWATCH

TermWatch is an application that allows the user to access terminology databases from any Windows application. Key combinations can be defined in such as way that, when selected, they will look up the selected word in the terminology database and paste the target term into the calling application, or copy the target term to the clipboard. Alternatively, all matches are presented in a table in the Déjà Vu translation memory system.

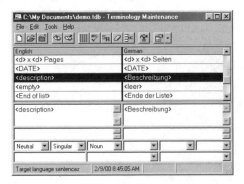

To import, export, create and maintain terminology databases, use the Terminology Maintenance utility, which is installed with the Déjà Vu translation memory system.

For more information on Déjà Vu and Terminology Maintenance, refer to the Atril Déjà Vu section on page 372 or visit the Atril web site at www.atril.com.

3.3   Glossary Management Tools

The following tools are designed for creating and maintaining large, bilingual terminology glossaries. Most of the tools work interactively with word processors and contain several search features.

3.3.1   LINGO TRANSLATOR'S ASSISTANT

Lingo offers a way to speed up the time-consuming task of creating, consulting and managing bilingual translation glossaries. Glossaries once created can be consulted using a dedicated search function. Glossaries can be imported and exported, and are compatible with any Windows word processor.

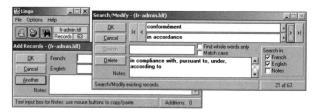

A special Microsoft Glossary Converter is also available that automatically imports Microsoft's CSV glossaries.

For more information on Lingo and the Microsoft Glossary Converter, visit the Julia Emily Software web site at www.lexicool.com.

3.3.2   AVALON GLOSSARY ASSISTANT

Glossary Assistant is an eight-language glossary, containing terms used in the Localization Industry. Avalon supplies the base glossaries, which can be customized and expanded by the users.

The Glossary Assistant interface is very simple and easy to use. The glossary tab displays the searchable list of terms, the Options tab enables the user to add terms to the list. A Glossary Assistant database can be shared over a network, so different users can work with the same glossary, by searching and adding terms simultaneously.

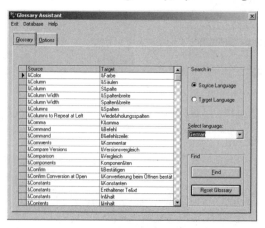

For more information on the Glossary Assistant, visit the Avalon Technologies Ltd. web site at www.lingualizer.net.

4 Software Localization Tools

Software localization tools are designed to help translators localize software user interfaces. Most of these tools combine resource editing, translation memory, leveraging (re-using), validation, and spell checking functionality.

4.1 Introduction

Software localization tools typically support editing of both text-only resource (such as RC) files, and binary program files (such as .exe, .dll, or Macintosh files). Here are some advantages of using software localization tools as opposed to software resource editors or development environments:

- Resource editors, as a rule, do not have glossary generation functionality, translation memory, statistics, spell checking, or validation functionality. This means that each new update must be translated from scratch.
- Localization tools prevent translators from inadvertently changing or deleting user interface items or encoding.
- Most localization tools contain review markers, indicating which translated strings have been recycled from previous versions, which strings need review, and which strings are signed off.
- Resource editors usually need to be installed as part of a development environment which takes up many system resources; localization tools are small, stand-alone applications.

Some software localization tools contain pseudo-translation features, which enable the user to "translate" strings using specified (accented) characters or string length parameters. The purpose of pseudo-translation is to anticipate problems that may arise during the translation cycle.

4.2 Windows Localization Tools

The following sections provide brief descriptions of the most commonly used software localization tools for Windows applications.

4.2.1 COREL CATALYST

Corel Catalyst is a software localization tool that can be used to translate binary, 32-bit Windows-based files, such as .dll, .exe, and .ocx files, and text-only software resource files, such as .rc and .dlg files. It can also be used to update translated files, to create glossaries from previously translated files, and to check resource files for common localization errors. Catalyst is used to translate and review text strings, menus, dialog boxes, and various custom resources supported by Windows.

Because Windows 9x does not allow changed resources to be saved back to .exe or .dll files, Catalyst provides a proprietary TTK format, with imports and extracts executable files. Changes can only be saved directly to binary files if Catalyst is run on Windows NT or Windows 2000.

Corel Catalyst provides functions for leveraging (re-using) existing translations, validating localized strings, creating software glossaries, pseudo-translations, filtering, and spell checking. Recent versions of Corel Catalyst also include support for Windows Help project files, such as .hpj, .rtf and .cnt files. Since the release of version 2.5 of Catalyst, translators can download the QuickShip version for free. QuickShip can be used to edit TTK project files, which have been created using the full Enterprise edition.

To translate software resource files using Corel Catalyst, follow these steps:

1. Start Corel Catalyst.

2. Create a new project using the Document Selection dialog box.

3. Choose File > Insert Files to import the files to be translated.

4. Next, in WYSIWYG mode or non-WYSIWYG mode, translate the resources.

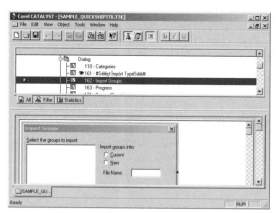

5. After translation, extract and save the translated file to its native format using the Extract Files command from the File menu.

For more information on Catalyst, visit the Catalyst web site at www.corel.ie/catalyst.

4.2.2 APPLOCALIZE

AppLocalize is a tool developed by Software Builders, which is used to translate binary resource (.res) or executable (.exe) files. Please note that resource changes in executable files can be saved under Windows NT or Windows 2000 only.

Follow these steps to translate .res or .exe files using AppLocalize:

1. Start AppLocalize and choose the New command from the File menu to create a new project.

2. Choose the Languages command from the Description menu to enter the source and target language(s).

3. Choose the Add/Merge from Base Resources File command from the Actions menu.

4. In the Add/Merge from Base Resources File dialog box, select the .res or .exe files to be imported.

5. In the main translation window, translate dialog boxes, menus, and strings.

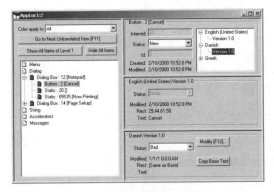

6. Export the translations to a new .res or .exe file using the Generate translated Resources File command from the Actions menu.

7. Build a program file, for example a .dll, using the translated .res file.

For more information on AppLocalize and a demo version, visit the Software Builders web site at www.sbuilders.com.

4.2.3 RC-WINTRANS

RC-WinTrans by IBS Software is a tool that can be used to translate Windows resource script (.rc) files. The user can create, translate and maintain multiple language versions of the resource file from projects. RC-WinTrans can also be used to leverage (re-use) existing translations, and to resize dialog box items using its built-in dialog editor.

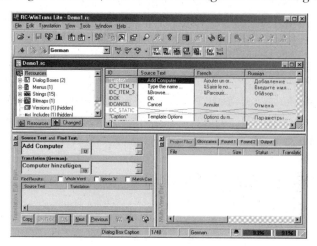

For more information on RC-WinTrans, visit the IBS Software web site at www.schaudin.com.

4.2.4 PASSOLO

Passolo by PASS Engineering is a tool for localizing software files. It helps the user to isolate localization from software development. It exports translatable text from software resource files and imports it after translation. Passolo also includes dialog box resizing functionality and several automated localization tests.

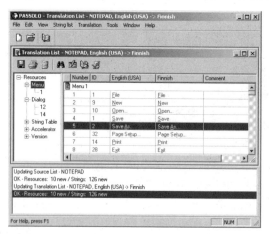

Recent versions of Passolo are tightly integrated with Trados Translator's Workbench for translation memory functionality.

For more information on Passolo, visit the PASS Engineering web site at www.passolo.com.

4.2.5 VISUAL LOCALIZE

Visual Localize is a tool developed by AIT GmbH in Germany, for localizing 16-bit and 32-bit application files, including .dll, .exe, and .drv files. A project in Visual Localize contains all the information on the translated file, such as resources and limits applied to the number of characters, and dictionaries contain source and target terms.

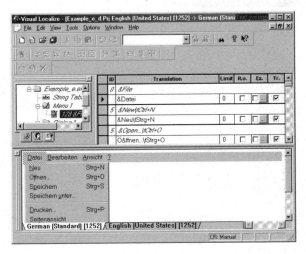

For more information on Visual Localize, visit the AIT web site at www.visloc.com.

4.2.6 VISUAL TRANSLATE

Visual Translate is a tool developed by AlShare, for translating Visual C++ .rc files. It enables the user to import several .rc files into one dictionary project.

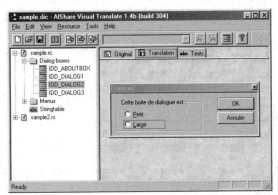

For more information on Visual Translate, visit the Alshare web site at www.alshare.com.

4.2.7   VENONA TRANSLATION TOOLKIT

Venona is a software translation tool for C++ resource files. It contains resizing, advanced search and replace options, automatic hot key assignment, pseudo-translation, and project statistics features.

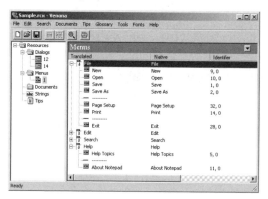

For more information on Venona Translation Toolkit, visit the Sajer Software web site at www.sajer.com.

4.2.8   PROPRIETARY TOOLS

Many large software developers have developed tools for localizing their products. Microsoft has developed LocStudio, for example, which is an advanced version of older tools like RLToolSet and Espresso.

Other examples of proprietary software localization tools are listed in the following table.

Company	Software Localization Tool
Autodesk	Autodesk Localization Studio
Intel	IIDS
Lotus	Domino Global Workbench, RED
Microsoft	LocStudio
Oracle	HyperHub, TTT
Symantec	Pebbles

These tools are normally only available to in-house translators working for publishers, and localization vendors working on their projects.

4.2.9   TRANSLATION MEMORY TOOLS

Most computer aided translation tools have capabilities for translating text-only resource files. Trados Translator's Workbench, IBM TranslationManager, and Atril Déjà Vu, for example, offer import filters for software resource (.rc) files.

More information on these tools can be found in the Translation Memory Tools section of this chapter.

4.3 Macintosh Localization Tools

Since Macintosh applications have a different design and format from Windows applications, several tools have been developed to help translators localize Mac OS applications and re-use previous translations.

As a rule, translators would combine a resource editor such as ResEdit with a localization tool such as AppleGlot and MPW scripts to localize applications. PowerGlot is a tool that is comparable to Corel Catalyst in that it contains both resource editing, glossary extraction, and translation memory features.

4.3.1 APPLEGLOT

AppleGlot is a Macintosh software localization tool developed by Apple Computer. It has been designed to speed up the process of localizing Macintosh applications and resource files. Here is a brief outline of the localization process, using AppleGlot:

- AppleGlot extracts text from resources within files, and later merges the translations back to create localized resources. These extracted text files can be used to translate all user interface text, such as menus, dialog boxes and strings.

- AppleGlot does incremental updates from previously localized versions of the software. This minimizes the amount of effort needed to update a new release of a file by preserving previously localized resources, or portions of resources. Refer to the AppleGlot section on page 133 for more information on updating software using AppleGlot.

Follow these steps to translate a Mac OS application using AppleGlot:

1. Create a new environment by selecting the New Environment command from the File menu. An environment is a set of specifically named folders that AppleGlot uses to handle a project.

2. Copy the files to the appropriate folders. When localizing a new software application, move a copy of that application into the _NewUS folder within the Environment folder.

3. If language glossaries from other translated applications are available, copy them to the _LG folder. All translations found in these language glossaries will be stored in the work glossaries as potential translations, or "guesses". Apple provides language glossaries with standard Apple interface terminology on the Apple FTP server at ftp.apple.com/devworld/Tool_Chest/Localization_Tools/ Apple_Int'l_Glossaries.

4. Return to AppleGlot and open the environment using the Open command from the File menu. Locate the environment folder, select it – but do not open it – and click the Select Folder button.

5. In the AppleGlot environment window, mark the files to be translated, and click the Translate Only button.

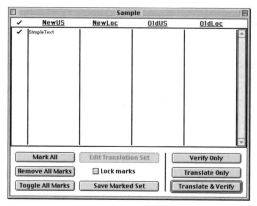

6. Save the batch file in the environment folder. The batch file contains all information produced automatically by AppleGlot, or that was entered manually in the Environment window.

7. AppleGlot now starts extracting the text from the resources, and creating work glossaries.

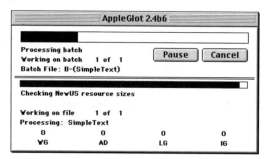

8. When text extraction is completed, translate the work glossary file(s) in the _WG folder using a text editor, word processor or a translation memory tool.

Before giving work glossary files to translators, add comments to the file containing specific localization instructions. Comments in work glossary files must be enclosed in { and } braces.

An AppleGlot work glossary contains the text from the resources in the following format:

```
Resource type, ID and item number [item information]
<Source text>
<Translation>
```

Typically, a work glossary file looks like this:

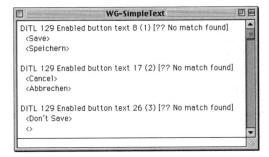

AppleGlot creates work glossaries in one of the following file format: MPW, MS Word, MacWrite, SimpleText or Microsoft Excel. The file format is specified in AppleGlot's Preferences dialog box. SimpleText format is normally used, which can be handled by most word processors and text editors.

If the work glossary is too big to be opened in SimpleText, use an alternative text editor, such as BBEdit. For more information on BBEdit, visit the Bare Bones web site at www.barebones.com.

When translating work glossaries, it is very important to look at the resource information line that indicates the resource and item type. Refer to the Resource Types section on page 86 for a complete list of resource types.

Follow these steps to compile the translated strings into the application file:

1. Copy the translated work glossary files to the _WG folder. Make sure to overwrite the old files, using the same file names.

2. Start AppleGlot and open the batch file that was saved in step 6 in the previous section.

3. Select the Translate & Verify button. This command will also compare and verify the resources in the original and localized files.

The localized application version will be placed in the _NewLoc folder.

AppleGlot can be downloaded from the Apple FTP server at ftp.apple.com/devworld/Tool_Chest/Localization_Tools.

4.3.2 POWERGLOT

PowerGlot is a Mac OS localization tool that extracts, sorts, and presents all translatable text contained in an application in a comprehensive way. It was developed by Florent Pillet, a French Macintosh developer. PowerGlot has advanced features for creating word counts from Macintosh applications, leveraging (re-using) previously translated versions, and creating error reports.

Follow these steps to translate a Macintosh application using PowerGlot:

1. Make a copy of the program file to be translated.

2. Start PowerGlot, and select Add Work Files from the Database menu.

3. PowerGlot reads the resources of the application and displays the resources in the database window.

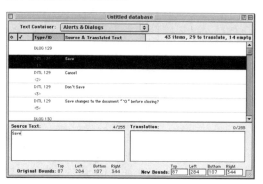

4. Choose the Database Settings command from the Edit menu. Specify the project settings, such as source and target language.

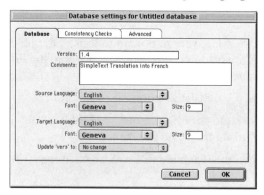

5. From the Text container drop down list, select the resource type to be translated, for example, Menus.

6. Click on a menu item and type the translation in the Translation field.

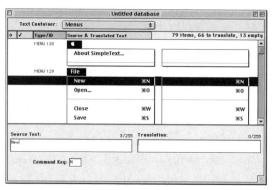

7. Translate the other resource types, such as alerts and dialog boxes, strings, and window titles.

8. Choose the Generate Localized Files – From Original Files command from the Database menu to build a localized version of the application.

For more information on PowerGlot, visit the PowerGlot web site at www.powerglot.com.

4.4   Dynamic Localization Tools

A dynamic localization tool is a software program that translates the user interface of an application on-the-fly, while it is running. Translations are entered in dictionaries that are used to dynamically translate the interface components of specified applications, such as dialog boxes, menus, and strings.

4.4.1   JARGON

Jargon is a dynamic localization utility that works by matching text used in application user interface controls (menus, buttons, list boxes, etc.) with texts found in its Phrasebooks. The Phrasebooks contain foreign language translations of the text used by applications and system menus or buttons such as Cancel, Apply, and OK.

The source code of the application remains unchanged. You can use the Phrasebook Editor to customize Phrasebooks for an application, and to add translations. If the phrase is not found in one of the Phrasebooks, it is displayed in the source language.

You can set the elements of the user interface to be translated, as well as the source and target languages, in the Translation Defaults dialog box. When using Jargon's Discovery mode, all user interface strings that are not found in one of the Phrasebooks are automatically entered in a Phrasebook for translation.

To manually add translations to a phrasebook, click the Edit button in the Application Preferences dialog box, and add the source and target terms in the Phrasebook Editor.

For more information on Jargon, visit the MDR Technologies web site at www.mdr.com.

4.4.2   SUPERLINGUIST

The SuperLinguist application was developed by KT International. It consists of four software products: SuperLinguist, SuperLinguist Terminal Manager, SuperLinguist Resource Editor, and SuperLinguist Resource Manager.

SuperLinguist is used to dynamically translate the user interface of any Windows application to another language, while the application is running. The SuperLinguist Manager captures the source user interface strings and builds an application dictionary. The application dictionary can be translated using the Manager. Once the dictionary has been translated, the SuperLinguist Engine performs the real-time translation. The SuperLinguist interface is very basic, i.e. the user opens a language dictionary and selects the application to be translated.

For more information on SuperLinguist, visit the KT International web site at www.kt-international.com.

4.4.3 WIZTOM

WizTom by WizArt is an internationalization and dynamic user interface localization workbench. Working with Windows and Java applications, WizTom intercepts the contents of the screen before it is displayed and replaces the original texts with a translation in the appropriate language.

WizTom consists of three modules: The Workbench for text extraction, thesaurus import/export, and control resizing, The Controller for dynamic language switching, and The Audit for testing of the user interface translations.

For more information on WizTom, visit the WizArt Software web site at www.wizart.com.

5 Machine Translation Tools

Although machine translation has not been used extensively in the localization industry, this situation may change in the near future. A number of publishers have successfully implemented pilot projects designed to assess the viability of the technology for localization projects. These tests have shown positive results from the perspective of both cost and productivity.

The following sections provide some basic information on how machine translation can be integrated with translation memory, and which machine translation tools are currently used.

5.1 Translation Memory vs. Machine Translation

Translation memory (TM) should not be confused with machine translation (MT). The major difference is that in machine translation a computer translates the text, whereas in translation memory systems, a computer only stores translated sentences. Where an MT system tries to *replace* a translator, a TM system *supports* and assists the translator with the translation tasks. Interestingly enough, only low-end MT systems make claim that they can replace the translator. The more powerful the MT tool, the more likely it is to be marketed as a translation productivity tool, rather than a replacement for the translator.

Although there have been very few significant improvements in MT systems over the past few years, porting to PC, Internet compatibility, and price reductions have revitalized the interest in machine translation systems. More and more translation memory systems offer support for MT. Trados Translator's Workbench, for example, is fully compatible with the LOGOS and Systran machine translation systems.

In a typical setup where TM and MT are used, the computer first searches the translation memory for a match of the sentence to be translated. If no (fuzzy) match is found, the translator can ask the MT system to translate the sentence, edit the result and store the translation in the translation memory. In most cases, this can also be done in batch mode, where source text is first pre-translated by running it against a translation memory. Any remaining untranslated segments are then processed by a machine translation system. The output is post-edited by a human translator, who confirms the translation of each segment and automatically stores it in the translation memory database.

Here are some examples of commonly used machine translation systems:

- Systran – more info at www.systransoft.com
- LANT@MARK – more info at www.lant.com
- L&H iTranslator and Power Translator – more info at www.lhsl.com
- Logos Translation System – more info at www.logos-ca.com

Machine translation is applied on many levels, from processing large-volume mission-critical product descriptions to online "gisting" offered on many web sites. Many web sites offer online translation services, using a back-end machine translation engine. One of the first web sites to offer machine translation gisting was Altavista (babelfish.altavista.com). Altavista enables users to translate web content or search results using the Systran machine translation engine.

Since the quality of the output from most gisting engines is questionable, to say the least, gisting is not used by professional localization vendors. Improper use of MT systems for the wrong types of documents, will make MT a costly, inefficient and time-consuming exercise.

Machine translation has been proven to be effective only when used by vendors to translate very controlled input that has been carefully planned for by the post-editing team. Machine translation will only provide a return on investment once large investments have been made to make the source text suitable for machine translation processing, and the system has been properly "loaded" with the specialized terminology that is likely to occur in the specific texts to be translated. This means pre-editing all text to identify potential problems the MT system may encounter, and adapting the text, if necessary. For more information on this so-called structured authoring or controlled language, refer to the Controlled Language section on page 29.

6   Word Counting Tools

Word counting is an everyday task for many translation and localization vendors, and special tools have been developed to provide accurate counts for the most frequently used file formats: HTML/XML/SGML and PDF.

6.1   WebBudget

Counting words in large batches of markup language files has always been somewhat problematic. Some tools only process one file at a time, others skip translatable text in unrecognized sections. This is why Aquino Software developed WebBudget. WebBudget is a tool that generates detailed word counts of SGML, XML or HTML files in batch mode, and it also has the functionality to specify word prices for automated billing reports.

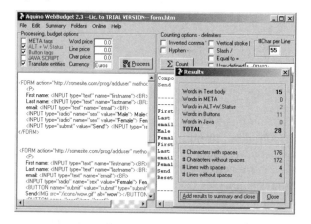

Aquino Software has also released a tool called FreeBudget, which can be used to generate word counts from RTF, DOC, and TXT files.

For more information on WebBudget and FreeBudget, visit the WebBudget web site at www.webbudget.com.

6.2   PDF Count

PDF Count is a plug-in for Adobe Acrobat developed by 4Translation. It generates statistical information on PDF documents. Information will include statistics on word counts, character counts, and number of pages.

For more information, visit the PDF Count web site at www.pdfcount.com.

Chapter 12:
Terminology

This chapter is aimed at translators or linguists who deal with terminology issues in localization projects. The chapter contains information on terminology management issues in localization projects, creation and management of glossaries, and useful terminology resources.

This chapter includes the following sections:

1. Introduction
2. Terminology Setup
3. Terminology Reference Materials
4. Terminology Standards
5. Creating User Interface Glossaries
6. Further Reading

Related chapters are Chapter3, which contains information on translating software applications, Chapter 6, which deals with of online help translation, and Chapte r8, which contains information on translating documentation.

1   Introduction

Terminology management is a frequently underestimated task in localization projects. Time constraints infrequently allow for thorough research to find the correct translations for specific terms or to maintain professional terminology management databases (termbases). Nevertheless, terminology is a critical task for both the publishers and vendors involved in localization.

For software publishers, terminology management is essential for maintaining consistent terminology in a product and across different products and releases. Managing and controlling terminology is vitally important, particularly when a publisher is using a number of translation suppliers. Terminology also plays an important role in controlled authoring processes designed to reduce and to improve translation speed.

For vendors, terminology is of key importance during the following three phases of a translation or localization project: the startup, the production, and the review cycle. First of all, at the start of a project, a list of key terms must be created which will form the basis for a terminology list to be developed during translation. During the production cycle, i.e. during translation and editing, glossaries containing terminological equivalents will be linked to translation memory tools for automatic term lookup. Finally, during review stages, terminology needs to be checked for accuracy and consistency. For example, a review phase must be scheduled to check whether translations for user interface terms match the actual translated software. This is called a software consistency check.

Translators or linguists responsible for terminology management in multilingual localization projects typically have the following responsibilities:

- Review and approval of generic and product specific terminology
- Maintenance of terminology databases (TDB or termbase), ensuring that all terminology is of verifiable quality and consistency
- Terminology research in instances where no translations are available, or where several different translations are possible
- Guidance for translators, both internal and external, in establishing accurate and complete terminology glossaries
- Evaluation and customization of terminology management and glossary tools
- Monitoring the deployment of terminology and glossary management tools

To ensure consistent terminology use, most localization agencies use terminology and glossary management software. These tools typically have the following features and functionality:

- Storage of terms, equivalents, definitions, and contextual information
- Advanced lookup features for quick searches of specific terms and fuzzy-matching capability for broad searches of entire resources
- Automatic insertion in the translation environment, eliminating the need to copy and paste or re-type terms

To prevent glossaries or termbases from becoming too large or cluttered, many localization agencies separate their terminology information into the three types that are described later in this chapter:

- Operating environment glossaries
- Client glossaries
- Project glossaries, including software user interface glossaries

It is important that both publishers and localization vendors be involved in the terminology management process. Publishers should create a database containing source language terms used in their products, for example, while localization vendors provide target language equivalents for these terms before and during the localization cycle. These terms are entered manually or automatically in multilingual terminological entries, which are then populated to form a master database for future project reference.

Traditionally, terminology management and terminology research involved locating documentation about a certain subject matter in the source and target language and extracting the key terminology in both languages. This activity is accompanied by contextual information, definitions, and other specifications. In software localization, terminology research is complicated by the fact that many software products use the latest in computer technologies, and very often little or no reference material is available. Many terms are often new to English and therefore pose difficulties when terminologists search for an equivalent in another language. The term may not even exist, and it may mean that the translator has to come up with an equivalent that accurately reflects the source term. One way to find equivalents for English terminology is to search for articles describing the subject matter in specialized magazines in the target language.

The greatest benefits can be gained, however, if terminology management has been consciously planned during the development cycle. There are many benefits to be gained from working on terminology management issues at this early stage, such as:

- Unambiguous source language documentation that is easier to read and translate

- A standardized, company-wide vocabulary that helps establish a corporate image

- Substantial time efficiencies for the translation, particularly when using computer aided translation tools or machine translation systems

- Cost savings through increased consistency and terminology leveraging among products

Terminology management focuses on defining *concepts* in a source language, and finding equivalents in the target language. A concept is a unit of thought or knowledge made up of a unique set of characteristics. Concepts are mental abstractions that allow us to think about real or conceived objects. By giving names (assigning terms) to concepts, we are able to talk or write about them. Terminological entries in termbases provide a collection of data about a particular concept. These data can include the terms and phrases associated with the concept and other information, such as definitions, target language equivalents, grammatical information on terms, and contextual information.

Although most software localization service providers will not be in a position to dedicate the time and resources required to maintain professional terminology management systems that include a full range of terminological data categories, each localization vendor will have to pay attention to how terminology is used and maintained in localization projects.

Terminology management for software localization focuses mainly on keeping terminology consistent within and between products and teams of translators. Consistency with the operating environment terminology is also important.

Here are some examples of common terminology issues encountered in software localization projects:

- How should terminology setup for a new project or new client be handled?

- How can consistent use of terminology be guaranteed when a large team of translators, editors, reviewers, and proofreaders is working on a project?

- Who is responsible for setting terminology standards, maintaining terminology resources, and ensuring consistent use of terminology?

- How can consistency with the target operating environment be guaranteed?

- What is the best way to set up a publisher-specific multilingual terminology database?

As a rule, several translators and editors will be working simultaneously on different components of a localization project, so it may be difficult to maintain consistent use of terminology. Setting up a project glossary during the project can help avoid many of these problems.

2   Terminology Setup

The first task in a software localization project normally involves setting up a terminology list and finding the appropriate equivalents for the terms, phrases, and even text chunks included in the list. The project glossary, as described in the Project Glossaries section on page 403, is usually based on this initial terminology list.

A terminology list can be created in many ways; here are some examples of how this can be done:

- Check whether the online help or printed documentation delivered with the domestic product contains an explanatory glossary of terms. This glossary can be used to start a terminology list, and it will automatically provide translators with a definition of terms.

- Use the search keywords feature from an online help file or the index entries and table of contents in a printed manual to create the initial project glossary.

- Check whether the publisher's technical documentation department, i.e. the people writing the documentation and online help, are maintaining a glossary of English terms for internal consistency purposes. It is important to bear in mind, however, that the terms selected for a help glossary, an index, or for technical documentation will probably not include all the terms that need to be documented for purposes of translation.

- Run a terminology extraction tool on the online help or documentation source files. Some terminology management tools offer this functionality, although in a very basic way without support for compounds, for example. Professional extraction tools are similar to analysis tools in machine translation systems.

- Include all product names, help file titles, manual titles, and possible chapter titles for the product. Verbs or phrases that are commonly used in the documentation or online help, for example "right-click", may also be included.

- If possible, extract the core software user interface terms, i.e. the options in dialog boxes and the menu items, to be included in the terminology list. Most software localization tools will enable the user to do this.

The translator working on the terminology list should be provided with sufficient reference material to produce accurate translations, such as a copy of the running software product, including online help or printed documentation, and glossaries of the target operating environment of the application, for example Mac OS or Windows.

Tip: One issue which is very important in terminology setup is the identification of the target audience for the translated material. When a reference guide for network administrators is translated, for example, several key terms may remain in English. In the case of a getting started guide for novice computer users, however, the translator may want to translate some of the more basic terminology.

After equivalents have been proposed for the terms in the terminology list, it is very important to have it validated immediately by the publisher before the translation cycle begins. Software publishers will usually assign a sales representative or product manager in the target language country to validate the terminology translations. As a rule, these language reviewers will be actively involved in selling the translated product, so it is important that they are involved in the terminology research process; terminology should be approved by them before the translation starts. Any new terms or changes in terminology should be communicated to them throughout the project.

Establish direct communication between the lead translator and the language reviewer to prevent any potential problems with the final acceptance of the localized product.

3   Terminology Reference Materials

Translators working on a software localization project should have access to the following terminology resources:

1. Project glossary – This glossary is dynamic and is constantly modified and expanded throughout the project. Project glossaries are a combination of the terminology list created during the terminology setup and the software glossary, which was created based on the translation of the main user interface and which normally includes all menu items and dialog box options.

2. Operating environment glossary – These glossaries are usually fairly static and should be accessible in some sort of searchable online format. A quick way to search all Microsoft glossaries with a single query, for example, is to convert all glossaries to Adobe Acrobat PDF files. After indexing these files using Acrobat Catalog, the translators only need to download the free Acrobat Reader with the Search plug-in to search the complete set of glossaries.

3. Multilingual client terminology database – This is a generic termbase that contains key terminology and equivalents used for this particular publisher. It covers all the publisher's products and all versions of these products.

4. Subject matter or industry specific dictionaries – When translating an application that covers financial administration, for example, obtain multilingual dictionaries or glossaries specific to this subject.

5. World wide web – Many web sites are now accessible in multiple languages and search engines support queries in different languages, so the world wide web has become an invaluable source of terminology information, both monolingual and multilingual. Care must be taken, however, when using web resources. Try to evaluate or verify the quality of multilingual web sites in order to ensure that the terminology used is reliable. Many poorly translated web sites only perpetuate bad source and target language equivalents.

In each translation team, one of the senior translators will be responsible for adding new terms to the project glossary, reviewing the work of the other translators, and checking whether it is consistent with the glossary. To make sure the project glossary is complete, ask all translators on the team to maintain lists of key terms they encounter while translating. The lead translator should then assemble all lists and enter new terms in the project glossary.

The main reason for assigning one responsible person to the maintenance and updating of the project glossary is to maximize consistency and accuracy across the glossary. It is also wise for one person to be responsible for validating the terms to be included in the project glossary.

Synchronizing different language lists can be quite complicated. Different spellings, different forms, or the input of remarks in term fields can make the automatic merging process virtually impossible. In canonical form, nouns are entered in singular form, unless they are uniquely used in plural form, and verbs are entered in the infinitive form. Terminological databases that offer input profiles are very useful. These profiles force users to enter data correctly. As soon as data are entered in an incorrect format, the tool will prohibit the user from leaving the data entry screen and saving unauthorized data.

Project glossaries will normally be linked to a networked translation memory tool to provide automatic terminology lookup for the translators. This means that terms in the source text found in the project glossary will be displayed automatically with matching equivalents.

Always develop a plan that identifies those who need access to the terminology databases, and ascertain whether all people involved in the translation project need to have simultaneous access. It is important to think about the glossary setup. Using different tools for different glossaries can be time-consuming for translators as they will have to cross-check terms. Switching from one tool to another, or changing active glossaries in one tool is not practical. Translators working in a translation memory tool would be less inclined to use terminology resources if this process is too cumbersome or time-consuming.

3.1 Project Glossaries

If a previously translated version of a product does not exist, translators create a preliminary glossary with key words and phrases before the translation cycle begins, i.e. during the terminology setup phase. This glossary should be carefully reviewed by a senior translator or by the publisher.

A project glossary would typically contain the following terms:

- Industry-specific terminology
- Equivalents for keywords, both verbs and nouns, appropriate for the product
- Product-related names that should not be translated
- Words or even phrases that are repeated throughout the project, such as "Note", and "Select"
- Feature and concept names
- Names of help files or manuals

This glossary will function as a base terminology source for the project, so it is important that term equivalents be correctly established from the very beginning.

In a software localization project, once all software resource files have been translated and reviewed, a glossary of the software user interface strings should be generated and included in the project glossary. Ideally, a comment field should mark which terms are generic and which ones come from the user interface.

In addition to source terms and target terms, software glossaries may also include:

- Hot keys
- Product name and version
- Category, i.e. button, menu, dialog box title, etc.

Several software localization tools create text-only glossaries from software resource files or binaries. For more information on these tools, refer to the next section, Creating Software Glossaries.

3.2 Operating Environment Glossary

When translating a product for a specific operating system, such as Windows or Mac OS, it is important to maintain consistency with the terminology used in the localized version of the operating system. When the localized application contains many standard menu commands such as File, Open, Print, Edit, and View, for example, the translations chosen for these commands should correspond with the translations used in the operating environment.

Some software developers, such as Microsoft, maintain their own style guides and glossaries. Complete Microsoft operating system and application glossaries can be downloaded from Microsoft's FTP server. All basic Microsoft Windows 3.x terminology can be found in the Microsoft Press publication *Microsoft GUI Guide*. The GUI Guide also contains translations for standard software elements, such as dialog boxes, drop down lists, and check boxes. Please note that the GUI Guide has not been updated since Windows 3.x.

3.2.1 MICROSOFT GLOSSARIES

The operating system and application glossaries from Microsoft can be found on the Microsoft Developer Network CD-ROMs and on the Microsoft FTP server at ftp.microsoft.com/developr/MSDN/NewUp/Glossary.

These glossaries are comma-delimited .csv format files, and can be opened using a spreadsheet application or word processor. The glossaries include the operating systems as well as several Microsoft applications, such as the Office programs.

Most terminology management applications contain import filters for these files, but considering the size of the glossaries, it is advisable to use other search methods.

To search these Microsoft glossary files, use the Find function from a word processor or spreadsheet, or use a utility called MSG Browser. This tool enables the user to find translations, not just for any English term included in the glossary files, but also for entire text segments (phrases, sentences, and even paragraphs), thus demonstrating the use of terms in context. For more information on MSG Browser and a free working demo version, visit the MSG Browser web site at www.icactive.com/msgb.

3.2.2 APPLE GLOSSARIES

Apple Computer provides operating system glossaries in all languages of the Mac OS.

Apple's international glossaries can be found on the Apple Developer Connection CDs and on the Apple FTP server at ftp.apple.com/devworld/Tool_Chest/Localization_Tools/Apple_Intl_Glossaries.

The glossaries are available in three different formats: AppleWorks spreadsheet (SS) tables, tab-delimited text (TXT), and AppleGlot language glossaries (LG). The AppleGlot versions can be used to pre-translate products. For more information on translating applications with AppleGlot, refer to the AppleGlot section on page 133.

3.2.3 NOVELL GLOSSARIES

Novell product glossaries, available in several languages, can be found on the Internet, on the Novell FTP server at ftp.novell.com/pub/updates/other/tresorce. The glossaries are in tab-delimited text format. The folder also contains translation style guides for several languages.

3.2.4 SILICON GRAPHICS GLOSSARIES

Silicon Graphics software glossaries, available in several languages, can be found at www-europe.sgi.com/developers/library/local/glossary.html.

3.2.5 LOTUS GLOSSARIES

Lotus product glossaries, available in several languages, can be found on the Internet on the Lotus FTP server at ftp.lotus.com/pub/lotusweb/product/ngd. The glossaries are in Lotus Notes database format, as they are part of the Domino Global Workbench translation environment, which is used to translate Notes database files.

For more information on Domino Global Workbench, visit the Lotus Globalization web site at www.lotus.com/international.

3.3 Multilingual Client Terminology Database

When working on a product with multiple versions or languages for a publisher, it may be a good idea to start building a terminology database that stores all terms specific to that publisher. A client termbase typically contains:

- Generic terms from the publisher's products
- Terms from the marketing or documentation group
- Feature and concept names

All bilingual project glossaries from the different languages and products must be assembled and merged into one database. An entry in a client termbase treats a single concept and may include the following fields:

- Subject field reference
- Source term
- Context, i.e. a text segment where the term(s) is used
- Definition of the concept
- Synonyms or acronyms
- Target language terms and synonyms associated with the concept
- Source of terms or of textual material, e.g. definitions or contexts
- Product, version, project, etc. identifiers

The following image displays an entry from one of the sample databases shipping with Trados Multiterm, a commonly used terminology management system.

If the terminology database is manageable with respect to size and volume, consider identifying each entry with a client identifier and then combining the termbases of several clients into one general database, along with a client specification. If you have localized several products for publishers that produce software in the field of e-commerce, for example, create an E-Commerce Terminology Database that includes terms used for all these publishers.

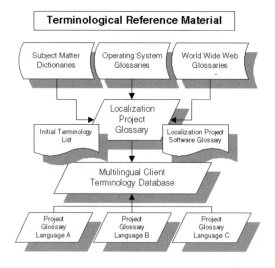

This chart shows possible sources for a dynamic multilingual client termbase environment. First a localization project glossary is created from translations found in static sources such as subject matter dictionaries, operating system glossaries, and glossaries found on the world wide web. The project glossary then incorporates the initial terminology list, which is created during the terminology setup phase, and the software user interface glossary. Once a project glossary for one language has been validated and reviewed, it can be merged with project glossaries for other languages to create a multilingual terminology database.

Merging means that different lists are integrated into one. Most translation projects do share a common source language which automatically leads to bilingual terminology lists that all share one source language. Use this language together with other commonly shared features to help you with the synchronization during the merge process. Experience indicates that it is not sufficient to compare two English entries from say, an English-Spanish and English-French list. Features like capitalized first letters for proper nouns, subject matter code and grammatical information can help to create an English-Spanish-French list.

4 Terminology Standards

Many standards have been developed for terminology. In terminology management, for example, we can distinguish the following types of terminology standards:

- Operating environment standards
- Subject matter or industry standards
- Terminology format standards

In the localization industry, Microsoft glossaries are often considered to be the "standard". Even though this is true for software user interface terms for Windows-based applications, other standards should also be carefully considered. When translating a financial software package, for example, terminology standards in the financial industry should be adhered to. When designing termbases, you can choose from a variety of standard formats for modeling your terminological entries. Once you have modeled your entry, however, care should be taken to maintain consistency within the termbase in order to ensure the integrity of your data over time.

4.1 Industry Standards

Many countries have developed standard terminology for particular industries, such as the automotive, pharmaceutical, and financial sectors. When translating a software application or web site for a specific industry or subject matter, translators should adhere to these standards in order to ensure the quality and user acceptance of the localized product. If there is any question concerning which standards to use, it is wise to consult with the client.

Even though many countries are developing country-specific terminology standards, the International Organization for Standardization (ISO) and the ISO/IEC Joint Technical Committee 1 (JTC) are important producers of international terminology standards.

4.2 Terminology Format Standards

In the early 1990s, ISO developed terminology standards, including *Principles and methods of terminology* (ISO 704), *Presentation and layout of terminology standard*

(ISO 10241), *Vocabulary of terminology* (ISO 1087), and *International harmonisation of concepts and terms* (ISO 860). For more information on these standards, visit the ISO web site at www.iso.ch.

The following sections provide the names of some standards and file formats that have been developed for terminology exchange. Most of them are incorporated into SALT (Standards-based Access service to multilingual Lexicons and Terminologies), a consortium of academic, governmental and commercial groups. The members of SALT are testing, refining, and implementing a universal format for leveraging both human-oriented terminology resources and machine translation lexicons for application in integrated localization environments where a variety of tools and approaches are being used, e.g. computer aided human translation, translation memory, machine translation, and various other localization tools. For more information on SALT, visit the Translation, Theory, and Technology web site·at www.ttt.org and the SALT web site at www.loria.fr/projets/SALT.

4.2.1 MARTIF

The MAchine-Readable Terminology Interchange Format (MARTIF), is an international standard (ISO 12200) for human-oriented terminology interchange. It is an SGML-based method for exchanging and sharing terminological information between concept-oriented termbase systems.

For more information on MARTIF, visit the Translation, Theory, and Technology web site at www.ttt.org.

4.2.2 OLIF

The Open Lexicon Interchange Format (OLIF) is a format developed within the European OTELO project for machine-translation dictionary interchange. In addition to dealing with these so-called *lexbases*, i.e. primarily word-based machine-translation lexicons, OLIF also facilitates access to more traditional *termbase* systems, but without accommodating the complex hierarchical structures allowed by MARTIF.

For more information on OTELO and OLIF, visit the OTELO web site at www.otelo.lu.

4.2.3 TBX

TBX (TermBase Exchange) is a project of LISA's OSCAR group and will provide a standard exchange format featuring a LISA subset of ISO 12620, which provides an exhaustive list of terminological data categories, plus a declared structure designed to facilitate so-called "blind" interchange among LISA partners. TBX is an XML environment and will function as a subset of the SALT family of interchange standards.

For more information on TBX, visit the LISA web site at www.lisa.org.

5 Creating User Interface Glossaries

In most cases, the translation of help and documentation files will begin before the software translation is finalized. To provide the translators working on the help and documentation with sufficient terminology reference, it is advisable to create a software glossary from the menu and dialog box items only. By doing this, translators will have translations for most of the software references in the help files and documentation.

Tip: It is not advisable to include all software strings in a software glossary. By including all error messages, status messages, and other long strings, the glossary may become unmanageable for a terminology management system and slow the translators down.

It may be useful to provide translators with information on the situational context for each glossary item. It may be useful, for example, to know whether a term is a menu item, a dialog box option, or a dialog box title. Some glossary tools will add this information; in other cases, it may be worthwhile to add this information manually, in cases where the contextual reference is unclear.

5.1 Windows

As discussed in Chapter 3, Windows-based applications can be translated in two ways, either in text-only resource files that are compiled into binary files, or the translator can work directly in the binary program files. Glossaries can also be created in two ways. Most software localization tools contain glossary extraction features. For more information on these tools, refer to the Software Localization Tools section on page 383.

With Corel Catalyst for example, software glossaries can be created from one or more program files, such as .exe, .dll, and .ocx files, or software resource files such as .rc and .dlg files.

Follow these steps to create a software glossary using Catalyst:

1. Create a new Catalyst project, and insert the source file(s) using the Insert Files command from the File menu.

2. In the resources window, click on the file name of the imported file.

3. Choose the Import Translations command from the Object menu, and select the translated program or resource file.

4. Choose the Extract Glossary command from the Tools menu.

5. In the Extract Glossary dialog box, type a name and specify a path for the glossary file.

6. The glossary is saved in tab-delimited text format.

For more information on Corel Catalyst, visit the Catalyst web site at www.corel.ie/catalyst.

5.2   Mac OS

Mac OS applications are usually localized by editing directly in the program files. It is possible to create software glossaries from these files using software localization tools. AppleGlot is the most commonly used tool for software glossary creation.

Follow these steps to create a software glossary using AppleGlot:

1. Run AppleGlot.

2. Create a new environment by selecting the New Environment command from the File menu. An environment is a set of specifically named folders used by AppleGlot to process a project.

3. Use the Finder to copy the files to the appropriate folders. Move copies of the previous English version into the _OldUS folder and the _NewUS folder, and a copy of the accompanying localized version into the _OldLoc folder.

4. In the AppleGlot environment window, mark the files to be "translated", and click the Translate Only button.

5. Save the batch file in the environment folder. The batch file contains all the information that AppleGlot produced automatically or that was entered manually in the Environment window.

6. When text extraction is completed, the _AD folder will contain an application dictionary that contains all localized strings.

Follow these steps to convert an AppleGlot language glossary to tab-delimited format:

1. Open the AppleGlot glossary in Microsoft Excel or another spreadsheet application.

2. Delete the first column.

3. Copy the remaining column to a word processor document.

4. Search and replace the > character followed by a paragraph mark with a tab character (search >^p and replace with ^t).

5. Search and replace all < and > characters with an empty string.

6. Save the document as text-only.

There is one disadvantage to this method: If strings include carriage returns, the section after the carriage return is deleted when the first column is deleted. For common resource items, however, such as menu and dialog box items, this should pose no problems.

For more information on AppleGlot, refer to the AppleGlot section on page 389.

6   Further Reading

The books listed below cover different aspects of terminology management.

Cabré, M. Teresa. 1999. *Terminology: theory, methods, and applications*. John Benjamins, ISBN 1-55619-788-8.

Sager, J.C. 1990. *A Practical Course in Terminology Processing*. John Benjamins, ISBN 1-55619-113-8.

Wright, Sue Ellen and Gerhard Budin. 2000. *Handbook of Terminology Management*. John Benjamins, ISBN 1-556-19502-8.

Chapter 13:
Project Evaluations

This chapter contains information on evaluating localization projects.

This chapter includes the following sections:

1. Introduction
2. Activities
3. Word Counts

Regardless of the type or nature of a localization project, a thorough evaluation of the source material will always help prevent surprises, problems, and rework later on in the process. Project evaluations are important not only for awarded projects, but are also required to create project proposals and quotations which include rates and price breakdowns for all project activities and services.

This section provides information on evaluating different components of a localization project, in order to quickly generate statistics such as word counts and estimated production hours for engineering and desktop publishing activities.

1 Introduction

Localization kits or requests for quotation (RFQ) received from software developers often include some guidelines or instructions, but, as a rule, these will not be sufficient to clearly define the total project scope.

A source file analysis performed by the localization vendor is focused on finding answers to the following questions:

- What are the costs, time frame, resource requirements, potential issues, project scope, and necessary quality assurance steps?
- What are the required deliverables?
- Are all required files included?
- Are all files to be translated? Old versions of files or unused files are often included by software developers. These need to be identified.
- Are the word counts provided by the publisher accurate?
- How many translations can be recycled from previously translated versions? Refer to the Translation Memory Tools section on page 362 for more information on re-using translations.

- Is it possible to perform a pseudo-translation? A pseudo-translation allows the localizer to replace all source text with, for instance, accented characters or with characters of a different length, e.g. Chinese or Japanese double-byte characters, to assess the potential for file corruption or execution problems.
- Where applicable, is the publisher's proprietary translation tool stable and useful?
- Can the source material be test-compiled and test-generated properly?
- What is the most efficient way to localize the product?

Compiling the English software and online help will indicate whether all required files are included, and whether the software source material is functional. If errors in the source material are not fixed before the translation cycle, all mistakes will need to be corrected a number of times across languages in the localized versions of the software!

2   Activities

Here is a list of activities normally associated with a localization project:

- Project preparation
- Translation and review
- Engineering and testing
- Graphics localization
- Desktop publishing
- Project management

Activities such as project preparation, engineering, testing, and desktop publishing are typically quoted on an hourly basis, or in some cases on other metrics, such as the number of dialog boxes, number of pages, or number of graphics. As a rule, the evaluation should aim to establish both unit counts (e.g. number of words) and number of production hours. Usually the project manager will need both type of data for quoting and scheduling purposes.

Depending on the purpose of the project evaluations, a project scope overview can be created by combining the right tools with experience.

2.1   Project preparation

In many cases, project preparation can be a time-consuming task. When a non-standard online help or software file format needs to be localized, for example, special filters or parsers need to be developed in order to extract the text for translation in a translation memory tool. It may also be necessary to set up special computer or hardware configurations for the project, for example, as reference for the translators.

Here are some examples of project preparation tasks:

- Configuring computers
- Testing source material
- Preparing source material
- Assembling reference material
- Training translators
- Alignment of previously translated material
- Creating terminology list

During project evaluation, estimate the number of tasks required to prepare the project well, and the length of time required for these tasks.

2.2 Translation and Review

As indicated in the Creating Quotes and Proposals section on page 429, translation and review activities are usually priced on a per-word basis. For more information on generating word counts, refer to the Word Counts section on page 418.

Most localization vendors will have fixed word rates for each combination of source and target language pair. Note that the complexity of the source text and subject matter may require adjustments to these rates.

Generally speaking, certain text types will be charged at a higher rate, for example, legal texts, such as license agreements. If a software application contains a license agreement or copyright text, consult the publisher on whether the text should be simply "localized" or re-written in the target language by a lawyer familiar with the copyright laws of the target country. In the latter case, budget separately for this item. Never translate these texts without any consultation.

2.3 Engineering and Testing

The most difficult task in evaluating any software localization project is estimating the number of hours required for engineering and testing. Only experienced localization engineers will be in a position to accurately estimate the number of hours required to engineer localized versions of software or online help.

One way of calculating the hours is to compare hours spent on projects of similar size from the same publisher. Unless the evaluation indicates that it will be more complicated or time-consuming than other projects, it is safe to use statistics from similar projects.

2.3.1 SOFTWARE

Basic software localization engineering includes the tasks described in Chapter 4, i.e. compiling, resizing, hot key checking, and cosmetic testing.

The number of hours required for these tasks depends largely on the following factors:

- Platform and development environment (standard or non-standard)
- Number and complexity of dialog boxes in software
- Amount of resizing required
- Possible use of automated testing tools
- Level of internationalization in source code
- Complexity of build environment

Some localization vendors base the number of engineering hours on the number of dialog boxes in a software application. This is not the ideal way to do this, since menus and strings require engineering activities, and time required for compilation and cosmetic testing needs to be added as well. It is possible, however, to estimate the time required for resizing based on number of dialog boxes. To count the number of dialog boxes, open the resource file or application file in a resource editor or localization tool and count the number of the resources in the Dialog section. Some software localization tools, such as Corel Catalyst, automatically calculate the number of items for each resource type. By multiplying the total number of dialog boxes by the average time needed to resize per dialog box, it is possible to estimate the length of time needed to resize the dialog boxes.

Each localization vendor will have different standards for estimating the time required for testing localized software. It is important to know the level and type of testing required, whether it is cosmetic testing, linguistic testing, or functional testing. In most cases, linguistic and cosmetic testing will be included in the time estimated for engineering. Functional testing is usually a separate step. This can only be calculated based on the test scripts to be used or executed. Creating a test script may also be part of the project scope. For more information on levels of testing, refer to Chapter5, Software Quality Assurance.

2.3.2 ONLINE HELP

As a rule, engineering and testing online help files are considered to be a single activity. Testing localized online help systems is an integrated part of online help engineering, unless customers request separate functional testing phases. This could include tests using several different platforms or browser versions.

The number of hours required for these tasks depends largely on the following factors:

- Platform and development environment (standard or non-standard)
- Complexity of file contents, for example scripting
- Number and length of online help topics
- Level of testing required

- Possible use of automated testing tools, for example HtmlQA
- Number of image maps and hypertext links

Tip: If online help or HTML files contain heavy scripting, form elements, or Java components, it is advisable to handle these files as software. Even though no compilation is required, it may be necessary to resize and test these components.

Online help engineering and testing is often quoted or scheduled based on the number of topics or screens in the help file. This is not the most accurate way to do this, because online help topics can contain a single sentence or a three page text. The automated help testing tools HtmlQA and HelpQA will display the number of topics in the help file.

2.4 Graphics Localization

Graphics will normally be linked to source files through a separate graphics folder. To determine how many graphics are included in an online help file or document, count the files in this graphics folder. If it is not clear whether all graphics are actually linked, or if graphics are embedded or pasted in the documents, count the graphics manually.

The number of hours required for localizing graphics depends largely on the following factors:

- Types of graphics, i.e. regular screen captures or complex line-art
- Availability of screen capture scripts
- Complexity of backgrounds, fonts, and layout
- Availability of layered graphics with separate text layer
- Availability of blank graphics without text
- Complexity of graphics editor

Please note that some graphics included in a help file or document may not require localization. Bullet or icon symbols, for example, are also included in graphics folders but, as a rule, require no modification. Check the graphics visually before including the total graphic count in a quotation. Some graphics editors such as Paint Shop Pro include an image browser. The Windows 2000 image thumbnail preview feature can also be used.

If the graphics are regular screen captures or if they all require similar editing effort, use a price per graphic. However, if some of the graphics require a great deal of manual editing and retouching and some require very little, it is advisable to quote and schedule on an hourly basis, or to quote separate prices for simple and complex graphics.

Tip: Check whether different versions of the graphics need to be created, for example gray scale for printed documentation and colored graphics for online documentation or help. It is easier to create colored images and to automatically convert them to gray scale than to manually create two different versions of each image.

2.5 Desktop Publishing

Even though desktop publishing is usually charged on a per-page basis, in some cases it may be necessary to estimate the number of hours required for desktop publishing.

The number of hours required for desktop publishing depends largely on the following factors:

- Platform and application used for DTP (standard or non-standard)
- Language support for target language
- Complexity of layout, fonts, and graphics
- Conversions from or to other file formats
- Creation of one document containing multiple languages

Some desktop publishing applications may not support Asian languages. If this is the case, a close substitute should be selected, which will, in most cases, result in additional work. As a rule, Asian languages often require more DTP time than non-Asian languages.

Most word counting features in desktop publishing applications will also show how many pages the document contains. Otherwise, count the pages by going to the last page of the document, and adding the preface, table of contents or title pages, where applicable.

3 Word Counts

Determining or verifying word counts is an important part of evaluating a localization or translation project. Since different tools may generate different word counts from the same source material, it is important for translators and agencies to agree with publishers on the tools used for analyzing and processing the source files.

For quotation, scheduling and resourcing purposes, project managers will typically focus on the following information:

1. Total number of words
2. Internal repetitions
3. Leverage (translation re-use) percentage, including fuzzy matches

The total number of words can usually be generated using the application used to create the source files, such as FrameMaker for documentation files. If additional information is needed, such as number of internal repetitions or matches with previous translations, use a translation memory tool, such as Trados Translator's Workbench, or a software localization tool. To determine the percentage of leverage from previous translations, a translation memory or previously translated version is required. Refer to the Translation Memory Tools section on page 362 for more information on translation memory. If previous versions were translated without the use of translation memory, these texts can be aligned in order to create a translation memory database. Refer to the Alignment section on page 365 for more information.

Tip: Please note that different translation memory tools will generate different results, which are mainly due to the differences in the fuzzy matching engines. As a rule, never rely on the word counts from a single tool. Always validate word counts using at least one other tool or method.

Words included in graphics or illustrations are often overlooked in the word counting process. Not all images in manuals are regular screen captures. They often contain sample text or captions, which need to be localized separately.

The sections below describe the tools best suited to counting words within certain standard file formats.

3.1 Software

On the Windows platform, it is possible to generate word counts from text-only software resource files or from compiled .dll or executable files. For compiled .dlls, a software localization tool such as Corel Catalyst is required. When generating word counts from the text-only software resource files, it will take more time to determine translatables, but the count will be more accurate, particularly if all non-translatable strings are removed from the files. In some cases, it may be necessary to create a script or macro to automatically identify or externalize all translatables from the text files. The scripting language best suited for language processing is Perl.

Several things need to be considered when creating software word counts:

- Remember to include components such as installers, wizards, generated reports, or third-party utilities in the total word count.
- Check whether the software application contains graphics with text, by opening the program file in a resource editor and browsing through the Bitmap resources.
- If user interface text is hard-coded in the executable, it is not possible to generate word counts. In this case, contact the developer and obtain the source code files.

The following sections explain how to count words in text-only resource files on the Windows platform, and program files on Windows and MacOS.

3.1.1 SOFTWARE RESOURCE FILES (WINDOWS)

The easiest way to generate word counts from text-only software resource (.rc) files is to use a software localization tool such as Corel Catalyst. Refer to the Binary Program Files (Windows) section on page 420 for more information. Counts can also be generated, however, using a word processor such as Microsoft Word.

To generate word counts quickly from .rc files using Microsoft Word, follow these steps:

1. Open the .rc file in Microsoft Word.

2. Select all text and choose the Sort command from the Table menu. Sort all text by paragraphs.

3. All comment text, define statements, string sections, captions, controls, and menu items are now included in separate blocks in the document.

4. Browse through the file and delete all lines that do not contain translatable text. Translatable text is enclosed in double quotation marks.

5. After deleting all non-translatable lines, select all text and convert the text to a table, using the double quote character (") as a delimiter.

6. The second column of the table will now contain all translatable text. Copy this column to a new document and count the words using the Word Count command. This will generate an estimate of the number of translatable words.

Tip: To count multiple .rc files, concatenate the files for counting purposes by copying them all to one folder and typing the following DOS command: COPY *.RC ALL.TXT . The ALL.TXT file will contain the strings from all .rc files.

Another way to generate word counts is to import the .rc files into a translation memory tool that supports resource files, such as Trados Translator's Workbench. After importing the .rc files, run the diagnosis or statistics command that generates word counts. These tools will also display information on internal or external matches. For more information on using these tools, refer to the Translation Memory Tools section in Chapter 11, Translation Technology.

3.1.2 BINARY PROGRAM FILES (WINDOWS)

To generate word counts from binary program files, such as .dll or .exe files, use a software localization tool that provides word count features, such as Corel Catalyst.

If a set of setup disks or a CD-ROM containing the running software application has been provided, the .dll or .exe files containing the user interface text need to be identified by a localization engineer. To locate the program files containing the interface text, install the application, choose an option from a dialog box, and search the program folder for files containing the text of that option. Use the Windows Find feature to search a folder for files containing a certain text string. Once the files containing interface text have been located, use a software localization tool to count the words in these files. Always confirm with the publisher which files need to be localized.

To generate word counts from a .dll or .exe file using Corel Catalyst, follow these steps:

1. Start Corel Catalyst and create a new project.

2. Use the Insert Files command from the File menu to import the .dll or .exe file to be processed.

3. Select the file and click on the Statistics tab to see detailed word counts for each resource type.

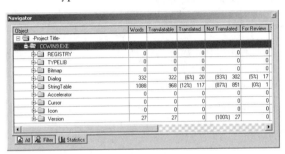

Alternatively, save the files as text-only .rc files using Microsoft Visual Studio and follow the procedures described in the previous section.

3.1.3 BINARY PROGRAM FILES (MAC OS)

The easiest way to generate word counts from Ma cOS application files is using the PowerGlot utility. For more information, refer to the PowerGlot section on page 391.

An alternative method would be to create project glossaries using AppleGlot, and to count the glossary files using a word processor. For more information, refer to the AppleGlot section on page 389.

3.2 Online Help

Since online help is typically the largest component of localization projects, it is very important to generate an accurate word count of all source files. Online help source files are usually translated in a translation memory tool, and most translation memory tools contain advanced statistics features outlining the number of words, number of fuzzy and exact matches with previously translated material, and number of internal repetitions.

For online help files, three tool types are used to generate word counts:

- Translation memory tools, such as Atril Déjà Vu or Trados Translator's Workbench

- Source document editors, such as Microsoft Word for RTF and DOC, or FrontPage for HTML

- Online help testing tools, such as HelpQA for WinHelp and HtmlQA for HTML

When generating word counts using a translation memory tool, remember to generate counts using the applications used to create the source files. If the counts match, the translation memory tool has correctly recognized and filtered out all translatable text. For more information on generating word counts with translation memory tools, refer to the Statistics section on page 363.

3.2.1   HTML

Counting words in HTML files can be particularly tricky, because it is not always easy for a user or a word counting tool to identify the strings that need to be translated. HTML files and other markup languages contain markup and text. In order to create accurate word counts, a tool should be able to distinguish markup tags from translatable text.

Tip: If a compiled HTML Help .chm file has been provided, this should be de-compiled to its source (.html, .hhc, .hhp) using the HTML Help Workshop compiler which can be downloaded from web sites such as www.helpmaster.com.

HTML files may contain custom tags or scripts containing text that is not always easy to identify as translatable. Here are some examples of translatable text often omitted from counts generated by editors or translation memory tools:

- Text in META tags, such as keywords
- Image placeholder text
- Button or forms text
- Text in mouseover statements
- Text included in embedded code and scripting

HTML files are usually made up of small documents and it is not always efficient to count 100 files by opening and counting them individually. There are several online help testing tools available now to analyze sets of HTML files and automatically generate word counts. The following image shows the statistics generated by HtmlQA. For more information on HtmlQA, refer to the Using HtmlQA section on page 269.

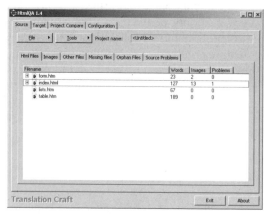

WebBudget is a tool that was specifically designed to count words in HTML, XML, or SGML files. For more information, refer to the WebBudget section on page 396.

It is not uncommon now to have standard HTML pages replaced by Active Server Pages (ASP) or customized HMTL or XML files. This enables the browser or server to run scripts that allow users to enter or retrieve specific information. These files are hybrid files, consisting of HTML and scripting language, and are particularly difficult to count. To analyze these files, spot check the generated counts from one or two of the files manually to check that all translatable words were found. Remember to check the graphics used in the online help file for translatable text.

3.2.2 WINDOWS HELP

Remember to include the following file types for WinHelp projects: .rtf files, .cnt files, .hpj files, and images.

Tip: If a compiled .hlp file has been provided, this should be de-compiled to its source (.rtf, .bmp, .hpj) using one of the freeware Windows Help decompilation tools that can be downloaded from www.helpmaster.com.

When a localization kit has been provided including all help source files, such as .rtf, .hpj, and .cnt files, the easiest way to generate word counts is to use HelpQA. HelpQA generates detailed statistics on the help project, including word counts, number of images, number of files, number of topics, and number of links. Click on the Reports button to create a text document with all of the statistics.

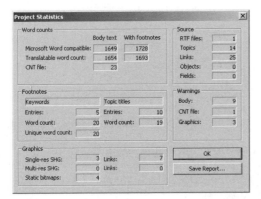

To generate word counts on a Windows help project without using HelpQA, create word counts in Microsoft Word or another word processor. Rich Text Format (RTF) files can be opened using most word processors. Please note that different word processors or even different versions of a word processor may generate slightly different word counts.

Consider the following points when doing word counts on RTF files in Windows Help or Mac OS QuickHelp:

- A proper word count from the RTF files would not include some of the footnote types, such as the # and [A] footnotes. These footnote types are never translated.

- If the RTF files contain many bitmap references, such as {bmc bullet.bmp}, these references should be deleted before generating a word count.

- [K] keyword footnotes separated by semi-colons without spaces are usually counted as a single word. If a [K] footnote contains the words "file;print", for example, this will be considered as a single word.

This last problem can be avoided by clicking in the body text and using the find/ replace command to replace all # and [A] characters with spaces. Next, click in the footnotes area and replace all semi-colons with semi-colon-space. Now run the word count command to generate word counts on the RTF file. Do not save the files after making these modifications!

Help Project (.hpj) files usually contain very few translatable words, so these can be counted manually. For more information on how to identify translatable text in .hpj files, refer to the .HPJ Files section on page 190.

To count the words in a help contents (.cnt) file, follow these steps:

1. Open the .cnt file using a word processor.

2. Select all text and convert the text to a table using the equal symbol (=) as a separator.

3. Copy the first column to a new document and count the words.

CNT files typically contain help file topic titles, which are considered as full internal matches by a translation memory tool.

Remember to check whether the graphics in the online help file contain translatable text.

3.3 Documentation

Most word processors or document editors have a word counting function. If no such feature exists, export the text to a word processor or translation memory tool and generate a word count. Chapter 8, Documentation Translation, contains information on how to create word counts using different word processors and desktop publishing applications.

To generate a quick word count from PDF files, copy all text from the PDF file to a word processor and use the word count feature in the word processor. To do this, open the PDF file using Adobe Acrobat (this will not work with Acrobat Reader), choose Edit > Copy File to Clipboard, open Microsoft Word, select Edit > Paste and run the word count function. When using Acrobat Reader, open the PDF file, select the Continuous command from the View menu, choose the Select All command from the Edit menu, and paste the text into Word for counting.

An alternative way of generating word counts from PDF files is to use the PDFCount plug-in which can be downloaded from www.pdfcount.com. This tool can be run using Acrobat Reader.

Tip: It is important to note that generating word counts from PDF files will not necessarily produce accurate counts. If each page contains a heading, for example, this text will be counted on every occurrence.

For more information on Adobe Acrobat, refer to the Portable Document Format (PDF) section on page 342.

3.4 Web Sites

Evaluating web sites for localization purposes can be a complex task. In the case of highly dynamic, database-driven web sites it is often difficult to generate an overview of the total number of words to be translated.

Roughly speaking, web sites may contain the following components with translatable material:

- Static HTML pages
- Dynamic server pages, such as ASP or JSP files
- Web-based applications
- Graphics

To generate word counts for static HTML pages, follow the instructions in the HTML section on page 422. Please note that HTML pages may contain scripting information, for example JavaScript, with translatable strings that are not recognized by the majority of standard word counting tools or translation memory systems. These sections should be counted separately.

Dynamic server pages usually combine static content with content retrieved from a database. Counting the words in the ASP or JSP files will only handle the static content, which means that all information retrieved from the database is disregarded. To obtain an accurate word count, export the database tables that publish information to the web pages. Contact the site developer to obtain a database export file, then run the (tab- or comma-delimited) text file through a word counting tool or translation memory system. In many cases, a custom filter will need to be created to include only the relevant database content in the word count.

For web-based applications, follow the instructions provided in the Software section on page 419. For graphics, follow the instructions provided in the Graphics Localization section on page 417.

It is important to note that very few web sites are *translated* in their entirety. Most web sites combine translated and local content, i.e. in many cases information on a web site is too market- or country-specific to be translated. Identify which sections of a web site need to be translated before generating word counts or quotations for localization.

Here are some other important issues to consider when evaluating web sites for localization:

- Frequency of updates – Web sites changing on a daily basis require a special tool or technology that will manage the workflow of multilingual content.
- Internationalization – New web technology often does not support double-byte character sets.
- Content providers – Many web sites contain content provided by third-parties; check who will be responsible for localizing this information.

Some localization service providers offer consulting services where consultants work with web publishers to determine the scope of a web globalization initiative. These consulting engagements may include a full analysis of the current site infrastructure, categorization of sections to be translated or re-created for local markets, and possible implementation of multilingual content management technology solutions.

Chapter 14:
Project Management

This chapter contains information for localization project managers. Topics include tasks and responsibilities of project managers, and organizations and tools for project management.

This chapter includes the following sections:

1. Introduction
2. Tasks and Responsibilities
3. Organizations and Training
4. Tools and Applications
5. Further Reading

Related chapters are Chapter 1, which provides an overview of localization and typical localization project processes, and Chapter 13, which contains information on evaluating localization projects.

1 Introduction

Project managers are key resources in any localization project. They serve as the central point of communication for people involved in a localization project. A project manager is generally responsible for scheduling and monitoring all project components and activities. Most large localization companies have dedicated project managers assigned to localization projects. Depending on the number and size of the projects, project managers can be dedicated to a single client, or to one or more projects. As an industry standard, project management is invoiced as a percentage of the total project cost. This is currently around 10%.

Project managers usually have a wide range of tasks and responsibilities, including creating quotes and proposals for new projects, coordinating project setup, planning projects, monitoring project finances, managing resources and quality assurance steps, and change management.

Most localization vendors expect project managers to have the following skills as a minimum:

- General project management skills
- Experience dealing with localization or multilingual translation projects
- Excellent communication, reporting, and negotiation skills

- Strong organizational skills for production tasks
- Experience with planning, budgeting, resource management, project tracking, risk management, and quality assurance
- Understanding of localization processes and benefits and limitations of translation technology
- Flexibility and adaptability
- Foreign language skills (preferred)
- Technical skills (preferred)

Many smaller localization agencies do not have dedicated project managers. As an alternative, senior translators often double as project managers or localization engineers.

Localization project managers need a wide range of software applications to enable them to complete their tasks effectively. In addition to all standard Office, spreadsheet, and Internet applications, the "toolkit" for a project manager will most likely include the following:

- A project management application, such as Microsoft Project
- Standard templates for status reports, change approval forms, tracking sheets
- A human resources database application

In addition to these software tools, reference works such as *A Guide to the Project Management Body of Knowledge* by the PMI Standards Committee are invaluable. Although many consider localization project management to be a very different discipline, many standard project management practices can be applied in the localization industry.

2   Tasks and Responsibilities

As mentioned in the introduction to this chapter, localization project managers are responsible for many activities. In the following sections the key tasks and responsibilities listed below will be discussed:

- Creating Quotes and Proposals
- Project Setup
- Resourcing
- Scheduling
- Finances
- Quality Management
- Communication

These tasks all focus on the three important goals in managing a localization project: time, quality, and budget. Successful projects are completed on schedule, within budget, and according to previously agreed quality standards.

2.1 Creating Quotes and Proposals

As explained in the Localization Process section on page 17 in the Introduction to this book, most localization projects start with a pre-sales evaluation phase where publishers send out a request for quotation (RFQ) or a request for proposal (RFP) to multiple localization vendors to obtain the most competitive bid.

The procedure for most localization vendors is for account managers or business development managers to create quotations or proposals for new clients. For new projects from existing clients, project managers often create quotes.

2.1.1 INTRODUCTION

Professional RFQs and RFPs generally include an introduction to the project, an overview of the project components, (estimated) project scope and volumes, expected services and deliverables, and deadlines. There are currently no industry standards for RFQs or RFPs. Publishers generally send completed source-language product to localization vendors in order to ascertain how quickly and at what cost a localized version can be delivered. Publishers with well-established processes will generally send out full localization kits, with a questionnaire for the vendors to complete and return. This enables the publisher to obtain a clear picture of how complete the localization kit is and whether the vendor requires any additional files or further tools to complete the project.

It is important to establish what a publisher expects from a quotation or proposal. Is the publisher looking for a general cost estimate and some general company information, or is the publisher expecting a very detailed breakdown of all project costs and procedures? Work with the publisher to establish the time frame allowed for completing the quotation or proposal.

If the publisher has not provided sufficient project-specific information, ask more detailed questions about the project. Here is a list of the type of questions to ask to ensure that a comprehensive proposal is submitted to the publisher:

- Into which languages should the product be translated? When the product is translated into several languages, the preparation work can be performed for all languages simultaneously. This will also help to control project costs.

- Which components should be translated, i.e. software, help and/or documentation, sample files, web pages, etc.?

- Which other tasks need to be performed, for example page layout, printing, software functionality testing, and online help testing?

- Will there be any updates or milestones during the translation cycle? If yes, how many updates will there be, and how extensive will they be? Updates are often estimated in percentages, for example "10% new, 20% changed, 70% unchanged". This is often based on statistics from translation memory tools.

- Is there a requirement to create glossaries? What format should be used? Are any existing glossaries available?

- Is there a requirement to use a specific translation memory tool or other computer aided translation tool? Are any existing translation memories available?

- What final deliverables/output is expected? How should the files be delivered?

- Is any special software or hardware required for localizing the product? Examples are a client/server setup or a specific version of an operating system.

- Does the product require any specialized knowledge or experience of the subject matter?

- What reference materials will be provided by the publisher, e.g. marketing materials, previously localized versions of the product, or the domestic version of the running software?

- What is the time frame for delivering the localized product?

Providing general cost estimates without conducting a thorough project evaluation introduces a number of financial risks for both the vendor and the publisher. For the purposes of this book, it is assumed that the publisher provides a localization kit containing all source material, the request for a detailed cost breakdown, a preliminary project plan, and information on the services that can be provided by the vendor.

2.1.2 PROJECT EVALUATION

The project evaluation task at the quotation stage of a project is often underestimated or neglected by localization vendors. This is often because of a lack of sufficient resources dedicated to project evaluation. This task is all too often performed by people working in production who tend to give priority to real, live projects in production rather than evaluation projects which may never be awarded. Localization vendors should consider assigning dedicated resources to this task.

Providing a comprehensive evaluation to a publisher, where all costs and issues have been identified upfront, will be beneficial to both publisher and vendor, with few surprises as the project progresses. Furthermore, it helps build the publisher-vendor relationship and gives the publisher a certain level of confidence that the project is in good hands.

From a vendor perspective, it is important to identify all costs upfront to ensure that respectable margins are made on the project. A poorly evaluated project can have a negative financial impact on a vendor, particularly when dealing with a multi-million dollar project.

When creating a quotation for a potential localization project, ensure that all translatable project components have been identified, and all activities necessary to localize the product are covered. This can only be achieved by treating the evaluation as a "real" project that has already been awarded. The only difference is that real project evaluations focus both on project scope (word counts, time estimates) and source material integrity (compilation, completeness). For pre-sales evaluations, focus on the project scope, i.e. word counts for all components, time estimates or implications for engineering tasks, testing and desktop publishing. The quality of the source material is less of an issue at this point, because the localization kit will probably include an updated version of the source materials.

Refer to Chapter 13, Project Evaluations, for detailed information on evaluating localization projects.

Translation Volumes

Project evaluators should provide project managers with the word count volumes for all components. If possible, this should include the following:

- Total word count
- External matches – if a translation memory exist, how many words can be leveraged or re-used?
- Internal matches – how many words are repeated within the same document and only need to be translated once?

Most of this information will be provided by the analysis utilities in a translation memory tool. Always check the word counts in at least one other tool, for example the application used to create the source files. If possible, use the word counting tool used by the publisher. For more information on word counting, refer to the Word Counts section on page 418.

Word counts should be listed according to each project component, because different word rates apply to individual components such as software, online help/documentation, graphics, multimedia, or marketing material. Software, for example, is more difficult to localize than documentation, and is normally priced at a higher rate.

Engineering Scope

Estimating engineering and testing times for online help, web pages, or software is probably the most difficult task in evaluating a localization project. Many factors can influence the time required to build localized software applications or online help projects, such as file format, level of internationalization, level of testing required, etc. Many localization vendors have an average turn-around time for standard online help files, which is normally linked to the number of words in a file. As a project manager, it is advisable to always ask for a second opinion on the estimated time required for engineering a product. A very experienced software engineer should be able to scope a project fairly accurately, taking into account some of the factors listed above.

For more information, refer to the Activities section on page 414.

Desktop Publishing Scope

Desktop publishing is usually charged per page for standard documentation formats, such as Word or FrameMaker files. Desktop publishing is becoming more and more complex and involves many other tasks, such as image editing, creating PostScript files, or converting printed documentation files to online documentation or online help format. It is important to ensure that all of these additional tasks are factored into the costs quoted per page.

For more information, refer to the Activities section on page 414.

2.1.3 PRICING

Most software publishers will reserve a budget for localized versions of their products. These budgets may be assigned to the marketing budget or the product development budget. Localization vendors should be aware that most people on the publishing side responsible for localization budgets often have a hard time convincing upper management in their organizations that localizing a product is expensive and is more than just a translation project. It is not unusual for publishers to ask several vendors for quotes, then compare these several quotations or proposals and finally select the lowest bid. Publishers are becoming increasingly price conscious and are being forced to keep a cap on their budgets by asking for fixed prices on projects or fixed prices on project components. They are moving away from hourly rates often quoted on engineering tasks, because of the risk of cost overruns.

After all project components and tasks have been identified and evaluated, each component or task needs to be linked to a price. Most localization vendors maintain standard rates for certain tasks, for example a fixed word price for software translations into German, a fixed rate for online help translation into Italian, and online help testing rates that are based on the number of topics or hours.

Although standard prices are used, they may not necessarily apply to the project being quoted. The complexity of the translation or engineering work, for example, may be much higher than average. In such cases, consider adjusting the standard unit prices.

Here are some general guidelines for creating a competitive quotation:

- Instead of general time estimates, software publishers increasingly demand unit prices, which give them a more objective way to budget all work for the different languages.

- Use as many fixed unit prices as possible. Quoting too many tasks with a general hourly rate will make the quotation less competitive. In cases where "units" such as graphics or dialog boxes are very complex, quoting on an hourly basis could be an option.

- Indicate clearly which activities are included in each unit price. For example, does the word rate for translation work also include editing, and proofreading? In most cases, these tasks will be included in the word rate, plus one client review pass.

- Once a localization vendor has established a good working relationship with the publisher and successfully completed some projects, the vendor should consider issuing quotations that are based on post-calculation. This implies that all hours spent on certain tasks are calculated after the project and then invoiced to the publisher.

Many publishers will provide vendors with a standard template listing project scope and volumes, where only the rates and total project pricing need to be filled out. Some publishers also provide a task list with guidelines on what is expected in the word rate. This makes it easier for the vendor to provide an accurate quote. Working this way also makes it easier for the publisher to compare quotations received from different vendors. If all of the tasks are not listed in the template, highlight this when returning the quotation to the publisher.

2.1.4 PROPOSAL OR QUOTATION CONTENTS

A professional quotation or proposal should provide publishers with the following information:

- Cost breakdown, including number of units for all tasks, unit rates, prices per task and per language, and grand totals
- List of deliverables
- Assumptions or potential issues
- Billing schedule
- Preliminary schedule
- Preliminary project plan with work breakdown
- Change management procedure
- Company info

Quotations should be as specific as possible and should clearly define all tasks and activities. On the other hand, the quotation should leave room for modifications and changes in the course of the project. Of course, all quotations are subject to revision if there are additional files, updates, or services that should be invoiced.

Costs Breakdown

The following table shows typical contents of a quotation, where activities and project components are linked to fixed unit rates:

Activity	Component	Charged By
Research	terminology	hour or term[1]
Translation	software	word[2]
	html/xml	word[3]
	help/documentation	word
	sample documents	hour or word
Engineering	software	dialog box or hour[4]
Testing	software (linguistic)	hour
	software (functional)	hour
	html/help	topic or hour[5]
Desktop Publishing	documentation	page or hour
	collateral material	page or hour
Graphics	software	screen or hour[6]
	html/help/documentation	screen or hour
Printing & Conversions	html/help	hour
	documentation	page or hour
Project Setup & Preparation	all	hour
Project Management	all	% of total or hour[7]

Here are some important notes on the items listed in the table above:

1. Research to determine the equivalents of product-specific terms should be charged per hour or per term, depending on the complexity of the terminology list and the amount of time required.

2. The word rate for software translation is usually costed about 20-30% higher than the word rate for online help and documentation. Some localization vendors may increase the costs twofold, but this unit price will often include resizing and linguistic testing of the software. For more information on software translation, refer to Chapter 3, Software Translation.

3. If HTML files contain a great deal of scripting, such as JavaScript or CGI, a software rate could be applied. Scripts and forms require additional effort. They

may need to be resized or tested, which is very comparable to tasks associated with localizing software files.

4. Engineering typically includes resizing dialog boxes, checking hot keys and compiling the software. Quoting engineering activities based on the number of dialog boxes is not an accurate way to cost the tasks. These activities should be quoted per hour or per dialog box, depending on the complexity of the dialog boxes, how they need to be resized, and any related activities. Resizing that can be done directly in the resource editor is easier than manually changing coordinates of boxes in text-only resource files (reverse engineering). For more information on resizing dialog boxes, refer to the Dialog Box Resizing section on page 120.

5. Help topics, or *help screens*, are quoted per hour or per topic, depending on the size of the topic or screen. A help topic can be ten A4 sized pages long or it can be three lines. If the average size of a help topic is an A4 sized page, it is safe to quote on a topic basis. If topics vary a lot in size, quote on an hourly basis. For more information on help testing, refer to Chapter 7, Online Help Engineering and Testing.

6. Where images are very complex and require a significant amount of manual editing, it may be risky to quote a fixed price per screen. Graphics can be composed of screen captures that are captured in seconds, or complex graphics with bitmapped backgrounds that require hours of editing. In the latter case, getting layered source images (with the translatable text on a separate layer) can be a huge time and cost saver. For more information on graphics editing, refer to the Editing Graphics section on page 353.

7. As an industry standard, project management is costed at 10 to 15% of the total project costs. Sometimes, an additional 2 to 5% is charged for communication costs. Some publishers request that these be included in the unit rates and prefer not to see the additional cost as a separate line item.

Please note that in some countries it is common to charge translations per line – about 55 characters – or per number of translated words, i.e. target text. In localization, however, it is common to count the words of the source text.

List of Deliverables

Include a list of deliverables in the proposal to ensure that vendor and publisher have the same expectations. In many cases, such a list will be part of the RFQ or RFP, which can then be copied or referenced in the proposal.

Here is a list of items that could be included in a list of deliverables:

- Fully localized, engineered and tested online help (compiled and source files)
- Fully localized, engineered and tested software (compiled and source files). Note that the level of testing as outlined in the preliminary project plan normally covers cosmetic testing.

- Fully localized and formatted documentation files, both in PostScript and PDF format, and source files
- Translation memories and up-to-date product glossaries in all languages

Include a note stating that if any additional deliverables or services are required, the quotation would need to be adjusted accordingly.

Assumptions

It is advisable to add assumptions and risks to the project proposal. Examples of assumptions that can be included are:

- Project volume or scope changes result in modifications in schedule and quotation.
- Project schedules depend on timely hand-off of source material by the publisher.
- If linguistic reviewers assigned by the publisher request many stylistic, preferential changes to translations, additional time needed for entering these will be invoiced.
- Project work will not start until a purchase order is received.
- Project milestones or delivery will not be delayed by late receipt of comments from the validator.

Note that assumptions should not give the publisher an impression of inflexibility. Assumptions should create clarity, but not pose restrictions.

Billing Schedule

A billing or payment schedule must be included in a project proposal, particularly for large projects. A billing schedule outlines how much will be invoiced and paid at which stages in the project.

An example of a billing schedule is 50% upfront at project award and 50% upon completion, or 30% upfront, 30% at an agreed milestone during the project, and 40% upon completion.

Preliminary Schedule

In most cases, RFQs or RFPs will contain a schedule from the publisher stating the project start date and end date for each component. Create your own preliminary schedule based on this schedule and link schedule items to the number of resources required for each stage or phase of the project.

A preliminary schedule should give a general overview of staggered deliveries, for example, localized software will be delivered first, with online help and documentation being delivered at later intervals.

Always include a note stating that the schedule is provisional and may change, depending on quality of the source material and the timely hand off of the source materials from the publisher.

Preliminary Project Plan

Project plans should include an overview of how the project will be managed by the localization vendor. For each component, there should be a process overview and details of tools to be used.

Most project plans will also contain a resource plan, i.e. the resources assigned to each task, a training plan for all people involved in the project, short biographies for the key people in the team, and a list of potential issues that may come up during the project. A good project manager will assess and manage all potential risks.

The list of potential issues may also include comments on the localization kit that is delivered with the RFQ or RFP. Avoid criticizing the localization kits, include valuable suggestions on how the localization kit could be improved and how this will positively impact the schedule and costs.

Company Info

The quotation or proposal provides you as a vendor with an ideal opportunity to highlight the strengths of your organization, its technical infrastructure, the resources available, and other relevant company information that will underscore the competitive advantage you can offer to the publisher.

When selecting localization vendors, software developers are not only interested in costs. They will also be looking at issues such as

- Company profile, services offered
- Quality of services
- Discount policies for large volumes
- Available resources
- Existing customers and references
- Engineering skills, project management skills
- Translation tools used
- Marketing materials expertise
- Formal quality assurance mechanism

Other things that publishers may be interested in are how the localization vendor manages cost overruns, and any similar projects which have been completed successfully, i.e. on time and on budget.

2.2 Project Setup

A project manager for a new localization project should lead the effort in the project setup. During the project setup phase, project managers should focus on getting started as quickly as possible without ignoring potential problems associated with the project, considering all of the standard risk factors. A well-prepared project will have a higher chance of success.

Here is a list of important steps to take in setting up a project:

- Organize a project evaluation for all project components
- Create a project folder for all material
- Create a project schedule and resource plan
- Organize preparation for all project components
- Create a project budget and a quality plan
- Create a communication plan

Each of these activities is explained in further detail in the following sections under Resourcing, Scheduling, Finances, Quality assurance, and Communication.

2.2.1 PROJECT EVALUATION

In most cases, a project evaluation will have been carried out during the project quotation phase. Evaluations on awarded projects, however, often need to provide project managers with much more information than estimated volumes and schedules. A project evaluation should also check the integrity of the source material. Any errors that can be fixed before a localization project starts will save time later on in the project.

If no statement of work listing components, tasks, volumes, deliverables, and other expectations has been provided by the publisher, start the project by finding out what exactly is expected by the publisher. Scope the project in detail, and create a task list, which should serve as a template for the project schedule.

To avoid surprises during the localization project, ask the publisher questions before it starts. Here are some examples of questions to ask:

- All questions listed under Creating Quotes and Proposals section on page 429.
- Who will be the contact person? Will there be different contacts assigned to engineering or desktop publishing?
- What is the preferred communication method?
- Will there be a language, software or desktop publishing review by the publisher? It is advisable to request a preliminary client review of translated material very early in the project.
- How often should status reports be provided?
- Is there a project schedule available? Deadlines are often closely linked with the the shipping date for the English product, or trade shows where localized versions need to be presented.

- Will there be different language tiers? Large software developers release different language versions of their applications in tiers. This is often based on the importance of the target markets. As a rule, the main European languages are Tier 1, i.e French, Italian, German, and Spanish (FIGS). Nordic languages are considered as Tier 2, i.e. Danish, Finnish, Swedish, and Norwegian. Dutch may also be included in the Tier 2 languages. This varies from one publisher to another.

Never start a project without clearly identifying the project scope and any potential problems or issues. In practice, however, projects will can only be scoped as the project progresses and as different source components or updates become available.

For more information on project evaluations, refer to Chapter 13, Project Evaluations. This section also details the information evaluators should provide to project managers to enable them to create a schedule, resource plan, project plan, and quality plan.

2.2.2 PROJECT FOLDER

Project managers are responsible for ensuring that all files are stored in a central location, and that all team members work with the most recent versions of the project materials. To structure work and avoid loss of information, create a work directory or folder on the network in which all material is stored. This should include the source and translated files.

A network folder structure would normally organize projects by client name and project number and name. A project folder should contain the following files:

- All deliverables to and from the publisher
- All hand-offs to and from project team members and translators
- The latest versions of all source and target language files
- Reference material and proprietary tools
- Templates and style sheets
- Translation memory databases and glossaries
- Administrative information, including schedules, quotations, and project plans

The main advantage to storing all project files in a central work folder, with a standard folder structure is that it is easier to locate and backup all essential project files for everybody involved in the project. It also makes it possible to track deliveries at a later point, for example to identify the source of errors found in the final delivery.

Here is a typical folder structure for localization projects:

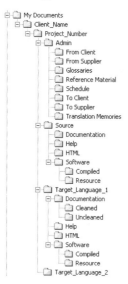

The \Admin folder contains all files sent and received, and general project information such as schedules and status reports, reference material, glossaries, and translation memories. The \Source and \Target folders contain all project components. The \Cleaned and \Uncleaned folders in the \Documentation folder contain translated files before and after processing with a translation memory tool.

Apart from storing files in a standard folder structure, it is also important to deliver translated files in an organized, structured manner. The deliverables should mirror the source material exactly, in both structure and content. Delete any old versions of translated files or internally used instruction files. If files are delivered electronically in a compressed file, number the delivery. The translated help files for the DataLink project, for example, should not be called dlink_hlp.zip but dlink_hlp1.zip. If files are updated after delivery or corrections need to be implemented, number deliveries sequentially: dlink_hlp2.zip, dlink_hlp3.zip, etc. For multilingual projects, include a language code in the delivery file, for example dlink_hlp_deu1.zip.

2.2.3 PROJECT SCHEDULE AND RESOURCE PLAN

Project managers should be able to create a schedule and resource plan based on the project evaluation report.

The schedule should contain the start and end date for each component and each activity, for example for preparing terminological resources, online help engineering, or creation of screen captures. Project managers should only create a schedule based on discussions with all production line managers involved in the project. If the project includes an online help engineering activity, for example, consult the engineering manager, to ensure sufficient engineering will be available during the time scheduled for that task. For more information on creating project schedules, refer to the Scheduling section on page 443.

The resource plan is closely linked to the schedule, and should list all of the resources required to complete the project within the specified schedule. For example, how many translators will be needed to translate the word volumes within the time scheduled? Will sufficient desktop publishers be available to format files once the translation is completed in all target languages? For more information on resource management, refer to the Resourcing section on page 448.

The schedule should only be submitted to the publisher once the resources and contingency plans have been confirmed.

2.2.4 PROJECT PREPARATION

Once a schedule and resource plan have been created, the project setup phase can begin. Project preparation involves assigning the components of a localization kit to the individuals involved in the project and providing tailored instructions for each participant. Based on the schedule and resource plan, for example, translators should receive a kit which will provide them with all source material needed to get started immediately. It should also provide them with sufficient reference material to produce a quality translation.

Translators are typically provided with the following information:

- A schedule detailing translation delivery dates
- Instructions on deliverables and services required, such as translation, editing, entering reviewer corrections, spell-checking, and glossary updating
- The source files to be translated, i.e. software, help and/or documentation. These files should be provided in native format for reference, and in a computer aided translation tool format, i.e. as translation memory files.
- A running version of the application to be translated, including online help files, and previously translated versions of the application, if available
- Instructions and details on the contents of the kit, information on the translatable components, tools to be used, and procedures to be followed
- Non-standard tools required to complete the translation
- Reference material, such as a product overview, a project glossary, glossaries from previous versions of the product, other applications from the same publisher, previously translated versions of the product, publisher style guides, relevant web sites, or operating system glossaries, and lists of questions and answers
- Procedures, i.e. the order in which components should be translated, file management, and the review process

It is important to provide translators with sufficient reference material for the following reasons:

- A clear understanding of the functionality of each software option ensures a more accurate and higher quality translation.

- The first deliverable of software translations should be as final as possible. Changing software translations later in the localization process will require you to update the online help files and documentation. If they have been (partly) translated already, and contain references to the first software translations, reworking and further editing will be required to reflect any of the changes to the software. This will inevitably impact the project budget and schedule.

In addition to preparing material for translators, it may also be necessary to prepare kits for other outsourced tasks, such as engineering, desktop publishing, or testing. Always analyze the entire localization kit and customize each package for each resource and related task. If desktop publishing is outsourced to a third party, provide them with the documentation components of the localization kit, as well as the evaluation results and schedule.

2.2.5 PROJECT BUDGET AND QUALITY PLAN

Once a project schedule and resource plan are in place, develop the project budget and quality plan. In most cases, the budget will have been considered during scheduling and resourcing, but a complete project budget can only be created once a schedule has been finalized and resources assigned. For more information on budgets, refer to the Finances section on page 451.

The quality plan is closely linked to the project budget. If project managers elect to skip several quality steps in an effort to speed up the process, this may well reduce the costs, but will have a considerable impact on the final quality. A quality plan should define all quality steps to be implemented during the project, such as review steps, client review steps, and proofreading. For more information on quality plans, refer to the Quality Management section on page 453.

2.2.6 COMMUNICATION PLAN

A communication plan is a critical part of a localization project and should be prepared during the project setup phase. It is the only way to ensure project managers monitor projects effectively and highlight potential problems.

A communication plan should outline the responsibilities assigned to each team member; it should identify resources responsible for resolving questions and sending files, and it should also identify the escalation path for any problems. Project managers should create communication plans both for internal use, targeted to internal and external production staff working on the project, and for external use, targeted to the publisher, identifying the contacts at the vendor site. For more information on communication plans, refer to the Communication section on page 458.

2.3 Scheduling

Time to market is critical in software localization projects. In many cases, software publishers are aiming for simultaneous shipment (simship) of all language versions of an application on a single CD.

To ensure simultaneous or timely shipping of localized software products or web sites, translation work usually starts before the domestic product is finished or shipped. Consequently, change management and scheduling dependencies caused by updates are among the most important responsibilities for localization project managers.

2.3.1 PROJECT PLANNING

The first task required of project managers, when creating a schedule for a localization project is to define all tasks and activities. Most of this information should be generated from a thorough project evaluation. Detailed scheduling can only be performed once the material has been received and analyzed. Analyze new material using existing translation memories from previous versions of the product in order to accurately budget the amount of time required to translate help or documentation files.

A project manager creates a time schedule at the very beginning of the project, outlining the start and end dates for all activities in the localization project. These activities would include:

- Terminology setup and multilingual glossary preparation, including client review
- Project setup and preparation, including evaluation of source material and extraction of translatable text
- Translation of software, online help and documentation, including all review steps and proofreading
- Engineering and testing of software and help, including screen capture creation
- DTP of documentation, including screen captures and output to PostScript or online documentation format
- Quality assurance and final production

Make sure to allow time for activities such as conversion to and from the translation memory tool, compilation of localization kits, preparation of files for delivery, etc. These tasks are easily forgotten, which may lead to schedule problems, particularly with multilingual projects.

When all tasks have been defined, project managers should evaluate the following aspects of the project, which are critical to creating an accurate project schedule:

- Dependencies, i.e. which activities need to be completed before another activity can start?
- Sequence of activities
- Workload and duration of each activity

- Resource assignments

Each task will cover a certain period and a certain resource will be assigned to each activity.

Dependencies

Localization projects usually contain many dependencies. The most important dependency is the receipt of the source material on time. If no source files have been received from the publisher on the agreed date, there is very little that can be done to expedite the project.

Examples of dependencies between project activities are:

- Translation of online help or documentation files containing references to a software application cannot be completed unless the software has been translated and tested.
- Translated material cannot be proofread until the translations have been edited.
- Client reviews cannot proceed until material has been translated and edited.
- Engineering of software and online help cannot proceed until translation has been completed.
- Software screen captures cannot be created until the software has been localized, engineered and tested.
- DTP on documentation and testing of online help files cannot be completed until all screen captures and other graphics have been localized.
- Localized online help cannot be converted to other formats until the help has been completely localized, engineered and tested.

When defining project activities, mark these dependencies clearly.

Sequence

Once all activities and dependencies have been listed, put the activities in a logical sequence, carefully considering all dependencies. An example of a typical localization project sequence can be found in the Localization Process section on page 17 of the Introduction.

Here is a typical localization project sequence:

1. Identification of terminology and of target language term equivalents
2. Software translation
3. Translation of online help and documentation
4. Engineering and testing of software
5. Screen captures
6. Engineering and testing of online help

7. Desktop publishing

8. Quality assurance and delivery

Sometimes it may be necessary to start translating help and documentation *before* the software is translated. In this case, instruct the translators to translate all software references and to create a glossary of these translated references. This glossary can then be used to translate the software resource files automatically.

If the project contains sample files or templates, it is advisable to start translating these in conjunction with the software files. These types of files typically contain sample data that can be translated by a translator other than the translator working on the software. Screen captures can be started early in the project because screen captures in help and documentation often contain graphics with data from these sample files.

Note that many activities can also be performed simultaneously. Project preparation can be done while terminology lists are being prepared, for example, online help engineering can be done while documentation is being translated, and screen captures can be created while the functionality of the software is tested.

Workload and Duration

Define the workload and duration of each project activity. If project evaluations have concluded that the online help file contains 10000 words for translation, for example, estimate the length of time it would take to translate these words, edit these translations, and proofread the final output.

There are no standard metrics for productivity in translation and localization, because too many factors can influence productivity levels, such as:

- Complexity of the source material
- Quality of the source material
- File formats of the source
- Tools used

The use of translation memory or machine translation tools can increase productivity significantly. Productivity normally increases during the project, because translation memories generate an increasing number of matches as each component is translated, or as additional products are localized.

Most localization vendors assume that a translator can translate approximately 1500 words of software per 8 hour day, and 2000 to 2500 words of running text in online help or documentation per day. For Asian languages, these numbers would generally be lower, because of the complexity of entering and processing Asian characters. These estimates are only guidelines on new text, and exclude fuzzy or full matches retrieved from translation memory. Editing translations accounts for 20 to 30% of the time required to produce the translations. Most proofreaders can work through approximately 2000 to 3000 words per hour. These estimates may vary depending on the complexity of the subject matter and the target language.

For all other activities project managers will rely on evaluation findings to scope the workload and duration for each activity. Even for translation work, it is advisable to ask linguists to assign a complexity factor to the source text. It is important to monitor throughput of completed projects. By recording statistics for projects completed by the vendor, it is possible to calculate an aggregate throughput for certain types of projects.

It is important to build in a contingency plan when scheduling workloads and durations for the various project activities. Many project managers add 10% to the duration of each task to allow for slippages or other unforeseen problems. Another option is to add a few days of contingency at the end of the project schedule.

Resource Assignment

Once all activities, their dependencies, sequence, and durations have been established, assign resources to each activity. Availability of resources could also have a huge influence on the project planning. Finding translators for localization projects with Japanese as source language and German as target language, for example, will be much more difficult than finding resources for standard English into German translation work.

The combination of volumes, resource availability, quality, and deadlines will dictate how many resources need to be assigned to a particular task. A 50,000 word project with a one week delivery schedule would require five translators. Assuming they will all translate 2,000 words of raw translation per day, they may be forced to skip editing and proofreading. Assigning so many people to a relatively small job will almost certainly damage language consistency and overall quality.

For projects that are localized into multiple languages, determine where certain activities need to take place, such as engineering or desktop publishing. Centralizing these activities has the advantage of leveraging experience across languages, but may cause a bottleneck towards the end of the project, because all languages need to be finalized and delivered within the same period. It is advisable to stagger these activities for each language to avoid resource problems.

Note that each scheduled activity has a cost estimate attached to it. The cost estimates from the quotation need to be compared with the costs of the resources that have been scheduled.

Milestones

Once all required information is present, set milestones for the project. A milestone is a task with no specific duration. It normally refers to a delivery to or from the publisher. This could be a new version or updated version of the product. In localization projects, a milestone usually is a point in time where a predefined set of deliverables is ready.

Delivery of the source material from the publisher to the localization vendor is also a milestone which needs to be included in the schedule. All other project milestones depend on this first one.

Project managers can put as much detail in milestones as they want. Usually the milestones communicated to the publisher only include deliveries or hand-offs to the publisher, either final deliveries or review steps. For production staff, project managers will create many more milestones, for example hand-off of source material to translators, delivery of translated material to QA, hand-off of engineered software to testing, and delivery of screen captures to DTP.

Project milestones will be linked to dates, and the project activities will be scheduled between milestones.

2.3.2 CREATING SCHEDULES

Simple, straightforward localization projects containing few complex tasks and activities can be scheduled using a spreadsheet application or even a word processor. Most localization projects have many complex and variable components, with different team players, various project milestones, and many dependencies. For the more complex projects, a project management software application is a necessity to keep track of the project in an efficient way.

Project schedules can be created in many different ways, for example, using flow charts or Gantt charts. A Gantt chart is a bar chart used as an aid in planning and scheduling, in which project activities or tasks are shown graphically as bars drawn on a horizontal time scale.

Task Name	Duration	Start	End	1997			
				29/06	06/07	13/07	20/07
Software translation	83.00 d	30/06/97	22/10/97				
Prepare/check glossary	5.00 d	30/06/97	04/07/97				
Prepare software files	2.00 d	07/07/97	08/07/97				
Datalink core resources	71.00 d	09/07/97	15/10/97				
Translate	5.00 d	09/07/97	15/07/97				
Internal linguistic review	3.00 d	16/07/97	18/07/97				
Preliminary build & review	3.00 d	21/07/97	23/07/97				
Client review	5.00 d	28/07/97	01/08/97				
Update to 4.01	8.00 d	06/10/97	15/10/97				
Remaining software (excl samples)	70.00 d	14/07/97	17/10/97				
Translate	5.00 d	14/07/97	18/07/97				
Internal linguistic review	3.00 d	21/07/97	23/07/97				
Preliminary build & review	2.00 d	24/07/97	25/07/97				

In theory, localization projects can be scheduled in two ways: backward and forward. In backward scheduling, the publisher sets a milestone for an activity or deadline for the project. In this case, the project manager will schedule resources and tasks based on these milestones, if possible. In forward scheduling, the project manager will schedule all tasks and resources based on workload, optimum size of teams, and most workable sequence of activities, and propose milestones for the project to the publisher. In practice, localization projects usually will combine these two methods to get the best results and meet the project schedule and requirements.

To create a project schedule using a project management application, follow the steps listed in the Project Planning section on page 443 and enter the data in the application. For more information on these types of applications, refer to the Tools and Applications section on page 463.

Most of these tools will enable the user to enter the tasks, link dependent tasks, add milestones, assign resources, enter or change task durations, and adjust deadlines.

Once a preliminary schedule has been created, it should be sent to production staff for approval, and then to the publisher. If the schedule has been approved by all parties involved in the project, the project work can start.

2.3.3 PROJECT TRACKING AND REPORTING

Once the project has started, dates will more than likely slip. These changes should be monitored by the project manager in a tracking sheet or in the project management software. A tracking sheet shows the differences between the estimated start and end dates in the project schedule and the actual work in progress. It will also show whether the project is on schedule, ahead of schedule, or behind schedule.

An important part of project tracking is anticipating potential problems with resources or deadlines. In order to get a complete overview of the progress of the project, project managers should ask all project team members for regular status reports and time sheets. If one activity is moving faster than expected, which happens occasionally, project managers should aim for an early delivery. This will help maintain good relations with the publisher, and may help bring a project in under budget. It may also serve to compensate for any delays that may occur in the other stages of the project, thus avoiding time or cost overruns that might otherwise occur.

The Gantt charts in Microsoft Project offers very effective ways to track the status of a project. The user can automatically display and process project interruptions, changes in resources, and other changes affecting the workflow of the project. A task usually has one predecessor and one successor. Changing the duration of one of these tasks will automatically adjust the Critical Path of the project, which is the sequence of tasks that determines the end date of the project. In Gantt charts, each activity will be shown with two different bars, one showing the initial estimates, and the second one showing the actual progress.

When there is a risk of the project going off track, project managers should take corrective actions by adding additional or alternative resources, or by adjusting the schedule to avoid impacting the entire project.

Tracking sheets may be sent to the publisher on a regular basis, along with or included in a general status report. The status report should list any outstanding project-related issues. If any cost changes arise during the project, these should also be included in the status report with reasons and estimated amount. Many localization vendors use online scheduling and tracking systems where customers can access a secured area of an Intranet to see the progress of a project.

2.4 Resourcing

As part of project management, resources, including translators, engineers and desktop publishers, need to be scheduled and allocated. The goal is to make the most effective use of the people assigned to the project.

Resource management for localization project management involves setting up a project team, finding the right resources, and adding additional resources if necessary. Most localization project managers do not manage corporate human resource activities, such as staff employment, performance management, salary surveys, and legal issues. Project managers assign production staff to projects, but production staff usually reports to line managers.

Use of external contractors and agencies is very common for most localization vendors. A dedicated resource manager is usually responsible for negotiating prices and contractual agreements with these resources.

2.4.1 RESOURCE PLANNING

Determine first the number of resources and the necessary skills required to complete the project. These factors will affect both the duration, quality, and the cost of the project. If a relatively high proportion of unexperienced people is put on the job, the costs may be low, but the quality will most certainly be affected. If more experienced, and more expensive resources are used, the costs and quality will improve accordingly.

At this point in the project, focus on job categories, rather than individual resources. For example, how many software translators, online help translators, engineers, desktop publishers, or programmers are needed to complete the project successfully? The best way to determine this is to talk to the line managers responsible for the respective resources.

2.4.2 RESOURCE ALLOCATION

Once the roles, skill sets, and responsibilities have been identified for the project, begin setting up a project team. Create an organization chart, listing all the roles defined in the previous section, and then assign names to each role.

In a typical scenario, translation activities are outsourced by localization vendors and performed in-country either by local offices, partners, or freelance translators. All other activities, such as engineering and desktop publishing, may either be performed in-country or centralized in one location, preferably the location where the project manager is based.

When setting up a team of linguistic and technical staff, focus on the following:

- Translation should always be performed by native speakers, preferably in-country.
- If multiple translators are working on the same project, assign one of them as project lead who will be responsible for terminology management, contacting the publisher or reviewer about linguistic issues, and ensuring stylistic consistency.
- Limit the number of translators working on a project as much as possible to maintain consistency.
- Find translators who have worked on similar projects or previous versions of the same product.
- Find the right mix between freelance and internal staff.
- A localization engineering team should ideally be a mix of people with linguistic and technical backgrounds.

- For engineering and DTP, assign the same person to work on a single task across all languages rather than assigning each language to different resources. This will ensure consistency across languages. If a mistake occurs in one language, it is likely to occur in others.

- It is not essential for engineering and DTP staff to be native speakers of the languages they are working with in the localized files. Knowing the language may even be a distraction from the task at hand, where their function is to engineer or format files for a localized product.

- Make sure all people working on the project track their hours accurately for each task completed. This will help to track the costs and clarify any deviations from the budget to the publisher.

Many of the larger localization vendors employ resource managers to source the appropriate resources for all project activities. It is important for the resource managers to communicate with the project managers to identify the number of resources and skill sets required.

As part of resource management, project managers should evaluate training needs at the start of the project. This is particularly important when translators or other team members are new to the product or technology. In many cases, customers are willing to train localizers in their products before the project starts, as both parties will benefit from this: Translators who have a good understanding of the product will produce higher quality translations, and will feel more motivated to work on the project.

Here is a typical profile of a software localizer required for a financial software application, working from English into German:

- Native speaker of German with translation degree
- Experience using translation memory tools
- Experience translating financial software
- Experience with user interface localization tasks
- Available from week 32 to week 40

Here is a typical profile of a software localization engineer required for a software application developed in Java, working from English into Japanese:

- Experience compiling software using the Java Development Kit
- Knowledge of Java internationalization and localization issues
- Experience using layout managers
- Experience dealing with multi-byte languages, preferably Japanese
- Available from week 42 to week 45

Most localization vendors maintain databases with the data on internal staff and freelance staff skill sets that can be searched for suitability for any given localization project. Several language portals were launched in the late 1990s to assist translation agencies and publishers in locating translators. Examples of such portals are www.aquarius.net and www.proz.com.

During resource planning and team setup, it is important to consider contingency or backup options. For each key project team member assigned to the project, ensure that there is a backup resource, should this person be unavailable for any reason during the project.

2.4.3 RESOURCE MONITORING

Resourcing does not stop when the project manager has set up a project team and project work has started. Project managers should continually monitor the performance of each resource and take action when resources are jeopardizing quality or project delivery schedules. This is not always easy, especially where project managers are working with geographically distributed human resources.

During the project, project managers should build in quality assurance steps between each of the activities to check that all resources are performing as expected. Where a translation is completed by one translator and then passed for editing to another translator, add a spot check step to assess whether the translation is acceptable. For more information on quality checks, refer to the Quality Management section on page 453.

If team members repeatedly perform below standard, project managers should take corrective action by replacing the underperformers. Likewise, if team members are under too much pressure, project managers should also react, by changing the schedules or adding resources.

In some cases, it may also be necessary to employ additional external resources, for example, consultants with expertise in a certain field or discipline. Translators should never be expected to have in-depth knowledge on all subjects. The best translations are produced by having a combination of strong linguistic skills and strong subject-matter expertise.

Project managers are also expected to share knowledge among team members. This applies specifically to multilingual projects, where establishing direct contact between translators in the different target languages will positively impact the final quality and productivity. For more information on team communication, refer to the Communication section on page 458.

2.5 Finances

Once a project has been awarded to a localization vendor, the project manager is responsible for creating a project budget. A project budget is a financial plan which details the size of the budget and how it allocated. A project budget is normally calculated based on the expected revenue minus the gross profit margin determined by the localization vendor. The total costs expected should be equal to or lower than the project budget.

Throughout the project, the initial budget should be continuously checked against the actual or direct costs. It should include payments for staff and outside suppliers or equipment; any budget overruns should be monitored carefully.

2.5.1 BUDGET SETUP

When setting up a localization project budget, project managers should pay attention to the following:

- Expected volumes and word rates for outsourced translation
- Resource costs, e.g. usually hourly rates for each individual project team member
- Expected number of hours allocated to all project activities, whether or not these are billable directly to the publisher
- Additional investments required for the project, e.g. purchase or leasing of software or hardware just for this project
- Additional costs required for the project, e.g. travel costs
- Contingency percentage for unanticipated expenses, e.g. rework or higher overtime rates

With these data, project managers can develop a system based on activity-based costing (ABC), to determine the total project cost estimates, which can be used to develop a budget. Most localization vendors have an accounting system where the profit margins are all amounts invoiced to the publisher minus all direct and indirect costs. Direct and indirect costs are defined and interpreted differently by each vendor. Some vendors include communication and project management costs as indirect costs, while others will charge these costs as direct costs to the project. This is the reason why many localization vendors still have a hard time establishing detailed profitability figures on completion of a project.

2.5.2 BUDGET CONTROL

Budgets need to be monitored and controlled continually by the project manager. This means that the actual project costs need to be compared on an on-going basis with the budgeted costs. In the event that budget overruns occur, project managers should record these in the cost baseline and take corrective action.

When reviewers take twice as long as the estimated time to edit a translated text, project managers assess whether the translation quality was poor or the editor too slow. In either case, corrective action should be taken to prevent this from happening again. If the quality of the translation is below standard, project managers either switch resources or request a rework by the original translator. Project managers can only monitor budgets by comparing time sheets and internal invoices with initial schedules and estimated costs.

An important aspect of budget control is asking clients for approval before any non-budgeted work is started. Project managers are responsible for deciding when to stop work. Likewise, when additional services are requested by the clients, project managers need to ensure these are included in the quotation and invoiced.

Most project management applications enable the user to track the estimated costs against the actual costs, and to generate budget reports. For more information, refer to the Tools and Applications section on page 463.

2.6 Change Management

It is very common for the scope of a localization project to change after the translation starts. It is, therefore, absolutely critical that a reliable change management solution is implemented. One of the most important tasks of a project manager is to monitor the scope of the project and compare it to the specifications and schedules estimated in the initial quotation. Monitoring and rescoping tasks also require that the project manager highlight and invoice any extra activities or updates to the original files.

It is important to agree with the publisher on a change management procedure before the project starts. Here are some general guidelines:

- Any change to the initial project scope or deviation from the original quotation must be communicated to the publisher using a change request form.
- Once the project has been finalized, a reconciliation step should summarize the differences between the actual project and initial quotation. Any cost differences should be included in the final payment.

Change management is only possible when project managers continuously monitor time spent on the project by each team member. If actual volumes or production times differ substantially from the estimates in the original quotation, project managers should pinpoint whether this is an actual project scope change or resource issue.

2.7 Quality Management

Quality management is one of the responsibilities often assigned to a localization project manager. This does not mean that project managers should check or review all localized deliverables, but that they must ensure that all necessary quality checks are in place for all activities and services required by the publisher.

At the start of each project, project managers should create a quality plan which outlines all quality checks to be integrated in the process and schedule. Examples of quality checks are proofreading translated material, cosmetic testing on localized software, or language reviews by the publisher. During the project, project managers should ensure that the quality checks are actually carried out.

2.7.1 QUALITY PLANNING

Quality planning must be integrated into the overall project planning and defines all activities that guarantee the required objectives and quality standards. Scheduling items such as project evaluation, translation review steps, publisher reviews, and proofreading will lead to quality deliverables. Selecting resources is also part of quality planning. Using inexperienced resources on a complicated localization project will undoubtedly generate quality problems. The ideal setup is to mix the teams, so that experienced team members drive the project and take responsibility for the quality of the deliverables, while giving the less experienced team members the opportunity to learn.

Many localization vendors have incorporated ISO 900x quality assurance processes (see below) for all their services and activities, including translation, engineering, and even project management. Others use ISO for parts of their processes, and have defined internal quality systems. In such cases, most of the QA steps that project managers need to build into the schedule have been pre-defined. Note that formal quality procedures do not always guarantee quality. Many projects will require additional or customized quality assurance steps based on publisher requirements or project specifications.

For companies without formal quality standards or processes, there are many things a project manager can do to ensure quality deliverables, such as providing translators with well-prepared source material and implementing several language review steps. It is advisable to implement sign-off forms for all team members to sign once their tasks and activities have been completed. These sign-off forms could state that they have taken all of the necessary quality control steps.

Preparing Source Material

As explained in the Project Preparation section on page 441 of this chapter, well-prepared projects should provide translators with detailed project information and reference material.

Translators working on online help or documentation files which contain references to localized software, for example, should be supplied with a copy of the localized software. Translators who can refer to a running version of the localized software not only produce accurate software reference translations, but may also be able to track any linguistic or functional problems. This will help the software quality assurance engineers during the testing cycle.

Software user interface glossaries should normally be merged with the project glossary and linked to the translation memory system. The translation memory tool will provide automatic terminology lookup when the help and documentation files are translated. When the help files are translated using Trados Translator's Workbench, for example, the software glossary would be loaded in MultiTerm. For more information, refer to the Trados MultiTerm section on page 380.

Language Review Steps

A typical translation workflow involves translation, revision/editing, and proofreading. First, translators should review their own work and run a spell-check on their documents. This review is a linguistic one, which can be performed on-screen in the translation memory tool and is part of the translation process.

Depending on the complexity of the text and the experience of the translator, an editor will edit the entire text on-screen in the translation memory tool. When a group of translators are working on one project, for example, one senior translator will act as project lead and review all translations completed by different team members to ensure stylistic and terminological consistency. Make sure that any translations completed by new or inexperienced translators are reviewed at a very early stage!

As a project manager, there are some issues to focus on when translated documents are being reviewed and edited:

- Verify that any suggested edits are actually necessary. Rephrasing perfectly clear sentences just for stylistic reasons is a waste of time and often creates consistency problems. Online help and documentation files do not require a perfect style. Accuracy and consistency are factors that are far more important.

- Make sure that all edits are implemented by – or at least seen by – the original translator of the document. This is the only way to avoid repeated errors in a translation cycle.

- Ask the reviewer or editor to keep a list of the most common errors for future reference.

- Pay special attention to generated components, such as a table of contents or keyword index in online help files or documentation. It may be necessary to first generate the index or to compile files. For more information on indexes, refer to the Translating Indexes section on page 307.

Terminology changes are often introduced in the translated software. This is often due to length restrictions in software strings, bugs found in the localized software, or linguistic reasons. In this case, or where the help translation was started before the software translation was finalized, verify that all software references in the translated online help or documentation are consistent with the actual running software. Most localization vendors include this software consistency check in their standard procedures.

The last language-related check is proofreading. Proofreading does not necessarily focus on translation quality, but more on the final linguistic quality of the localized product. Proofreaders should focus on obvious mistakes such as spelling errors, typos, incorrect captions, etc. For more information on editing and proofreading, refer to the Reviewing Documentation section on page 315.

Client Review

Most software publishers will request samples of the translated material for internal evaluation during the localization project cycle. This review is usually scheduled between editing and proofreading and will concentrate on aspects such as accuracy of translations, terminology, language quality, and local usability. It is important to agree with the publisher on the number and frequency of scheduled client review cycles. It is advisable to schedule a small sample review early on in the project so that any suggestions for change can be reported by the client reviewer and implemented immediately by the translators.

The result of this review is often referred to as a *pass* or a *no-pass*. If a no-pass is returned by the publisher, implement the suggestions and corrections and return the revised translations for a new quality check. Direct contact between translators and client reviewers often helps to prevent or resolve language or terminology problems.

Make it clear to the publisher that delivery of translated material is dependent on the timely arrival of the publisher's review comments. If the reviewer is late, this will impact the schedule for the remainder of the project. This review is often performed by marketing personnel who do not place a high priority on this work, as it is not part of their core tasks. Discuss the impact of a delay on the project with the publisher. This is an internal problem that the project manager at the publisher's side needs to resolve with their language reviewers.

2.7.2 QUALITY STANDARDS

For many people, the term *quality standards* is often associated with ISO, the International Organization for Standardization. ISO is a non-governmental organization that links national standards bodies with representatives in each country.

The ISO definition (ISO 8402: 1986, 3.1) of "quality" is "The totality of features and characteristics of a product or service that bear on its ability to satisfy stated or implied needs."

The ISO definition (ISO 8402: 1986, 3.6) of "quality assurance" is "All those planned and systematic actions necessary to provide adequate confidence that a product or service will satisfy given requirements for quality."

The ISO definition (ISO 8402: 1986, 3.7) of "quality control" is "The operational techniques and activities that are used to fulfill requirements for quality."

The main goals of quality assurance and quality control standards are to produce a better quality product, save time and money, increase client satisfaction, and hence provide a competitive edge. In localization projects, project managers are responsible for ensuring that both quality assurance and quality control are well-managed. During the planning phase, quality assurance steps should be integrated into the schedule, and during the project, checks should be in place to ensure that quality control steps are actually carried out.

Assessing the quality of localized deliverables can be a complicated task and much has been discussed and written on this topic. Everybody agrees that a quality translation has to be accurate and consistent as far as terminology, writing style and format is concerned. However, not many standard metrics for assessing translation quality have been developed and applied as a standard world-wide.

Because existing standards were too complicated, expensive or not applicable to translation or localization, several initiatives have been undertaken by industry sectors, local translation organizations, and universities. A good example is the Translation

Quality Metric Task Force by the Society of Automotive Engineers. For more information, visit the SAE web site at www.sae.org (search for "translation quality").

A national standard under development in the U.S. is the ASTM Standard for Language Translation, a standard developed by the National Foreign Language Center (NFLC) and the American Translators Association (ATA), under the auspices of the American Society for Testing and Materials (ASTM). For more information on this standard, visit the ASTM web site at www.astm.org (search for subcommittee F15.48).

No system has been developed, however, that can be applied to all types of multi-lingual projects, covering all activities, aspects, and project components. In the localization industry, the two most commonly used translation quality assessment tools are the LISA QA Model and the DIN 2345 translation quality standard, *Translation Contracts*.

LISA QA Model

The Localisation Industry Standards Association QA Model was prepared by a group of companies active in the localization industry, including publishers and localization vendors. It aims to help organizations manage the quality assurance process for all activities and components in a localization project.

The LISA QA Model consists of reference manuals and templates. The reference manuals explain the localization process and QA checkpoints for documentation, online help, software, computer-based training, and packaging components. Two sets of criteria are given for each of the components, one for language and one for functionality. It also contains quality check lists and templates which can be used to track errors.

The following image shows one of the quality assurance form templates included in the package:

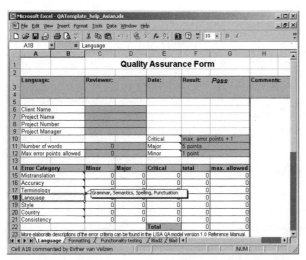

For more information on the LISA QA Model, refer to the LISA web site at www.lisa.org.

DIN 2345 Translation Quality Standard

The DIN 2345 translation quality standard was prepared by a technical committee with representatives from professional organizations in Germany, Austria, and Switzerland. It focuses on translation activities only, and contains sections on work procedures, source and target text correctness, contracts, translation content, and checking and revision. It regulates the conditions under which translation contracts are performed and defines many terms and activities associated with those contracts.

According to the foreword, "Freelance translators, in-house translation departments and translation agencies or companies may declare on their own responsibility that their work complies with this standard. This declaration of conformity may well serve to increase the client's confidence in the quality of the services provided, as compliance with the standard is verifiable for every translation."

For more information on the DIN 2345 Translation Quality Standard, refer to the DIN web site at www.din.de (search for "2345").

2.8 Communication

Communication is critical to the management success of a localization project. Project managers will be communicating with publishers, translators, technical staff, linguists, client reviewers, and all people involved in the project.

For project managers, it is important to clearly distinguish between external communication and internal communication, and to include a communications plan section in the project plan.

2.8.1 COMMUNICATIONS PLANNING

The questions that should be asked when creating a communications plan are: who needs specific information, when will it be needed, and in what format should it be delivered? For internal communications, determine information distribution strategies for the project team; for external communications identify the team member responsible for communicating with the publisher on specific issues, such as how often will a status report be sent to the publisher and whom questions should be directed to.

Numerous projects have been hampered by problems caused by a lack of communication. On the other hand, many projects have been delayed or concluded with misunderstandings because of overcommunication. Project managers should find the right balance by communicating the right amount of information in a timely manner to the right people.

A good communication plan clearly answers the following questions:

- Where can project information be found, and how will updates to the information be distributed?
- Who will receive specific information, and how often? For example, who will receive status reports and schedules, and how will this information be distributed? Who will be copied on distributed information?

- Who can answer questions on different aspects of the project, for example on terminological issues? Who will serve as a backup, if the first contact is unavailable?
- Where will questions and answers be stored for future reference?
- What are the preferred communication methods, and what is the second preferred method?
- Who will handle issues or difficulties with any of the team members?
- Who has the final say in conflicts that may arise?
- Who will communicate with the publisher, and on what issues?
- How often are time sheets or work in progress updates required?
- How frequently and when will status reports be sent to the publisher?

In most cases, the project manager will be the point of contact for clients on all issues related to schedules, finances, quality, deliveries, and project status. Some publishers allow direct communication between their development staff and the engineering team at a vendor site, or between publisher reviewers and the translators. If this distributed model is applied, ensure that the project manager is copied on all communication to maintain an overview of the project and potential issues.

2.8.2 INTERNAL COMMUNICATION

Because localization projects contain many interrelated components and dependencies, project managers should inform all team members of their responsibilities of any steps that precede or may be related to their own tasks, and the support people they can contact. Project managers should actively encourage information exchange within the project team. Because most localization project teams are geographically distributed, project managers need to ensure all team members are up-to-date with the latest developments, changes, or updates in the project. It is good to keep every person involved in the project informed of the overall status of the project. However, avoid overloading people with unnecessary information. When communicating with production staff on issues that may influence their workload or availability, copy their line managers, who should be aware of changes in schedule or volume for internal planning purposes.

As a rule, translators will be native speakers of the target language(s). They should be familiar with computer and software terminology, but not necessarily with project and process-related terms. Communicate project-related information using language and terminology that is understandable and clear for non-native speakers.

In dealing with freelance translators, contractors, in-house staff, partner vendors, and publisher reviewers, avoid conflicts on terminological or stylistic issues. Discussions about details or regional preferences should be avoided and it should be clear who has the last say in such issues, and who is responsible for which decisions. Organizing meetings between project team members always helps.

An issue which is very important in projects involving multiple languages is the management of questions from translators and corresponding modifications across different languages. Setting up online question forms or databases containing questions and answers, accessible for translators in all target languages, is one way to ensure that each language version will contain consistent modifications or interpretations.

2.8.3   EXTERNAL COMMUNICATION

Project managers typically deal with localization or product managers from several clients. As a rule, clients expect project managers to act independently, pro-actively, and to be open and honest in their discussions. Some publishers may adopt a more formal approach, others will try to integrate the vendor in their processes and team. Regardless of how the vendor communicates with the publisher, it is never easy to inform publishers of missed deadlines or other project problems. Procrastinating will only compound the problem. It is preferable to inform the publisher about delays or other problems as soon as they occur. This will allow the project manager to rectify the problem quickly with the help of the publisher. Avoid communicating bad news by means of e-mail or fax. A telephone call will show commitment and give the project manager a chance to explain the situation and discuss possible solutions.

Establishing clear agreements on deadlines, possible updates, and status reporting at the start of the project will help prevent most misunderstandings or conflicts. Ensure that revised milestones are communicated clearly in a status report.

The best way to get a project started is to set up a kickoff meeting where the vendor project manager meets with the publisher to discuss the schedule, communication issues, and any other project-related issues. It is not unusual for a publisher to expect regular status reports, conference calls, or additional meetings once the project is underway.

Status Reports

Status reports are typically sent weekly by the localization vendor to the publisher, unless the vendor provides online access to a project tracking system where clients can log in and check the status of their projects on a daily basis. Some clients ask localization vendors to use their proprietary status reporting procedures or forms in order to create some level of reporting standards.

A status report from a localization vendor to a publisher usually contains the following information:

- Project specifications, i.e. project number, name, and languages
- Scheduled start and end dates versus actual start and end dates (tracking sheet)
- Deviations from schedule or budget
- Outstanding and resolved issues and problems
- Work in progress
- Expected progress for the following week
- List of materials received from publisher, and deliveries made to publisher

If the status report includes deviations from the original schedule, causes and corrective measures need to be mentioned as well. In most cases, delivery of a status report is followed by a meeting or conference call to discuss the issues raised in the report.

Client Complaints

Not all projects run smoothly, and the most well-managed and planned projects run into problems. The publisher may raise concerns about the quality of a deliverable or service. Localization project managers often have a hard time explaining slippages or quality issues in translated materials. Project managers will react in different ways, with some promising the impossible to rectify the problem, while others become very defensive finding endless excuses as to why the problem occurred. The best way to handle complaints or problems with a project is to acknowledge the problem exists and to agree with the client that everything will be done to rectify the situation as quickly as possible.

Here are some guidelines on how to react to and handle client complaints in a professional manner:

- Listen carefully to complaints, make notes, and agree to first establish the facts at the vendor site and then to schedule a follow-up meeting in order to find a solution to the problem.

- Establish the nature and possible reason for the complaint. Ask the publisher for additional information, if necessary.

- Check whether the complaint is justified by first asking the person responsible, then possibly a third party.

- Find a solution and take corrective action.

- Inform the client of the solution and actions taken to ensure that no further errors or problems of this nature arise.

- Report the error to the relevant line manager or quality manager.

No project is ever completed without some glitches, and no client can expect 100% quality all the time. True professionalism can be shown by resolving problems in a calm and committed manner.

3   Organizations and Training

Most organizations providing training for project managers focus on general project management theories and practice rather than on translation or localization. As mentioned in the introduction, however, most standard project management practices can easily be applied to software localization. Professional project management is an important component in developing a mature and professional localization industry.

The following web sites contain general information on project management, case studies, training opportunities, software tools, publications, useful links, national organizations, and companies offering project management services.

3.1   International Project Management Association

The International Project Management Association (IPMA) is a non-profit organization that functions as a promoter of project management at an international level through its membership network of national project management associations around the world. The IPMA also has many individual members, as well as co-operative agreements with related organizations world-wide.

For more information on the International Project Management Association, visit the IPMA web site at www.ipma.ch.

3.2   Association of Project Management

The Association of Project Management (APM) is affiliated to the IPMA and is dedicated to advancing the profession of project management and the professional development of project managers. Activities include developing and running project management training courses, providing project management consultancy, and assessing training needs for project managers.

For more information on the Association of Project Management, visit the APM web site at www.apm.org.uk.

3.3   The Project Management Forum

The Project Management Forum is an information resource for everything related to project management. It is hosted by LODAY Systems Ltd., but has no connection to any national or international project management organization, nor does it reflect the policy of any project management professional or commercial organization.

For more information on the Project Management Forum, visit the PMF web site at www.pmforum.org.

3.4   Project Management Institute

The Project Management Institute (PMI) is one of the largest organizations in the world for project management professionals. PMI is a nonprofit professional association that sets project management standards, provides seminars, educational programs and professional certification.

PMI have published *A Guide to the Project Management Body of Knowledge*, the PMBok Guide. It provides an excellent overview of the project management profession and can be downloaded from their web site.

For more information on the Project Management Institute, visit the PMI web site at www.pmi.org.

3.5   ETP – The Structured Project Management Company

ETP is a company based in Ireland that specializes in project management workshops aimed at the localization industry. ETP's approach is called Structured Project Management, which is based on a number of standard, consistent steps. ETP have also developed a software application called Silver Bullet, which is a desktop decision support system for project managers. ETP's CEO Fergus O'Connell has published books on the subject of project management (see below).

The Localisation Industry Standards Association (LISA) has selected Structured Project Management as the preferred and most dynamic project management method for use by the localization industry.

ETP's top ten reasons why projects fail were listed in Deborah Fry's article on localization project management in Language International, Vol 10.3 (1998):

1. The goal of the project is not defined clearly.

2. The goal is defined properly, but changes to it are not controlled.

3. The project is not planned properly.

4. The project is not led properly.

5. The project is planned properly but then is not resourced as planned.

6. The project is planned such that it has no contingency.

7. The expectations of project participants are not managed.

8. Progress against the plan is not monitored and controlled properly.

9. Project reporting is inadequate or non-existent.

10. When projects run into trouble, people believe that the problem can be solved simply, e.g. by working harder, extending the deadline, or adding more resources.

For more information on ETP and Structured Project Management, visit the ETP web site at www.etpint.com.

4   Tools and Applications

According to LISA's 1998 Industry Survey, 96% of the respondents to the survey use project management tools in whole or part. In localization, several types of project management tools are used, including:

- General project management tools
- Translation project management tools
- Customized automated workflow and project tracking tools

Most of these tools enable project managers to create and track schedules, assign resources, set milestones, and track costs. Only a few examples are discussed below, because many of the tools will have similar functionality. The web sites mentioned in the previous sections contain many links to project management tools and applications.

Workflow and project tracking tools aim to automate some of the project management tasks. They automatically transfer material to the next step in the pre-defined process, for example, and allow customers to check the status of projects online, 24 hours a day.

4.1 Microsoft Project

Microsoft Project is probably the most commonly used project management software application in the localization industry.

Project integrates well with other Microsoft Office applications and contains advanced features for breaking a project into tasks, phases and milestones, creating a sequence of tasks, specifying milestones, assigning resources and resource costs, and monitoring the project progress and costs.

Possible views include sheets, charts and graphs, and forms for tasks or resources, including Gantt charts and PERT charts. The following image shows a project schedule viewed in a Gantt chart.

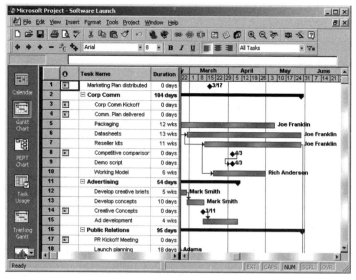

For more information on Microsoft Project, refer to the Project web site at www.microsoft.com/office/project.

4.2 LTC Organiser

The Language Technology Centre (LTC) is a company developing and providing language technology solutions. LTC provides localization and translation, training and consulting services.

Their project management tool, LTC Organiser, is tailored to the translation and localization industry and supports and facilitates multilingual translation projects.

The LTC Organiser contains a translator's database that can be used to identify appropriate translators, allocate them quickly, and track the status, progress, and cost of translation projects. The client database is another feature of the LTC Organiser which enables the user to store all relevant client information. The Project Management feature keeps track of projects, and documents within projects at the different stages of development. The Finance Module allows the user to create, print, save, export, and customize invoices, quotations and purchase orders. The following image displays a screen in the Project Management module.

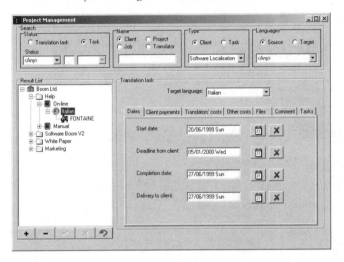

For more information on LTC Organiser, visit the Language Technology Centre web site at www.langtech.co.uk.

4.3 Silver Bullet

The Silver Bullet from ETP is a so-called "decision support system" for project managers. It is a companion product to Microsoft Project which gives the user a high-level overview of projects. The Silver Bullet is also a knowledge management system, in that it stores information from previous projects to achieve better results in new projects.

The tool enables the user to reuse existing project plans and build new ones very quickly, and it evaluates project plans to identify potential errors in the plan. The following image displays a project outline in Silver Bullet.

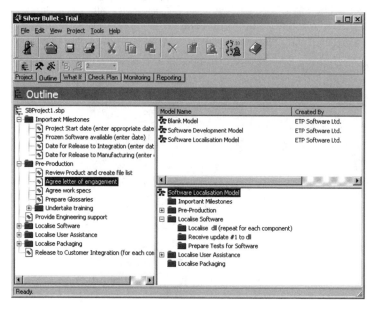

For more information on Silver Bullet, visit the ETP web site at www.etpint.com.

5   Further Reading

The books listed below cover different aspects of project management.

Lewis, James P. 1999. *The Project Manager's Desk Reference : A Comprehensive Guide to Project Planning, Scheduling, Evaluation, and Systems.* McGraw-Hill, ISBN 0-071-34750-X.

O'Connell, Fergus. 1999. *How to Run Successful, High-Tech Project-Based Organizations.* Artech House Publishers, ISBN 1-580-53010-9.

O'Connell, Fergus. 1996. *How to Run Successful Projects, The Silver Bullet.* Prentice Hall Europe, ISBN 0-132-39856-7.

Rea, Kathryn P. and Bennet P. Lientz. 1998. *Breakthrough Technology Project Management.* Academic Press, ISBN 0-124-49970-8.

Rea, Kathryn P. and Bennet P. Lientz. 1998. *Project Management for the 21st Century.* Academic Press, ISBN 0-124-49966-X.

Appendix A:
Glossary of Terms

8-bit Unicode Transfer Format - *See* UTF-8

accelerator key - *See* hot key

accented character - A character with a diacritic, i.e. a mark placed over, under, or through a Latin character. Diacritics usually indicate a change in phonetic value, for example in ä or ç.

alignment - Creating a translation memory database by matching segments in two sets of translated documents (source language and translated version). With modern text alignment tools, this is a semi-automated process.

bi-directional language - Language, such as Hebrew or Arabic, where text is displayed and read from right-to-left, but where left-to-right display is also supported, for example for English words or trademarked names.

build environment - Set of files necessary to build or compile a software application.

Cascading Style Sheet (CSS) - An external document that determines the layout of tagged file formats such as HTML.

CAT - *See* computer aided translation

character set - Mapping of characters from a writing system into a set of binary codes. Examples are ANSI, which uses eight bits to code one character, or Unicode, which uses 16 bits for each character.

CJKV - Short for Chinese, Japanese, Korean, Vietnamese

code page - A character set and character encoding scheme which is a part of a related series. Unlike characters sets, each character in a code page has a numerical index.

collateral - Relatively small localization project components such as quick reference cards, disk labels, product boxes, and marketing material.

computer aided translation (CAT) - A term used to describe the computer technology that automates or supports translators in the translation of one natural language into another language.

concatenation - The process of adding text elements or strings together to form a larger string. This is often problematic for translation because in many languages the word order in sentences differs from the English word order.

consolidation - In the context of the localization industry, consolidation refers to mergers and acquisitions of localization service providers.

control key - A key combination of Ctrl and a letter or number that immediately executes a command.

controlled language - A subset of a natural language, used mainly to write technical material, which is more structured and easier to understand than uncontrolled language.

cosmetic testing - Testing the user interface of an application.

CSS - *See* Cascading Style Sheet

Cyrillic - The writing script used to represent characters in Slavic languages, such as Greek or Russian.

DBCS - *See* double-byte character set

desktop publishing (DTP) - Formatting and layout of text and images on a computer prior to output on paper, CD-ROM, or any online format.

Document Type Definition (DTD) - A file which specifies the rules for the structure and mark-up of an SGML or XML document.

double-byte character set (DBCS) - A character encoding system that uses one or two bytes. Languages using double-byte character sets are Japanese, Chinese, and Korean.

double-byte enablement - Internationalizing a product in a way that it supports the input, processing, and display of double-byte characters used in Asian languages.

DTD - *See* Document Type Definition

DTP - *See* desktop publishing

dynamic web site - As opposed to static web sites, dynamic sites produce web pages dynamically, using a combination of database content, style sheets, scripting, and HTML.

extended characters - All characters in the ASCII range 128 to 255.

Extensible Markup Language (XML) - A metalanguage, i.e. a language for describing other languages, used to create customized markup for specific purposes. XML is a subset of SGML and has been designed specifically for the web.

Extensible Stylesheet Language (XSL) - A language for expressing stylesheets, controlling formatting and other output behavior, which is based on DSSSL (SGML) and CSS (HTML).

FIGS - Short for French, Italian, German, Spanish

full match - A source text segment which corresponds exactly (100%) with a previously stored sentence in a translation memory tool.

functional testing - Testing the functionality of a product, i.e. the tasks or commands performed by running a software application.

fuzzy matching - A method used in translation memory tools to identify text segments that do not match previously translated segments 100%. This approach allows translations of similar texts to be leveraged. For example, "Press OK to continue" is a 75% fuzzy match with "Click OK to continue".

g11n - *See* globalization (11 letters between "g" and "n").

Gantt chart - A bar chart used as a tool for planning and scheduling, in which project activities or tasks are shown graphically as bars drawn on a horizontal time scale.

gisting - Using machine translations to produce translations that will merely convey the approximate rather than the full and literal meaning of documents such as e-mails, news articles, letters, and web pages.

globalization (g11n) - Globalization addresses the business issues associated with launching a product globally. In the globalization of high-tech products this involves integrating localization throughout a company, after proper internationalization and product design, as well as marketing, sales, and support in the world market.

glossary - In the context of translation/localization projects, a bilingual list containing keywords or phrases and equivalent translations.

glyph - The actual shape of a character. A sans-serif **A** and a serif A, for example, are two different glyphs of the same character.

hard-coding - The embedding of translatable strings in the body of programming code rather than in separate resource files.

help compiler - Utility used to build online help files, i.e. it converts sets of source files (for example HTML) and images into one binary, searchable online help document.

Hiragana - A small set of characters used for words of Japanese origin. Hiragana and katakana scripts represent individual syllables used for Japanese pronunciation.

hot key - The underlined letter or number in a menu command or dialog box option which can be pressed in combination with the Alt key to activate the command or option.

hotspot - An area of an image in an online help document that links to another topic.

HTML - *See* HyperText Markup Language

HTML Help - HTML Help is a follow-up to Windows Help (WinHelp). It is the Microsoft standard for online help, which is based on the HTML file format.

hypergraphic - Image in an online help file or web page containing "hotspots" or links to other pages.

HyperText Markup Language (HTML) - A subset of SGML, defining a set of tags used mainly for display of pages on the web.

i18n - *See* internationalization (18 letters between "i" and "n").

ideographic - A writing system in which symbols or ideographs representing words or syllables that represent pronunciation and meaning. Ideographs are used in Japanese Kanji, Chinese Hanzi, and Korean Hanja.

IME - *See* input method editor

input method editor (IME) - A utility which converts keystrokes and ideographs to other characters, usually allowing the user to choose one entry from the characters retrieved from the dictionary.

internationalization (i18n) - The process of generalizing a product so that it can handle multiple languages and cultural conventions, without the need for re-design. Internationalization takes place at the level of program design and document development.

internationalization testing - Testing the international support and localizability of a product.

International Organization for Standardization (ISO) - A worldwide federation of national bodies governing standards in approximately 130 countries, one from each country.

ISO - *See* International Organization for Standardization

Kanji - Japanese name for basic ideographs from Chinese origin which represent a single word.

Katakana - A character set which consists of a different set of symbols for the same sounds as expressed in hiragana. However, katakana is often used for writing English and other foreign words and names.

kick-off meeting - A meeting before the start of a new localization project where representatives, typically key project team members from the localization vendor and publisher, discuss project plans, schedules, and other project-related issues.

l10n - *See* localization (10 letters between "l" and "n").

language engineering - The application of knowledge of written and spoken language to the development of information, transaction and communication systems, so that they can recognize, understand, interpret, and generate human language.

language tier - In the context of localization, a set of languages released simultaneously. French and German, for example, are usually "tier one" languages.

layered graphic - An image file in which translatable text is stored on a separate layer for efficient translation.

leverage - In the context of translation or localization, re-using or recycling previously translated words.

linguistic testing - Testing all language-related aspects of a localized product in context.

LISA - *See* Localisation Industry Standards Association

locale - A collection of standard settings, rules and data specific to a language and geographical region.

Localisation Industry Standards Association (LISA) - An organization which was founded in 1990 and is made up of mostly software publishers and localization service providers. LISA organizes forums, publishes a newsletter, conducts surveys, and has initiated several special-interest groups focusing on specific issues in localization.

localization (l10n) - Localization involves taking a product and making it linguistically and culturally appropriate to the target locale (country/region and language) where it will be used and sold.

localization kit - Set of files, tools, and instructions created by software developer and sent to localization vendor when a software localization project is started.

localization testing - A combination of linguistic and cosmetic testing to ensure the quality of the user interface in a localized application.

localization vendor - A business that provides localization services, ranging from translation and project management, to engineering and testing.

machine aided translation - *See* computer aided translation

machine translation (MT) - A methodology and technology used to automate language translations from one human language to another, using terminology glossaries and advanced grammatical, syntactic, and semantic analysis techniques.

markup - A sequence of characters or other symbols inserted in a text or word processing file to indicate how the file should look when it is printed or displayed or to describe the document's logical structure.

markup language - Set of codes and tags, combined with text that need to be processed and displayed using an application, for example a web browser for HTML.

match - In the context of translation memory, a segment in the source text which corresponds exactly (full match) or partly (fuzzy match) with a segment stored in the translation memory databases.

MBCS - *See* multi-byte character set

Microsoft Developer Network (MSDN) - Microsoft's online subscription service, which publishes a set of CDs containing development kits and tools, localized versions of Microsoft operating systems and applications, glossaries, beta versions of new releases, etc.

MLV - *See* multi-language vendor

mnemonic - *See* hot key

MSDN - *See* Microsoft Developer Network

MT - *See* machine translation

multi-byte character set (MBCS) - A character set in which each character is represented as either a 1-byte or 2-byte value. The standard ASCII character set is a subset of the MBCS, which is used for languages that require a set of more than 256 characters.

multi-language vendor (MLV) - A localization vendor capable of localizing products in a wide range of languages. Most MLVs centralize project management for multi-language projects and have offices or partners all over the world.

national language support (NLS) - Function that allows a software application to set the locale for the user, identify the language in which the user works, and retrieve strings — representing times, dates, and other information — formatted correctly for the specified language and location. National language support also includes support for keyboard layouts and language-specific fonts.

NLS - *See* national language support

outsourcing - In the context of localization, contracting certain activities to third parties. Most localization vendors, for example, outsource translation work to freelance translators, and publishers often outsource the full localization process to localization vendors, including translation, engineering, and testing.

PDF - *See* Portable Document Format

Portable Document Format (PDF) - File format developed by Adobe which is based on the PostScript standard; PDF files can be created from any other application and are used mainly for electronic file distribution.

post-mortem - In the context of localization projects, a meeting between representatives from the publisher and the localization vendor, held after a project is completed, to evaluate the project and suggest process modifications for future projects.

PostScript - A programming language which is used to describe the appearance of text, graphical shapes, and sampled images on printed or displayed pages.

pseudo-translation - An automated or manual process where each translatable text string in the software is replaced with a longer string or a series of accented characters, in order to spot any potential problems in compiling and executing the localized files.

quality assurance (QA) - The steps and processes in place to ensure a quality final product.

quality control (QC) - Verification of the quality of products produced by the QA process.

RC file - *See* resource script file

request for proposal (RFP) - A request sent out by a publisher to a localization vendor, usually including a localization kit, which is used to create a proposal for localization services.

request for quotation (RFQ) - An RFQ is sent by a publisher to a localization vendor with source material to obtain a quote listing all project components and costs.

resizing - Adjusting the size or position of elements of a screen, form, or dialog box to ensure translated text fits in the space available.

resource editor - A stand-alone tool or feature in a development environment that enables the user to edit a user interface, e.g. dialog boxes and menus.

resource-only .dll - A dynamic link library (.dll) containing application resources, e.g. menus, dialog boxes, icons, and messages. In well-internationalized applications, resource-only .dll files are combined with single worldwide binaries to enable users to run applications in any locale.

resource script (RC) file - A text file containing descriptions of resources from which the resource compiler creates a binary resource file. For Microsoft Windows applications, resource-definition files usually have a .RC filename extension.

RFP - *See* request for proposal

RFQ - *See* request for quotation

Romaji - Characters used to write Japanese sounds with Roman letters.

screen capture - Picture of interface item of a software application, for example a dialog box or menu item.

screenshot - *See* screen capture

segmentation - Division of text into translatable units, such as sentences or paragraphs. Most translation memory tools contain customizable segmentation rules.

SGML - *See* Standard Generalized Markup Language

shortcut key - *See* control key

Simplified Chinese - Chinese ideographs used in mainland China and Singapore. Compared to Traditional Chinese, Simplified Chinese has thousands of characters altered by deleting or changing strokes.

simship - Simultaneous release of localized versions with the domestic product, for example English, version. Simship is only possible when the translation cycle starts during development.

single language vendor (SLV) - Localization vendor that offers translation service to one target language.

single source publishing - A publishing method where content (text and images) is created once, and published to several different formats, such as PDF, HTML or online help.

single worldwide binary - One binary or set of binaries that meets the requirements of all users, regardless of language or geographic location. This single source is developed, compiled, and tested by one team, with no conditional compiles. The text language is either bound into one executable file, or is user-callable from separate language .dll files.

SLV - *See* single language vendor

software consistency check - A quality assurance step in which translators compare translated software references in online help or documentation files to the actual localized software interface to check whether they match.

Standard Generalized Markup Language (SGML) - An international standard for information exchange that prescribes a standard format for using descriptive markup within a document, defining three document layers: structure, content, and style.

static web site - A web site that consists mainly of HTML pages with text and graphics that are manually updated. The concept of the "static" web site contrasts the evolution of the dynamic web site.

stop list - A list of frequently used words, such as *the* and *or*, which will not be included in a search index, for example the search index created for an online help file or a set of PDF files.

TDB - *See* terminology database

termbase - *See* terminology database

terminology database (TDB, termbase) - A data collection that defines concepts, generally in a specific specialized subject field, and documents the terms associated with those concepts.

terminology management system (TMS) - Software application that stores and encodes terminology resources in dictionaries. Examples of terminology management systems are STAR TermStar and Trados MultiTerm.

text expansion - A feature of translated text where some languages use more text or longer words to express ideas than was the case in the source language. German or French texts, for example, are on average 30% longer than English texts.

tier - *See* language tier

TM - *See* translation memory

TMS - *See* terminology management system

TMX - *See* Translation Memory Exchange

Traditional Chinese - Chinese ideographs used in Taiwan and Hong Kong. Differences with Simplified Chinese include character encoding schemes, terminology, and linguistic style.

translation memory (TM) - Translation memory is a technology that enables the user to store translated phrases or sentences in a database.

Translation Memory Exchange (TMX) - An open standard, based on XML, which has been designed by a group of tool developers to simplify and automate the process of converting translation memories from one format to another.

translation portal - Web site that offers automated translation workflow solutions, where translation jobs can be automatically distributed to freelance translators, using the latest in translation technology. Examples of translation portals are www.uniscape.com and www.e-translate.com.

UI - *See* user interface

Unicode - A 16-bit character set capable of encoding all known characters and used as a worldwide character-encoding standard.

user interface (UI) - All elements of a software application used to interact with the user, such as dialog boxes, menus, and messages.

UTF-8 - An encoding form of Unicode that supports ASCII for backward compatibility and covers the characters for most languages in the world. UTF-8 is short for 8-bit Unicode Transfer Format.

W3C - *See* World Wide Web Consortium

Windows Help (WinHelp) - An online help system which consists of a compiled .hlp with a .cnt contents file. Windows Help files are created by creating sets of RTF files and bitmap images.

WinHelp - *See* Windows Help

World Wide Web Consortium (W3C) - The organization that considers and approves additions and updates to the HTML and SGML standard within the framework of the Internet or World Wide Web. For more information, visit www.w3c.org.

XML - *See* Extensible Markup Language

XSL - *See* Extensible Stylesheet Language

Appendix B:
Localization in the New Millennium

The following article is an edited version of an article published in Language International magazine, in December 1999, entitled *The End of Translation as We Know It*. It paints a picture of how the localization industry and localization models may evolve over the next few years.

Nobody knows how translation and translation technology will develop over the next few years. It is very obvious, however, that there will be many changes. The New Economy, which is so much characterized by Globalization, will also have a profound impact on translation technology and the localization industry.

Although the art and theory of technical translation will remain largely unchanged, there will undoubtedly be changes in process workflows and the management of the translation process. The next few years may very well change the way we look at translation. The following sections contain a quick overview, and some possible scenarios in which translation technology and the industry may develop.

1 Localization Models

In the early nineties, the localization industry as we now know it was finding a niche for itself, straddled between the software industry and translation world. Many companies have emerged as so-called specialists in managing, translating, and engineering complicated software products. After years of mergers and acquisitions, we now see an industry that has consolidated into a dozen MLVs (multi-language vendors) with an international presence, and thousands of smaller SLVs, the single-language vendors or traditional technical translation agencies.

Traditionally, localization projects did not start until the entire source – usually U.S. English – product was finalized and shipped to the customer. Customers in non-English speaking countries often had to wait for several months before they could purchase the product in their native languages. When the software and localization industry matured and globalized, product lifecycles, time-to-market, and the simultaneous shipment ("simship") of different language versions became important issues for software developers. Publishers wanted to ship all language versions simultaneously, or within an acceptable period following the release of the English product. As a result, a different localization model evolved, where translation was started while the English product was still in the development cycle. This new, parallel model created the need for translation leveraging tools, such as translation memory and software localization tools, to enable localization vendors to re-use translations with each intermediate product update or release.

It is now apparent that this model has a limited life cycle, mainly because localization projects will soon change into continuous localization flows, i.e. steady streams of updates and product revisions. In the next few years, for example, more and more software applications will be run from servers, mainly through the internet. Static software products shipped in boxes will gradually disappear, and localization projects will no longer have clearcut start and end dates. Furthermore, the frequency of web site updates will become an important competitive advantage for a software publisher. If a web site is published in 6 languages, for example, each change made in the English version will have to be made in the other 5 languages within days, or in the case of important news announcements, within hours of the English change. As a direct result, translation and localization will evolve as processes that run in parallel with development and content creation.

The only way to manage frequent updates and modifications is to store all information in a database format, using a content management system. Documentation, along with software, online help, and web site text and graphics, will be created, managed, and published using database technology. Today, most e-commerce web sites selling products online are already based on giant databases containing product information that generate web pages on the fly using scripting languages and active server pages. In order to translate these so-called dynamic or live web sites quickly and efficiently, advanced translation technology will need to be utilized.

2   Translation Technology

With the change in general software and documentation creation and publishing technologies, translation technology will also have to evolve to reflect these developments. Because the translation turnaround time will become the key factor in industry competitiveness, the number of steps between content creation and translation will need to be reduced to a minimum. Ideally, translators should sit at the same desk as the software developers and technical authors, and translate all of the content simultaneously. The closest we can get to this is to grant translators or translation agencies access to the source information database, to enable them to work directly on the source and to translate batches of new material as soon as it is released or signed-off.

Changes or additions to the database should be tracked automatically and transferred to the translators. A real-life scenario would be a situation where technical authors add a new piece of text to a web-publishing database, and then indicate that there is new information to be translated in a specified set of languages. The new text would be forwarded automatically to previously selected translators or translation agencies. This new project would be forwarded to their "translation inbox". Once the text has been translated using a translation memory system, the translated text is automatically transferred to the correct language section of the multilingual database for validation, QA and publication.

In this setup, there will be two databases running simultaneously:

- A multilingual database containing all source language text and all language versions of the web site, online help system, documentation set, and software applications.
- A bilingual translation memory database maintained by the translator or localization vendor.

A much more efficient solution would be to integrate a translation memory engine in this large, multilingual database that contains both source and translated material. This engine would automatically analyze all new content created, and pre-translate text using full or fuzzy matching before sending it out for translation. The translation memory engine could run in parallel with a structured authoring/controlled English tool which guarantees maximum leverage, both in source and target languages. If structured authoring is used, and the language pairs are feasible, the multilingual database could also be linked up to a machine translation engine to pre-translate material that was not found in the translation memory.

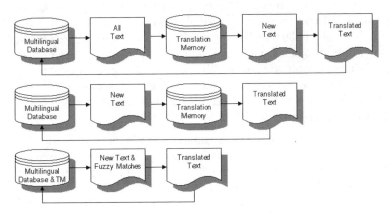

The figure above illustrates three translation technology models:

1. All information is extracted from the database, processed by translation memory so only new text is translated.

2. Only new or changed information is extracted from the database and processed by translation memory.

3. The content management database contains a translation memory engine that pre-translates all new or changed content so translators will only receive new text or fuzzy matches.

In this scenario, translators would only need a translation editor or limited version of the translation memory engine, which would only process internal matches. Translators should eventually be able to maintain real-time translation memory connections with an Oracle or SQL database through TCP/IP, and be able to enter their translations over the Internet. The same database should be accessible for reviewers, both from the localization vendor and from the publisher to avoid delays caused by file transfers.

With a fragmented translation model, it is critical to run a final QA of all translated material before it is published.

3   Localization Industry

How would a database-driven structured translation model affect the localization industry? First and foremost, there would be no more fixed projects, with clearcut start and end dates. The main advantage to this approach for translation vendors would be workload distribution. Translators could actually work in tandem with the developers and authors. It would be quite easy for translators to be linked directly to certain publishers. If a particular software company or e-commerce firm updates its web site on a daily basis, for example, a translator or group of translators could be assigned by the localization vendor and publisher to take full ownership for any and all updates. This would ensure a consistent style, and optimize the company and product knowledge among these translators. The number of translators required could be directly linked to the average throughput generated by technical authors or developers.

This model would pose problems with many small updates or additions, as translators would probably end up working on several small projects every day. If publishers generate an average of 600 translatable words per day, for example, one translator will need at least three projects from each publisher to generate sufficient revenue. Leverage tracking systems will monitor the number of words sent out for translation or review, so the work can be invoiced at agreed times. Establishing long-term relationships and contracts between publishers and vendors would be critical to the success of these automated translation workflows.

In this scenario, even the project management and file distribution performed by translation or localization agencies would hinder the speed at which translations could be turned around. The information should be communicated directly between publishers and translators. So where does that leave the vendors, or the large MLVs? First and foremost, translation quality needs to be verified. Although translation can be outsourced to freelance translators or third-party agencies, most large publishers will have to depend on vendors to guarantee the overall quality of the delivered translations, to manage terminology and translation resources, and to select and assess the resources used.

Multilingual database publishing only works for technical content that can be translated almost literally. It does not apply to true localization, i.e. the creation of local content for different countries. Most companies will want to adjust their web site pages to reflect a local context, for example, in situations where there is a requirement for regional content, such as marketing information, local offers, and regional office information. MLVs will need to have the expertise and resources to truly localize or re-write information in as many different languages as possible.

4 Structured Translation

Companies that want to go global in the most efficient and cost-effective way possible cannot ignore the power of multilingual database publishing. Structured translation will go hand in hand with structured content creation. In a few years, content will be replicated automatically from a central database to locations all over the world, translations will be transferred automatically back into the central repository, and localization vendors will find themselves managing people and processes instead of temporary projects.

The localization industry and translation technology still have a long way to go over the next few years...

Index